NOTE

Oxford Historical Monographs will consist of books which would formerly have been published in the Oxford Historical Series. As with the previous series, they will be carefully selected studies which have been submitted, or are based upon theses submitted, for higher degrees in this University.

THE NAZI PARTY
IN LOWER SAXONY
1921-1933

BY

JEREMY NOAKES

OXFORD UNIVERSITY PRESS

1971

Oxford University Press, Ely House, London W.1

GLASGOW NEW YORK TORONTO MELBOURNE WELLINGTON
CAPE TOWN IBADAN NAIROBI DAR ES SALAAM LUSAKA ADDIS ABABA
DELHI BOMBAY CALCUTTA MADRAS KARACHI LAHORE DACCA
KUALA LUMPUR SINGAPORE HONG KONG TOKYO

PRINTED IN GREAT BRITAIN
BY WILLIAM CLOWES & SONS, LIMITED
LONDON, BECCLES AND COLCHESTER

FOR INGRID

ACKNOWLEDGEMENTS

This book is a revised version of a D.Phil. thesis prepared at St. Antony's College, Oxford. I am extremely grateful to the Warden and Fellows for enabling me to spend two years in the intellectually stimulating atmosphere of St. Antony's and for financing research trips to Germany. I am particularly grateful to Professor James Joll, formerly Sub-Warden of the College, for his patience and sympathy with my problems and for valuable advice.

I also owe a debt of gratitude to the Deutscher Akademischer Austauschdienst and to the Volkswagen Foundation for helping to finance my research in Germany.

Thanks are due to the staffs of the various archives which I consulted in Germany. I am particularly grateful to Dr. Werner Jochmann of the Forschungsstelle für die Geschichte des Nationalsozialismus in Hamburg, who gave me valuable help and advice at various stages in my research. Dr. Dieter Brosius of the Niedersächsisches Staatsarchiv kindly corrected errors in Lower Saxon topography in the manuscript.

I have benefited greatly from discussion with fellow scholars in Germany, and in this connection would like to mention Dr. Gerhard Schildt and Dr. Ulrich Wörtz. Dr. Ernst-August Roloff gave me the benefit of his extensive knowledge of Brunswick in the Weimar Republic. Herr Albrecht Tyrell read an earlier draft and made some helpful suggestions.

I am indebted to several scholars in England. I benefited from the help of Dr. Alan Bullock who read an earlier manuscript as did Dr. Robert Benewick and Dr. Geoffrey Pridham. Mr. A. J. Nicholls was kind enough to read the book before publication. I am particularly grateful to my friend, Dr. Jonathan Wright, who has given me advice and encouragement at every stage in my research.

Acknowledgements are due to the publishers of the following works for permission to quote from them: W. S. Allen, *The Nazi Seizure of Power. The Experience of a Single German Town 1930–1935* (Eyre and Spottiswoode, London, 1965); Rudolf Heberle, *Landbevölkerung und Nationalsozialismus. Eine soziologische Untersuchung der politischen Willensbildung in Schleswig-Holstein 1919 bis 1932* (Deutsche Verlagsanstalt, Stuttgart, 1963); Ernst von Salomon, *Die Geächteten* (Rowohlt, Hamburg, 1962); and Ernst von Salomon, *Der Fragebogen* (Rowohlt, Hamburg, 1951). I am also grateful to Messrs. Weidenfeld and Nicolson for permission to use parts of my article 'Conflict and

ACKNOWLEDGEMENTS

Development in the NSDAP 1924–7' which appeared in the *Journal of Contemporary History*, Vol. I No. 4 October 1966.

My thanks are due to the Clarendon Press for their help with the preparation of the manuscript for publication and I am grateful to my father for undertaking the laborious task of proof-reading and indexing.

I should perhaps add that although these and other sources of assistance made a significant contribution to the book, the responsibility for any errors belongs to me alone.

Finally, I owe a special debt to my wife who during my long absences abroad had to bear the burden of a family crisis. Without her this book would not have been written.

CONTENTS

CONTENTS

CONTENTS

LIST OF MAPS
at end

ABBREVIATIONS

Parties and other Organizations

AG	Arbeitsgemeinschaft der nord und west-deutschen-Gaue der NSDAP
ApA	Agrarpolitischer Apparat
DDP	Deutsche Demokratische Partei
DHP	Deutsch-hannoversche Partei (Guelphs)
DHV	Deutscher Handlungsgehilfenverband
DNVP	Deutschnationale Volkspartei
DSP	Deutschsozialistische Partei
DVFB	Deutschvölkische Freiheitsbewegung (January 1925–)
DVFP	Deutschvölkische Freiheitspartei (1922–1924)
DVP	Deutsche Volkspartei
DVSTB	Deutschvölkischer Schutz und Trutz Bund
Gau H-E	Gau Hanover-East
Gau H-S-B	Gau Hanover-South–Brunswick
Gau W-E	Gau Weser-Ems
GDAP	Grossdeutsche Arbeiterpartei
GVG	Grossdeutsche Volksgemeinschaft
HJ	Hitlerjugend
KPD	Kommunistische Partei Deutschlands
NSBO	Nationalsozialistische Betriebszellenorganisation
NSDAP	Nationalsozialistische Deutsche Arbeiterpartei
NSDSt.B	Nationalsozialistischer Deutscher Studentenbund
NSFB	Nationalsozialistische Freiheitsbewegung (August 1924–January 1925)
NSFP	Nationalsozialistische Freiheitspartei (June–August 1924)
SA	Sturmabteilung
SPD	Sozialdemokratische Partei Deutschlands
SS	Schutzstaffel
Uschla	Untersuchungs und Schlichtungsausschuss
USPD	Unabhängige Sozialdemokratische Partei
V-S-B	Völkisch-Sozialer-Block (April–May 1924)

Newspapers

GT	*Göttinger Tageblatt*
NB	*Niedersächsischer Beobachter*
NfSL	*Nachrichten für Stadt und Land*
NS	*Niedersachsen-Stürmer*
NTZ	*Niedersächsische Tageszeitung*
VB	*Völkischer Beobachter*

ABBREVIATIONS

Archives and Journals

BA	Bundesarchiv
BDC	Berlin Document Center
BSA	Stadtarchiv Braunschweig
FGN	Forschungsstelle für die Geschichte des Nationalsozialismus in Hamburg
NSAA	Niedersächsisches Staatsarchiv Aurich
NSAH	Niedersächsisches Staatsarchiv Hannover
NSAO	Niedersächsisches Staatsarchiv Oldenburg
NSAOsn	Niedersächsisches Staatsarchiv Osnabrück
NSAS	Niedersächsisches Staatsarchiv Stade
NSAW	Niedersächsisches Staatsarchiv Wolfenbüttel
SAD	Staatsarchiv Düsseldorf
SAG	Stadtarchiv Göttingen
Vjhfzg	*Vierteljahreshefte für Zeitgeschichte*

Other

Pf	Pfennig
RM	Reichsmark
TH	Technische Hochschule

INTRODUCTION

Previous histories of the rise of National Socialism have tended to concentrate either on the political, economic and social conditions which produced a situation favouring the rise of the party, or, if they dealt with the development of the party itself, then only briefly or by concentrating on the activities of the Reich party leaders.[1] Detailed study of the NSDAP itself has been confined almost entirely to the period 1919–23 in Bavaria.[2] There has been no attempt to examine the emergence of the party in North Germany before 1925 or the structure and activity of the party's organization and propaganda machine at regional and local level after 1925. Even Professor Allen's interesting study of a small town in Lower Saxony, while it tells us much about the milieu in which National Socialism flourished and the success of its propaganda, does not, as the author admits, tell us much about the way the party *organized* its successful propaganda:

Exactly how much was initiated locally and how much was promoted by the example of other Nazi groups or by the District and National Nazi leadership remains to be determined. It would be extremely interesting to know exactly what means were used by the NSDAP to instil the sense of purposefulness and initiative into its local groups which were then used by the movement as a whole. It would be useful to know how co-ordination was combined with flexibility in this authoritarian instrument. The material available for this study of Thalburg did not supply the answers to these questions.[3]

By concentrating on the NSDAP in one particular area between 1921 and 1933, it is hoped to provide a case study of the growth of Nazi organization and propaganda at regional level, and thereby to provide an answer to these and other questions. Above all, this study hopes to give a picture of the development of the party, the phases through which it moved, and the changes in orientation which occurred at various periods.

The rise of National Socialism may be seen as a process involving two stages. The first stage saw the emergence of Hitler as the *Führer*

---

[1] E.g. A. Bullock, *Hitler. A Study in Tyranny* (London, 1952; revised ed. 1962).

[2] E.g. W. Maser, *Die Frühgeschichte der NSDAP* (Bonn, 1965). I was unable to see a copy of D. Orlow, *The History of the Nazi Party: 1919–1933* (Pittsburgh University Press, 1969), until after the manuscript had gone to press.

[3] W. S. Allen, *The Nazi Seizure of Power. The Experience of a Single German Town 1930–1935* (London, 1966), p. 274.

INTRODUCTION

and the NSDAP as the major political organization in the *völkisch* movement. This was a precondition for the second stage—the struggle of Hitler and the NSDAP for control of the state. The emphasis therefore in the first part of this book is on an analysis of the first stage as it affected the anti-Semitic movement in Lower Saxony. The major questions which arise are first, what were the factors which distinguished the NSDAP from its *völkisch* rivals and were responsible for its success? And second, how was it that Hitler not only emerged victorious in his conflicts with rival individuals and groups, but also succeeded in creating a unique form of leadership—that amalgam of charismatic and bureaucratic aspects of authority which was embodied in the position of the Führer of the NSDAP?[1]

Lower Saxony is a very convenient area in which to study this process. In the years 1921–6 Lower Saxony was important in the struggle between the NSDAP and its *völkisch* rivals and in Hitler's assertion of his authority within the party. The base of the NSDAP was in Bavaria, but it was Hitler's success or failure in extending the authority of the NSDAP and of his leadership within the *völkisch* movement outside Bavaria which would ultimately determine his chances of winning power.

The second part of this book concentrates on how the NSDAP set about gaining the support necessary to win control of the state. It deals with the development of the party organization in Lower Saxony and the tensions which existed within it. Even after Hitler's frustration of the Strasser group's attempt to win some independence from the party head-quarters, Munich's control over the party in Lower Saxony was only loose until after 1929. From 1930 onwards, therefore, the book concentrates on analysing how policies and directives largely framed at Reich level were applied on a regional and local basis. There is also an attempt to analyse why various sections of the population in Lower Saxony were vulnerable to the appeal made by National Socialism and a study of the propaganda themes and techniques used by the party to exploit its opportunities.

Lower Saxony is again a convenient area in which to study these developments. The three Reichstag electoral districts which it embraced —Hanover-South–Brunswick, Hanover-East and Weser-Ems—were among those with the highest NSDAP vote in Germany in the years 1930–3. On the other hand there were *Kreise* in which the NSDAP vote was well below the Reich average. In both its social structure and political background Lower Saxony contains considerable variety.

[1] On the combination of charismatic and bureaucratic aspects of authority within the NSDAP, see H. Gerth, 'The Nazi Party: Its Leadership and Composition', in *American Journal of Sociology* (1940), pp. 517 ff.

INTRODUCTION

One problem which faces all students of Nazi organization at local level should finally be mentioned: the question of sources.[1] The first stage in the Nazi rise to power is extremely well documented, thanks largely to the individuals involved who preserved their documents. For the second stage, however, the documentation is vast (particularly from 1930 to 1933), but rather poor in quality. There is a large amount of material which can give a fairly clear picture of the routine operations of the party machine, but there is very little which sheds light on what went on behind the scenes, particularly in the relations between the party's regional organizations (*Gaue*) and the Reich head-quarters in Munich. There are also no documents whatever on the policies of the leadership regarding the Nazi governments in Brunswick and Oldenburg. The reason for this dearth lies partly in the loss and destruction of documents in the war, but also, as Jochmann points out, in the development of the NSDAP itself. As the party grew, it tended increasingly to conduct its important business less through correspondence and more through meetings of individuals and groups of party functionaries, for which minutes were either not kept because they were informal or, if kept, have been lost.

For the purposes of this study, the term 'Lower Saxony' is taken to mean the area formed by the boundaries of the Prussian province of Hanover (comprising the *Regierungsbezirke* Hanover, Hildesheim, Lüneburg, Stade, Aurich and Osnabrück), and by the boundaries of the Free States of Oldenburg (excluding the Provinces of Birkenfeld and Lübeck), Brunswick and Schaumburg-Lippe.[2] Agriculture employed the largest number of people in Lower Saxony—38·5 per cent of the working population compared with 30·5 per cent for the Reich as a whole;[3] 33·3 per cent worked in industry (Reich average 41·4 per cent); 16·6 per cent in business and trade (16·5 per cent) and 11·6 per cent in administration and other professions (11·6 per cent). North and Central Lower Saxony were overwhelmingly agricultural, the Harburg, Wilhelmshaven–Rüstringen and Unterweser areas being the only significant exceptions. Even in the south, in the Labour Office districts of Northeim, Göttingen, Hameln, Helmstedt, Peine and Stadthagen, there was also a large percentage employed in agriculture. The type of agriculture and the size of holdings varied with the soil. In

[1] See the remarks in Werner Jochmann, *Nationalsozialismus und Revolution. Ursprung und Geschichte der NSDAP in Hamburg 1922–1933* (Frankfurt, 1963), pp. VII–VIII.
[2] Excluding Bremen. Before the Allied occupation the term Lower Saxony was used in a rather vague geographical or cultural sense and had no political content.
[3] For the following see *Die Wirtschaftsstruktur im Bezirk des Landesarbeitsamtes Niedersachsen.*, hrsg. Wirtschaftswissenschaftliche Gesellschaft zum Studium Niedersachsens, C.V., Reihe A, Heft 14 (Hanover, 1930), pp. 3 ff.

INTRODUCTION

the northern coastal areas such as Hadeln and Norden, the lush water meadows or 'marshes' encouraged cattle-grazing and rather large isolated farms with wealthy and independent peasants. Further away from the coast the so-called *Geest* began, infertile land made up of low lying moors west of the river Weser, while to the east it was dryer, sandy heath land. The *Geest* was used for growing rye and potatoes and above all for animal breeding, particularly cattle and pigs. According to an animal census of 1 December 1928 only Bavaria had a larger number of cattle than Lower Saxony, while Lower Saxony had the largest number of pigs of any province or state in Germany.[1] Cattle and pig breeding were particularly prominent in the north-west, in Oldenburg and East Friesland. The *Geest* area was characterized by small and medium-sized family-run farms arranged in compact villages with close community ties.[2] In the south between Hanover and the Harz mountains and the Weserbergland, the soil is a rich loam, producing corn, sugar beet and vegetables, with slightly larger farms and wealthier peasants.

Industry, with the exception of one or two isolated cities such as Osnabrück and Wilhelmshaven, was concentrated in the south-east, in *Regierungsbezirk* Hildesheim, in and around the city of Hanover, and in the state of Brunswick. There was little heavy industry—ore mining in the Harz, potash mining near Hanover and Hildesheim, the iron and steel complex of Ilseder Hütte in Peine, and an important chemical industry with the Pelikan-Werke and the big rubber firm of Continental, both in Hanover. There were, however, a considerable number of light industries such as the canning factories of Brunswick, which produced much of Germany's supply. Handicrafts were particularly important in Lower Saxony. Including Bremen, there were about 106,000 businesses employing 88,500 journeymen and 58,000 apprentices. If one includes the masters, there were 253,000 employed in handicrafts—34 per cent of all those employed in industry and approximately 11 per cent of the working population of Lower Saxony.[3]

The economic structure of Lower Saxony was summed up in the 1930 report of the *Landesarbeitsamt* in the statement that 'in all branches of economic activity one can observe the predominance of small and medium-sized concerns. Big businesses and huge concerns are rare both in agriculture and industry. Handicrafts have also not yet taken on an industrial character.'[4]

[1] *Die Wirtschaftsstruktur*, p. 8.
[2] For important details on the *Geest* see R. Heberle, *Landbevölkerung und Nationalsozialismus* (Stuttgart, 1963), pp. 92 ff.
[3] *Die Wirtschaftsstruktur*, p. 44.
[4] Ibid., p. 3.

4

Politically, Lower Saxony also showed considerable diversity.[1] In the Province of Hanover political opinion in the period 1867–90 had been divided between those who accepted the Prussian victory at Langensalza in 1866, and those who resented the Prussian invasion and wished to restore the Guelph dynasty and an independent Hanover. The latter were organized in the *Deutsch-Hannoversche Partei* (DHP), known by their opponents as the Guelphs. They consisted of the old Hanoverian aristocracy and above all the rural middle class—peasantry, shopkeepers and artisans—particularly in the oldest Guelph lands, the former principalities of Calenberg, Lüneburg, Göttingen and Grubenhagen, and the counties of Hoya and Diepholz. Their support for the Guelph dynasty was based firstly, on the fact that its policies, particularly the inheritance laws and the rules governing the emancipation after 1833, had consistently favoured the peasantry at the expense of the big landowners; secondly, on the fact that the Prussian conquest had had unpleasant consequences such as national service, billeting, and higher taxes; and last but not least from loyalty springing from a deep-rooted conservatism. The Guelphs were supported in their opposition by the Catholic Centre Party, strong in *Regierungsbezirk* Osnabrück, whose hostility to the new Reich, with its Protestant if not Erastian basis, had been sharpened by the *Kulturkampf*.

Opposed to the Guelph and Centre alliance, which accounted for approximately 43 per cent of the vote in the Province, were the National Liberals, and after 1880 the Progressives and the Free Conservatives who won approximately 46 per cent of the vote between them. By far the strongest were the National Liberals who won approximately one-third of the vote. They were supported by the majority of the urban population except in the former royal city of Hanover, and by much of the rural population in the Guelph lands which had been acquired more recently—in Hildesheim in the south, and above all in the northern territories of Stade, Verden and Bremen which had a tradition of political liberalism. In East Friesland (*Regierungsbezirk* Aurich), which the Guelph dynasty had only acquired in 1815 and which from 1744 to 1807 had been a part of Prussia, there was virtually no support for the Guelph cause; indeed there was a strong separatist movement in favour of leaving the Province of Hanover and joining the Province of Westphalia. The National Liberals and Progressives predominated here with some support for the Free Conservatives in the Norden area.

---

[1] For the following see B. Ehrenfeuchter, *Politische Willensbilding in Niedersachsen zur Zeit des Kaiserreiches* (Diss., Göttingen, 1951). H. Prilop, *Die Vorabstimmung in Hannover 1924. Untersuchungen zur Vorgeschichte und Geschichte der deutsch-hannoverschen Partei* (Diss., Hamburg, 1954) and Günther Franz, *Die Politischen Wahlen in Niedersachsen 1867 bis 1949* (Bremen, 1957).

With the exception of Brunswick where they were a small minority, the Guelphs were not of course represented in the Free States. Brunswick was dominated by the National Liberals, the Progressives, and increasingly by the SPD. In the state of Oldenburg the Liberals had an overwhelming majority and the Progressives were particularly strong. The Progressives led the opposition of the Oldenburg peasantry to high grain tariffs imposed by the Prussian Junkers which increased the cost of fodder for their cattle and pig rearing. In Catholic south Oldenburg the Centre Party was strong. Finally, in Schaumburg-Lippe the Free Conservatives and the Liberals were about evenly balanced.

After 1890 the political situation in Lower Saxony was transformed by two developments. In the first place, increasing industrialization and the lifting of the anti-Socialist laws enabled the SPD to make rapid progress largely at the expense of the Liberals. In 1890 the SPD had won one-fifth of the vote; by 1912 this had increased to one-third and they had become the largest party. The increase in the SPD vote had been particularly spectacular in the south-east of Lower Saxony where there had been a considerable amount of industrialization. In Brunswick the SPD were only 1·4 per cent away from the absolute majority in 1912.

Secondly, the Free Conservatives succeeded in increasing their percentage of the vote at the expense of the Guelphs. Thus while the Free Conservatives increased their vote from 3·3 per cent in 1890 to 14·2 per cent in 1912, the Guelph vote declined from 23·1 per cent to 10·8 per cent. In other words, the Guelphs were gradually coming to accept the new Reich.

Hence by comparison with the rest of the Reich, Lower Saxony was distinguished first, by the strength of the Liberal parties which tended to have a more rural basis than was usual elsewhere, and secondly, by the fact that Conservatism was expressed not through the German Conservative Party (DKP) which was entirely absent, but through the more moderate Free Conservative Party, through the deeply traditional and anti-Prussian Guelphs and even through the National Liberals who stood rather to the right of the party in comparison with other areas. Anti-Semitic parties had almost no support in Lower Saxony before 1914. At the beginning of the 1890s anti-Semitic agitation spread from neighbouring Hessen-Nassau into a few southern *Kreise* of Lower Saxony, but they never succeeded in winning more than 5 or 6 per cent of the vote. Anti-Liberal and anti-capitalist voters, who in other parts of Germany supported anti-Semitic parties, tended to support the *Bund der Landwirte*, which put up its own candidates, or the Guelphs.

PART I

I

THE BEGINNINGS OF NATIONAL SOCIAL-
ISM IN LOWER SAXONY 1919–1922

(i) *The development of post-war anti-Semitism*

NTI-SEMITISM as an intellectual movement in post-war Germany was derived almost entirely from pre-war thinkers.[1] This
continuity initially also extended to organization. The first anti-
Semitic groups to emerge in post-war Germany were the offspring of
racialist organizations which had already existed before 1914. The
most important development in anti-Semitism during the early years
after the war was the transition from groups characteristic of the pre-
war era with bourgeois leadership and political conventions, to a new
type of organization capable of exploiting the widespread social chaos
caused by war, revolution and inflation.

After the war, then, organized anti-Semitism began through the
activities of a number of *völkisch* groups which had their roots in the
pre-war period.[2] There was the *Reichshammerbund* which had been
founded in 1912, the *Deutschvölkischer Bund* which was the successor
organization of the pre-war *Deutschvölkische Partei*, and above all, the
Deutscher Schutz und Trutz Bund, which was established in February
1919 by the Pan-German League. Where the Pan-German League
appealed only to the élite, the *Deutscher Schutz und Trutz Bund* was
intended to win over the masses to the anti-Semitic movement, and it
was therefore far more radical than the pre-war anti-Semitic groups.
In June 1919, its headquarters were moved to Hamburg where there
was considerable support for *völkisch* ideas among the members of the
white-collar workers' union, the *Deutsche Handlungsgehilfenverband*
(DHV), which was based in Hamburg. The secretary of the DHV,
Alfred Roth, became the secretary of the *Deutscher Schutz und Trutz*

[1] On the continuity of German anti-Semitism as an ideology there is a considerable literature, e.g. P. G. J. Pulzer, *The Rise of Political Anti-Semitism in Germany
and Austria* (New York, 1964), p. 300 and K. R. Ehrlich, 'Judenfeindschaft in
Deutschland', in *Judenfeindschaft, Darstellung und Analysen*, hrsg. von Karl
Thieme (Frankfurt, 1962).
[2] For the following see *Ausgewählte Dokumente zur Geschichte des Nationalsozialismus 1933–1945*, hrsg. von Hans-Adolf Jacobsen und Werner Jochmann.
Kommentar, 9 ff; and A. Kruck, *Der Alldeutsche Verband 1890–1939* (Wiesbaden,
1954), pp. 130 ff.

Bund and under him the new organization launched a remarkable propaganda drive. Numerous meetings were arranged by its branches throughout the Reich and vast quantities of anti-Semitic literature were distributed. In the year 1920 alone, for example, it distributed 7·6 million pamphlets, 4·7 million handbills and 7·8 million stickers. By 1922, it had a membership of 280,000. Meanwhile, however, the organization had changed its name. Through its drive and through the resources which it could command, it had soon established itself as by far the most effective anti-Semitic group. As a result, by the Autumn of 1919 it had succeeded in absorbing the *Deutschvölkischer Bund* and therefore adopted a new name, the *Deutschvölkischer Schutz und Trutz Bund* (DVSTB).

In Lower Saxony organized anti-Semitism was soon very much in evidence. By the summer of 1919, for example, in the relatively small university town of Göttingen there were branches of the *Reichsham-merbund*, the *Deutschvölkischer Bund*, and the *Deutscher Schutz und Trutz Bund*.[1] Moreover, a new *völkisch* organization was established, the *Verband zur Befreiung vom Judenjoch* (League for the Liberation from the Jewish Yoke), which was intended to incorporate the other anti-Semitic groups to form a united movement. At a membership meeting on 15 July 1919, which was addressed by a Professor Will-rich, it was joined by 170 members.[2] The League maintained that it was 'independent of any political party' and that its sole aim was the 'effective repression of the excessive Jewish influence on our public life'. Although, significantly, it described itself as a 'workers' league', in fact its chairman was a member of the Board of Works and its secre-tary, a student. The League does not appear to have been very success-ful in unifying the *völkisch* movement in Göttingen and it was not until 19 February 1920 that the four *völkisch* groups united to form a branch of the *Deutschvölkischer Schutz und Trutz Bund*.[3]

Elsewhere in Lower Saxony the DVSTB established itself some-what earlier. In the Autumn of 1919 a branch was formed in the small town of Wolfenbüttel near Brunswick.[4] It was started by a bookseller who had been active in the anti-Semitic movement before the war, and lectures by two professors from Giessen and Heidelberg helped to in-crease its membership to over 100 by 1921. At the end of 1919 and the beginning of 1920 branches were founded at Wilhelmshaven and

[1] For the following see the issues of the *Göttinger Tageblatt* for 1919.
[2] *GT*, 15 July 1919.
[3] *GT*, 20 Feb. 1920.
[4] See *Die Geschichte der NSDAP im Kreise Wolfenbüttel*, 1937 in Niedersächs-isches Staatsarchiv Hannover (in future NSAH) Hann. Des. 310 I A, Nr. 92 and Kurt Schmalz, *Nationalsozialisten ringen um Braunschweig* (Braunschweig, 1933), pp. 12 ff.

Oldenburg by members of a mine-sweeper flotilla.[1] By 1922 the branch in Wilhelmshaven had a membership of 192, mainly officers, civil servants, white-collar workers and artisans.[2] At the beginning of February 1920 the branch in Hanover was already advertising in the *Göttinger Tageblatt*, offering to send informative literature on the Jews for fifty pfennigs.[3] By 1921, the DVSTB had branches in the villages of Wittingen and Hankensbüttel in the agricultural *Kreis* Gifhorn.[4] In short, the DVSTB had constructed a network of support throughout Lower Saxony. It was laying the foundations on which future anti-Semitic movements would build.

What sort of people were attracted by the DVSTB? In the first place, there were ex-officers and ex-professional soldiers who resented the loss of the war, for which they blamed the 'stab in the back' by the home front, and their treatment under the revolution which contrasted so sharply with the social prestige they had possessed under the empire. Many of them, in addition, had been axed under the provisions of the Versailles treaty. Secondly, there were artisans who under the Empire had had a status which clearly separated them from the proletariat and who had been linked with the established order by their acceptance of its values. This group, which had already come under pressure from the accelerated economic and social change of the war period, now felt their whole position jeopardized by the apparent triumph of the proletariat and its political representatives. Thirdly, there were *Akademiker*, particularly teachers who had acted as missionaries of the Pan-German ideology during the Wilhelmine period. Finally, there were the young: students and apprentices for whom defeat meant the collapse of the world in which they had been brought up and in which national prestige was one of the most important values. For them defeat meant burning resentment and an uncertain future, neither of which encouraged them to settle down. Many of these young men hurled themselves into activity by joining the Free Corps—men like the ex-military cadet, Ernst von Salomon who described their predicament in his autobiographical novel, *Die Geächteten*:

The picture of my father in uniform taken at the outbreak of war, pictures of friends and relations, who had been killed in the war, the army sash, the bent Hussar's sword, the epaulettes, the French helmet, the shot-through wallet of my brother—the blood had already become quite dark and spotty—the epaulettes of my grandfather with the heavy silver tassels which had now

---

[1] *Aufzeichnungen aus meinem Tagebuch von Paul Opitz* in Hoover Institution NSDAP Hauptarchiv, Reel 7, Folder 163.
[2] See the membership list in NSAH Hann. Des. 122a 76e.   [3] *GT*, 5 Feb. 1920.
[4] *Wir waren dabei. Berichte über die nationalsozialistische Bewegung im ehemaligen Kreise Isenhagen.* In the Bundesarchiv (in future BA) Slg. Schumacher 202, I).

turned black, a packet of letters from the front on mildewed paper—but I couldn't face it any more—all that stuff. No, I couldn't face it. It was all no longer valid. It all belonged to the period of those victories, when the flags hung out of all the windows. Now there were no more victories, now the flags had lost their shining significance. Now in this confused moment, when everything was turning to ruins, the road which was intended for me was buried. I stood uncomprehendingly in front of the new order . . . without any certainty . . . except that that world with which I was bound up, for which I did not need to declare myself because I was a part of it, was now finally and irrevocably sinking into the dust and would never rise again.

Although the DVSTB organized and propagated anti-Semitism, it was not a political organization, nor was it committed to any political party. The majority of anti-Semites at this period found political expression in the German National People's Party (the DNVP), for the DNVP was not only the heir of the two old Conservative parties, but also of the pre-war anti-Semitic parties. Yet although a large number of members were anti-Semitic and although thanks partly to the activity of the DVSTB there was a powerful minority within the party which wished to give anti-Semitism more emphasis, the conservative and Christian Socialist elements remained dominant.[1] Anti-Semitism was essentially used as a tactical device. In the words of a member 'we sought and found in the toleration and encouragement of anti-Semitism a distinctive policy for the party to distinguish it from all the others, particularly from the DVP (German People's Party), and we expected great successes from it.'[2] In the 1920 *Reichstag* election it was used in an attempt to make the party acceptable to urban voters in Berlin and West Germany who might otherwise have been put off by its Junker image.

A number of anti-Semites, however, were not satisfied with the lack of definite political aims of the DVSTB and disliked the reactionary nature of the DNVP and the lukewarmness of its anti-Semitism. Above all, they objected to the bourgeois conventions of these organizations—their *Spiessigkeit*.[3] It was these men who formed the main support for organizations which sought a radical *political* solution to their problems.

One anti-Semitic organization, however, had already felt the need for political activity within the *völkisch* movement and, in particular,

[1] For the following see L. Hertzmann, *DNVP. Right-Wing Opposition in the Weimar Republic 1918–1924* (University of Nebraska Press, 1963), pp. 124 ff.

[2] Quoted in ibid., pp. 130–1.

[3] For examples see Schmidt, *Zwanzig Jahre Soldat Adolf Hitlers*, and H. Preiss, *Die Anfänge der völkischen Bewegung in Franken* (Erlangen, Diss., 1937), pp. 39–40.

the importance of winning over and organizing the working class. The *Germanenorden* had been founded in 1912 to unite all the various anti-Semitic groups and clubs which proliferated in the pre-war years.[1] At a meeting of the Order in Berlin in December 1918 it had been agreed to found a 'German Socialist Party' which would be '*Deutschvölkisch* and socialist'. The initiative was then taken by the Bavarian representative of the Order, Freiherr von Sebottendorff, who in May 1919 established a *Deutschsozialistische Arbeitsgemeinschaft* (German Socialist Working Group). The Thule Society—the camouflage name of the Bavarian head-quarters of the Germanen order—had already assisted in the formation of a 'German Workers Party' (DAP) on 5 January 1919 by a journalist, Karl Harrer, and a railway workshop employee, Anton Drexler, which was soon joined by an army agent, Adolf Hitler.[2]

The programme for the new *Deutschsozialistische Arbeitsgemeinschaft*, a combination of nationalism, land and financial reform, and anti-Semitism, was provided by a Düsseldorf engineer, Alfred Brunner. Unlike its fellow offspring of the *Germanenorden*—the German Workers Party—it soon founded branches throughout the Reich. At a meeting in Hanover from 24 to 25 April 1920 a new name—the *Deutschsozialistische Partei* (DSP)—was agreed upon and Brunner was elected leader.[3] It was also agreed at this meeting that, temporarily at any rate, the head-quarters should be in Hanover, perhaps because of its favourable position as a communications centre between North and South, East and West. Eight members of the Hanover branch attended this meeting and a Hanover policeman was elected chairman, though Brunner retained the actual leadership. But in comparison with the branches in Munich (400 members) and Nuremburg (300 members), the Hanover branch was small. Its report of its activities to the meeting mentions 'still only a few, though active colleagues'.[4] Even its alleged activity is questionable. It appears to have failed to expand outwards from the city. There is evidence for only one other branch being founded in Lower Saxony—Hildesheim, shortly after the Hanover meeting.[5] This failure of the DSP to increase its support reflected a lack of drive which encouraged discontent within its ranks and offered opportunities for a more dynamic alternative. This alternative was provided by the NSDAP.

[1] R. von Sebottendorff, *Bevor Hitler Kam* (München, 1933), pp. 33 ff.
[2] Cf. W. Maser, *Die Frühgeschichte der NSDAP* (Bonn, 1965), pp. 147 ff. and G. Franz-Willing, *Die Hitler-bewegung 1919–1922* (München, 1962).
[3] See Tagesordnung für den Vertretertag in Hannover in NSDAP Hauptarchiv, Reel 4, Folder 109.
[4] Ibid.
[5] Abteilung: Leitung Deutschsozialistische Partei to Kiel branch, 5 May 1920 in NSDAP Hauptarchiv, Reel 41, Folder 839.

(ii) *The founding of the Hanover City branch of the NSDAP*

In the Spring of 1921, the DVSTB branch in Hanover was joined by an unemployed businessman named Bruno Wenzel.[1] Wenzel had returned to Germany from Spain in 1920 just before the Kapp putsch. His period abroad had made him an ardent nationalist and while in Spain he had already organized a petition with 2,000 signatures which he had sent to the National Assembly in Weimar, demanding the franchise for *Auslandsdeutsche* to a new Economic Parliament which would replace the Reichstag, and which was an old racialist dream.

On his return to Germany, Wenzel had moved about the country finding work where he could and became a member of the DVSTB after reading a street pamphlet. One of his temporary jobs was distributing *völkisch* pamphlets at the Leipzig Fair and among these pamphlets were the first Nazi issues of the *Völkischer Beobachter* and the booklet, 'My Political Awakening' by Anton Drexler. Wenzel, according to his own account, now saw in the aims of the NSDAP the political conclusions which the DVSTB had failed to draw from its own *völkisch* premises. When attempts to persuade the Hanover DVSTB branch to amalgamate itself with the NSDAP failed because of its desire to remain above party, a desire characteristic of German bourgeois contempt for party politics, Wenzel corresponded directly with Munich[2] and on 17 May 1921 became Member No. 3368.

Wenzel now began to proselytize for the NSDAP among the members of the DVSTB in Hanover. Here he met a former policeman, now working in a factory, Gustav Seifert. Seifert, a carpenter by training, had joined the police in Hanover before the war and had shown his ambition by learning languages.[3] This had led to a posting to the German occupation forces in Warsaw during the war. It was in Warsaw, Seifert later maintained, that he had first come into contact with the 'Jewish question' and after the war he published a pamphlet 'Honour truth' about his Warsaw experiences. After the war he had left the police for health reasons and had been forced to take a job in a factory. The experience of the November revolution had interested Seifert for the first time in politics, and he joined the SPD. 'I came to trust this party because of its tremendous victories at the polls; and slogans such as "Freedom for the efficient", "Fight all criminals and bad elements", "Creation of an ideal state", encouraged me to work for it.' But he soon found that 'the inner comradeship which I had expected was lacking, everything went according to the rule book'.[4] After his

---

[1] Wenzel Autobiography in NSDAP Hauptarchiv, Reel 6, Folder 141.
[2] Munich to Wenzel 16 Apr. 1921; in NSDAP Hauptarchiv, Reel 6, Folder 141.
[3] The following account is based on Seifert's autobiography, ibid.
[4] Ibid.

attempt to draw the attention of a district party meeting to the 'Jewish problem' had been rebuffed, he resigned and, having been converted by anti-Semitic literature, joined the DVSTB on 24 January 1920. Soon, however, disillusioned with its lack of activity, he joined the DSP. But here too he failed to find what he was looking for and, as a result, was excited by what Wenzel told him of the Munich NSDAP when they met in the early summer of 1921. They decided to contact Munich and try and establish a branch of the NSDAP in Hanover.[1]

At the time when they applied, however, the NSDAP organization was about to be involved in a serious crisis.[2] This crisis had been sparked off by a decision which was reached at the international National Socialist meeting held at Zeitz on the 26–28 March 1921. Anton Drexler, the NSDAP representative at the meeting, had been persuaded by the DSP leader, Brunner, to amalgamate his party with the DSP and the Austrian and Czech parties to form a 'German National Socialist Party' with its head-quarters in Berlin and which was to have a federal organization. During the summer, some members of the NSDAP who resented Hitler's increasingly powerful position within the party and his autocratic behaviour pressed for the carrying out of this amalgamation as part of a general challenge to Hitler's role within the party. Hitler, however, was prepared for the threat and met it with a counter-attack. He handed in his resignation which, since he was responsible for its recent success, the party could ill afford to accept. He only agreed to withdraw it in return for the introduction of a new set of statutes giving him absolute power within the party and ending the 'nonsense' of decision-making by committee.[3] Hitler was supported in his *coup* by a group of young activists who, admiring his energy and ruthlessness, had totally committed themselves to his leadership. They were led by Hermann Esser, a former member of the SPD, a man who rivalled Hitler as a demagogue and who possessed an extremely dubious personal reputation. In effect, a complete transformation of the party had occurred, with the older ineffective, conventional leaders who had founded the party replaced by a group of young extremists who were personally committed to Hitler. Moreover, the NSDAP was no longer governed by the constitutional principles according to which political parties in Germany were traditionally organized and through which power was diffused. It had acquired a unique structure of authority in which decisions were made by the

[1] Seifert-Wenzel correspondence, 6–9 June 1921, in NSDAP Hauptarchiv, Reel 6, Folder 141.

[2] For the following see Maser, op. cit., pp. 263 ff.; Franz-Willing, op. cit., pp. 106 ff.; and D. Orlow, 'The Organizational History and Structure of the NSDAP 1919–1923', *Journal of Modern History* (June 1965), pp. 217 ff.

[3] For Hitler's own views on the change see A. Hitler, *Mein Kampf*, translation, pp. 263 ff. (New York, 1939).

leader without reference to the other party members or functionaries. The basis of this authority was both formal and informal. It was embodied in the official statutes and was in this sense institutional. Yet its real basis was not legal but charismatic, the unqualified commitment of young activist followers to a successful leader.

The application of Wenzel and Seifert to form a Hanover branch of the NSDAP reached Munich a few weeks before this crisis reached its climax. Relations between the NSDAP and the DSP were still extremely confused. At the first international meeting of National Socialists which had been held at Salzburg in August 1920, it had been agreed to divide the areas north and south of the Main between the DSP and the NSDAP respectively. The decisions of the Zeitz meeting had made the situation even more complicated. The Munich head-quarters of the NSDAP still regarded the DSP as 'the National Socialists in North Germany' and therefore advised Seifert not to go ahead until further discussions had taken place with the leader of the DSP.[1] Wenzel and Seifert, however, were not prepared to wait. They sent out about 100 invitations to known sympathizers for a meeting on 2 July at a public house in the Gustav Adolf Strasse.

This determination to go ahead with the founding of an NSDAP branch in what was still DSP territory is of considerable interest because it helps us to understand why the NSDAP proved to be the most successful of the numerous *völkisch* organizations which existed at this period. What was it about the NSDAP which made it so much more attractive to many *völkisch* activists than the DSP, its biggest rival at this period? Fortunately, one of the founders of the Hanover branch, Seifert, has explained his motives very clearly. He wrote to a *völkisch* colleague:

I am not a follower of every new group that comes along. I joined the NSDAP because of my conviction that it is run by men who, above all, know what they want. You must agree with me that our educated classes have not the vestige of a talent for organization and, even though their theories may be well-meant, they almost always fail in practical work unless others do the work for them. Hitler and Drexler are men of action (Männer der Faust), who follow clearly defined policies, although they have not been to university.[2]

In contrast, as he explained to the Munich head-quarters, 'the DSP executive committees are packed with too many graduates'.[3] Seifert and others like him, who were disenchanted with the bourgeois composition and style of the *völkisch* movement, welcomed the NSDAP as

[1] Munich to Seifert, 25 June 1921; in NSDAP Hauptarchiv, Reel 6, Folder 141.
[2] Seifert to W. Kellerbauer-Augsburg, 6 Jan. 1922; in Hauptarchiv, Reel 6, Folder 141.
[3] Seifert to Munich, 22 July 1921, ibid.

a party with radical aims which projected an image of dynamic activity and showed an understanding of how to appeal to the masses. Here, those who were barred by the social exclusiveness of the DNVP found the type of political environment and activity which they were seeking: comradeship among those of similar status and outlook and grass-roots propaganda among the masses instead of endless intellectual discussion. Above all *action*.

Estimates of those who attended the founding meeting on 2 July 1921 vary between twenty and forty-five.[1] Of these thirteen agreed to join—nine men and four women. Munich must have meanwhile decided to give its blessing to the venture because the meeting was also attended by its representative, *Regierungsrat* Lauboek. It is significant for the characterization of the NSDAP that, at Wenzel's suggestion, it was Seifert who was elected chairman—'because he was a worker with his hands', while Wenzel himself became vice-chairman and the real leader.[2]

A second and rather badly attended meeting of the branch was held on 16 July.[3] The statutes were formally read out, approved and signed by all the members.[4] Munich was named as the party head-quarters and the *Völkischer Beobachter* as the official organ. People of 'alien race' were excluded from membership. The statutes reflected more democratic than autocratic principles of organization. The leadership was in the hands of an executive committee, composed of a chairman, vice-chairman with executive powers (Geschäftsführer), the secretary, and two other members. The committee was elected for a two-year period in a membership meeting and was responsible for appointing subordinate officials. With the important exception of the rule governing the expulsion of members, which was decided by the executive committee without requiring explanation, and the rather unclear distribution of powers between the committee and the meetings of the membership, the majority principle governed decision-making within the branch. Also interesting is the emphasis on the responsibility of the leadership to hold frequent meetings for propaganda purposes, which shows the determination to avoid a club atmosphere. Membership dues were fixed at an entrance fee of Reich Marks (RM) 2 and RM 2 per month for men, RM 1·50 for women, and RM 1 for those under 18.

Meetings were held regularly on Wednesday evenings for members

---

[1] Accounts of this meeting in Wenzel, op. cit., p. 4; Seifert, op. cit., p. 28; and Ludolf Haase, 'Aufstand in Niedersachsen. Der Kampf der NSDAP 1921–1924, (mimeo, 1942), pp. 11 ff.
[2] Haase, op. cit., p. 11.
[3] Seifert to Drexler, 17 July 1921; in Hauptarchiv, Reel 6, Folder 141.
[4] Copy of the statutes, ibid.

and their guests. But initially propaganda proved difficult.[1] On 6 October there were still only twenty-two members. The Party's terminology—the combination of 'national' and 'socialist'—met with a lack of comprehension from both Left and Right. There was not the same reservoir of students and ex-Freecorps men as existed in Munich. Hanover had voted 48·8 per cent SPD even in the election of 1920 which had seen a big swing to the Right throughout the Reich; and the middle classes in Hanover voted for the more moderate German People's Party and the traditionalist Guelph Party rather than for the more extreme right-wing DNVP, which only won 6·8 per cent of the vote in the same election.[2] Seifert complained to Hitler in the winter of 1921 that the biggest problem was the question of money:

The better-off circles refuse help . . . their whole aim is to win back their pre-war position of superiority, but if possible get other people to pull their chestnuts out of the fire for them. My two years membership of the *Deutsch-Völkischer Schutz und Trutz Bund* has opened my eyes.[3]

Soon after the foundation of the branch, on 26 August 1921, Erzberger, the leading Catholic politician, was assassinated by right-wing extremists; and the infuriated reaction of the Left intimidated the membership, so that for several weeks they stayed away from the meetings.[4] Nor could they rely on the authorities being sympathetic as could the Party in Bavaria. The *Oberpräsident* in Hanover was Gustav Noske, a tough right-wing Social Democrat who suppressed extremism from whatever quarter it came.[5]

The main propaganda effort was concentrated on the distribution of pamphlets and the putting up of posters, some of which were ordered from Munich and others which were printed in Hanover.[6] The pamphlets were aimed at the middle class, but above all at the workers. They were violently anti-Semitic. One of the most widely distributed pamphlets, printed in Munich by the *Völkischer Beobachter*, was titled 'Sensational Revelations in *The Times*' and purported to quote from a *Times* article, containing excerpts from the Protocols of the Wise Men of Zion. In a pamphlet aimed at the middle class, they appealed to

Artisans! Civil Servants! Artists! Graduates! War-pensioners! Pensioners! Officers! Shopkeepers! Small manufacturers! Have you not yet realized that you have already sunk below the so-called proletariat and are victims of the

[1] Seifert to Hitler, 6 Oct. 1921, in Hauptarchiv, Reel 6, Folder 141.
[2] G. Franz, op. cit., p. 126.
[3] Seifert to Hitler, 6 Oct. 1921, NSDAP Hauptarchiv, Reel 6, Folder 141.
[4] Ibid.
[5] See G. Noske, *Erlebtes aus Aufstieg und Niedergang einer Demokratie* (Offenbach, 1947).
[6] For the following handbills see NSDAP Hauptarchiv, Reel 6, Folder 141.

international Stock Exchange and currency speculation? Then you must organize yourselves politically. Political neutrality is disastrous. If you want to go on living you must fight. Individually you are nothing; united a power which no one can resist. The only popular movement which represents your interest is the NSDAP.

Above all, however, they tried to appeal to the workers. For example, in a pamphlet ironically titled for shock effect 'National Socialist Betrayers of the Workers Party', the workers were assured that the party was not 'yellow', that they favoured Trade Union organization to protect the economically weak; but the term 'exploiter' in the pamphlet was limited to the description of the 'international finance capitalists'. In another handbill headed 'New Treachery against the Workers!! Jewish-international Bank and Stock Exchange bandits under the protection of the USPD', they pointed out that although the Constitution had promised a decent human existence to all, only speculators and racketeers were profiting from the new republic. Later, in a further attempt to win the workers, Seifert was to suggest to Hitler the formation of a party Trade Union and a party consumers co-operative.[1] Yet what membership details survive seem to confirm the results of previous studies that it was the lower middle class which was most attracted to the party. The list of occupations of the first twenty-five members contains only one worker, and one fitter; of the remainder five were businessmen, seven artisans, three civil servants, two manufacturers, a clerk, a writer and four housewives.[2]

Another important method of propaganda was to make speeches at meetings held by other parties and organizations. As Seifert wrote to a friend,

the DSP which has already been in existence for two years does not dare to go out into the public and therefore does not make progress. Our main task must be to carry the living word into the mass of our people and make them aware of the incredible danger of Juda's fiendish activities.[3]

Seifert and Wenzel made particular use of protest meetings organized by others—artisans' associations protesting against the new trade tax or protests about the housing shortage. On the 4 August 1922, for example, the party demonstrated in the street for the first time, using a protest march against the housing shortage which had been organized by the SPD and KPD to draw attention to their own swastika banners. As inflation increased and discontent grew during 1922, the

[1] Seifert to Hitler, 15 June 1922, ibid.
[2] Membership list, NSDAP Hauptarchiv, Reel 6, Folder 141.
[3] Ibid., Seifert to T. F. Viergutz-Hellerau bei Dresden, 6 Sept. 1921.

party increased its membership and by May there were ninety members. The increased membership enabled the party to book a number of outside speakers. On 2 May 1922 for example, Herman Esser, an important figure in the Munich organization, spoke to an audience of 600; the meeting brought in more than 1,500 RM and above all 'from now on an uninterrupted stream of requests for membership and newspaper orders'.[1]

(iii) *The NSDAP outside Hanover 1921–1923*

The leaders of the Hanover branch did not limit their activities to the city of Hanover itself, despite a warning from Hitler of the 'great danger of dividing your energies' and his advice to concentrate on Hanover and build it into a bulwark.[2] During the winter of 1921 and the spring of 1922, Wenzel and Seifert began to hold meetings in neighbouring *Kreise* such as Gifhorn, Nienburg, Göttingen, Brunswick and Wolfenbüttel.[3] In February 1922 a branch was formed in Göttingen with twelve members and by the end of the year this had been followed by branches in Gifhorn, Wolfenbüttel, Grasdorf/Hanover, Bergen/Celle, and Hildesheim.[4] In Wolfenbüttel, after the banning of the DVSTB branch by the state government of Brunswick, its members joined Kunze's Deutsch-Soziale Partei, another *völkisch* group.[5] In November–December 1922, however, after this party had also been banned, they decided to join the NSDAP. Dr. Kahle, the Medical Officer of Health in Gifhorn, who had been won over by Wenzel, had given them a talk on the party programme and a member of the branch had visited Hitler in Munich. Soon afterwards, on 15 February 1923, a branch was founded in nearby Brunswick which by arrangement with Munich took the title of the 'Brunswick department of the Munich branch of the NSDAP', in order to avoid a ban. These two branches received considerable support from Hanover. Thus between February and August 1923 Wenzel held fifteen meetings for the Brunswick branch.[6]

Invariably, the platform for the NSDAP speakers was provided by members of the DVSTB. An interesting example is the invitation from the Helmstedt DVSTB branch to Seifert: 'We do not want a Jürgen von Ramin or a *Landrat* or suchlike, but men who have fewer

[1] Wenzel, op. cit., p. 8.
[2] Hitler to Seifert, 6 Sept. 1921, in NSDAP Hauptarchiv, Reel 6, Folder 141.
[3] Wenzel, op. cit., pp. 6–7.
[4] Seifert, op. cit., p. 33.
[5] Die Geschichte der NSDAP im Kreise Wolfenbüttel. 1937 in NSAH Hann. Des. 310 I A Nr. 92 and report of the Fremdenpolizei Braunschweig, 25 July 1923, NSA Wolfenbüttel 12 A Neu Fb 7 4004.
[6] See the list of Wenzel's speeches; in NSDAP Hauptarchiv, Reel 6, Folder 141.

titles and more common sense, and the gift of speaking to the hearts of common men.'[1] It was also activists of the DVSTB who took the initiative in founding the new NSDAP branches:—a medical student in Göttingen,[2] Dr. Kahle in Gifhorn,[3] and teachers in Bergen and Grasdorf.[4]

In the north-western part of Lower Saxony the first NSDAP group was formed by a young student, who had heard Hitler in Munich and brought back home with him to Oldenburg a copy of the NSDAP programme.[5] Several members of the group had been excluded from the local *Stahlhelm* because of their *völkisch* extremism. The *völkisch* movement in general and the NSDAP in particular were comparatively strong in the northern part of Oldenburg and in East Friesland. The first evidence for *völkisch* activity in the area is a report on the founding of a branch of the DVSTB in Wilhelmshaven by members of a minesweeper flotilla at the end of 1919.[6] Among other places, members of this branch staged meetings in Neustadt-Gödens, a village in Kreis Wittmund with a considerable Jewish settlement.[7] By the beginning of 1923 two *völkisch* organizations which had established themselves in Bremen and Wilhelmshaven—the *Treudeutscher Bund* and the *Bund deutschdenkender Arbeiter*—were active in East Friesland, holding speeches and distributing pamphlets.[8] They made a particular effort to reach the workers and were led by a schoolmaster, Dr. Rüthnick of Bremen, by a former naval officer, and by a businessman who had fought with the Free Corps in the Baltic states; in fact a typical group of early *völkisch* activists. Their contact man in East Friesland was a lawyer in the town of Norden. The *Treudeutscher Bund* appears to have been connected with the NSDAP since Seifert from Hanover was a frequent speaker. It was probably a cover organization for the NSDAP supporters in East Friesland after the banning of the party in Prussia in November 1922. Another group associated with the NSDAP existed in North Oldenburg (Friesland and Butjadingen).[9]

---

[1] DVSTB branch in Helmstedt to Seifert 3 Mar. 1922, ibid. Ramin was a leading member of the *völkisch* movement.

[2] See below.

[3] 'Wir waren dabei. Berichte über die nationalsozialistische Bewegung in Isenhagen' in BA Sammlung Schumacher 202 I.

[4] Report of the Oberpräsidium Hannover, 6 July 1922, NSAH Hann. Des. 122 a XI Nr. 76 and 'Geschichte der Ortsgruppe Grasdorf' in NSAH Hann. Des. 310 I A, Nr. 67.

[5] Haase, op. cit., pp. 91 ff.

[6] See p. 10 above.

[7] Report of a public meeting in the hotel *Zur deutschen Eiche* in Neustadt-Gödens, 26 Jan. 1920, in NSDAP Hauptarchiv, Reel 7, Folder 163.

[8] For the following see the reports of the Landespolizeistelle Willhelmshaven for 1923 in NSAA Rep. 21a 4731 and Oldenburg police reports in NSAO 136 2858.

[9] Haase, op. cit., pp. 92 ff.

It was led by a group of young teachers who published the *Butjadinger Beobachter*, a weekly which relied on Seifert in Hanover for its material.

(iv) *The NSDAP in Göttingen 1921–1922*

The most important of the new NSDAP branches to be formed outside Hanover at this period was Göttingen, which was indeed soon to replace Hanover as the most effective group in Lower Saxony. The first member in Göttingen was a painter who joined the Hanover branch in September 1921, but the initiative was taken by a young medical student, Ludolf Haase.[1] Just before the war Haase had organized weekly readings for a group of fellow grammar school pupils out of *The Struggle against the Jews* by a doctor of medicine called Stille, a book which he had 'dug out of his father's cupboard'. Dr. Stille had been a member of the *Deutsch Sozialen*, a pre-war anti-Semitic party. Through this book and through his own 'observations', Haase had discovered that 'right among us there lived a deadly enemy, a carrier of physical and spiritual plague'—the Jews.

Immediately after the war, in company with some of his former fellow-pupils, Haase began distributing anti-Semitic leaflets in Hanover and joined a volunteer battalion, part of the Free Corps. Then, after moving to Göttingen to begin his studies, and together with two other students, he succeeded in overthrowing the leadership of the local branch of the DVSTB which they considered to be inactive and, in 1921, he was elected chairman. Yet despite the comparatively large membership of the branch (200), and despite the presence within it of a considerable number of young officers and students, Haase felt that it lacked *élan*. Disillusioned with the nationalist bourgeoisie, he began to look for a more active movement and one more aware of the 'social problem', that is to say of the need to win mass support. He worked for a short time with Kunze's *Deutsch-Soziale Partei*, but then having heard stories of 'a completely new type of organization, which was really aggressive', he travelled to Munich. Haase described his feelings on attending his first Nazi meeting as follows:

It was like a dream. Instead of the usual feebleness, he (the author) saw real workers' storm troops, tough boys with horny hands and felt the hot breath of the uncorrupted, fighting soul of the people. Herman Esser, who spoke on the 'Protocols of the Elders of Zion' used language that was unparalleled in comparison with what we were used to in the rest of Germany. At once it was clear: only this movement, if any, had a chance of winning power.

On his return to Göttingen, Haase contacted a few members of the DVSTB who were sympathetic to his ideas. Then he met Wenzel on

[1] For the following see Haase, op. cit., p. 101 ff.

a visit to a DVSTB gathering in Hanover and arranged to organize an NSDAP branch in Göttingen.

The branch in Göttingen was founded on 7–8 February 1922 with twelve members. Because of the dislike of students among the workers, a caretaker was elected chairman, while Haase controlled the branch from the background; intellectuals were temporarily banned from joining. Only nine of the first twelve members' occupations have been recorded. These were two caretakers, a medical student, a printer, a milk salesman, a gamekeeper, a foreman, a lathe operator, and a sculptress.

Soon after its foundation the Göttingen branch was active, establishing NSDAP groups in the surrounding countryside. The most successful of these was in the neighbouring town of Northeim. The initiative here was taken by two brothers, Karl and Ernst Girmann, the owners of a small ironmonger's shop, and Karl Ernst, an unsuccessful salesman.[1] Between 1920 and 1922 they had been members of the nationalist paramilitary organization *Jungdeutscher Orden*. But they had found its aims 'insufficiently clear and consistent' and gladly accepted the invitation of a NSDAP contact man to attend the first mass demonstration in Göttingen on 18 November 1922. The image of Haase speaking passionately to the crowd in his *Räuberzivil* made a deep impression and they joined the party at once. They were also impressed by the fact that the list for signatures of those who wished to join was headed 'We are looking for men ready to help us fight (*Mitkämpfer*) not passengers (*Mitläufer*).' Haase continues:

the new members at once began an active propaganda campaign, through which significantly they attracted above all the young people, apprentices, students, grammar school boys. These were joined by several workers, mostly unemployed, together with a few artisans and tradesmen. They began at once with the SA exercises. . . . There was no separation between political work and service in the SA, everyone took part in the SA exercises and vice versa.

The character of this activity is clear from the anecdotes which Haase believes worthy of record. Thus he describes with amusement how the Northeim SA broke up a meeting of a student supporter of the bourgeois German People's Party and then forced him to buy them a round of drinks, and mentions with contempt the shock of a factory owner and previous supporter of the NSDAP when he heard of the event. Haase sums up the attitude of the NSDAP supporters in Göttingen by stating 'that the atmosphere of the University made us opponents of "refined intellectualism" that attitude which rejected every deed as "exaggerated", "youthful excess", etc.'.[2]

[1] For the following see Haase, op. cit., pp. 272 ff. W. S. Allen, *The Nazi Seizure of Power*, pp. 75–6 gives their occupations.
[2] Haase, op. cit., p. 626.

(v) *The creation of an SA*

As the Party enlarged its activities, it increasingly provoked opposition from the Left. A public meeting on the 17 August 1922, at which about 100 people listened to a speech on 'The Struggle against those responsible for the insane inflation', ended in uproar, provoked by Communist hecklers.[1] Partly for this reason, and partly because, as Haase put it 'the spirit of what we said and the image which the party presented to the spectator had to correspond',[2] the NSDAP had soon organized storm troops in both Hanover and Göttingen. In the second meeting of the Hanover branch on 16 July 1921 a heckler had been ejected and Seifert had then begun a course in jiu-jitsu for the male membership. An SA was formed of those members who were active in other paramilitary organizations, war veterans, or those trained in sport, for which a special account was opened on 1 February 1922 and which was put under the quasi-military command of a former aristocratic officer.[3] In Göttingen strong-arm stewards with swastika armbands were introduced in the first meetings, although, according to Haase 'strictly speaking they did not yet have much to control'.[4] Apart from the defence of meetings and the intimidation of hecklers, the storm troops were also useful for attack. Thus on the 22 November 1921 Seifert informed Hitler that he was training a storm troop 'so that I can visit the meetings of opponents with it'.[5] Finally, as in Munich, the SA acted as an advertisement for the party among those who were already involved in paramilitary activities, and who provided the main body of new recruits.

The period 1919–1922 then saw the NSDAP emerge as the most radical group in the *völkisch* movement in Lower Saxony. This was important since potential supporters were all seeking the most effective among the considerable number of *völkisch* groups which existed and effectiveness was judged essentially in terms of both the radicalism of the party's aims and methods and the extent to which it mobilized the individual in its cause, giving him the impression of active participation in a movement. This activism distinguished the NSDAP from other *völkisch* political parties, who were offering a similar 'socialist' political programme in an attempt to organize the lower middle class and working class who were alienated from the reactionary and socially exclusive

[1] Hanover political police monthly report, 22 Aug. 1922, in NSAH Hann Des. 80 Hann II No. 718.

[2] Haase, op. cit., p. 133.

[3] Seifert, op. cit.; and Gerhard Nodewald, Aus der Geschichte der ersten SA in Hanover in den Jahren 1921/5, in Hoover Institution NSDAP Hauptarchiv, Reel 6, Folder 141.

[4] Haase, op. cit., p. 133.

[5] Seifert to Hitler, 22 Nov. 1921, in NSDAP Hauptarchiv, Reel 6, Folder 141.

DNVP. But it was the political programme which distinguished the NSDAP from the activist paramilitary groups which derived from the Free Corps movement. The NSDAP, therefore, succeeded in synthesizing two major components of the extreme Right in post-war Germany: the *völkisch* elements among the lower middle and working class, and the Free Corps activists. Through its combination of political and paramilitary activity, the NSDAP could harness the tremendous energy and enthusiasm of former members of the Free Corps and other paramilitary organizations to the propaganda activities of a political party. The *élan* which it thereby acquired and communicated were in turn effective in winning new recruits.

(vi) *Relations with Munich*

It should be emphasized that in this early period there did not exist the disciplined parties within the *völkisch* movement which were to emerge after 1925. The situation was exceptionally fluid and confused. In the words of the historians of the Nazi movement in Oldenburg: 'In those days one really belonged to all the groups. They were all members of the DVSTB, also of the Ehrhardt Brigade, the National Association of German Officers or the Association of Nationalist Soldiers, of the *Deutscher Herold* etc. It was always the same people.'[1] It was only after 1925 that Hitler was successful in overcoming this multiple membership of *völkisch* organizations, in order to create a disciplined party. He had begun to lay the foundations of such a party through his resistance to amalgamation with the DSP and through his redrafting of the statutes, but he had much less success in establishing a tight control over his party outside Bavaria.

During the first few months after the founding of the NSDAP branch in Hanover, the position *vis-à-vis* the DSP branch in the City remained unclear. For although Seifert far preferred the NSDAP, he nonetheless believed that it should only be part of a wider *völkisch* movement: 'Presumably', he wrote to a colleague, 'we are all quite clear about the fact that as a single organization we can never achieve what could be won by a unified movement.'[2] He kept trying to persuade Munich of the need to maintain contacts with similar groups.[3] Hitler, who had resigned to prevent the amalgamation of his party with the DSP, opposed Seifert's arguments and insisted that 'what we need is to bring in an energetic mass if possible from the extreme Left

[1] Haase, op. cit., p. 91.
[2] Seifert to J. Seidel. Führer des Deutschen Volksbundes, Dresden, 24 Nov. 1921. NSDAP Hauptarchiv, Reel 6, Folder 141.
[3] E.g. Seifert to Munich, 18 Aug. 1921; NSDAP Hauptarchiv, Reel 6, Folder 141.

and the extreme Right'; Seifert should therefore 'let things ripen'. 'Whether you succeed in winning over the valuable parts of these groups will depend on how effective you are; therefore propaganda and still more propaganda.'[1] Seifert, however, remained unconvinced and attended a DSP meeting at Magdeburg in the hope that an agreement might be reached.[2] His experience here of the disunity and sterile bickering of the DSP finally convinced him of its worthlessness.

Hitler expressed his satisfaction at Seifert's change of mind. He emphasized that while there was 'no reason to attack all groups with different views to us, we must attack those who pretend to have the same views'.[3] But it had also become clear to Hitler that it was essential to lay down basic lines of policy for the party if he wished to avoid deviations on the part of branches outside his immediate control.

At the NSDAP Congress in Munich in January 1922, delegates including Wenzel and Seifert assembled to hear Hitler speak on what he described as the two important topics of the meeting: the clarification of the party's position in relation to similar movements, and the further development of the party's organization.[4] In his speech Hitler made two points.[5] First, he attacked the other groups on the Right: the Conservatives were cowards who 'while mouthing patriotic slogans' in fact 'trembled in front of every thug' and 'compromised every other day', and the *Völkische* were a crowd of academic dreamers who forgot 'that they were not living in the year 600 or 700 but in 1920'. In particular he attacked their political style—'the incredible cowardice, the weakness which expressed itself in the apologetic phrase about 'a dignified, *bürgerlich* decent, intellectually based "political style"''. Secondly, Hitler attacked the decentralization of the *völkisch* movement and insisted on the need for a 'ruthless, tight organization' with a definite head-quarters, and claimed that the NSDAP and Munich had, through their success, demonstrated their right to that organization and head-quarters. He directed that in the future all branches would receive statutes and membership cards from Munich. After the meeting, where Hitler's proposals had been unanimously accepted, the Hanover branch complained about the postal charges involved in this plan and suggested that Munich should send blank party cards which the branch could then issue themselves, rather than having to send for each card individually.[6] It appears, in fact, that Hitler had overestimated the organizational efficiency of his own head-quarters. Four

[1] Hitler to Seifert, 6 Sept. 1921, ibid.
[2] Seifert to W. Kellerbauer-Augsburg, 6 Jan. 1922, ibid.
[3] Hitler to Seifert, 5 Jan. 1922, ibid.
[4] Report on Parteitag by Wenzel, ibid.
[5] Copy of speech in Haase, op. cit., p. 122 ff.
[6] Seifert to Hitler, 24 Apr. 1922; NSDAP Hauptarchiv, Reel 6, Folder 141.

months later, the Hanover branch was asking what had happened to the plan.[1]

After the Munich meeting there were no more suggestions from Seifert of association with the DSP. In fact, during January, the DSP branch had been dissolved. Its chairman was elected vice-chairman of the NSDAP branch and part of its membership was absorbed. But the influence of Munich in this period remained limited judged by later standards. The tone of the correspondence from Munich was one of exhortation rather than command. In fact, only rarely did the branch receive advice and there were few directives.[2] Repeated visits to Munich were necessary to find out the wishes and plans of the headquarters. Furthermore, the Hanover branch had not been transformed into an autocratic organization as had happened in Munich after Hitler's seizure of power; it still appears to have been more like a club, with a careful emphasis on procedure. Thus Seifert reported that after the exclusion of the vice-chairman, the former leader of the DSP, for lack of interest, his successor had been 'duly elected in our membership meeting on 17 March'.[3]

[1] Seifert to Hitler, 20 May 1922, ibid.   [2] Haase, op. cit., p. 190.
[3] See footnote 1.

II

THE PERIOD OF ILLEGALITY (FIRST PHASE) 1922–1923

(i) *The banning of the NSDAP in Prussia—17 November 1922*

O N 24 June 1922 Walther Rathenau, the Jewish Foreign Minister, was assassinated by members of the extreme right-wing 'Organization Consul'. The reaction to this murder, particularly from official quarters, threatened to make political activity for the extreme Right more difficult. Two days later, a Decree for the Protection of the Republic was published making it easier for the authorities to take action against anti-Republican meetings and speeches. This was followed on 1 July by a decree of the Prussian Ministry of the Interior banning the DVSTB in Prussia. Despite this, however, the Hanover branch of the NSDAP continued with its celebrations of the first anniversary of its foundation on 2 July and membership continued to rise. On 2 July the branch had 104 members, by 17 November the figure had increased to 316.[1] The November report of the Hanover political police noted 'great activity' on the part of the NSDAP.[2] A potential new source of support were the members of the ex-servicemen's association, the *Stahlhelm*, which had been banned in the Province of Hanover on 6 July 1922. Hitler's name had already appeared for the first time in the North German press over his threatened deportation by the Bavarian government as an alien in the spring. Attracted by his extremism, a number of the more activist former *Stahlhelm* members made contact and joined the branch.[3]

In the middle of this steady, though by no means spectacular, progress came the news that the SPD Prussian Minister of the Interior had banned the NSDAP from 17 November. At first the Hanover branch answered the ban with defiance. Ten days later, Seifert placarded Hanover with large posters attacking it; and the party carried through its Christmas celebrations as if nothing had happened.[4] But it soon became apparent that the ban represented a serious obstacle to

[1] Wenzel, NSDAP Hauptarchiv, Reel 6, Folder 141, pp. 9–10.
[2] Monthly report for Nov. of the Hanover political police. NSAH Hann. Des. 80 Hann II, No. 718.
[3] See F. Kopprasch, 'Erinnerungen verflossener Tage', *Die Nationalsozialistische Bewegung 1921–24* (Hanover, 1933), p. 22.
[4] Seifert, NSDAP Hauptarchiv, Reel 6, Folder 141, p. 88.

political activity. The laxity of the police in permitting the Christmas celebrations had been attacked in the SPD newspaper, *Volkswille*, on 28 December, and from now on the police broke up attempts by the party to hold meetings.[1]

This ban on the NSDAP created an entirely new situation, particularly since it coincided with the emergence of a new anti-Semitic party—the *Deutsch-völkische Freiheitspartei* (DVFP). This new party had been founded on 17 December 1922 in Berlin by three leading members of the DNVP, von Graefe, Wulle, and Henning, who had resigned from that party because of the unwillingness of the leadership to adopt a more extreme racialist position.[2] The Hanover branch was founded on 23 December 1922 by a number of former officers and businessmen, of whom the most important were a Major Dietlein and the former secretary of the Hanover DNVP branch, Major Dincklage.[3]

Over the next few years the founding of the DVFP was to have an important effect on the development of anti-Semitism in North Germany in general and Lower Saxony in particular. It meant that just as the NSDAP was banned, a new specifically racialist party emerged possessing important advantages. In the first place, it began with the support or potential support of the majority of racialists who had joined or voted for the DNVP since 1919. Secondly, while the NSDAP had only a few branches concentrated in the Hanover and Göttingen areas and a few members elsewhere, particularly in the State of Oldenburg,[4] the DVFP possessed an organization which spanned the whole of Lower Saxony since a number of influential DNVP members in various parts, including Major Henning, the DNVP *Reichstag* deputy for Weser-Ems, and Pastor Voss, the Prussian *Landtag* deputy for Hanover-East, had joined the secession. Finally, its three leaders were members of the *Reichstag* and this gave the party immunity from police interference until it too was banned on 23 March 1923.[5]

A number of members, however, particularly in the Göttingen area, bitterly resisted the attempt of the DVFP to absorb them and

[1] Wenzel, op. cit., p. 11.

[2] Hertzmann, *DNVP. Right-Wing Opposition in the Weimar Republic 1918–1924* p. 124 ff.

[3] Hanover political police report for Dec. 1922, NSAH Hann. Des. 80 Hann II, Nr. 718 and Seifert, op. cit., pp. 41–2.

[4] For the NSDAP in the state of Oldenburg see Haase, 'Aufstand in Niedersachsen' (mimeo, 1942), p. 91 ff.

[5] Severing advised the Reichskommissar für Ueberwachung der öffentlichen Ordnung, in a letter of 12 Mar. 1923, that they would have to proceed cautiously with regard to the DVFP, because it was represented in the *Reichstag*—see NSAS G VII 10 27.

began a struggle which was to dominate the *völkisch* movement over the next two years. This conflict was not limited to Hanover; it was to split the movement throughout North Germany. What were the issues at stake?

In the eyes of its opponents, the DVFP, despite its racialist programme, had little to distinguish it from the other bourgeois parties. It was too much like the pre-war anti-Semitic groups which had failed because of their lack of mass appeal and because they had become infected with 'Jewish parliamentary compromise'. Significantly, in order to define their position *vis-à-vis* the DVFP they quoted an old memorandum of Hitler's in which he had attacked the *völkisch* movement which had emerged since 1918 in organizations such as the DVSTB. This movement, according to Hitler, was

similar to that of the 80s and 90s and, just as in those days, control over it was acquired by entirely honourable but fantastically naïve scholars, professors, *Land-*, *Studien-* and *Justizräte*, in short middle-class idealists. It lacked the warm breath of youthful energy. The impetuous drive of enthusiastic hotheads was rejected as demagogy. As a result the new movement was a *völkisch* but not a popular movement (*Volksbewegung*). It remained alien above all to millions of our working class compatriots.[1]

He also attacked its 'lack of determination when necessary to act with the most brutal ruthlessness' and its lack of strict discipline and organization. It was the weakness of this movement, Hitler maintained, which had necessitated the foundation of the NSDAP. His arguments were now repeated verbatim by the opponents of the DVFP in defence of their own independence. In effect, the real distinction between the NSDAP and its *völkisch* rivals lay in the desire and ability of the NSDAP to evolve a political style adapted to the radicalized political conditions of post-war Germany and in particular to the 'Front generation' and its heir, who, in the words of one of their most articulate spokesmen, were 'still marching . . . marching for the revolution, for another revolution, . . . discontented when they disperse, dynamite when they remain together'.[2] From the point of view of its opponents, the desire of the DVFP to unify the *völkisch* movement into a parliamentary party endangered the existence of the NSDAP as, in Hitler's definition, a *Kampforganisation* dedicated to the overthrow of the Weimar political system.

(ii) *Developments in Hanover during 1923*

In December 1922, however, this struggle lay in the future. The immediate problem was how to get round the ban on the NSDAP.

[1] Werner Jochmann, *Nationalsozialismus und Revolution. Dokumente* (Frankfurt, 1963), pp. 88–9.
[2] E. von Salomon, *Die Geächteten. Neuausgabe* (Hamburg, 1962), p. 29.

One possible way out was offered by the Free Corps leader, Rossbach, who had been introduced to Hitler by Wenzel at the big German Day in Coburg in the autumn of 1922 and who had become a member of the NSDAP.[1] Rossbach, who felt that the Severing ban threatened to wipe out the remnants of his own Free Corps (many of whom were members of the NSDAP), decided to form a new party with a virtually identical programme to operate in Prussia in place of the banned NSDAP.

At the end of November, therefore, Rossbach founded the *Grossdeutsche Arbeiterpartei* (GDAP) in Berlin with Wenzel as its political director. The Hanover branch of the new party was founded at a meeting in the Landesheim on the 6 December 1922, organized by a ' Herr Oertzen' who was clearly a front man for Wenzel and Seifert.[2] The meeting was attended by approximately 500 people and the party immediately began a vigorous propaganda campaign with pamphlets and speeches at the meetings of other parties. But the founding of the new party had not gone unnoticed by the authorities and, on 10 January 1923, Severing banned it on the grounds that it was a continuation of the NSDAP under another name.[3]

The former members of the NSDAP were now back where they had started. In this situation Rossbach thought the only solution was an alliance with the DVFP, which was to some extent protected against Severing by its *Reichstag* deputies. At a meeting of *völkisch* leaders in the *Reichstag*, therefore, he agreed that his organization should come under the aegis of the DVFP with a new name—the *Grossdeutsche Arbeiterbewegung*.[4] The DVFP hoped thereby to win mass support and in particular to penetrate the working class.

Wenzel, however, was discontented with the result of the Berlin meeting, construing it as a sell-out to the DVFP. Thus although initially the GDAP in Hanover were prepared to co-operate with the DVFP (at a meeting in Hanover on 21 February they agreed to join the DVFP in return for a seat on the committee[5]), within a week the arrangement was breaking down due to disagreement over the NSDAP representatives on the committee and over the conditions which the GDAP insisted had been laid down at the *Reichstag* meeting.[6]

[1] Wenzel, 'Die Gründung der Ortsgruppe Hannover, ihre Vorgeschichte und Entwicklung', in *Die nationalsozialistische Bewegung 1921–1924* (Hanover, 1933), p. 13.
[2] Hanover political police reports in NSAH Hann. Des. 80 Hann II, Nr. 718.
[3] Ministerialblatt für die Preussische innere Verwaltung 10 Jan. 1923, in Niedersächsisches Staatsarchiv Stade (in future NSAS) G VII b.27.
[4] Wenzel, op. cit., p. 13.
[5] Hanover political police report of 10 Mar. 1923, in NSAH Hann. Des. 80 Hann II, Nr. 718.
[6] Dietlein to Wenzel 27 Feb. 1923, in NSAH Hann. Des. 310 I A, Nr. 70.

The situation in Prussia remained extremely confused throughout 1923, particularly in Hanover. As Wenzel put it, the ban on the NSDAP and its successor organization, the GDAP, together with the existence of the DVFP, until it too was banned in March, caused 'conflicts among our members who tended to prefer either the practical advantages offered by a permitted "club life" or the strict principle of the national socialism which had been banned'.[1] Even the leadership was not immune to the temptation offered by the DVFP. Wenzel later hesitated for a time when offered the leadership of the DVFP branch in Hanover, thereby confusing his supporters and losing the confidence of Hitler.[2] Attempts were made to found front organizations such as a 'Verein zur Hebung des Deutschtums im Inlande' (Club for the strengthening of Germanness at home), but they were only partially successful. It was possible to hold quite large private meetings, but effective propaganda was ruled out.

In this situation Wenzel and Seifert turned their attention to those areas in Lower Saxony which were independent of Prussia: Brunswick, where they succeeded in building up quite a successful organization composed largely of discontented Independent Socialists,[3] and Bremen and Oldenburg where they were rather less successful. These activities were financed by the Pan-German League. At the Berlin meeting Wenzel had met a Free Corps colleague of Rossbach, Heinz Hauenstein, who put him in touch with the League. The Pan-Germans, who objected to the take-over of the *völkisch* movement by the DVFP leadership, saw an opportunity for undermining the DVFP by supporting Wenzel's national socialist activities with a sum of RM 1 million. Wenzel at once visited Hitler in Munich to ask permission to accept the money and was told: 'If you can get 10 million instead of 1 million all the better. It is the same source that I am tapping at the moment. Politically we all depend on the Pan German League, of which we can only complain that, despite its correct analysis and the long existence of such an influential organization, up to now it has done no practical work. But now we can make up for this by using its resources.'[4]

The banning of the NSDAP had created something of a vacuum on the extreme right at a time of increasing political crisis. Into this vacuum moved a figure whose character and activities throw interesting light on the atmosphere of the post-War *völkisch* movement. Georg

[1] Wenzel, op. cit., p. 19.
[2] Wenzel, Autobiography, p. 17, NSDAP Hauptarchiv, Reel 6, Folder 141.
[3] Ibid., p. 13.
[4] Ibid. Hitler denied knowledge of Wenzel's affiliation with the Pan German League in a letter to Seifert, 23 Aug. 1923 in NSDAP Hauptarchiv, Reel 6, Folder 141 but Wenzel's account of his interview with Hitler sounds convincing.

Quindel had some claim to be regarded as the most active anti-Semitic agitator in post-war Hanover. Quindel, a convicted confidence trickster, had spent nearly two years distributing anti-Semitic pamphlets before founding the first anti-Semitic paper in Hanover, the weekly *Der Sturm* on 1 May 1921.[1] Using his new influence, Quindel succeeded in having the head-quarters of the DVSTB and of a paramilitary group *Jungsturm im Landesverband Niedersachsen* transferred to his publishing house.[2] Then, after the ban on the DVSTB, he founded a *Lesergemeinde deutschvölkischer Blätter* on 15 September 1922 with regular meetings every Thursday, often with outside speakers.[3] After the NSDAP increased in importance during 1922, Quindel persuaded them to use *Der Sturm* as the Party organ.[4]

In March 1923 Quindel was arrested for his racialist activities, spending the next two months in prison, and *Der Sturm* was banned until 1 May.[5] Initially it was agreed among the leaders of the banned NSDAP that they should keep the paper going until Quindel's release. However, Wenzel and the SA leader, Schreiber, then decided to take over the publishing house and start a new paper, buying off Quindel with a settlement of RM 4–6,000 a month for the next six months. Quindel was extremely indignant at receiving such an ultimatum and refused to co-operate. He had the advantage of possessing a paper and countered their move by publishing accusations against them. This forced his opponents to found their own newspaper, which appeared on 20 May with the title *Der Niedersächsische Beobachter*, and which printed an attack on Quindel exposing his prison record, entitled 'Swindle Quindel'. But Quindel had taken the initiative and succeeded in winning over many former NSDAP supporters, including most of the SA. He now built up his own organization, which was financed, as his paper had been, by appeals to businessmen and landowners for resources with which to fight the Communist threat. Quindel, Seifert, and Wenzel appealed repeatedly to the NSDAP head-quarters in Munich for official recognition.[6] But Munich was too preoccupied with the important developments in Bavaria to pay much attention to the infighting in the North. Quindel vastly exaggerated the number of his followers. Nevertheless, he astonished his rivals with his success in

[1] For the Quindel affair see Haase, op. cit., pp. 201 ff.

[2] Report of Hanover police to the Oberpräsident in Hanover, in NSAH Hann. Des 122a, Nr. 76.

[3] Monthly report of Hanover political police, 20 Sept. 1922, in NSAH Hann. Des 80 Hann II, Nr. 718.

[4] Haase, op. cit., p. 206.

[5] For the following see Seifert to Hitler, 26 Aug. 1923, National Archives T-84, Reel 4, Frames 3803, and Haase, op. cit., p. 207 and pp. 226 ff.

[6] See the correspondence with Hitler of Oct. 1923, in National Archives T-84, Reel 4.

acquiring financial support.[1] His technique was to organize a storm troop, by winning them with uniforms and money; and then to send them to protect landowners and peasants, frightened by tales of the Communist threat. In return for this service, Quindel received a stream of food deliveries which could then be sold or distributed among his supporters. On 26 May 1923, the day when Schlageter was executed by the French for sabotage in the Ruhr, Quindel gave his backing to the formation of a new organization of storm troops, known as the *Schlageter-Gedächtnis-Bund*. This organization rapidly spread beyond Hanover and a considerable number of branches were founded throughout the Reich.[2] In Hanover itself there were three troops with together approximately 350 men.

(iii) *Developments in Göttingen during 1923*

In Lower Saxony the lead in the struggle against the DVFP was taken by the Göttingen branch. Haase had already shown his resourcefulness by the way he met the ban on the NSDAP in November 1922.[3] The Göttingen branch had planned its first mass meeting for 18 November. When the police banned it, Haase won the support of the local branches of the right-wing paramilitary organizations, *Orgesch* and *Jungdeutscher Orden*, and a large number of student associations for a mass protest march through the city which lasted for several hours. The demonstration was a great success—the branch doubled its membership from twenty-five to fifty as a result. Among the new members was a Dr. Jander of the University Institute of Chemistry, who began successfully canvassing for members among his own University colleagues. An SA with forty-five members—largely ex-soldiers and Free Corps—was quickly formed and began holding regular exercises with a few weapons in the Eber valley outside the town.

On learning from Hanover of the founding of the GDAP, Haase at once established a branch in Göttingen and held a meeting on 9 December to capitalize on the publicity created by the protest march.[4] Wenzel was the main speaker and this meeting too was very successful —seventy new members joined, mostly students. Apart from the activity of the SA, the branch concentrated on placarding the town with posters. The police, despite directives from the *Oberpräsident* in Hanover, were unable to catch the offenders, partly because a number of police sympathized with the aims of the GDAP.[5] They were also

[1] Haase, op. cit., pp. 215 ff.
[2] See *Schlageter-Gedächtnis-Bund* material, in NSAH Hann. Des. 310 I H.
[3] Haase, op. cit., pp. 152 ff.   [4] Ibid., pp. 163 ff.
[5] Ibid., and correspondence between the Polizeidirektion Göttingen and the Regierungspräsident in Hildesheim in Stadtarchiv Göttingen (SAG) XXVII, 156, No. 2.

fortunate in having the continued support of the leading bourgeois paper in the city—the *Göttinger Tageblatt* whose proprietor, Gustav Wurm, had been a racialist since before the war, and which printed propaganda material for them free.[1] Financing their organization, however, presented serious problems, for the membership dues were insufficient. It required 'a laborious effort to establish connections with the commercial world and with industry. The shopkeepers were easiest; with industry only small firms co-operated, while the large ones remained without exception doggedly reactionary.'[2]

Under Haase, the Göttingen branch was dominated by a group of student activists, some of whom were to reach important positions within the NSDAP at *Gau* and even at Reich level, most notably Herbert Backe, Darré's successor as head of the Reich Food Estate. Significantly, these men used support for Adolf Hitler as their programme and their badge of independence. Just as in Munich, where the Esser group had backed Hitler in his struggle with the older more moderate leadership of the party, in Lower Saxony it was the young and radical members who were unwilling to be absorbed and neutralized in the bourgeois and *spiessig* DVFP and who declared Hitler to be the only acceptable leader. For these men, Hitler not only represented a radical *völkisch* stance but also his party was a form of organization which had great appeal. The *Führerprinzip* and the SA, both of which were unique to the NSDAP among the political parties, gave the party features similar to the organizations of which they had experience and in which they had been moulded—the army and the Free Corps.

Haase and the Göttingen group devoted great attention to the technique of organization. The banning of the NSDAP posed similar problems for the branch in Göttingen as it had for the branch in Hanover. But unlike in Hanover where the leadership was divided between Wenzel, Seifert, and even the SA leader, Schreiber, Haase had taken over absolute control of the branch after the ban and this was to be of vital importance in maintaining cohesion in the confused period which followed.[3] On occasions when there was a serious disagreement within the branch, Haase would give instructions to the SA to throw the dissenters out.[4] Furthermore, Haase had established a *Deutscher Arbeiter und Mittelstandsverein* as a front organization, which provided a cover for meetings and other activity during the ban.[5] They even succeeded in founding branches in neighbouring towns—the most successful were in Northeim and Moringen.

[1] Haase, op. cit., p. 282 and Seifert to Hitler, 20 May 1922; in NSDAP Hauptarchiv, Reel 6, Folder 141.

[2] Ibid., p. 271.   [3] Ibid., p. 163.   [4] Ibid., pp. 312–13.

[5] Ibid., p. 176. That the authorities were, in fact, misled is clear from the correspondence between Regierungspräsident in Hildesheim and the Oberpräsident in Hanover during 1923, is NSAH Hann. Des. 122a 76e.

By the autumn of 1923, the disintegration of the *völkisch* movement and, in particular, the struggle with the DVFP had persuaded other former NSDAP leaders in Lower Saxony of the need for tighter organization. As a result, it was agreed to give Wenzel similar powers over the whole Hanover region as Haase had secured over the Göttingen branch in November 1922. But shortly after they had secured the agreement of Munich, Wenzel began making plans to leave for Spain and therefore handed over his authority to Haase and the SA to Schreiber.[1] On 6 March 1924, Haase received confirmation from Munich that he was empowered 'to bring together and organize the NSDAP groups in the Hanover area', to take over their political direction and to collect money for their finance.[2] Haase had in fact already acted on the assumption that he possessed such power. In February, for example, he had issued an important directive to the NSDAP branches of his *Landesverband* as he described it, in which he had laid down that

> our preparation for the coming dictatorship as well as our experience in the movement have occasioned the need for a dictatorial constitution for our regional organization. It is essential for the leaders to have absolute authority within their branches. . . . The committee is there only in an advisory capacity. Membership meetings together with parliamentarism, that is 'voting' are absolutely forbidden as seeds of corruption. The leadership of the regional organization is equally permitted to interfere in the affairs of the branches at all times.[3]

After his official appointment, Haase followed this memorandum up with a series of important directives. On 26 March, for example, he emphasized to the branches Hitler's principle of only founding a branch where there was an adequate leader:

> whatever happens we must not make the mistake of the *Schutz- und Trutzbund* which neglected this fundamental principle and in the end existed everywhere and yet nowhere. . . . A farmer's boy who has got complete control of his village is of more value to the movement than so-called 'leading personalities' whose activity is practically worthless.[4]

Haase's aim was to 'bring together a group of really *völkisch* men who, while conceivably going without big, immediate and superficial successes, will in the end form such a store of controlled energy that the continually fluid and wavering mass will crystallize around this core when the time has come'.[5] An essential aspect of this organization was the *Kampfstil* which was developed.

[1] Haase, op. cit., p. 364.   [2] Ibid., pp. 365–6.
[3] Ibid., pp. 383–4.   [4] Haase, op. cit., pp. 402–3.
[5] Ludolf Haase, 'Notwendigkeiten. Denkschrift über die Fortsetzung der Nationalsozialistischen Parteiarbeit in Norddeutschland', in Jochmann, op. cit., p. 66 ff.

To yield to an enemy superior in numbers was absolutely forbidden. .... It was common for the holders of nationalist meetings to be compelled to close down because of continual bellowing and this was only too successful with the bourgeoisie. But with us it had to be different; it was preferable for chairs and tables to be smashed to pieces and blood to flow than for a National Socialist branch leader to give up his right to continue the meeting. If he did so, he could be sure of a severe reprimand. For even if we lost, the fact of our opposition to the finish would win respect and even make our enemy think about the bases of such energy.[1]

Haase compared this with the style of the DVFP which had never had the courage or determination for ruthless self-defence and had indeed relied on the SA for protection at its meetings.

The Hanover-South NSDAP successor organization was probably unique in the *völkisch* movement in North Germany at this period. *Völkisch* groups were normally organized on traditional lines with decisions taken by a majority vote. The *Führerprinzip* had been introduced into the *völkisch* movement with Hitler's seizure of power within the Munich branch in July 1921; but it had not been followed at regional or branch level until Haase acquired absolute authority in the Göttingen branch in November 1922. It was this tight organization which gave cohesion and effectiveness to the Göttingen area at a time when 'in Hanover every group and virtually every single member messed around on his own, picked and chose whether to join or reject this or that organization'.[2]

The banning of the NSDAP in Prussia created a new situation in the relations between the party in Lower Saxony and the head-quarters in Munich. Munich found it increasingly difficult to follow developments in the Hanover area, let alone exercise any control over them. The extent to which Hitler was dependent on his northern branch leaders for information is clear from a letter which he wrote to Seifert in August 1923.[3] He complained that Wenzel had persuaded him that it was necessary for the Nazis in Hanover to join the DVFP which forced him (Hitler) to leave all members in North Germany free to do the same. Then, after persuading Hitler to have a meeting with its leader, von Graefe, Wenzel had suddenly declared that he was unable to continue working with the DVFP. Hitler concluded the letter rather desperately: 'The day will come which will bring clarity into this too.'

In any case the efforts of the party leadership were now entirely dominated by the SA's preparations for the 'March on Berlin' and they had little sympathy for the dissensions which bedevilled the party

---

[1] Haase, op. cit., pp. 444–5.
[2] Wenzel, op. cit., p. 22.
[3] Hitler to Seifert, 23 Aug. 1923, NSDAP Hauptarchiv, Reel 6, Folder 141.

in North Germany. The party leadership was no longer trying to insist on the exclusiveness of the NSDAP but ordering its followers 'to use every means to end all dissensions, since, in a very short time, we may be needing every *völkisch* comrade for our great aim'.[1] This also meant that they had little sympathy for the opponents of the DVFP. The Munich leadership respected the desire of the Haase group to remain independent, but was itself working loosely with the DVFP and insisted therefore that 'if a close co-operation cannot be achieved then, however unfortunate that may be, you must work side by side with a minimum of friction'.[2]

(iv) *The Hitler-Putsch*

There were a number of paramilitary organizations in Lower Saxony in 1923. The largest, but least militant organization in the Province of Hanover was the *Vaterländische Vereinigung Nordhannover* which was founded in August 1921 to unite the remnants of the anti-Communist *Orgesch*.[3] It acted as a loose co-ordinating association of 'citizen's leagues' or *Heimatbünde* which had been formed to meet the Communist threat and many of which became branches of the *Stahlhelm*. It was backed in the countryside by the *Landbund* organization and in the towns by the Employers' associations. Its membership in July 1922 was estimated to be 15,000. There was also a battalion of ex-Silesian Free Corps men organized in the *Verband Hindenburg* under a Major von Waldow, who had been axed from the *Reichswehr* in 1920 and was now an executive in the big firm of Hanomag.[4] These groups occasionally came together for quasi-military exercises. In July 1923, for example, about 1,000 men from Hanover, Harburg, Göttingen, Hildesheim and Brunswick held a Field Day in the Lüneburg heath at Ebstorf/Uelzen. The SA in Hanover, Göttingen and elsewhere co-operated with these groups from time to time.

In March the police smashed a so-called 'small committee' of right-wing activists, which was under the leadership of a Captain Julius Brinckmann from Munich, to which the Hanover SA leader belonged.[5] The Hanover SA was in fact disguised as a *Stahlhelm* troop and worked with the Hanover *Stahlhelm*. In July the Brunswick and

[1] Der Chef des Stabes—Das Oberkommando der SA to Rektor Fetz—Bremen; in NSDAP Hauptarchiv, Reel 16, Folder 298.

[2] Der Chef des Stabes—Das Oberkommando der SA to Schreiber, 7 Aug. 1923, ibid.

[3] Report from Regierungspräsident Lüneburg to Oberpräsident Hannover, 23 July 1922, in NSAH Hann. Des. 122a XI, No. 76.

[4] Police reports to the Regierungspräsident Lüneburg in NSAH Hann. 80 Lüneburg III XXV 15.

[5] Haase, op. cit., p. 199.

Werningerode SA groups took part in a big march with ex-servicemen's leagues and other paramilitary formations in Goslar.[1] On the other hand, the Hildesheim branch of the *Stahlhelm* disliked the radicalism of the SA.[2] Its leader, General Ulrich, remarked: 'If I had the power I would have that Hittler [*sic*] arrested. . . . We shall call on our formation at the appropriate time, but we shall not let ourselves be involved in adventures.' The *Reichswehr* was also involved in these paramilitary activities, since it was attempting to recruit volunteers for action in the Ruhr.[3] The leader of the *Stahlhelm* branch in Goslar, the retired General von Oven, who had been dismissed because of his ambiguous attitude during the Kapp Putsch, acted as a liaison between the army and the right-wing paramilitary groups. The National Socialists were among the groups which were intended to strengthen the *Reichswehr* and the Göttingen SA, for instance, co-operated.[4]

As the general political situation became more and more tense during the autumn of 1923, Wenzel and Haase sent Munich their summing-up of the situation in the Province of Hanover.[5] They had heard from press reports that Hitler was coming under pressure to join a coalition of the *Vaterländische Verbände* with Kahr, Ehrhardt, the Bavarian People's Party and Prince Rupprecht, and now informed him that a similar reactionary-separatist coalition was being formed in Hanover between Ehrhardt, the *Nationalverband deutscher Offiziere*, the DNVP, and the Guelphs. They declared their agreement with the views which were being expressed in the *Völkischer Beobachter*—the determination to resist the danger of being neutralized in such a coalition. Shortly afterwards, during the same month, Wenzel and Haase attended a meeting in Nuremberg at which Hitler told the assembled branch leaders his views on the situation.[6] In case of emergency while he was away, Haase had left behind instructions for the 'leading November criminals of the area' to be taken before a drum-head court martial under a former officer, Major von Riepenhausen, who had offered himself for the job with the words 'that is something I'd like— to have the others shot'.

There is no record of what Hitler said to his branch leaders in October, but in Hanover and Göttingen preparations for a *putsch* from the Right and to meet the possibility of a *putsch* from the Left were made

[1] Ibid., p. 87.

[2] Offener Brief an die Leitung der Organisation 'Escherich' Hildesheim, 3 Apr. 1923, in BA R 72/9.

[3] F. L. Carsten, *The Reichswehr and Politics 1918–1933* (Oxford, 1966), pp. 155–6.

[4] Haase, op. cit., p. 254.

[5] Wenzel and Haase to Hitler, Hoffmann and Rosenberg, 1 Oct. 1923, in National Archives T-84, Reel 4, Frames 3552–3.

[6] Haase, op. cit., p. 340.

with some care.[1] A false alarm occurred shortly before the Hitler *putsch* when it was reported that a Red battalion was marching on Hanover from Misburg; the remnants of the Hanover SA and the *Verband Hindenburg* marched out to meet it. Then, a few days before 8 November, the Hanover SA was called together, given final instructions and then transported to the Lüneburg heath, where it was joined by the *Schlageter Gedächtnisbund*[2] and two other paramilitary formations, the *Siedlungskameradschaft Schmude*, clearly a settlement of former Free Corps men, and the *Schutz bei Aller und Leine*. Here they awaited the signal for action, passing the time with marches and shooting practice. Their presence had been reported to the headquarters in Munich. Meanwhile, a small group remained behind in the city itself under permanent alarm. In Göttingen too preparations were made. Haase nominated an acting *Bürgermeister* and the SA was assembled in the Kaiser-Wilhelm Park, 200-men strong.

But although there was a general awareness that something was about to happen, no definite news was received of when the *putsch* was to take place and its actual timing came as a surprise.[3] By the time the news came through, it was too late and the party in Lower Saxony played no part in the *putsch*.

[1] For the following see ibid., p. 351 ff.
[2] The association of former SA men founded by Quindel.
[3] Haase, op. cit., p. 72; and Wenzel, op. cit., pp. 20–1.

III

THE PERIOD OF ILLEGALITY
(SECOND PHASE) 1923–1925

(i) *Renewed conflict with the DVFP—the founding of the 'Directorate'*

ALTHOUGH the Reich ban of the NSDAP did not directly affect the position of the former members in the Hanover area, since the party had already been banned, the arrest of Hitler offered the leadership of the DVFP the opportunity to extend their influence within the *völkisch* movement. On 24 October 1923, von Graefe and Esser, as the representatives of the DVFP and NSDAP, had reached agreement on co-operation between the two parties but had published a communiqué before Hitler's approval had been obtained, though this was not known until much later.[1] Now, after the failure of the *putsch*, the DVFP was anxious to use the opportunity to consolidate its position in the North by amalgamating with the remnants of the NSDAP. On 31 January 1924 at a meeting in Salzburg, an attempt was made to persuade Rosenberg, now the official acting leader of the NSDAP, to agree to united party organizations at provincial level, whose leadership would be determined according to the proportion of the party's membership.[2] This would have given control of what was left of the NSDAP in North Germany to the DVFP. Initially, Rosenberg refused to accept this plan, despite DVFP references to the October 1923 agreement. He was only prepared to accept an electoral alliance. But the DVFP announced nonetheless that agreement had been reached and in fact on 24 February a new agreement was signed, whereby the NSDAP accepted a division of the country between the parties on a proportional basis with mixed provincial organizations where neither party predominated.[3] Rosenberg also agreed to general policy being decided by the two head-quarters consulting together.

The Hanover–Göttingen NSDAP group were extremely concerned about the danger of DVFP influence in Munich. They were reassured by a letter from 'Rolf Eidhalt' (the code name of the Munich

[1] Haase, 'Aufstand in Niedersachsen. Der Kampf den NSDAP 1921–1924,' (mimeo, 1942), p. 385.
[2] Serge Lang and E. von Schenk, *Portrait eines Menschheitsverbrechers nach den hinterlassenen Memoiren des ehemaligen Reichsministers Alfred Rosenberg* (St. Gallen, 1947).
[3] Copy of the agreement in Hoover Institution. NSDAP Hauptarchiv, Reel 44, Folder 894 and Haase, op. cit., pp. 386–7.

SA head-quarters) dated 10 January 1924, which laid down that the NSDAP branches would remain completely independent of the DVFP and that the October 1923 agreement merely meant that the DVFP head-quarters in Berlin would be informed of directives issued by the Munich NSDAP head-quarters to its North German branches.[1] But during January, Major Henning, one of the DVFP leaders whose *Reichstag* constituency was the Weser-Ems district, toured Lower Saxony trying to persuade the former NSDAP branches and members to join the DVFP and this activity increased after the Salzburg meeting.

On 17 February, Haase reacted to this in a memorandum which he addressed to the branch leaders of the illegal NSDAP warning them that the Salzburg agreement had not been accepted by Rosenberg and that this was just another example of the DVFP's attempt to absorb the NSDAP.[2] With the agreement of 24 February, however, the situation had theoretically changed. For the Province of Hanover was a 'mixed' area with both DVFP and NSDAP organizations, so that under the terms of the agreement they were obliged to form a joint regional committee. Haase, however, agreed only to co-operate with the electoral alliance which had been set up for the spring elections— the Völkisch-Social-Block (V-S-B).[3]

Haase and Wenzel were encouraged in their stand against the DVFP by a letter from Munich, dated 27 February, which laid down that 'the NSDAP works completely independently of all other *völkisch* organizations or parties and the regional organizations join together with the DVFP on a purely organizational basis for the election period to form a Völkisch-sociale-Block'.[4] This point was then confirmed by a representative from Munich who visited Hanover on 2 March.[5] The NSDAP head-quarters in Munich had thus agreed to take part in the election despite the decision which Hitler had forced through at the 1922 National Socialist Congress in Salzburg against participation in elections. The reason they gave was that 'we do not want to let the energies of our movement lie fallow, but use them in a great propaganda campaign for the *völkisch* idea in general and the national socialist one in particular'.[6] In fact, Rosenberg had already been compelled to face the paradox that an anti-Parliamentary party which had had to renounce the use of force—as the NSDAP had to after the failure of the *putsch*—could only survive by participating in elections, since this was the only activity open to it and the only way of winning power.

[1] Printed in Haase, op. cit., p. 378.

[2] NSDAP Hauptarchiv, Reel 44, Folder 894 also printed in Jochmann, *National-sozialismus und Revolution*, pp. 61 ff. This book contains a selection of documents from this reel.

[3] Haase, op. cit., p. 390.   [4] Letter printed in Haase, op. cit., p. 390.

[5] Ibid., p. 388.   [6] Ibid., pp. 390–3.

The NSDAP leaders in the Hanover area only agreed to work in the V-S-B because of the directive from Munich. The Hanover DVFP, however, hoped to out-manoeuvre the Haase group by ignoring their offer of assistance and claims for representation on the V-S-B list of candidates.[1] Haase's reaction to this was in the first place to initiate an independent campaign in the Göttingen area, with the assistance of Wenzel; and secondly, to tighten up his own organization.[2] This second task was particularly important, in view of the splintering of the *völkisch* movement which had even increased since November 1923. In a letter to Munich on 24 February, Haase described four different *völkisch* groups apart from his own which were active in the Hanover area: the DVFP, a group round Seifert and Quindel, a group in Brunswick, and a group created by a representative from Munich who had been sent to form an electoral alliance.[3]

The *völkisch* electoral alliance—the *Völkisch Sozialer Block*—achieved considerable successes in both the provincial and *Reichstag* elections of Spring 1924. In Lower Saxony it succeeded in winning 150,000 votes (7·5 per cent), compared with the Reich average of 6·6 per cent.[4] But success in the elections only added to the conflict within the *völkisch* movement. In Bavaria, for example, former leaders of the NSDAP objected to the fact that the majority of the new V-S-B deputies had only recently joined the movement, some only just before the election; and many of the old members of the NSDAP were critical of their bourgeois background and attitudes.[5] At a meeting in Munich in June 1924, Hermann Esser, the spokesman of these former NSDAP members, attacked the V-S-B *Reichstag* deputies and demanded that they 'accept Hitler's programme unconditionally and not merely make vague protestations of loyalty. For Hitler was not only *völkisch*; above all he was a national socialist. The deputies must not forget the workers and should support the eight-hour day.' He was supported in this radical view by Streicher, the Nazi leader in Nuremberg, who declared in an article in the *Münchner-Augsburger Abendzeitung* that 'there was little to distinguish between the aims of the *Völkische* from those of the Communists, apart from a number of differences on the racial question'.

Esser and Streicher had gone into open opposition to the Bavarian

---

[1] Ibid., pp. 393–6.
[2] See above p. 36.
[3] Letter printed in Haase, op. cit., p. 399.
[4] Franz, *Die Politischen Wahlen in Niedersachsen 1867 bis 1949* (Bremen, 1957), p. 56.
[5] This account of the events in Bavaria is based on the reports of the Reichskommissar für Ueberwachung der öffentlichen Ordnung, in the Niedersächsisches Staatsarchiv in Oldenburg (from now on NSAO), 136 No. 2915 and Friedrich Plümer, *Die Wahrheit über Hitler und seinen Kreis* (Munich, 1925), pp. 25 ff.

branch of the V-S-B, the *Völkisch Block* led by Rosenberg, and captured the Bavarian successor organization of the NSDAP—the *Grossdeutsche Volksgemeinschaft* (GVG) which they built up as a rival organization. They were later joined by Arthur Dinter, the leader of the V-S-B in the Thuringian parliament, and by a number of other powerful supporters such as Max Amann, the head of the *Eher Verlag*, the NSDAP publishing house. And they managed not only to become the most powerful *völkisch* group in Bavaria, but also managed to found branches elsewhere. The GVG in fact provided a convenient cover for the opponents of the DVFP in North Germany, including the Haase group in South Hanover.

After the election the V-S-B in Lower Saxony soon broke down, for the DVFP maintained its pressure on the NSDAP members who refused to accept amalgamation. On 11 May, the DVFP arranged a meeting in the *Hannover Landbundhaus* for *völkisch* representatives from the Hanover area.[1] At this meeting the Haase group was criticized by a number of speakers and some of their supporters changed sides. It was now clear to Haase that if his group was not to be isolated and neutralized by the more powerful DVFP organization, it was essential to organize the opponents of the DVFP over a wider area.

At the Berlin meeting of the V-S-B in March, Haase had made contact with other groups of former NSDAP supporters who were involved in a similar struggle with the DVFP, in particular a group in Pomerania.[2] A member of this group, Joachim Haupt, a student, now took the initiative with a plan to co-ordinate the opposition to the DVFP in North Germany. In a memorandum which was circulated among interested groups, Haupt laid down certain objectives:[3]

(1) The restoration of the independence of the National Socialists.
(2) Non-participation in a parliamentary coalition or government.
(3) An attitude of reserve on the part of the national socialist deputies.
(4) The formation of a North German Directorate to create a solid organization.
(5) The working out of an NS programme of action which consciously bases itself on the *völkisch* class (*Stand*)—the peasants, the workers, and the *Mittelstand* and not the *völkisch* movement (i.e. the political organizations).

On 3 June the North German opponents of the DVFP met in Hamburg.[4] The meeting was attended by representatives of the

---

[1] Haase, op. cit., pp. 447–8.
[2] Haase, op. cit., p. 410.
[3] Joachim Haupt, 'Ueber die organisatorischen Massnahmen zur Fortsetzung der nationalsozialistischen Parteiarbeit in Norddeutschland', in Jochmann, *op. cit.*, pp. 69–72.
[4] Jochmann, op. cit., p. 73.

regional organizations of the GVG in Pomerania, Schleswig-Holstein, Hamburg, Bremen, Hanover-South and of groups in Hanover-East and Westphalia. It was agreed to set up a 'Directorate' of three and, significantly, 'following the example of South Hanover, to change over to the principle of dictatorship in all the regional organizations'. The man chosen to lead the Directorate, Adalbert Volck, was an experienced *völkisch* propagandist who was probably meant to remove the rather too youthful image which the organization might otherwise have had. Certainly Volck saw himself in this role.[1] Volck was a Baltic German refugee from Dorpat, who had moved to Lüneburg after the war and from 1919 onwards had spread *völkisch* propaganda throughout Lower Saxony.[2] He had been a member of the DVSTB and then had been present at the founding of the DVFP in Berlin in 1922. But he disagreed with the DVFP over their attitude to parliament and came to regard them as 'a continuation of the DNVP'. He also disliked their association with Ludendorff, the war hero, who was now a leading anti-Semite. He feared that Ludendorff, as a Prussian General, would alienate the Guelph peasants among whom he was seeking support. As a result he broke with the party. He had then come into contact with Hitler supporters opposed to the DVFP, in particular with Haase, and, impressed by their *völkisch* radicalism, he joined them. The other two members of the Directorate subordinate to Volck were Haase and Sunkel, a student at the University of Greifswald in Pomerania. Almost immediately, however, Volck handed over his powers to Haase for a period of two months on the grounds of pressure of work; and it was Haase who drafted the first directives, introducing the *Führerprinzip* into the new organization and ordering the subordinate groups 'continually to emphasize that Adolf Hitler is our example and our leader'.[3]

The emphasis on Hitler was crucial to the success of the organization. In their struggle with the DVFP it was essential to show that they had Hitler's support—such was his prestige within the *völkisch* movement. Yet, although these men resisted amalgamation in the name of Hitler and this was important in strengthening Hitler's influence in North Germany during his imprisonment, he nonetheless refused to commit himself by openly supporting them. He had no intention of tying his hands before his release. He did not wish to become dependent on the members of the Directorate and furthermore, there were influential men within the DVFP whom he wished to win over. The supporters of the Directorate were mostly young and without social or financial weight and, since he was the only radical *völkisch*

[1] Volck to Sunkel, 11 Aug. 1924; NSDAP Hauptarchiv, Reel 44, Folder 895.
[2] Volck Lebenslauf, ibid.
[3] Directives 1-3 and 5 in Jochmann, op. cit., pp. 83-9. Directive N.4, ibid.

leader of any importance, they would have to support him in any case. Meanwhile, the conflict between the two groups served his purpose by preventing the emergence of a viable *völkisch* organization and by encouraging the movement to regard him as the only leader capable of reviving their fortune.

That this was Hitler's policy was to become clear through the correspondence between the members of the Directorate and Hermann Fobke, a young activist who had worked with the Göttingen group, but was now with Hitler in Landsberg for his participation in the *putsch*.[1] On 16 June Hitler had informed Haase in reply to an attempt by the Directorate to enlist his support that he had 'resolved to withdraw from public politics until I have the freedom to act as a real leader'.[2] Fobke summed up the situation by reporting that although Hitler had told him that 'he particularly liked the young ones who do not want anything to do with Berlin', i.e. the DVFP, he 'at the moment considers things to be in such a mess that he is convinced that he will have to start again from the beginning when he is free'; Fobke admitted being 'somewhat horrified by the apparent indifference with which he regards our cries for help'.[3]

In Hanover the DVFP made use of Hitler's refusal to support the Directorate. At the beginning of June, Rust, the DVFP *Gauleiter*, had tried to reach a *rapprochement* with Haase.[4] In return for agreeing to amalgamation Rust offered him a free hand in the Göttingen area. The most interesting aspect of the offer was the attitude to Hitler which it revealed. Rust made it clear that as far as he was concerned the final decision on amalgamation would rest with Hitler after his release. He concluded his letter: 'once again, let us work together. Then Hitler can come and see what the situation is and make his decision.' The fact that the DVFP leader in Hanover, Rust, already clearly regarded Hitler as the real *völkisch* leader is of the utmost significance. Many *völkisch* leaders did not share his view, but the fact that some now accepted Hitler's leadership is vital to an understanding of how, after his release, Hitler could reorganize the NSDAP outside Bavaria with such a wide basis of support, despite the fact that prior to 1923 the NSDAP possessed a minute organization in Prussia and had then been banned for two years. The main reason for Hitler's prestige in the *völkisch* movement during this period appears to be his behaviour during the Munich trial in February–March 1924. His proud assumption of responsibility for the *putsch* contrasted very favourably in the eyes of

[1] Cf. Jochmann, op. cit., pp. 90 ff.
[2] Ibid., p. 77.
[3] Ibid., pp. 90 ff.
[4] NSFP Hannover-Süd an die Reichsleitung in Berlin, 25 June 1923, NSAH Hann. Des. 310 I A, Nr. 1.

members of the *völkisch* movement with the attempts by the army and conservative leaders to disclaim responsibility for the affair.[1]

Haase, however, rejected Rust's overture, whereupon Rust moved onto the attack. At a meeting of DVFP representatives from the Province of Hanover on 22 June, he secured his unanimous recognition as leader of the region and, thus strengthened, summoned a meeting for 27 June in Hanover, to which representatives of those former NSDAP groups which did not support Haase were invited.[2] At this meeting a *Nationalsozialistische Freiheitspartei* regional organization for Hanover was created through the amalgamation of the two parties, and Bernhard Rust was elected chairman with Seifert as a member of the three-man executive committee.[3] The new party declared that the Haase group had cut itself off from the amalgamation and that further co-operation with them was therefore impossible. Finally, the DVFP took the initiative nationally. On 9 July the DVFP announced in the *Deutsches Tageblatt* that Hitler had resigned the leadership and asked Ludendorff and von Graefe to take over in his place, and that for the period of Hitler's imprisonment Ludendorff had nominated Gregor Strasser, the NSDAP leader in Landshut in Bavaria, to represent the former NSDAP in the *Reichsführerschaft* in place of Rosenberg.[4] The announcement concluded:

Forwards is our slogan. Towards the unity of the *Völkische*! At the great *Reich* party meeting in Weimar on 15–17 July the unification of both parties will be consummated as a powerful manifestation of the idea of *völkisch* unity. Then there will be no more reason for small-minded people to make stupid pin-pricks. Then there will be only one mighty *völkisch* army reaching as far as the German tongue is spoken. And Ludendorff and von Graefe will be its leaders until the day when the free Hero of Munich can step once more into their circle as the third leader.

This announcement and in particular the patronizing reference to Hitler returning as the 'third leader' infuriated the Directorate.[5] Haase had already received an invitation to the proposed meeting in Weimar and he decided that the Directorate should attend in force to

[1] It is remarkable, for example, that many of the contributors to Theodore Abel's survey on the early history of the Nazi movement report that they established contact with the movement after reading press reports following the *putsch* and in particular the trial, which was given massive front-page coverage in the provincial press. See Theodore Abel, *The Nazi Movement* (New York, 1965), p. 69.

[2] Dincklage to the Kreisleiter des bisherigen völkischen Blocks, 16 June 1923, in NSDAP Hauptarchiv, Reel 44, Folder 895 and Niedersächsischer Beobachter, 13 July 1924.

[3] Landesverband Hannover-Süd der Nationalsozialistischen Freiheitspartei Entschliessung. 23 June 1924, NSDAP Hauptarchiv, Reel 44, Folder 895.

[4] Haase, op. cit., pp. 520–1.

[5] Ibid., p. 522.

make a definite stand against the DVFP.[1] To prepare tactics for Weimar and to discuss a number of other issues that had arisen out of the disorganization caused by the Ludendorff declaration, a meeting of the North German NSDAP leaders was held at Harburg on 13 July.[2] The meeting was attended by representatives from Pomerania, Hamburg, Schleswig-Holstein, Hanover-East, Hanover-South and Westphalia. The most important question was whether or not Hitler had appointed Strasser as his representative. Volck was therefore directed to make enquires from Fobke in Landsberg. Secondly, there was the question of the attitude of the Directorate to the new paramilitary organization, the *Frontbann*, which was being established by Röhm with Ludendorff as its patron. Here it was agreed to accept Ludendorff as the military leader, but to authorize only the Directorate to put storm troops under his command, to avoid the danger of losing control over the SA. Finally, all those present agreed to oppose participation in elections and a number of representatives were chosen to attend the DVFP meeting in Weimar.

Fobke replied to Volck's enquiry about Strasser in a letter dated 18 July.[3] He reported that Hitler had not appointed Strasser or anyone else as his successor. It was Ludendorff who had nominated Strasser in the capacity of Bavarian representative within the *Reichsführerschaft*; and, although Hitler accepted this, he had only given up his leadership *for the period of his imprisonment*. Armed with this information, Volck determined to use support for Hitler as the main argument against amalgamation at the Weimar meeting. He concluded his directive on tactics for the meeting: 'Our programme consists of two words: "Adolf Hitler."'[4] He also decided that they would not accept a majority decision.

The meeting which took place on 20 July in Weimar was attended by approximately eighty National Socialists, including the three members of the Directorate.[5] As Volck put it: 'the whole point of the thing was to use Ludendorff's authority to compel obedience' and he noted that when Ludendorff appeared at eleven o'clock 'one could really feel how the majority jumped'.[6] After a confused tirade by Esser, the meeting continued with a long speech by Rosenberg in which he gave a history of his experience with the DVFP.[7] He described their behaviour over the Salzburg meeting in January; their refusal to satisfy the NSDAP demands for adequate representation on the V-S-B list of

[1] Haase to Heinze, 8 July 1924, in NSDAP Hauptarchiv, Reel 44, Folder 894.
[2] Jochmann, op. cit., p. 93.   [3] Ibid., pp. 94–5.   [4] Ibid., pp. 90–7.
[5] There is an account of the Weimar meeting by Volck, ibid., pp. 98–102 and by Sunkel, in NSDAP Hauptarchiv, Reel 44, Folder 894.
[6] Dr. Adalbert Volck, 'Vertraulicher Bericht über die Nationalsozialistische Vertretertagung in Weimar am 20 July 1924', in Jochmann, op. cit., p. 98.
[7] 'Rede Alfred Rosenbergs auf der Tagung in Weimar', ibid., pp. 103–19.

Reichstag candidates; their failure to mention the NSDAP in the announcements of election results so that it appeared as if the DVFP had won all the votes on its own; and, most interesting of all, gave an account of the attempts during May to persuade Hitler to support amalgamation. According to Rosenberg, Hitler himself had suddenly and surprisingly taken the initiative in favour of amalgamation. He had given up the negotiations when he became aware of the widespread hostility to amalgamation among his supporters and decided to opt out of the struggle until his release. The major point in Rosenberg's speech lay in his assertion that

in its active core the *völkisch* movement is national socialist. The *Welt* and *Staatsanschauung* of the future is National Socialism, the content of this political thought we all owe to Adolf Hitler. He is the creator of the movement, its inevitable leader. . . . In the intended amalgamation we National Socialists will provide the intellectual capital, the drive, the masses, in fact really everything. The DVFP will provide a few clever parliamentary representatives and a better organization. And simply because we have a weaker organization amalgamation represents a great danger.

In other words, Rosenberg had now come to the same conclusion as the members of the Directorate.

Rosenberg's speech was followed first by a demand from Ludendorff for amalgamation and then by a statement by Volck of the Directorate's position to the effect that they only regarded themselves as keeping Hitler's seat warm for him ('*Platzhalter Hitlers*'). No vote was taken; delegates were simply asked publicly to state their position. The result was chaos. The majority favoured amalgamation; some were confused and voted for both Hitler and Ludendorff; a few joined the Directorate in definitely opposing amalgamation.

(ii) *The founding of the Nationalsozialistische Arbeitsgemeinschaft— 7 September 1924*

From the point of view of the Directorate, the most important result of the Weimar meeting was the conviction they had acquired that Bavaria could no longer be the base of the movement. In a report circulated to the regional organizations, Sunkel summed up this view by declaring that the Weimar meeting represented 'the total disintegration of the old NSDAP' and stating that the future of National Socialism lay in North Germany.[1] Two days later, therefore, Volck wrote off to Fobke asking Hitler to come to North Germany after his release but insisting that he drop Esser.[2]

Part of the reason for the conviction that Bavaria was finished was the performance of the leaders of the *Grossdeutsche Volksgemeinschaft*,

---

[1] Jochmann, pp. 98–9.   [2] Ibid., pp. 120–1.

Esser and Streicher. Esser and Streicher had not only taken up completely contradictory positions on most of the points at issue; they had also made vicious personal attacks on members of the Directorate. Furthermore, Esser had already committed a cardinal sin in the eyes of the racialists by taking his dispute with conservative *völkisch* leaders in Bavaria to the 'Jewish' *Frankfurter Zeitung*, threatening to disclose all he knew.[1] Sunkel summed him up as 'the picture of a *völkisch* demagogue who is leading a movement without plan or direction. So far as he is to be taken seriously at all, he has too much of what the Rosenberg school lacks [i.e. aggressiveness]. But Esser is not to be taken seriously.'[2]

These views of the Directorate, the idea that Hitler should come to North Germany; the dislike of Esser and Streicher; and the desire to get a definite statement of support from Hitler for the stand of the Directorate, found expression in a series of letters from Volck and Haase to Fobke in the weeks following the Weimar meeting.[3] Hitler, however, refused to be drawn. He agreed with them that Ludendorff's activity should be limited to the military side of the movement, and he agreed that Esser was impossible as a leader despite his demagogic qualities. But on the main point at issue he remained immovable. As Fobke reported:

Hitler said he had to keep completely neutral so that after his release he could organize the Party without having compromised himself with any commitment. Those who did not submit would be kicked out. . . . He therefore has no sympathy for the desperate struggles of the North German National Socialists.[4]

Hitler's lack of concern for his North German supporters caused growing resentment within the Directorate. The younger members, Haase and Sunkel, felt this merely as frustration and a continual fear that Hitler might still agree to amalgamation. But it began to become apparent that Volck did not feel the same devotion to Hitler as his young colleagues. On the one hand, he admired Hitler as the leader of the pure anti-parliamentary wing of the *völkisch* movement and he believed in the *völkisch* principle of autocratic leadership. On the other hand, he felt that as a veteran of the movement his views should be taken into account, particularly when dealing with North Germany— which in any case he considered racially superior to the South. As he summed it up in a letter to Haase: 'I have frequently been in so-called leading positions and have no intention of letting a South German interfere in North German affairs or he must do it alone.'[5] And he added

---

[1] Copy of Esser's letter, in NSDAP Hauptarchiv, Reel 44, Folder 893.
[2] Jochmann, op. cit., p. 99.   [3] Ibid., pp. 120 ff.
[4] Fobke to Volck, 29 July 1924, in Jochmann, op. cit., pp. 122–4.
[5] Volck to Haase, 6 Aug. 1924, in NSDAP Hauptarchiv, Reel 44, Folder 895.

both a criticism of Hitler's methods—'all ideas of a *putsch* are ridiculous'—and the prophecy that 'because Hitler is to be deported, he will need us all the more'.[1] Volck was gradually broken on the horns of a dilemma. While continuing to maintain that Hitler was the real leader and that he himself was only the *Platzhalter Hitlers* in order to defeat the attacks of the NSFB leadership, he became increasingly disillusioned by Hitler's arbitrary and dictatorial behaviour and his readiness to sacrifice principle to politics.

The question of Hitler's views on the dispute between the NSFP and the Directorate acquired new importance with an event which occurred in the middle of August. On 16 August, at a meeting in Weimar, the amalgamation of the DVFP and NSDAP in Prussia was carried through and a new *Nationalsozialistische Freiheitsbewegung* (NSFB) in Prussia was created.[2] The importance of this event for the Directorate was not only that it emphasized the separatist nature of their own organization, but also the fact that Hitler had sent a greetings telegram to the meeting of which the NSFP made full use in the press.[3]

The news of this telegram at once prompted a further enquiry from Haase as to whether or not Hitler supported their stand.[4] He emphasized the importance of a definite statement in view of the weakness of the position in South Hanover where they now awaited a general offensive from the NSFB, particularly since they had lost the vital support of the *Göttinger Tageblatt*, the main Göttingen paper, which was strongly *völkisch* and which had previously supported the NSDAP.

Fobke replied with an exceptionally interesting account of Hitler's plans for the period after his release.[5] Hitler had argued that a precondition for the fulfilment of National Socialist ideas was the freedom of Germany from external controls. To achieve this it was necessary to make the German people ready for war (*Frontreif*). But time was too short to achieve it solely with pure National Socialist ideas. 'We must therefore content ourselves with carrying through a programme of educating the German people in nationalism in co-operation with other nationalist elements to make them *Frontreif*. To achieve this compromises are necessary.' Hitler then discussed at length the difference between *Programmatiker* and *Politiker*. The *Programmatiker*—or ideologue—must always preach the pure doctrine; but the politician 'must consider apart from the great aim, the road that leads to it'. He

[1] At this time the Bavarian authorities were considering deporting Hitler to his native Austria.
[2] Protokoll Berlin, 18 Aug. 1924, gez. Wulle and Ludendorff, in NSAH Hann. Des. 310 I G.
[3] Copy of the *Völkischer Kurier*, in NSDAP Hauptarchiv, Reel 44, Folder 896.
[4] Haase to Fobke, 18 Aug. 1924, in Jochmann, op. cit., pp. 130–1.
[5] Fobke to Haase, 21 Aug. 1924, ibid., pp. 132–5.

left no doubt in which category he placed himself. In practical terms this meant that

> when, after his release, he began to assemble his forces, it would depend on what the individual had to offer him. . . . He would begin by creating order in Bavaria . . . and he would also use the *Reichstag* Parliamentary group as his instrument since it already existed and since, in his opinion, there were brains in it which in present circumstances we could ill afford to do without or alienate.

As a result Hitler found himself unable to sanction the position of the Directorate, but Fobke advised Haase to hold out.

Fobke's reply inevitably came as a disappointment. It coincided with a renewal of pressure from the NSFB and the first signs of weakening in the support for the Directorate. On 25 August, the *Reichsführerschaft*—Ludendorff, Strasser and von Graefe—published a statement to the effect that the Directorate possessed no authority from Hitler and was not recognized by them.[1] In the same week it became clear that the leader of the NSDAP opposition in Schleswig-Holstein, Hinrich Lohse, had recognized the NSFB leadership.[2]

The new situation created by the Weimar meetings clearly required some counter-measure on the part of the Directorate. The break with Esser and Streicher, for example, meant that the name *Grossdeutsche Volksgemeinschaft* was no longer a suitable cloak for the NSDAP opposition in North Germany.[3] It was decided, therefore, to hold another meeting of the North German opponents of the NSFB at which a new name for their organization could be decided and their opposition reaffirmed.

The meeting took place at Harburg on 7 September.[4] The list of those who attended shows that the Directorate had expanded its influence quite considerably since the previous meeting, probably as a result of the contacts made at the Weimar meeting in July. There were now representatives from Magdeburg, Berlin, Dresden and Karlsruhe apart from the original members. Volck began by rejecting accusations that he regarded the Directorate as an instrument for his own personal ends. He insisted that they considered themselves simply as the *Platzhalter Hitlers*. He defended his criticism of Ludendorff, which had evidently caused a certain amount of dissension, by claiming that Ludendorff had begun the controversy and that he was 'trying to turn

---

[1] Erklärung der Reichsführerschaft der Nationalsozialistischen Freiheitspartei: Der Fall Volck, Haase, Sunkel, ibid., p. 138.

[2] Ibid., p. 142.

[3] Haase to Heinze, 22 Aug. 1924, in NSDAP Hauptarchiv, Reel 44, Folder 894.

[4] Joachim Haupt, 'Bericht über die Tagung der Norddeutschen Nationalsozialistischen Verbände in Harburg am 7 September 1924', in Jochmann, op. cit., pp. 144–50.

the *völkisch* movement into a recruiting depot', a reference to his recent paramilitary activities in the *Frontbann*. He concluded that the *Reichstag* election and the attack of the DVFP against all the old National Socialists had completely devastated the *völkisch* movement and that they would have to begin again from the beginning. In the discussion which followed it was agreed to reject all participation in elections, though the final decision was reserved for Hitler; plans for the publication of a newspaper were considered; and finally, the name *Nationalsozialistische Arbeitsgemeinschaft* was chosen to describe the association of regional organizations under the Directorate.

The Harburg meeting had succeeded in its object of reaffirming opposition to the NSFB, though Gumm of Hamburg had reported the defection of a number of members to the NSFB and Lohse had declared himself not fundamentally opposed to representation in Parliament. On 10 September Volck wrote to Hitler, enclosing a report of the Harburg meeting and defending himself against reports by Strasser that he was too 'extreme' and had sought the quarrel with the DVFP.[1] He had evidently had reports that Hitler might dissociate himself from him, and the letter had a slightly defiant tone. Fobke's reply was important as a further definition of Hitler's plans for the period after his release:

After his release he will summon all the men in leading positions, in other words you too, to secure a clean break. This will be achieved through the reply to a single question: who shall be the political leader? Hitler does not recognize a *Reichsführerschaft* and he does not intend to participate in such a soldiers' council type arrangement. There will never be any question of an association of Hitler–von Graefe–Ludendorff. The discussion with the subordinate leaders after Hitler's release will be concerned with one simple question: who supports him as the sole leader?[2]

(iii) *The final phase of opposition—the Uelzen meeting of 2 November 1924*

The news that a *Reichstag* election was to be held on 7 December forced the Directorate to prepare once more to deal with the problem of electoral participation. In fact, it had already arisen in relation to the local election in Hamburg at the end of October. By refusing to speak at an election meeting in Cuxhaven, Volck had antagonized the party in Hamburg which felt he had missed an opportunity for propaganda.[3] But he was unrepentant. In a directive to the members of the *Arbeitsgemeinschaft* on 27 October, he reaffirmed that they were in favour of

---

[1] Ibid., pp. 152–3.
[2] Fobke to Volck, 21 Sept. 1924 in Jochmann, op. cit., pp. 154–5.
[3] Gumm to Volck, 23 Oct. 1924, ibid., pp. 168–9.

total abstention and opposed any electoral activity.[1] At the same time he summoned a meeting for 2 November at Uelzen near Hanover.

Volck's speech to the Uelzen meeting demonstrated the growing contradiction in his attitude to Hitler.[2] Thus while on the one hand he emphasized that 'Hitler remains for us *the* leader', despite the fact that he had not declared in favour of the Directorate, on the other hand he warned against 'adulation' of Hitler. On the question of the election, he laid down the principle of abstention, though without any attempt to control the individual's conscience. If, however, a supporter did vote 'then of course it must be "Black-white- and red"', i.e. for the DNVP.

Although Sunkel had concluded his report on the Uelzen meeting with the assertion that it represented the 'end of the foundation period of the *Arbeitsgemeinschaft*' which was now 'unexpectedly well-established', in fact differences of opinion had begun to emerge within it.[3] Lohse had not attended the meeting and now he was followed into opposition by Gumm, the Hamburg leader.[4] In Mecklenburg a dispute broke out over the ownership of *Die Vortruppe*, a *Völkisch* newspaper which had just been made the official organ of the *Arbeitsgemeinschaft*.[5] The editor also refused to carry a statement of the Directorate, condemning Esser and Streicher. More fundamental, Joachim Haupt, an important figure in the *Arbeitsgemeinschaft* and a fellow-student of Sunkel's, began to criticize Volck for being too romantic and not sufficiently activist.[6] Volck replied in a letter which shows the tension which existed between student activists like Haupt, Haase and Sunkel, and Volck, the older *völkisch* idealist.[7] He wrote,

It is not a good thing that so many young men want to lead us (please don't take that personally). When I was your age, perhaps I would have thought the same as you. . . . I was always in the thick of it and know what I am talking about. When we are 'ready', I shall be the first to act; but we are not yet. . . . As a much older man, I must warn you against anarchistic views.

On 15 December, Volck circulated a memorandum summing up the situation after the election.[8] He reaffirmed once more that 'We must never give up our basic position that Hitler is and remains *the* leader' and rejected the 'demagogy' of Esser and Streicher. But in referring to the possibility of Hitler's not returning from prison, he made

---

[1] Ibid., p. 170.   [2] Sunkel Bericht, ibid., pp. 172–7.
[3] Ibid., p. 177.   [4] Volck to Hans Ortmann, ibid., p. 183.
[5] See the correspondence between Körner, Priebke and Volck during November in NSDAP Hauptarchiv, Reel 44, Folder 895.
[6] Haupt's letter has not survived, but Volck mentions the criticism in his reply.
[7] Volck to Haupt, 4 Dec. 1924, in NSDAP Haupterarchiv, Reel 44, Folder 895.
[8] In Jochmann, op. cit., pp. 184–7.

the significant comment: 'we would then of course have to act independently, for the *völkisch* movement comes from the depths of the
people and is thus not dependent on individuals, otherwise it would be
finished if the leader died or became an invalid'. This distinction between the *völkisch* movement and its leader was in direct contrast to
Hitler's subordination of the conflict over policies in the *völkisch*
movement between the DVFP and the Directorate to the question of
who was to be the political leader—with the implication that nothing
else mattered. Hitler's release on 21 December 1924 was to bring this
contradiction to the point of head-on conflict.

IV

THE REFOUNDING OF THE NSDAP IN LOWER SAXONY AND THE ARBEITSGEMEINSCHAFT DER NORD- UND WEST-DEUTSCHEN GAUE DER NSDAP 1925–1926[1]

(i) *The resignation of Volck*

A MAJOR reason why Hitler had shown such a lack of interest in the north-west German Directorate was the fact that, as he emphasized to Fobke, he intended to begin by creating order in Bavaria. As early as the party congress of 1922, Hitler had insisted on the need for concentration on Munich, to provide the party with a definite head-quarters, thereby facilitating his control over it and preventing the splits which had bedevilled the *völkisch* movement hitherto.[2] He now reiterated these views in his directives about the internal structure of the movement contained in the first volume of *Mein Kampf*, written during 1924. Here he laid down

(a) Concentration of the entire work first in a single place, Munich. Formation of a community of absolutely reliable adherents. . . .

(b) Formation of local groups only after the authority of the central leading groups in Munich may be looked on as unconditionally recognized.[3]

On the question of the appointment of subordinates, Hitler had given Fobke two criteria which would determine his choice: first, support for him as the sole leader; and secondly, what the individual had to offer.[4] Both these criteria were involved in his selection of the leaders of the *Grossdeutsche Volksgemeinschaft* to man the new Munich party organization. Esser was appointed propaganda chief, while the actual

---

[1] There have been a number of recent studies of the *Arbeitsgemeinschaft* to which the author is indebted: G. Schildt, *Die Arbeitsgemeinschaft Nordwest. Untersuchungen zur Geschichte der NSDAP 1925/26* (Diss., Freiburg, 1964); R. Kühnl, *Die nationalsozialistische Linke 1925–1930* (Meisenberg, 1967); U. Wörtz, *Programmatik und Führerprinzip. Das Problem des Strasser-Kreises in der NSDAP* (Diss., Erlangen, 1966); and J. Nyomarkay, *Charisma and Factionalism in the Nazi Party* (Minnesota, 1967).

[2] For Hitler's congress speech see Haase, 'Aufstand in Niedersachsen. Der Kampf der NSDAP 1921–1924' (mimeo, 1942), pp. 122–30.

[3] A. Hitler, *Mein Kampf*, transl. (New York, 1939), pp. 483–4.

[4] See pp. 52 and 53 above.

running of the party organization was in the hands of Bouhler, Schwarz and Amann. Streicher and Dinter controlled the regional organizations of Franconia and the neighbouring province of Thuringia. All these men had been conspicuously loyal to Hitler during the pre-*putsch* period.[1] Furthermore, they were effective. The GVG vote in the *Reichstag* election in December was considerably larger than that of the Bavarian *Völkisch* Block.[2] The choice of the GVG leaders also demonstrated the ruthlessness with which Hitler was prepared to sacrifice unity to his two criteria. For the *Völkisch* Block deputies in the Bavarian *Landtag* had been alienated by the radicalism and bullying conceit of Esser and Streicher who were equally disliked by Hitler's loyal supporters in North Germany, the members of the *Arbeitsgemeinschaft*. But when reproached by Fobke for his choice, particularly of Esser and Streicher, Hitler only repeated 'that as far as he was concerned all that matters was what the individual had achieved. E.g., Streicher had won more than 60,000 votes in Nürnberg, more than the *Reichsführerschaft* in the whole of Bavaria.'[3]

Before he had reorganized Bavaria, Hitler took no action in North Germany.[4] He had no intention of making any prior commitments, which would be likely to bind him in any way. In particular, he did not take up any position regarding the North German directorate, despite repeated pleas from the Göttingen group that he should appoint Volck as leader of the Hanover regional organization of the NSDAP when it was refounded. Instead he pacified them with references to von Graefe as a 'parliamentary scoundrel' and vague promises 'to come up north'.[5] Hitler's silence deeply offended Volck; and when he had still heard no news by 12 January, he resigned from the Directorate and ordered the regional organization to seek directives from Hitler. His place as leader of the directorate was taken by Ludolf Haase.[6]

Volck's resignation was the culmination of a disenchantment with Hitler which had been growing since the summer of 1924. It was a combination of hurt pride, differences on matters of policy, and opposition to Hitler's autocratic methods and the intolerant adulation of his supporters.[7] The differences of policy hinged, in the first place, on a contrast between North and South Germany. According to Volck, the

[1] See Orlow, *Journal of Modern History* (June 1965), p. 217.
[2] See below.
[3] Fobke to Volck, 2 Feb. 1925; in NSDAP Hauptarchiv, Reel 44, Folder 899.
[4] Ibid., Fobke Rundschreiben, 10 Feb. 1925, reported a statement of Hitler that it was 'tactically impossible to do anything before the movement was free in Bavaria'.
[5] See footnotes 3 and 4.
[6] Two circulars of 12 and 21 Jan. 1925, ibid.
[7] See two long statements of his position in Jochmann, *Nationalsozialismus und Revolution*, pp. 188–92 and pp. 196–203.

völkisch renewal would come from North Germany where the *Arbeits-gemeinschaft* had already laid the foundations, particularly in Lower Saxony among the Guelph supporters. By refusing to come North, by supporting Esser and Streicher, and by putting up Ludendorff—who as a Prussian general was anathema to the Guelphs—as his presidential candidate, Hitler had jeopardized the whole movement. More import-ant, however, was his conception of the '*völkisch* renewal' as some-thing which had to emerge from the people itself, and which would be endangered if it was indissolubly linked with the fortunes of any one man. From this theory he derived his objections to the increasing glorification of Hitler. He insisted that

even leaders are only servants of the people's soul from which the movement stems. Of course the powerful appeal of Hitler's name should be used, but . . . even in political matters and particularly in intellectual-spiritual questions, absolute obedience is impossible; otherwise one breeds dependent creatures. . . . The misuse of the leader in the end went so far that at the mention of cer-tain names our stargazers broke out into hysterical shrieks of Heil! Those who do not shriek with us will be shot was the main precept of these screaming monkeys.

Some of Volck's views were shared by his former colleagues in the Directorate. They all disliked Esser and Streicher, and Haase agreed that the 'liberation' would come from North Germany (Lower Saxony).[1] But on the crucial question of his attitude to Hitler they had no sympathy with his views. Their idea of Hitler's position was summed up by a remark in a letter from Haase to Fobke that 'nothing should be undertaken in the *völkisch* movement without Hitler's agree-ment';[2] and their adolescent hero-worship emerged in Fobke's report from Munich that 'of course he's got a car again'.[3] It was important that this adulation was not limited to the Directorate, but was shared by the other National Socialists in Hanover. An enquiry about the position of the Directorate *vis-à-vis* Hitler must have given Volck no doubt about his isolation. For it insisted that 'basically all we Nazis in Hanover want is to agree with Hitler's views. If our views do not agree with his, then we shall have to alter our opinions.'[4]

Yet Haase and Fobke were upset by Volck's resignation. What particularly concerned them was the vacuum which it created in Han-over, into which they feared the NSFB might well move.[5] For their youth counted against them. They quickly refounded the NSDAP in Hanover and Göttingen unofficially, 'so that no-one can pinch the fine

[1] Haase to Fobke, 10 Jan. 1925; in NSDAP Hauptarchiv, Reel 44, Folder 899.
[2] Haase to Fobke, 2 Mar. 1925, ibid.
[3] Fobke to Haase, 3 Feb. 1925, ibid.
[4] Topf to Volck, 10 Jan. 1925, ibid.
[5] Fobke to Volck, 16 Jan. 1925, ibid.

old name'.[1] And they attempted to persuade Volck to change his mind, interceding with Hitler to try and win recognition for him.[2] But Hitler remained non-committal. He would obviously accept nothing but complete surrender. Volck was the first major victim, after the refounding of the party, of Hitler's totalitarian style of leadership. For his refusal to equate the *völkisch* movement with Hitler as *Führer* made him totally unacceptable. Volck's prophetic warnings on the dangers of Hitler's autocratic methods also illustrate the dilemma in which the racialists sometimes found themselves. He was not the last of those who, having glorified dictatorial leadership, found its realization unacceptable.

(ii) *The break-up of the Nationalsozialistische Freiheitsbewegung (NSFB) and the foundation of the Deutsch-völkische Freiheitsbewegung (DVFB)*

Although Hitler delayed recognition of the leaders of the *Arbeitsgemeinschaft*, he was also in no hurry to deal with the NSFB leadership. He had of course already told Fobke of his determination not to work with 'the Soldiers Council' type of *Reichsführerschaft*;[3] and he completely ignored a letter from von Graefe which demanded a definite commitment and complained about his support for Esser and Streicher.[4]

In view of this prevarication on Hitler's part, the NSFB, or rather the former DVFP leadership within it, determined to act themselves and present Hitler with a *fait accompli*. At a meeting of the Prussian regional organization of the NSFB on 14 January, leading members launched a bitter attack on Hitler.[5] In order to secure the lifting of the ban on the NSDAP in Bavaria, Hitler had been forced to promise the Catholic Minister-President, Held, not to make another *putsch*. The NSFB leaders now used these negotiations as the basis for accusations that Hitler was a lackey of Rome. They maintained that Rome (Ultramontanism) was an even greater danger than the Jews. This was an extremely effective propaganda line within the *völkisch* movement, for Rome had always been regarded as one of the 'international powers' undermining German *Volkstum*. Furthermore, great play was made with the danger of Bavarian particularism and the Prussian basis of the NSFB was emphasized in favourable contrast. Finally, Hitler was called variously a 'drummer' and a 'Pope', and it was denied that he

[1] Fobke to Sunkel, 28 Jan. 1925, ibid.
[2] Fobke to Hitler, 7 Feb. 1925, ibid.
[3] See above p. 53.
[4] Corswant-Cuntzow to Volck, 15 Jan. 1925, in NSDAP Hauptarchiv, Reel 44, Folder 899.
[5] Ibid.

was a politician, while his followers were described as 'young men who talk too much'. But these speeches from the leaders failed to win over all the delegates. A number of representatives, including the one from Hanover, declared their support for Hitler, and in the next few weeks at meetings up and down the country members were forced to choose whether to accept the leadership of von Graefe, Wulle and Reventlow and join a reconstituted DVFP to be known as the German *Völkisch* Freedom Movement (DVFB), or whether they should form branches of Hitler supporters, in anticipation of the refounding of the NSDAP.[1] The *Reichsführerschaft* of von Graefe, Strasser and Ludendorff resigned on 8 February. This was a decisive moment and it is particularly important to examine the initial membership of the reconstituted NSDAP and what distinguished it from the new DVFB.

In the first place, the criticism at the NSFB meeting of the youth of the Hitler supporters appears to be borne out by the limited evidence available. Thus the few NSDAP membership lists dating from 1925 that are still in existence show, with one exception (Schleswig-Holstein),[2] a striking age pattern. In Hamburg for example 64·5 per cent of the new members were under 25,[3] in Halle 66·1 per cent were under 30 and of these 65·1 per cent were under 25,[4] in East Prussia 68 per cent were under 30,[5] and in the local branch of Gifhorn in Lower Saxony 65 per cent were under 30.[6] This evidence is reinforced for the area of Lower Saxony by the report of the Bremen police on the split in the movement in the Weser-Ems area.[7] Here the majority of the NSFB members followed the leadership, probably because one of their leaders, Henning, was the *Reichstag* deputy for Weser-Ems. The Hitler supporters, who were in the minority, apparently consisted 'essentially of the young and activist elements'.

Secondly, many of the provincial leaders of the NSFB in North and West Germany declared for Hitler, including the regional leaders of Hanover-South, Rust and Major Dincklage, and the district leader in Hanover-East, Otto Telschow.[8] This demonstrates the strength of the position which Hitler had established for himself as the most effective *völkisch* leader. A number of factors contributed to this: first, by accepting full responsibility for the *putsch* at his trial in February 1924, while the Conservative and Army leaders denied having anything to do with it, Hitler created the myth of the sole responsibility of the

---

[1] Accounts of some of these meetings are contained in BA Sammlung Schumacher.

[2] BA Slg. Schumacher 208 I.   [3] BA Slg. Schumacher 201 I.

[4] BA Slg. Schumacher 207 B.   [5] BA Slg. Schumacher 201 I.

[6] BA Slg. Schumacher 202 I.

[7] Lagebericht Nr. 21, 16 Feb. 1925, in NSAO 136.2796.

[8] Hanover to the editor (of the *Völkischer Beobachter*), 25 Feb. 1925. NSAH Hann. Des. 310 I D, Nr. 3.

NSDAP and thereby became a hero to *völkisch* extremists.[1] Secondly, the chaos in the *völkisch* movement during 1924 had enhanced his own reputation.[2]

The account of the reasons for his joining the NSDAP rather than the DVFB reported later by Telschow, the former NSFB district leader in Hanover-East, give a good insight into the thinking of these new supporters of Hitler.[3] He declared his intention of leaving the NSFB at a meeting of the Hanover-East regional organization at Harburg on 16 January. The meeting had been addressed by Wulle, the leader of the Prussian NSFB organization, and on being questioned on the aims of the new DVFB, Wulle had replied that he wanted it to be 'the direct continuation of the old German-Social Party of the late Liebermann v. Sonnenberg', a pre-war anti-Semitic party. Telschow replied 'that in that case his party had no *raison d'être*, and he was the representative of an anachronistic *Mittelstandspartei*. He would go the way of the old anti-Semitic parties, the way into oblivion!'

The few activists who largely because of a dislike of what they considered to be the Catholic and un-Prussian nature of the NSDAP still remained in the DVFB, sooner or later had to go to Canossa and were appropriately rewarded. Thus, at the beginning of 1927, Reventlow, Kube, and Stöhr, three leading members of the party, resigned from the DVFB and joined the NSDAP. In his press statement Reventlow reported that within the DVFB there had emerged two wings, one led by Graefe and Wulle and consisting of former members of the conservative German National People's Party who had no interest in the 'radical social' question, and the wing led by himself. 'The future of Germany', he concluded, 'depends on whether the German worker —in the broadest sense—can be won for the German idea.'[4] In his view the NSDAP could achieve this, while the DVFB could not. Such people joined the NSDAP, in fact, because it had succeeded in becoming a mass party, not limited, as the DVFB largely was, to the anti-Semitic upper and upper-middle classes.

(iii) *The appointment of the Prussian leaders of the NSDAP—the Hamm and Harburg meetings of February and March 1925*

Hitler was now faced with the problem of organizing his supporters outside Bavaria—both those who had been in the *Arbeitsgemeinschaft*

---

[1] See H. H. Hoffmann, *Der Hitlerputsch* (Munich, 1961), pp. 266 ff.

[2] The Reich Commissar wrote that 'the very fact that the movement has collapsed has caused the vast majority of its supporters to set their hopes on Hitler, whom *völkisch* circles see as the only man with a definite political instinct.' Report of 20 Dec. 1924, NSAO 136, Nr. 2915.

[3] See the article 'Hitlerfahnen über Ost-Hannover' in the official newspaper for the NSDAP Gau Hanover-East—*Niedersachsen-Stürmer* (*NS*) of 19 Dec. 1931.

[4] *Der Nationalsozialist* NSAH Hann. Des. 310 I D 3.

and those who had just broken with the NSFB. Of the *Reichsführer-schaft*—Ludendorff, von Graefe and Strasser—which resigned on 8 February, neither Ludendorff nor Strasser had taken part in the founding of the new DVFB. Some time between 12 and 21 February, Strasser reached agreement with Hitler because, on 21 February, Hitler issued him with authority to confirm regional leaders in the state of Prussia.[1] Strasser was the obvious man to fulfil this role because, as a member of the *Reichsführerschaft*, he had established contact with the regional leaders in the North and West during 1924. He also had the advantage of possessing a free railway pass, the privilege of a *Reichstag* member.

At a meeting in Hamm in Westphalia on 22 February 1925, the leaders of the regional organizations of the NSFB in Westphalia, Rhineland-North, Rhineland-South, Hanover, and Pomerania, together with over 100 county leaders (*Kreisleiter*) declared for Hitler, and a number were appointed by Strasser as future regional leaders (*Gauleiter*) of the NSDAP, subject to confirmation from Hitler.[2] In Rhineland-South, there was a dispute over the leadership between members of the GVG and the NSFB. Strasser appointed his former colleague of the NSFB, and the GVG group was ordered to dissolve itself by the NSDAP head-quarters in Munich.[3]

The Hamm meeting, however, did not resolve the situation in Lower Saxony, where the old members of the Directorate were bitterly opposed to the ex-NFSB leaders, Rust and Dincklage. In fact, both sides had already been negotiating with Hitler. Fobke had interceded on behalf of Volck;[4] and Rust had visited Hitler some time before the Hamm meeting.[5] By the middle of February, however, it was becoming clear that Volck and Hitler would not reach agreement. Furthermore, at a meeting of the Hanover regional organization of the NSFB on 25 January, Rust had been unanimously confirmed as leader and instructed to negotiate with Hitler.[6] Haase and Fobke, therefore, decided to cut their losses and begin negotiations with Rust over the future organization of the party in the province of Hanover, though they continued to hope for a settlement over Volck.[7] On 25 February, an agreement was reached that Fobke and Haase should control the

[1] NSDAP secretary in Cologne branch to Amann, 2 Mar. 1925, BA Slg. Schumacher 203.
[2] Hanover to the editor (of the *Völkischer Beobachter*), 25 Feb. 1925, NSAH Hann. Des. 310 I D 3.
[3] Bouhler to Sitt, 20 Apr. 1925, BA Slg. Schumacher 203.
[4] Fobke to Hitler, 7 Feb. 1925. NSDAP Hauptarchiv, Reel 44, Folder 899.
[5] This is clear from Rust to Hitler, 25 Feb. 1925. Hann. Des. 310 I A, Nr. 8.
[6] Hanover to Munich undated, c. Mar. 1925, Hann. Des. 310 I A, Nr. 8.
[7] See the correspondence Fobke–Haase–Volck–Professor Hoffmann in NSDAP Hauptarchiv, Reel 44, Folder 899.

districts of Uslar, Einbeck, Northeim, Duderstadt, and Göttingen where they had always successfully resisted the intrusion of the DVSP and NSFB;[1] and three days later, Haase dissolved the *Arbeitsgemeinschaft*, ordering its members to join the NSDAP.[2]

The final decisions on the organization of the party in the province of Hanover were taken at a meeting in Harburg on 22 March, which was attended by Gregor Strasser.[3] One appointment, however, had already been made. On 12 March, Fobke proudly announced that the Hanover-South regional organization of the former *Arbeitsgemeinschaft* had been permitted to join the NSDAP *en bloc* and Haase had been appointed leader, with Fobke deputizing during his illness.[4] This unique dispensation, permitting the members to rejoin as a group instead of as individuals, was regarded by Haase and Fobke as a tribute to their struggle for the purity of national socialism during 1924 and their loyalty to Hitler during his imprisonment. It was probably also a compensation for the replacement of Volck by Rust.

At the Harburg meeting it was agreed to divide Lower Saxony into four parts:

(1) covered the *Regierungsbezirke*:—Hanover, Aurich, the Weser districts of the *Regierungsbezirke* Lüneburg and Stade,[5] Hildesheim minus the districts given to Haase at the meeting of 25 February; and the free states of Brunswick, Oldenburg and Schaumburg-Lippe. Rust was appointed leader of this area with his headquarters in the city of Hanover.

(2) The Elbe districts of the *Regierungsbezirke* Lüneburg and Stade of which Telschow was appointed leader with his head-quarters in Buchholz.

(3) The Hildesheim districts ceded to Haase and Fobke by Rust on 25 February.[6]

(4) The *Regierungsbezirk* Osnabrück which was ceded to Pfeffer von Salomon, the party leader in Westphalia.

In future the areas were to be known as (1) Gau Hanover-North, (2) Gau Lüneburg-Stade, (3) Gau Hanover-South, and (4) Gau Westphalia. This division was to remain with minor adjustments until the major party reorganization of 1928.

---

[1] Rust to Munich, 29 Mar. 1925, BA Slg. Schumacher 202 I.

[2] Haase 'Erklärung', 28 Feb. 1925, in NSDAP Hauptarchiv, Reel 44, Folder 899.

[3] Rust to Munich, 29 Mar. 1925, BA Slg. Schumacher 202 I.

[4] Fobke Rundschreiben, 12 Mar. 1925, in NSDAP Hauptarchiv, Reel 44, Folder 899. Haase was incapacitated during the first months of 1925, owing to a wound received during a fight with opponents at a meeting in Duderstadt, in June 1924. See Haase, op. cit., pp. 628 ff.

[5] Defined as Fallingbostel, Celle, Burgdorf, Gifhorn, Isenhagen and Lehe, Geestemünde, Blumenthal, Osterholz-Scharmbeck, Rotenburg.

[6] I.e. Uslar, Einbeck, Northeim, Duderstadt and Göttingen city and rural district.

(iv) *Hitler's directives for the refounding of the NSDAP*

The official refounding of the NSDAP took place on 27 February
1925 at a mass meeting in the *Bürgerbräukeller* in Munich, where
there was a demonstrative reconciliation between the leaders of the
Grossdeutsche Volksgemeinschaft and some of the Bavarian *Völkische*,
their former opponents.[1] The day before, Hitler had published an
article in the *Völkischer Beobachter*, entitled 'A New Beginning'.[2] He
began by insisting that he had no intention of bothering himself with
the dissension in the *völkisch* movement, and emphasized the point with
a veiled description of his attitude to the opponents of Esser and Streicher: 'I do not consider it to be the task of a political leader to attempt to
improve upon, or even fuse together, the human material lying ready
to hand.' Next, indirectly referring to the anti-Catholic stance of the
Deutschvölkische Freiheitsbewegung, he protested against 'the attempt
to bring religious disputes into the movement or even equate the movement with religious disputes'. The avoidance of anti-clericalism or
discrimination against Catholics was of course essential both for the
success of the party in the South and for the sake of its unity. It showed
the difference between Hitler's political realism and the ideologically
blinkered approach of his *völkisch* rivals. He concluded by demanding
that supporters should not weaken themselves with fraternal strife, but
unite for the external struggle.

Hitler followed this article with 'A Call to the Former Members of
the NSDAP', in which he promised that in a year's time he would
account for his leadership of the party to see whether 'it had again become a "movement", or whether the movement had been stifled
through being a party'.[3] At the *Bürgerbräu* meeting he repeated this
and asked that all criticism should be restrained until then, which in
effect amounted to asking for a free hand for the next year.

On matters of organization, he began by demanding in the *Call* that
the leaders should owe him 'the same obedience as we all owe to the
common idea', and then went on to define the organizational structure
more closely in his 'Basic Instructions for the Refounding of the
NSDAP'.[4] The first of these directives laid down that 'the new party
recognizes in its principles and programme the directives of the old
party ... the organization will be carried out according to the old
statutes'. This was intended to re-establish autocratic decision-making
which had existed since his seizure of power within the party in July–
August 1921. In the following directive on membership, however,

[1] VB, 7 Mar. 1925. For the following see also the account in A. Bullock, *Hitler.
A Study in Tyranny*, pp. 129–30.
[2] VB, 26 Feb. 1925.
[3] Ibid.   [4] Ibid.

Hitler insisted that all Nazis should sign a *new* membership form and that 'on entering the Party no conditions will be accepted either from leaders or from members'. Finally, the organizational structure of the party was completely centralized: 'each member is subordinate, in the first instance, to the party head-quarters'; local branches were to be approved by the party head-quarters; and finally, 'the leader must always precede the organization and not *vice versa*'.

(v) *The reactions of the Lower Saxony party leaders to Munich policies: 1925*

These organizational directives were put into effect by Bouhler, the party secretary. Bouhler immediately began to consolidate the control of Munich over the branches throughout the Reich, insisting on the necessity for the confirmation of senior party appointments, the sole validity of the membership cards issued at party headquarters, and on the remittance of membership dues: 1 RM entry fee and 10 pf of the 30 pf monthly due per member.[1]

This attempt to consolidate the authority of Munich over the rest of the Reich organization, though theoretically accepted, was to some extent resented by the provincial leaders in North West Germany. The collapse of the authority of the Munich head-quarters had completely undermined whatever centralized authority had existed before 1924. New men had come to the fore, who had gained self-confidence during 1924 and who, although enthusiastic supporters of Hitler, wished to exert some influence on party decisions, particularly those which directly affected their work. They had hoped that Hitler would come to North Germany. But now it appeared as if he had abdicated responsibility to the former GVG leaders, for he played no obvious role during the early part of 1925; he was banned from speaking outside Bavaria and Thuringia, and concentrated on writing the second volume of *Mein Kampf*. Yet the GVG leaders, Esser and Streicher, had been the *bêtes noires* of both the Directorate and the NSFB leaders, and dislike of Esser and Streicher was to play a crucial role in the coming months.

In April 1925, therefore, an attempt was made to win a measure of independence from Munich. The *Gaue* of Hanover, Göttingen, Hessen-Nassau, and Schleswig-Holstein wrote a joint letter to Bouhler in which they maintained that rigid centralization might have been necessary before 1923, but that since 'a stable organization has begun to emerge outside Bavaria', it would be better for individual *Gaue* to issue

[1] See the correspondence between Munich and the regional organizations in BA Slg. Schumacher.

membership cards and merely send Munich a monthly or quarterly report of the party's activities in the area.[1] To some extent this simply reflected a desire to cut down the secretarial work involved in correspondence with Munich, and also the fear that the local branches might correspond directly with Munich. This was a point, however, on which Hitler had given clear instructions and Bouhler replied that 'Herr Hitler considers it very important that the issuing of membership cards should be done centrally from the office in Munich. In return, he agreed that all business with the local branches should be carried on through *Gau* head-quarters.'[2]

Apart from the question of organization, another factor had emerged to disturb relations between the party in Lower Saxony and in Munich: the attitude to elections. At the international National Socialist meeting at Salzburg in 1922, Hitler had successfully insisted on abstention from elections. This had fitted in very well with the paramilitary style of the first NSDAP. The failure of the *putsch* of 8 to 9 November 1923, however, had fundamentally changed the situation. The violent recriminations which divided the Right, the attitude of the *Reichswehr*, and above all the gradual stabilization of the economy, meant that the concept of a 'march on Berlin' which had come to dominate the thinking of large sections of the Bavarian Right during 1923 was no longer relevant. But, assuming the party had repudiated a *putsch*, the only remaining method of winning power was the constitutional one. Hitler had probably been encouraged to accept this situation by the big successes gained by the *Völkisch*-Social-Block in the spring elections of 1924. In particular, the new government formed in Thuringia during that year had depended on the support of the V-S-B deputies and had been forced to raise the ban on the NSDAP,[3] a striking example of the potential influence of parliamentary activity. Sometime during 1924, therefore, Hitler had come round to accepting participation in elections.[4]

In his 'Call to the Former Members of the NSDAP', Hitler had been careful to pay a warm tribute to Ludendorff and, on the death of President Ebert, he succeeded in winning him as NSDAP candidate for the presidential election in March. This was something of a *coup* for Hitler because he thereby forced the rival DVFB to pledge its support for the other right-wing candidate, Jarres, thereby alienating its supporters who were still loyal to Ludendorff.[5] When Hindenburg was

[1] Fobke to Munich, 15 Apr. 1925, BA Slg. Schumacher 202 I.

[2] Bouhler to Fobke, 20 Apr. 1925, BA Slg. Schumacher 202 I.

[3] Frau Sauckel (wife of the Nazi leader in Thuringia), recounting the history of the paper *Der Deutsche Aar* in National Archives T-81, Reel 116, Frames 136781.

[4] Kurt Ludecke, *I Knew Hitler* (London, 1938), p. 217.

[5] The Bremen police noted confusion among the DFVB supporters in Weser-Ems, see Lagebericht, Nr. 24, 1 Apr. 1925, NSAO 136.2796.

put foward by the Right in the second ballot, Hitler could afford to drop Ludendorff with impunity.

Yet the participation of the party in the presidential election and in particular the candidacy of Ludendorff, long disliked by the Göttingen group, antagonized the party in South Hanover. At the beginning of April, Haase forwarded a memorandum to Munich entitled 'Necessities for the NSDAP'.[1] Here he advocated the extreme élitist approach which he had developed during 1924, condemning participation in elections in all circumstances and advocating the creation of small party cells on a highly selective basis. Instead of large meetings, which brought unreliable elements into the party, there should be careful canvassing and small study groups to prevent contamination by the mass. Within the organization at all levels democratic processes should be banned and a rigidly authoritarian system introduced. He concluded 'men of the north, who through years of persecution were compelled to study the inner life of the movement, observe the development of the new NSDAP with anxiety'. Haase could not conceive that Hitler would be able to combine successfully an organization based on the *Führerprinzip* and a revolutionary party with participation in elections and membership of the *Reichstag*.

The first official reaction came in a letter from Hess to Rust, in which he began by declaring that Hitler could not accept some of the points made, but then went on to emphasize that Hitler's attitude to parliamentarism had not changed:

As before he rejects it completely. But since we have already gone into Parliament against his will, he considers that 'parliamentary activity' is a weapon—among many others—that can be used. Not, however, activity in the sense of 'positive co-operation' which our members have pursued up to now, but obstruction and continual sharp criticism of the present system. To pursue parliamentarism within Parliament itself *ad absurdum*![2]

This official statement of the change of policy, which Hitler had described to Ludecke the previous year, was of course totally unacceptable to Haase. Even Rust, the former DVFP leader, was not satisfied. He replied that on the question of parliamentary elections he accepted 'emphatically and decidedly the standpoint of Herr Haase'.[3] The reasons for this seem to have been less doctrinaire than in the case of Haase; he conceded for instance that participation in the Bavarian election might be necessary. For Rust, unlike Haase, it was not a matter of principle but of tactics. The decisive factor was the situation *vis-à-vis* the DVFB. As he pointed out to Hess: 'We would lose all prestige and make ourselves look ridiculous, if we attempted to win

[1] Haase, Notwendigkeiten für die NSDAP in NSAH Hann. Des. 310 I A, Nr. 3.
[2] Hess to Rust, 25 Apr. 1925, NSAH Hann. Des. 310 I A, Nr. 8.
[3] Rust to Hitler, 30 Apr. 1925, NSAH Hann. Des. 310 I A, Nr. 8.

THE REFOUNDING OF THE NSDAP

votes within the sharply reduced *völkisch* electorate in competition with the DVFB.' In the first place, the party in the North was still only a rump organization whose finances were in very poor shape. Secondly, only three months previously the NSDAP had split off from the NSFB as the more radical wing of the *völkisch* movement. One of the features distinguishing the radicalism of the NSDAP had been its hostility to parliamentarism. It was impossible to expect the membership to perform a volte-face quite so soon.[1] Finally, Rust expressed his support for Haase's wish that the North German leaders should be consulted on matters of policy, but with the important qualification that 'the decision lies with the *Führer*, which must then be carried out without reservation'.

A further question which concerned the party in Hanover and elsewhere in North Germany was the need to organize a party trade union with which to win over the workers. Unlike the DVFB, whose support was centred in the agricultural areas, the NSDAP at this period tended to be based in the towns and to canvass support in the industrial areas round Hanover.[2] This attempt to win support in the industrial areas necessitated competition with the strongly entrenched Social Democratic and Communist parties, and for this a party trade union was considered vital.[3] But Hitler was opposed to the setting up of an NSDAP trade union.[4] He believed it would have inadequate resources with which to compete with the large Social-Democratic unions and, more important, he felt that 'the economic struggle will immediately draw the energy from the political fight'.[5] As a result, his Munich officials pigeon-holed demands for the formation of a party union.[6]

(vi) *The meeting of the North-West German Gauleiter at Hagen, 10 September 1925*

By September 1925, these conflicts of personality and policy were coming to a head. Hostility to local officials in Munich had been ac-

[1] The Hanover political police reported that the only difference between the meetings of the DVFB and those of the NSDAP, lay in attitudes expressed on the question of Parliament. See Monatsberichte, 30 Sept. 1925, in NSAH Hann. Des. 80 Hann II, Nr. 718.

[2] 'The stronghold of our movement in Lower Saxony and the main centre of attack, lies in the largest industrial area in the Province of Hanover, in the Ilseder Hütte', see Dincklage to Hanover, 1 Mar. 1926, NSAH Hann. Des. 310 I A, Nr. 12.

[3] E.g. the Brunswick leaders regarded the foundation of a National Socialist trade union as 'urgently necessary'. Dincklage to Munich, 30 May 1925, NSAH Hann. Des. 310 I A, Nr. 8.

[4] Hitler, *Mein Kampf*, pp. 880–1.   [5] Ibid.

[6] E.g. Bouhler to Klant, the Hamburg Gauleiter, 7 Apr. 1925, BA Slg. Schumacher 201 I.

centuated by Bavarian party conflicts in which Esser was seen as the main cause.[1] Hitler's old rival Drexler and another leading Bavarian racialist, Plümer, had resigned because of objections to Esser and Streicher, and had formed a *National-sozialer Volksbund* in opposition to the NSDAP. There was also frustration at Hitler's apparent indifference to the widespread opposition to Esser, and resentment of orders from Munich, such as those relating to the press and the creation of SS units, which were regarded as an attempt to impose measures suitable for Bavaria but not for North Germany. On the question of elections, Hitler had reaffirmed his change of policy at a meeting of leading officials in Weimar on 12 July:[2] but it was still opposed by the Göttingen leaders, who were joined in this by the deputy leader in Hanover, Dincklage.[3]

The leadership in the opposition to Munich was taken by Gregor Strasser. This opposition was not directed against Hitler personally, but rather against his leading party officials. It was based partly on real personal hostility to Esser and Streicher, and partly on a psychological rationalization imposed on the members of the opposition by the charismatic quality of their relationship with the *Führer*.[4] Thus, the NSDAP opposition talked in terms only of 'winning over Hitler',[5] while Esser and Streicher acted as a lightning conductor for hostility to the fundamental reorientation of the party which had taken place, and to Hitler's refusal to pay more attention to the needs of the party in the North, or to flatter the pride of its leaders by more consultation.

Strasser too does not appear to have wished to challenge Hitler's leadership. Hinrich Lohse, the *Gauleiter* of Schleswig-Holstein, recollected after the war that, at the Weimar meeting in July, Strasser had appeared resigned to his position as second in command.[6] For him, intense personal dislike of Esser and Streicher, dating from the conflict between the NSFB and the GVG in 1924, and a desire to reform the programme to emphasize the social question were decisive. Strasser's 'socialism' was a product of his service at the front. 'We young Germans of the Great War had nothing to do with the decadent world of

[1] See Jochmann, op. cit., p. 207.

[2] See 'Hitler in Weimar' draft article for the *Niedersächsischer Beobachter* in NSAH Hann. Des. 310 I D 1.

[3] Jochmann, op. cit., pp. 214–15.

[4] On this point, see Nyomarkay, *Charisma and Factionalism in the Nazi Party*, pp. 80 ff.

[5] E.g. Goebbels, 'Wir werden uns schon bei Hitler durchsetzen' diary entry, 21 Aug. 1925, in *Das Tagebuch von Joseph Goebbels 1925/6*. Hrsg. von H. Heiber (Stuttgart, 1961), p. 22.

[6] Hinrich Lohse 'Der Fall Strasser'. A memorandum dictated after the war and deposited in the Forschungsstelle für die Geschichte des Nationalsozialismus in Hamburg (in future FGN), p. 5.

the old system and felt no compassion at the collapse of its conventions —at the most we were astonished and angered by the cowardliness of the fall of this "bourgeois" world.'[1] Ideologically, it appears to have derived from Oswald Spengler's influential pamphlet *Preussentum und Sozialismus*, published in 1919, and its heroes were Freiherr vom Stein and Bismarck. In his maiden speech in the *Reichstag* as a member of the V-S-B, he had defined what distinguished them from the German nationalist parties:

> it is true that the German nationalist parties energetically support the demand for external security of the German state, but they forget that a truly national policy must be effective not only diplomatically, but also in home affairs. A domestic policy, however, means above all a social policy, not in the sense of charity, no German worker wants that, but in the recognition of the duties of the state towards the individual. In other words, a state socialism such as Bismarck aimed at and which he said he would force through.[2]

Strasser planned to achieve his aim of giving a new emphasis to the social aspect of national-socialism by bringing together party officials with similar views in a study group. This would have its own paper for the discussion of policy, in an attempt to enliven party thinking, particularly on the issues of social and foreign policy. In June and July 1925, Strasser made an abortive attempt to win Oswald Spengler as a future contributor. He described to Spengler the aim of national socialism as 'a German revolution through a German socialism'.[3] He conceded that 'our so-called programme neither expresses this very clearly, nor does it successfully suggest the means for reaching this goal—but that has a number of causes which lie primarily in the confusion of the two so-called *völkische* attitudes' (i.e. the conservative-nationalist and the national socialist anti-Semitic attitudes). The new paper would serve as a 'point of crystallization for a certain group of men with clear vision and political drive'.[4]

During 1925, Elberfeld in the Ruhr was establishing itself as the centre of a group which wished to place more emphasis on the 'socialist' aspect of National Socialism. The Ruhr even more than Hanover was faced with the problem of appealing to the workers. In August 1925, two young leading party members in Elberfeld, Karl Kaufmann and Dr. Joseph Goebbels, brought about the suspension of the *Gauleiter* of Rhineland-North, Axel Ripke, nominally on a charge of the embezzlement of party funds, but in fact because he was insufficiently

---

[1] G. Strasser, *Kampf um Deutschland* (Munich, 1932), p. 189.
[2] Ibid., pp. 21–3.
[3] Oswald Spengler, *Briefe 1913–36*, ed. M. Koktanek (Munich, 1963), pp. 397–401. I owe this source to Dr. Gerhard Schildt.
[4] Ibid.

radical.[1] It was to Elberfeld and to these men that Strasser now turned for support. He began by informing only Goebbels, Elbrechter (another Elberfeld leader), and the Göttingen group, whom he knew to be ardent opponents of the Munich officials, of his plan to create a centre of opposition to Munich. On 21 August Goebbels wrote in his diary:

Yesterday Strasser spent the whole afternoon here. Terrific chap. Huge Bavarian. With a wonderful sense of humour. Told a lot of sad things about Munich. About this chaotic mess in the Central Office. Hitler is surrounded by the wrong people. I think Hermann Esser is fatal for him. With Strasser we are now going to bring the whole of the West together in one organization. The basic negotiations are taking place at the beginning of September. We are going as far as Hanover and Göttingen. The west block is going to publish the *NS-Briefe*, with Strasser as publisher and me as editor. This will give us a weapon against the ossified bureaucrats in Munich. We are bound to convince Hitler.[2]

These negotiations over the formation of a western block took place at Hagen in Westphalia on 10 September 1925.[3] The meeting was attended by the majority of the Prussian *Gauleiter*, presumably in an attempt to get maximum support and to avoid suspicion of a plot. Strasser had had to visit his sick mother at the last moment, and Dr. Elbrechter presided at the meeting; because of Strasser's absence the anti-Munich aspect did not emerge explicitly; indeed a resolution was passed declaring that no hostility to Munich was intended. Most of the decisions taken were of a purely organizational nature: the need for improvement in the co-ordination of the *Gaue* in North-West Germany under a single leader—Strasser—with a central office and secretariat; the exchange of political and organizational experience, propaganda material and speakers; finally, where necessary, the working out of joint political statements. Elberfeld was designated as the headquarters of the new organization and the name '*Arbeitsgemeinschaft* of the north and west German *Gauleiter* of the NSDAP' (AG) was suggested. Finally, the publication of a journal to be called the *NS-Briefe*, under the editorship of Dr. Goebbels, was agreed upon.

But the decision to invite so many representatives already proved to be an error. On the two important questions to be raised—the attitude to Esser and the question of elections—there was considerable disagreement. When the issue of Esser was raised by Fobke, there were

[1] Goebbels and Kaufmann accused Ripke of telling Hitler that Goebbels was a Bolshevik. See the copy of the Protokoll of 25 July 1925, dealing with the dispute in BA NS/1. vorl. 341/419–20.
[2] Goebbels, *Tagebuch*, p. 21.
[3] Reports on the meeting in Goebbels to Strasser, 11 Sept. 1925, BA NS 1/vorl. 340, 399. Goebbels, op. cit., pp. 26–7 and Jochmann, op. cit., pp. 209–11.

cries of 'palace revolution', and the Göttingen representatives had difficulty in pushing through a decision to abstain from elections.[1] This latter question was particularly acute because provincial and district elections were due in October. The Munich head-quarters, evidently appreciating the delicacy of the problem sent different instructions to each *Gau* according to whether or not they favoured participation.[2] Faced with these tactics, the representatives at Hagen unanimously agreed to reject participation in all elections and a letter to this effect was sent to Hitler together with a criticism of the contradictory instructions issuing from Munich.[3]

(vii) *Divisions within the Arbeitsgemeinschaft—the Nationalsozialistische Briefe and reactions to the Strasser Programme*

This unanimity on the question of elections was in fact deceptive. Professor Vahlen of Pomerania and Haake of Rhineland South were both in favour of elections,[4] while soon after the meeting Pfeffer, the influential *Gauleiter* of Westphalia, was having to be gently reminded of the AG party line on this question.[5] Finally, in a foreword to an article by Haase in the *NS-Briefe*, Strasser doubted whether the question of participation in elections was of more than tactical interest,[6] thereby antagonizing the Göttingen group.[7]

The *NS-Briefe*, which became, as Strasser had intended, 'a platform for the airing of the competing forces, opinions and aims' within the AG, give an excellent insight into the diversity of its members' views and the extent to which they were contrary to those held in Munich.

The question of foreign policy, for example, was considered to be of great importance by the AG, and discussion of it filled the pages of the *NS-Briefe*. Goebbels, Kaufmann and Rust at this period all held 'national bolshevist' ideas common to many young right-wing intellectuals in Germany of whom Moeller van den Bruck, the author of *The Third Reich*, was perhaps the best known. These men saw in Russia 'the socialist national state for which consciously or unconsciously the younger generation in all countries long'.[8] For them socialism represented 'a final rejection of the materialism and capitalist mammonism

[1] Jochmann, op. cit., p. 210.
[2] See Bouler to Vahlen, 4 Sept. and Bouhler to Lohse, 8 Sept. 1925, BA Slg. Schum. 207 B and 208 I.
[3] Goebbels to Hitler, 12 Sept. 1925, BA Slg. Schumacher 203, 24.
[4] Jochmann, op. cit., p. 210.
[5] Dincklage to Pfeffer, 13 Oct. 1925, BA NS 1/vorl. 340, 347.
[6] *NS-Briefe*, Nr. 2, 15 Oct. 1925.
[7] See correspondence Haase–Goebbels, Nov. 1925, in BA NS 1/vorl. 341 Bd. 1, 249–50.
[8] Goebbels, 'Das russische Problem', *NS-Briefe*, 15 Nov. 1925.

of the West'.[1] They also admired the activism of the KPD compared with the bourgeois conventions of the other parties. In reply to the question of a Communist heckler as to what the NSDAP planned to do if a Western pact was signed, Kaufmann declared that from that moment on, 'the NSDAP would fight shoulder to shoulder with the KDP against the social-democratic crooks'.[2] Similarly, at a meeting in Hanover, Rust insisted that Germany could be saved only by an alliance with Russia. He also 'had more sympathy with the Communists than with any Social-Democrats or the so-called black-white-and-red leaders of Germany'.[3]

These doctrines were of course anathema to Munich, where foreign policy, and in particular the attitude to Russia, was governed by the anti-bolshevik and *Lebensraum* ideas which Hitler had just formulated in the second volume of *Mein Kampf*. In a reply to an article of Goebbels' in the *Völkischer Beobachter*, Rosenberg, who regarded himself as the party expert on foreign policy, severely criticized the author for regarding Russia as in the grip of a national-socialist revolution instead of under the domination of Jewish bolshevism.[4] Not only Munich opposed these 'national-bolshevist' ideas. Haase, in an article in the *NS-Briefe*, opposed a one-sided eastern orientation and maintained that Germany should wait and see how things developed.[5]

It was above all the social question which divided the members of the AG, and the differences soon became apparent. On the very evening of the day on which the AG was formed at Hagen, Goebbels reports a tough discussion: 'National and socialist. What comes first and what comes last. For us in the west there can be no doubt about the answer. First the socialist deliverance and then the national liberation will come like a tornado. Professor Vahlen thinks differently. The worker must first be made a nationalist'; and then significantly, 'the whole thing is a question of generations. Old or young. Evolution or revolution.'[6] But Vahlen was not alone. On 29 December Professor Schultz emphasized that the new 'national-communist' line was meeting with strong opposition in predominantly agricultural Hesse, while in the *NS-Briefe* Pfeffer was having to remind Goebbels that they needed *everybody*, workers *and* middle class.[7]

The divisions within the AG became very evident in the reaction to Strasser's draft programme.[8] One of his main objects in setting up the

[1] Ibid.

[2] Report by Duisburg police department, Staatsarchiv Düsseldorf, Reg. Düss. 16738.

[3] Report of Hanover police department, 31 Jan. 1926, NSAH Hann. 80 Hann. II 718.

[4] VB 14, Nov. 1925.   [5] *NS-Briefe*, 1 Jan. 1926.

[6] Goebbels, *Tagebuch*, p. 27.   [7] *NS-Briefe*, 15 Jan. 1926.

[8] NSDAP Hauptarchiv, Reel 44, Folder 896.

AG had been to create a basis of support for a new programme with which he planned to replace the Twenty-Five Points. This programme, composed during November, probably with the help of his brother Otto, was a hodge-podge of existing *völkisch* ideas—'back to the land', anti-Semitic, and favouring an authoritarian political framework, including increased powers for the President and a Chamber of Estates instead of the *Reichstag*. Its plans for foreign policy were a version of the *Mitteleuropa* idea: 'the organization and powerful concentration on a racial basis of the German nation in a greater German Reich: this greater German Reich to be the centre of gravity for a mid-European customs union and the basis for the United States of Europe'.[1]

The second meeting of the AG was held in Hanover on 22 November 1925.[2] Of the eighteen representatives who attended seven came from the Lower Saxon *Gaue*, though they did not form a united block. The main business of the meeting was to approve the statutes which are of some interest. The first justified the existence of the AG on the grounds that 'the economic structure and political peculiarity of the North-West German territory—that is of the Rhine–Ruhr area—requires more co-ordinated organization'. The second named the members of the AG as the *Gaue*: Rhineland-North, Rhineland-South, Westphalia, Hanover, Hanover-South, Hessen-Nassau, Lüneburg-Stade, Schleswig-Holstein, Greater-Hamburg, Greater Berlin, and Pomerania. The third statute emphasized that the AG was intended neither to interfere with the work of the *Gaue* and local branches, 'nor especially with the party head-quarters in Munich'. The seventh statute stated that 'the AG and the *NS-Briefe* exist with the express approval of Adolf Hitler'. These statutes demonstrate both the ambiguity of the AG's attitude and the strength of Hitler's position. For, while the formation of the AG had been clearly directed against the Munich head-quarters, they still wished to act with the approval of Hitler himself and to avoid the charge of being an anti-Munich Fronde.

The Hanover meeting also agreed that comments on Strasser's draft programme should be ready by 10 January and that the whole question would be discussed at another meeting in Hanover on 24 January 1926. Three of the critiques of Strasser's draft have survived, two of them from members of the Göttingen group.[3] Over the years 1923–6 the student leaders in Göttingen had spent a great deal of time discussing racial policies and advocated ruthless racial selection, in

---

[1] Ibid.   [2] See *NS-Briefe*, 1 Dec. 1925.

[3] NSDAP Hauptarchiv, Reel 44, Folder 896. The third was by 'Frederic' (Pfeffer) and was also negative. See also Reinhard Kühnl, 'Zur Programmatik der nationalsozialistischen Linken: Das Strasserprogramm von 1925/6' in *Vjhfzg* 1966.

which sterilization would play a vital role.[1] This was the basis for their opposition to participation in elections which, they considered, opened the party to the influence of the 'mass'. Their attitude to the Strasser draft derived from these ideas. They considered it far too moderate in a racialist sense and also tainted by liberal-democratic ideas, as in its support for the idea of an equal vote. They preferred the old programme on most points and objected in particular to Strasser's pan-European ideas. They were strongly influenced by one member of the group, Herbert Backe, an agricultural student and the son of a German officer who had emigrated to Russia before the Revolution.[2] Backe advocated the idea of a new German Order which would continue the work of colonization in the East begun by the Teutonic knights and, under his influence, Haase's statement read like a blueprint for later SS policy: the idea of Germany's future lying in the East, plans for the settlement of soldier peasants in the conquered territories, and in particular the resettlement of the *Auslandsdeutschen*. These ideas had, of course, much more in common with those expressed by Hitler in *Mein Kampf* than with Strasser's pan-European views or the national-bolshevik ideology of Goebbels and Kaufmann.

(viii) *The AG meeting in Hanover, 24 January 1926*

For some time Munich had been becoming increasingly suspicious of the activities of the AG. We have seen how Rosenberg had objected to the publication of views on foreign policy contrary to the party line, of which he was the architect. Furthermore, 'national-bolshevik' utterances by Kaufmann had been reported to Munich by a less radical party member, and Bouhler had demanded an immediate explanation of these 'enormities'.[3] Now a new dispute developed when, through an indiscretion, the Strasser draft was shown to Feder, who regarded himself as the father of the original programme. Strasser reported to Goebbels that Feder was furious at its circulation without the knowledge of Hitler himself, and a hurried attempt was made to persuade Hitler that it was innocuous and unofficial.[4]

The decisive meeting, at which both the matters dividing the AG among themselves and those which divided them from Munich came to a head, was held at Hanover in the house of the *Gauleiter*, Rust, on

[1] See the long discussions of ideology in Haase, 'Aufstand in Niedersachsen' (mimeo, 1942), pp. 633 ff.

[2] Ibid., pp. 651 ff. Backe was later a leading SS officer and head of the *Reichsnährstand*.

[3] Bouhler to Goebbels, 1 Dec. 1925, BA Slg. Schumacher 203.

[4] Jochmann, op. cit., p. 220.

25 January 1926.[1] In addition to the original members, it was attended by Hildebrandt of Mecklenburg and by Gottfried Feder, the party ideologue, who represented Munich. No *detailed* record of this meeting written at the time has survived. The first account to be published was by Otto Strasser, which appeared in London in 1940. He maintained that the meeting had agreed to accept the Strasser draft programme and that only Ley and Feder had not supported the campaign for the expropriation of the German royal houses, a live issue at the time. He also referred to critical remarks about Hitler made by Rust and Goebbels. The new sources which have since come to light, however, show that this account is only partially true. The most reliable of the new sources is a letter from Otto Strasser to Goebbels, written on the following day, giving him notes for the preparation of a report.[2] According to this account four major decisions were taken.

First, it was agreed to found a paper for the AG, under the editorship of Gregor Strasser, to be known as *Der Nationale Sozialist* and for which a new publishing house—the *Kampfverlag*—would be set up. The Lower Saxony *Gaue*, however, insisted on retaining their own newspaper, *Der Niedersächsischer Beobachter*.

Secondly, a resolution on the expropriation question was unanimously agreed upon.

Thirdly, on the question of the attitude to the *Vaterländische Verbände*, the various nationalist leagues, the decision of the last meeting was reaffirmed, that is co-operation with them was rejected.

Finally, on the question of the party programme, an important resolution was agreed upon:

recognizing that the general policy directives contained in the 25 points require the addition of a more detailed programme of action, particularly to enable propaganda to exploit the growing political crisis effectively, the meeting of the AG in Hanover on 25 January is handing over the drafts sent in by various party comrades to a study group under the direction of Party comrade Gregor Strasser for clarification and consideration, with instructions to send on the material, after it has been sorted through, to the Party head-quarters for further action.[3]

In other words, contrary to the account of Otto Strasser,[4] the Strasser draft was not accepted by the meeting as indeed was only to be expected after its rejection by the Göttingen group and Pfeffer.

No mention is made in this letter of criticism of Hitler, though

---

[1] Accounts of this meeting in Otto Strasser, *Hitler and I* (London, 1940), pp. 90 ff. Goebbels, *Tagebuch*, p. 55. Jochmann, op. cit., pp. 221–3 and the minutes of a conversation between Pfeffer and Dr. Gerhard Schildt, of Freiburg University, which were very kindly placed at my disposal by Dr. Schildt and of which I have a copy.　　[2] Jochmann, op. cit., pp. 221–3.

[3] Ibid., p. 223.　　[4] Otto Strasser, *Hitler and I*, p. 96.

there is a reference to the isolation of Feder and to Feder having 'taken down imprudent remarks which were made in the heat of the struggle'.[1]

On the second question discussed—the expropriation of the royal houses—there is more evidence in the shape of the resolution itself, which was subsequently published in the *NS-Briefe*.[2] This was a question which the parties of the Left had taken up in earnest, and the decision for or against would be regarded as a test of just how genuine a workers' party the NSDAP was. Pfeffer recalled that 'this question was extraordinarily embarrassing for everybody and they would much rather have avoided taking up a position on it'.[3] The resolution which emerged shows this only too clearly. It began with a denial of any desire to pre-empt the decision of the party head-quarters on the issue, another example of the anxiety not to alienate Hitler. It went on, however, to maintain that the crisis in Germany meant that the payment of hundreds of millions of marks to the former princes was not justified, particularly since the overwhelming majority had 'neither been aware of nor supported the *völkisch* tasks of Germany'. This was an important decision, since on this issue it aligned the AG on the side of the Left. Its significance was not really reduced by the fact that the resolution went on to criticize the deceit of the left-wing parties in view of the fact that they had turned down demands for expropriation in 1918 and 1919 when they were in power. Nor was it reduced by their attempt to assert their *völkisch* attitude by demanding the simultaneous expropriation of the property of all Jews who had entered Germany since August 1914 and of all capital gains since the beginning of the war.

The question of the alleged criticism of the leadership is the most difficult to prove one way or the other.[4] According to a recent source, Pfeffer, this was the main question discussed at the meeting.[5] Pfeffer describes how some delegates brought up the fact that Hitler was an Austrian and a Catholic, others that he was not an officer and therefore incapable of organizing paramilitary units. Above all, the Munich clique was held against him and the fact that he had virtually excluded Ludendorff from the movement. Apparently alternative leaders were discussed: Class, the pan-German leader was rejected as too reactionary; Graefe was at least a Protestant, but unfortunately not a revolutionary leader. Alternative methods of organization were also

---

[1] Jochmann, op. cit., p. 222.   [2] *NS-Briefe*, 1 Feb. 1926.
[3] Pfeffer minutes.
[4] This account revises that given by the author in his article 'Conflict and Development in the NSDAP 1924–1927', *Journal of Contemporary History* (Oct. 1966), pp. 3–36.
[5] See also Heinrich Bennecke, *Hitler und die SA* (Munich, 1962), pp. 128–9. Bennecke also relied on conversations with Pfeffer.

considered: whether a directorate was preferable to a leader, and whether the NSDAP should remain a party. But, according to Pfeffer, the meeting eventually decided that a leader was vital and that there was no alternative to Hitler. It was decided, however, that he should be compelled to take Strasser and a North German into the party headquarters; and after the meeting, Strasser, Rust and Pfeffer decided that Pfeffer should become the leader of the SA, which would give Strasser the necessary support in Munich.

But this account by Pfeffer, which was given forty years after the event, must be treated with reserve. There is no clear evidence for such extensive criticism of Hitler and neither Goebbels nor Otto Strasser, in their accounts written immediately after the meeting, make any reference to the decision to get Hitler to accept Strasser in a key position in the Munich office. The previous exclusion of Hitler from criticism and the care with which the AG had avoided antagonizing Munich lessen its credibility still further.

(ix) *The reaction from Munich—The Bamberg meeting of 14 February 1926*

Although the Pfeffer account of criticism of Hitler may not be accurate, there is considerable evidence for 'imprudent remarks' having been made at the meeting. Feder had been taking notes and Hitler received a full report. Hitherto, Hitler had been prepared to adopt a flexible attitude on matters of detail, provided his own authority was unquestioned. At the Weimar meeting of the North and West German *Gauleiter* in July 1925, he had declared that he had no intention of interfering in any details.[1] Now, prompted by Feder, he had to take determined action.[2]

In the first place, he could not tolerate discussion of the party programme. His attitude to the programme stemmed from his concept of discipline, understood as blind obedience, as the most important factor in effective political organization. For him the programme was not important as the basis for the formulation of the party's policies, and, in fact of course, it was later ruthlessly sacrificed to the demands of power. The enforcement of the programme, however, became a convenient means of ensuring ideological uniformity, which in turn secured a disciplined movement; discussion of the programme would undermine this discipline. 'For how does one think to fill people with blind faith in the correctness of a doctrine, if by continued changes in

---

[1] Dincklage to Eickelmann (branch leader in Brunswick), 13 Oct. 1925, in NSAH Hann. Des. 310 I A, Nr. 6.
[2] Cf. A. Tyrell, *Führer befiehl.... Selbstzeugnisse aus des 'Kampfzeit' der NSDAP. Dokumentation und Analyse* (Düsseldorf, 1969), p. 102.

its outward construction one spreads uncertainty and doubt.'[1] The important thing was that members should be committed to him as leader. The programme was a concession to contemporary political practice. To discuss it was to give it an importance which would undermine the independence of that leadership and create divided loyalties between programme and leader such as those which brought about the resignation of Otto Strasser in 1930. Furthermore, Hitler had recognized that to secure power legally the NSDAP would not only have to participate in elections but also persuade the social groups and institutions, such as big business and the army in which political and economic power was vested, to take the NSDAP seriously as a potential ally. It was primarily for this reason, and not simply to collect financial contributions, that Hitler began in 1926 his series of lectures to business groups.[2] He wished thereby to dissociate himself from the image of the party as it appeared at the level of the local branch. He needed complete control over the party to ensure that, unlike the other German parties, it was not committed to any particular programme or social group which would dictate its policies, but could appeal to a whole range of classes and interests. It was this ability which was to ensure its successes between 1930 and 1933. But the growing organizational independence of the AG threatened to create a regional block which would weaken the supreme authority of the Munich headquarters. And the attempt to make the programme more specific, even emphasize its socialist aspects as in the resolution on the expropriation of the princes, threatened to alienate the very groups whose sympathy Hitler was trying to win. Both threatened his autocratic leadership.

Hitler did not take long to act. Just over a week later, on 4 February 1926, invitations were sent out from Munich for a meeting at Bamberg on Sunday the 14th.[3] After a meeting with Hitler, Strasser wrote ruefully to Rust: 'Herr Feder has apparently been victorious right down the line', and told him that he would at once withdraw the programme and explain to Hitler that it was meant only as an incentive to clarify important questions.[4] Rust also began to prepare himself for retreat and replied that he welcomed Hitler's step: 'I shall be pleased if he grasps the tiller.'[5] Karl Kaufmann, however, wanted the AG to

[1] Hitler, op. cit., p. 678.

[2] See Werner Jochmann, *Im Kampf um die Macht* (Frankfurt, 1960), p. 25. This speech to Hamburg businessmen in Feb. 1926, was the first of a series. In June Hitler spoke in Essen to Ruhr employers and again in Dec. See Report of Essen Police Chief, 5 Feb. 1927 in Staatsarchiv Düsseldorf Reg. 16738.

[3] Contrary to the account in Otto Strasser, *Hitler and I*, p. 99, which maintains that the meeting was held on a weekday and that therefore only Goebbels and Strasser represented the AG.

[4] Strasser to Rust, 4 Feb. 1926, NSAH Hann. Des. 310 I A, Nr. 11.

[5] Rust to Strasser, 5 Feb. 1926, NSAH Hann. Des. 310 I A, Nr. 12.

initiate counter-measures. 'The intention of the Esser, Streicher, Dinter, Feder people is absolutely clear', he told Strasser.[1] 'The mines are laid and now everything depends on whether we as sappers are in a position to meet this attack with counter-mines.' He suggested that reliable members of the AG should be organized to take a common line and that Strasser himself should be the spokesman. Goebbels also noted: 'We shall act like a coy beauty and entice Hitler on to our territory. . . . No-one believes in Munich any more. Elberfeld will become the mecca of German Socialism.'[2] Significantly, however, both Kaufmann and Goebbels talked of opposition in terms of Munich or the 'Esser, Streicher, Dinter, Feder people', not of Hitler, and evidently still thought they could win over Hitler.

Kaufmann was not invited to Bamberg, according to Munich because they did not know he was a *Gauleiter*.[3] But although Kaufmann was not there and although Pfeffer declined because he feared a débâcle,[4] many members of the AG do seem to have attended. According to Goebbels, apart from Strasser and himself, Lohse, Vahlen, Rust, Klant and Schlange were also there.[5] Of the Göttingen group, Haase was too ill to attend and Fobke decided that it was a convenient moment to return to his studies.[6]

Before the meeting, Strasser, Goebbels, Rust and Vahlen had composed a plan of action.[7] Hitler, however, appears to have undermined it with a long and uncompromising speech. He began by repeating the foreign policy ideas which he had expressed in *Mein Kampf*, i.e. alliance with England and Italy, and Russia as the predestined field of German colonial expansion. Then, moving on to the question of the expropriation of the royal houses, his views may be summed up in the statement 'for us there are no princes, but only Germans'. Finally, he insisted that the original programme was completely adequate.

Strasser appears to have been overwhelmed both by the uncompromising nature of the speech and by the degree of acceptance which it had obtained from the ranks of the South German party leaders. He was faced with accepting the party line as laid down by Hitler, or making a definite break; for Hitler allowed no room for discussion or compromise. Yet if he tried to split the party on this issue who would follow him? The meeting at Hanover in January had shown the disunity of the AG on almost all points. Hitler was their leader. In these

[1] Kaufmann to Strasser, 8 Feb. 1926, BA NS1/vorl. 338, 155 ff.
[2] Goebbels, *Tagebuch*, p. 59.
[3] Bouhler to Kaufmann, 23 Feb. 1926, BA Slg. Schumacher 203.
[4] Pfeffer minutes.
[5] Goebbels, *Tagebuch*, pp. 59–60 and *VB*, 15 Feb. 1926, for a report on the meeting.
[6] Fobke to Hess, 10 Feb. 1926, BA Slg. Schumacher 202 I.
[7] Goebbels, *Tagebuch*, p. 59.

circumstances Strasser's reply could hardly be anything but hopelessly ineffective. His position was not made any stronger by Goebbel's complete silence. Goebbels also seems to have been overwhelmed by Hitler's unwillingness to hear their point of view. 'I feel knocked out. What is Hitler? A reactionary?' he wrote in his diary.[1] If we are to judge by his later performance, it was possibly also because, for the first time, he clearly saw where power in the party lay and that Hitler would only tolerate unconditional obedience. But, although Otto Strasser may be right in maintaining that Goebbels was impressed by the number of cars at the disposal of Hitler's associates, he is wrong to state that Goebbels went over to Hitler at this meeting.

(x) *The last months of the Arbeitsgemeinschaft*

At first, the AG refused to accept what had happened at Bamberg. It was still believed that Hitler could be removed from the influence of his evil advisers if they continued their pressure. During the following week, meetings were held at Göttingen and Hanover where, according to Goebbels, it was decided to concede Munich a pyrrhic victory, but to work hard to strengthen themselves for the struggle for socialism.[2] Furthermore, plans went ahead for the amalgamation of the *Gaue* Rhineland-North and Westphalia into a new *Gau* Ruhr which had been planned as 'a power factor which means something'.[3] At the inaugural meeting of the new *Gau*, the Elberfeld group gratuitously insulted Feder by allowing him only half an hour for his speech. Feder, very conscious of his importance as party ideologue, demanded at least an hour to an hour-and-a-half in view of the heretical views which had been emanating from their *Gau*.[4]

But these were essentially signs of sulky defiance. The real battle had taken place at Bamberg and it had been decided against the A.G. Both Strasser and Goebbels soon recognized the fact. On 5 March, Strasser wrote to the AG members asking them to return their copies of his draft programme because he had promised Hitler 'to withdraw all'.[5] On 15 March, Goebbels wrote an article in the *NS-Briefe* supporting Hitler's policy on South Tyrol—the sacrifice of the national aspirations of the German population to the need for an alliance with Italy.[6] On 10 March, Strasser was badly hurt in a car accident which

[1] Goebbels, *Tagebuch*, p. 60.
[2] Goebbels, *Tagebuch*, pp. 60–2. According to Goebbels it was suggested that he, Strasser and Kaufmann should go to Hitler and talk seriously with him. 'He must not let himself be tied by the rogues down there.'
[3] *Tagebuch*, p. 48.
[4] Feder to Goebbels, 26 Feb. 1926, BA NS1/vorl. 340.
[5] Jochmann, *Nationalsozialismus und Revolution*, p. 225.
[6] See article 'Der Apfelsinenkrieg' in *NS-Briefe*, Nr. 12.

put him out of action for several weeks. In the meantime, Goebbels made it up with Streicher, whom he described as a 'completely honest man',[1] and was being courted by Munich which invited him to make a speech there on 8 April. Strasser, however, was not so easily won over and replied that Goebbels' judgement of Streicher was a bit too favourable and warned him that in Munich they would carefully weigh every word he said.[2]

Goebbel's speech in Munich seems to have represented the beginning of his complete capitulation, for both Kaufmann and Pfeffer reproached him for it, while Hitler embraced him.[3] On the next day, 9 April, a meeting was held at which everything was discussed and at which Goebbels, at any rate, was completely won over. His diary was characteristically ecstatic:

> We come closer to each other. We ask questions. He answers brilliantly. I love him. Social question—quite new insights. He has thought of everything . . . I bow before the greater man, the political genius.[4]

The head-quarters in Munich soon began to take advantage of the decline of the AG to tighten its control over the provincial organizations of the party. For example, after the appearance of a pamphlet attacking the Hohenzollerns, a memorandum went out on 16 April to all *Gauleiter* insisting on the necessity for approval by head-quarters of all pamphlets issued by local party organizations.[5]

The Annual General Meeting of the party held on 22 May offered Hitler an opportunity to reaffirm his authority.[6] In his speech, he began by explaining that the only reason they were holding the meeting was to fulfil their legal responsibility as an authorized association. He poured scorn on the idea of democratic decision-making within the party and blamed the *völkisch* chaos of 1924 on the infection of the movement with democratic principles: 'the decisions of the movement cannot be taken by resolutions at conferences or conventions such as the Weimar congresses, for here too the natural balance of forces decides the issue; the stronger assert their will and the weaker fall into line'. He then went on to insist that they were not mesmerized by mere numbers, valuing energy and discipline much more. They would rather have 70,000 members who unconditionally obeyed every order of the leadership, than 500,000 who behaved like disobedient

[1] Goebbels to Strasser, 22 Mar. 1926, BA NS1/vorl. 340, 157.

[2] Strasser to Goebbels, 29 Mar. 1926 and 1 Apr. 1926, BA NS1/vorl. 341 BdI 156 and 154.

[3] Goebbels, *Tagebuch,* pp. 70-3.

[4] Ibid.

[5] Bouhler Rundschreiben an die Gauleitungen der NSDAP NSAH Hann. Des. 310 I A, Nr. 8.

[6] For the following see the report in NSDAP Hauptarchiv, Reel 3, Folder 82.

dogs. For this reason they had insisted that members of the party should be forced to choose between the party and other organizations of which they were members. 'We cannot serve two Gods at the same time.' Finally, he justified his position on the expropriation issue and on foreign policy, two of the matters which had been of most concern to the AG. The meeting concluded by approving changes in the statutes which were finally published in a definitive form on 30 June.[1] Those statutes were the same as those of 1921 with two additions: the introduction of an SA tax and a statute enabling whole branches to be excluded. But most important from the point of view of the AG was the reaffirmation that the programme of the Twenty-Five Points was immutable.

The fate of the AG as an organized group was sealed by the directives for *Gaue* and local branches of the NSDAP signed by Hitler and dated 1 July 1926.[2] They simply stated that 'since the NSDAP represents a large *Arbeitsgemeinschaft*, smaller *Arbeitsgemeinschaften* in the form of combination of individual *Gaue* have no justification'. These directives also confirmed Hitler's complete control over the party machine, already established by the statutes. Thus, while allowing for the election of local branch leaders by a membership meeting (though only by acclamation), the *Gauleiter* were in future to be nominated directly by the Munich head-quarters, and their choice of a deputy required confirmation from Munich.[3]

On the question of participation in elections which had been the main concern of the Göttingen group, the party leadership apparently attempted to soften the blow, by inviting them to hold a speech in opposition to participation at the party congresses of 1926 and 1927. This, however, resulted in a taunt from Streicher that the Göttingen

[1] The 1921 statutes were reaffirmed by Hitler in his article on the refounding of the party in the *VB* of 25 Feb. 1925, but he only signed them officially on 21 Aug., and they were only published in the revised form on 30 June 1926. The clause stating that the 25 points programme was immutable had been included in the 1921 programme (§2 and §12), but in the 1925 version Hitler had altered §12 in his own handwriting to read: 'Name, programme and orientation (Tendenz) of the movement may only be changed with the approval of the whole membership.' Hitler in the 1926 version was thus returning to the stricter 1921 version. See NSDAP Hauptarchiv, Reel 3, Folder 79, and Reel B, Folder 91.

[2] Richtlinien für Gaue und Ortsgruppen der NSDAP gez. Adolf Hitler in NSAH Hann. Des. 310 I A, Nr. 8.

[3] A few months later, Hitler removed another obstacle in the way of the totalitarian structuring of the party. After 1925, the multiple membership of paramilitary organizations which had hitherto characterized the *völkisch* movement continued with many members of the NSDAP being simultaneously members of the Stahlhelm. On 5 Feb. 1927, however, Hitler felt strong enough to issue a directive forbidding members of the NSDAP to belong to another paramilitary organization. See Rundschreiben an die Gauleitungen, 5 Feb. 1927, gez. Adolf Hitler NSAH Hann. Des. 310 I A, Nr. 19.

group were 'traitors to the movement' and, at the 1927 congress, the party leadership had to make it clear that the Göttingen group had been specifically asked to speak against elections, in order to protect them against abuse.[1]

On the question of personalities, whether or not Hitler compromised with the AG as Pfeffer maintains, the former members of the AG did have the satisfaction of seeing Esser replaced by Strasser as propaganda chief and Pfeffer brought into the party as commander of the SA in September 1926.[2] But, since the AG had ceased to exist, and since both Strasser and Pfeffer accepted Hitler's authority, the change brought no tangible results. Indeed, when Fobke continued to criticize the party for using the services of Esser, there was a sharp retort from Munich to the effect that 'the re-employment of Hermann Esser in a limited sphere was Herr Hitler's decision and therefore is beyond criticism'.[3]

(xi) *The Arbeitsgemeinschaft of the North and West German Gauleiter —a summary*

The AG was essentially an amalgam of different elements. In the first place, there were those like Strasser, Goebbels and Kaufmann who wanted to revise the programme to emphasize its 'socialist' aspect. This was partly a response to the requirements of propaganda activity in industrial areas. But perhaps more important in this context was the 'national bolshevik' ideology which they shared, and which in turn partly arose from their sympathy for Communist activists who were so much more like themselves than the *Spiesser* of the bourgeois parties. The views of the two Hanover leaders, Rust and Dincklage, tended in this direction. Dincklage had explained his decision to join the NSDAP rather than the DVFB by his recognition 'that the Berlin line (the DVFB) took no account of the basic question of the socialist renewal of our people',[4] and Rust favoured an alliance with Russia. Both had pressed the discussion of a possible party trade union on the AG.[5]

Secondly, there were the élitist racialist extremists, the Göttingen group, who refused to accept the participation in elections which was vital to the new policy of legality. They believed that the attempt to

[1] See the correspondence in NSDAP Hauptarchiv, Reel 44, Folder 900.
[2] *VB*, 26 Sept. 1926.
[3] The Uschla to Fobke, 9 Nov. 1926 NSDAP Hauptarchiv, Reel 44, Folder 900.
[4] Dincklage to Wenzel, 27 May 1925, NSAH Hann. Des. 310 I A, Nr. 4.
[5] Hanover to Goebbels, 11 Nov. 1925, NSAH Hann. Des. 310 I A, Nr. 6. The question of a party trade union was discussed at the Hanover meeting on 22 Nov. It was decided to leave the matter to party head-quarters, see *NS-Briefe*, 1 Dec. 1925.

win mass support would prevent the party from fulfilling its true function as a racial *élite*, and that it would turn the NSDAP from a 'movement' into a 'party'. In other words, they feared that if the party entered parliament, it would accept the existing system, acquire the parliamentary style of compromise which characterized the other parties, and lose the revolutionary *élan* which was its greatest attraction.

These groups were united above all by the desire to participate in the formation of policy. They accepted the authority of Hitler but wished at least for their views to be given a hearing in Munich.[1] They directed their opposition at leading officials like Esser and Streicher who, they considered, monopolized the ear of Hitler, encouraging him to ignore the North, and who were responsible for the dissension within the Bavarian movement. The background to this North/South division and personal rivalry lay in the year 1924, when the Directorate and the NSFB had acted independently of Munich. And, although the NSFB and the supporters of the Directorate had fought each other over the question of amalgamation, after the refounding of the NSDAP in February 1925 they could unite against the arrogance of the Munich organization, particularly since the leading officials there, the former leaders of the *Grossdeutsche Volksgemeinschaft*, had been a common enemy during 1924.

But apart from these two groups, there were a few members of the AG such as Ley–Cologne, Vahlen–Pomerania and Schulz–Hessen–Nassau, who shared few if any of these views, but who were included in the AG for the simple reason that their *Gaue* were in North and West Germany and it was desirable to avoid the appearance of a Fronde. They continually acted as a break on decision-making within the group, since they were suspicious of 'national bolshevik' policies, and in the case of Ley jealous of the influence of the AG leaders.[2] They tended to emphasize their loyalty to Munich.

Apart from the lack of unity within the AG, its weakness lay in its attitude to Hitler. The Göttingen group had fought the DVFP and then the NSFB in the name of Hitler during 1924 and its relationship to Hitler was one of complete hero-worship. The former DVFP and NSFB leaders had broken with their leadership—von Graefe, Wulle and Henning—and the new DVFB in the name of Hitler. Both groups had specifically tied themselves to Hitler's star. At first, they avoided the predicament of opposition to Hitler by opposing his leading officials and believing that they alone were responsible for the

---

[1] 'Dominant in the AG was the desire for the right of consultation. We wished to recognize the authority of the leadership but not to subordinate ourselves totally.' See Besprechung mit Karl Kaufmann am 27 Jan. 1964, in FGN.

[2] For a description of these men see Jochmann, *Nationalsozialismus und Revolution*, p. 208–9.

faults in the party which they criticized. After Bamberg, however, they could no longer be in any doubt and were faced with the decision to rebel or surrender. The divisions within the AG and (above all) their total commitment to Hitler—which had become the basis of their political creed—determined what their answer would be.

The foundation of Hitler's strength at this period was his success in projecting his leadership so that it came to be regarded as the most important factor in the *völkisch* movement. This had begun before 1923 when, even outside Bavaria, he was creating a core of young and devoted followers, like the Göttingen group. Then, by accepting full responsibility for the *putsch* at his trial in February 1924, while the conservative and army leaders denied having anything to do with it, Hitler created the myth of the sole responsibility of the NSDAP and thereby became a hero to the *völkisch* extremists. Moreover, by refusing to commit himself, he could watch while the chaos produced by the internecine rivalry in the *völkisch* movement enhanced his own reputation.

Refounded in 1925, the NSDAP attracted all the most anti-bourgeois elements in the *völkisch* movement—predominantly students, apprentices and young white-collar workers. This posed problems of adapting their views to the requirements of the legal path to power, problems which emerged with the AG and were to continue in a different form in the permanent state of tension which existed between the political organization and the SA, a tension which crystallized into revolt at moments when it appeared that the policy of legality was not likely to succeed. But the essential fact was that Hitler could rely on their support for his leadership. By developing a political style whose dominant feature was feverish propaganda activity combined with ruthlessness towards political opponents, he alone, apart from the Communists, offered them the type of personal commitment in politics which they were seeking. The other *völkisch* groups failed because what they were offering was anachronistic, a style of politics which was totally alien to the *déraciné* elements of a society formed by war, revolution and inflation, elements which provided most of the support for the radical Right.

PART II

V

THE NSDAP IN LOWER SAXONY
1925–1928: ORGANIZATION AND
PROPAGANDA

(i) *Problems of organization*

DURING the years 1925–7, apart from playing a leading role in the limited activities of the AG, the NSDAP leadership in Lower Saxony was faced with the main task of reorganizing and strengthening the party in their area. There were a number of difficulties to be overcome. In the first place, there was the problem of the existence of a rival racialist party, the *Deutsch-völkische Freiheits-bewegung* (DVFB). During January and February, the racialists had had to decide whether to join this successor organization to the DVFP and NSFB, or whether to declare their support for Hitler and await the refounding of the NSDAP. It soon became clear that the strongest support for Hitler was to be found in the southern part of Lower Saxony, particularly near the cities of Hanover, Brunswick and Göttingen. An analysis of the Nazi party membership in *Gau* Hanover-North in terms of their places of residence, dated 31 May 1926, shows that a majority of members and five of the six largest branches—Brunswick-City (255), Hanover-City (220), Wolfenbüttel (106), Hildesheim (66) and Goslar (50)—came from this area.[1] The significance of these figures is increased by the fact that they take no account of *Gau* Hanover-South which covered a significant part of this area, but for which no figures are available. Both the Hanover leaders of the NSFB and the Göttingen group in opposition to them had of course declared for Hitler.[2] Only a minority in this area preferred to support the new DVFB, though they were quite active during 1925, particularly in the city of Hanover itself.[3]

Unfortunately, there is very little evidence on the development of *Gau* Hanover-South during this period.[4] By the end of 1926, however, there had been a sharp drop in membership which aroused criticism in Munich; and it is clear that the *Gau* was no longer the driving force

[1] Gau Hannover-Nord Mitgliederbestand vom 31 May 1926, NSAH Hann. Des. 310 I A, Nr. 8.   [2] See p. 62 above.
[3] See the monthly reports of the Hanover political police for 1925–6 in NSAH Hann. Des. 80 Hann II, Nr. 718.
[4] What evidence there is is contained in BA Slg. Schumacher 202 I and SAG XXV 153, Nos. 23–4 and XXVII 156, No. 2.

behind the NSDAP in Lower Saxony which it had been during 1923 and 1924. Haase was still not completely recovered after his injury and, in any case, he and Fobke were disillusioned by the new parliamentary course introduced by Hitler. After 1926, they probably found it a convenient moment to return to their studies. Although Fobke was still dealing with important correspondence in October 1927, by the end of 1926 the *effective* leadership of the *Gau* appears to have devolved on an ex-agricultural student, Elsner von Gronow, who was making all the speeches in meetings in the surrounding area and who signed the announcements in the local party paper, the *Göttinger Beobachter*.[1] The local branch in Göttingen was run by a locomotive driver, Uhlendorff, as chairman, a post-office official as deputy chairman, a forestry official and a railway fireman as the two secretaries, and a caretaker and a baker as the two treasurers. It was quite active during 1925–6, holding periodic meetings addressed by outside leaders such as Goebbels and Feder with audiences of around 500. By the end of 1927, however, meetings were only collecting audiences of between 120 and 200.

In northern Lower Saxony, the balance was initially in favour of the DVFB who made great capital out of the alleged Catholic sympathies of the NSDAP among the protestant rural population, and attacked them as a socialist working-class party. The *völkisch Reichstag* deputy for Weser-Ems was Major Henning, a leader of the DVFB, and he succeeded in carrying with him a majority of the racialists in that area. There were only two NSDAP branches of any size: Oldenburg-City with fifty-six members and Osnabrück which at this period belonged to *Gau* Ruhr.[2] The great city of Bremen could only muster thirty-seven members in May 1926, though there were a few small branches in the Bremen area. During the first years, the situation hardly improved, despite the fact that the Oldenburg branch contained two effective propagandists in Heinz Spangemacher and Carl Röver, who was now the branch leader.[3] Between 1 January 1926 and 1 January

1 See the single issue of the *Göttinger Beobachter* in SAG XXVII 156, No. 2. The paper was printed by *Gau* Hanover-North for *Gau* Göttingen. See also the correspondence with Dincklage in NSAH Hann. Des. 310 I A, Nr. 16.

2 Gau Hannover-Nord Mitgliederbestand vom 31 May 1926, NSAH Hann. Des. 310 I A, Nr. 8

3 Heinz Spangemacher born 1885, from 1912–28 director of a private school in Oldenburg. Joined the NSDAP and the Ehrhardt brigade 1921 and very active in the *völkisch* movement before 1923. Rejoined the NSDAP in 1925, became Minister for Culture and Justice in the Nazi government of 1932. See personal files in BDC.

Carl Röver, born 1889, business training, 1911–13 business appointment in the Cameroons, 1916–18 served in the army propaganda department. After the war, worked in his father's not very prosperous draper's shop in Oldenburg. Already a member of the NSDAP before 1923. 1928 became *Gauleiter* of Weser-Ems and 1932 Minister-President of Oldenburg. See personal files in BDC.

1927 the NSDAP in the state of Oldenburg only increased its membership from forty-five to ninety-five, seventy of whom were in the city of Oldenburg itself and eighteen in the industrial town of Delmenhorst.[1] In May 1926 Rust had reported to Hess that the DVFB had collapsed in Weser-Ems;[2] but this was a far too optimistic assessment. During 1927, even in the industrial centres of Wilhelmshaven and Emden, where the NSDAP might have been expected to be strongest, the DVFB was far more active.[3] During the summer of 1927, Dincklage was persuaded to agree to the amalgamation of the party districts of East Friesland and Oldenburg to create a single unit within the *Gau* under the direction of Röver.[4] This had obvious organizational advantages and prepared the way for the creation of a separate *Gau*, Weser-Ems, a year later.

In the *Reichstag* constituency of Hanover-East, that is the Northern and Eastern part of the Lüneburg Heath, together with the Stade region near Hamburg, the *völkisch* deputies, Weidenhöfer and Pastor Voss, had also joined the DVFB and, during the first two years, the NSDAP found it exceptionally difficult to make any headway at all. In August 1925, the party secretary in Hanover, Otto Homann, complained to Dincklage that 'there is no work being done for the NSDAP in any of the Heath *Kreise* and there is not even an adequate list of sympathizers'.[5] This was not quite true since the party was quite active in *Kreis* Gifhorn, where the Medical Officer of Health was a tireless propagandist. But in general, the Lüneburg Heath remained for a long time a difficult area for the party to work in. This was felt particularly acutely by the NSDAP in *Gau* Lüneburg-Stade, which contained the greater part of the Heath, particularly after 1926 when it acquired the Heath *Kreise* belonging to *Gau* Hanover-North.[6] The *Gauleiter*, Otto Telschow,[7] complained about his difficulties in an interesting letter to Rust:

[1] Protokoll über die am 20 Feb. 1927, stattgefundenen Generalmitgliederversammlung des Bezirks Landesteil Oldenburg in NSAH Hann. Des. 310 I A, Nr. 8.
[2] Rust to Hess, 21 May 1926, NSAH Hann. Des. 310 I A, Nr. 8.
[3] See the fortnightly reports of the Landespolizeistellen Wilhelmshaven and Emden in NSAA Rep. 21a 9573, Bd. 2.
[4] Dincklage Verfügung, 21 June 1927, NSAH Hann. Des. 310 I A, Nr. 15.
[5] Homan to Dincklage, 7 Aug. 1925, NSAH Hann. Des. 310 I A, Nr. 4.
[6] Hitler to Hanover, 28 Dec. 1926, NSAH Hann. Des. 310 I A, Nr. 8. *Gau* Lüneburg-Stade acquired the *Kreise* of Lehe, Geestemünde, Blumenthal, Osterholz, Rotenburg, Achim, Verden, Fallingbostel, Celle-Town, Celle-County, and Isenhagen.
[7] Born 1876. Educated at a Prussian military cadet school. Served in the army from 1893–1901. From 1901–24 an official in the Hamburg police; axed in 1924. Joined the anti-Semitic Deutsch-soziale Partei of Liebermann von Sonnenberg in 1905. From 1922 a district leader of the DVFP. See Telschow's personal files BDC.

We are only just starting in the *Gau*. We began on 1 January with only 14 members and have now grown to about 130, a small number in view of the large area. But the *Gau* has an almost entirely agricultural population which is orientated towards the *Landbund*, the Guelphs, or the DNVP. In view of our lack of means the long distances complicate matters considerably. In the towns of Lüneburg and Stade we have not a single member. The DVFB district leader sits in Stade.[1]

Another problem was the fact that, apart from those racialists who joined the DVFB, there were also a number who wished to avoid joining either party, preferring to remain *völkisch* but above party. This was the case for example in the district of Norden in East Friesland which before 1925 had been a major stronghold of the *völkisch* movement.[2] Many of these joined the *Tannenbergbund*, which was established by Ludendorff to replace the *Frontbann*, and which campaigned against freemasons, Jews and Roman Catholics.[3] It attacked Hitler and the NSDAP as dependent on Rome (*Romhörig*). The organization, which was for a time loosely linked with the DVFB, had a considerable following, particularly among the anti-Semites in the rural areas of northern Lower Saxony, and proved to be an irksome rival in the period 1925–32.

Apart from the problem presented by the existence of the DVFB, there were also difficulties created by the need to adjust to the new legal course introduced by Hitler. Two questions were involved here. First, there was the new style of the SA. In his instructions for the refounding of the SA, published in the *Völkischer Beobachter* of 26 February 1925, Hitler had laid down that the reorganization should be based on the principles 'on which it operated before February 1923', i.e. before the influence of the *Reichswehr* became strong and the SA was progressively militarized.[4] Hitler insisted that 'its organization must respect the Law of Association (*Vereinsgesetz*). Armed groups or leagues are excluded from membership in the SA.' Hitler had to avoid offering the authorities an excuse to ban the party on the grounds of there being a danger of a *putsch*. From now on, the SA would have to serve the party purely as a propaganda and strong-arm squad with which the party could 'conquer the streets' from the Left. Yet strong objections were made to this new policy. It was totally unacceptable to

[1] Telschow to Rust, 3 Jan. 1926, NSAH Hann. Des. 310 I A, Nr. 11.

[2] Verbindungsmann in Norden to Hanover, undated c. Aug.–Sept. 1926, NSAH Hann. Des. 310 I A, Nr. 13.

[3] See Satzungen des Tannenberg–Bundes e.V. in National Archives T-84, Reel 159, Frames 525871–5 and Hannover–Süd-Braunschweig Gaupropagandaleitung to M. Freimuth–Berlin, 19 Jan. 1932, showing that it was still operating in 1932, NSAH Hann. Des. 310 I. B, Nr. 38.

[4] For the militarization of the SA during 1923 see H. Bennecke, *Hitler und die SA* (Munich, 1962), pp. 68–9 and 84.

Röhm, the leader of the *Frontbann,* who resigned on 1 May 1925 rather than carry it out.[1] There was also some opposition in Lower Saxony. In Bremen, for example, the Hitler supporters who were in a minority compared with the DVFB were organized in a paramilitary organization, the *Reichskriegsflagge,* under a Lieutenant Lindenberg, who was now a commercial traveller, having been axed from the *Reichswehr* after the Versailles treaty. This group refused to accept the new non-military role for the SA and joined the *Wiking* League of Captain Erhardt.[2] As a result, it took months to form an NSDAP group in Bremen. But the problem was not limited to Bremen. For a time, a similar danger existed in Göttingen, Hanover and Wolfenbüttel. The young SA men were tempted by free equipment and plenty of shooting practice which was supplied by the Ehrhardt organization. Indeed, the NSDAP believed it was financed by the Pan-German League to undermine the SA.[3] The problem was complicated by the fact that in some areas, initially, branches relied on help from the para-military organizations in protecting their meetings.

Secondly, there was the question of participation in elections. During 1925, the leadership in both Hanover and Göttingen had given instructions to the party not to participate in the local elections in November.[4] But during 1926, a rift developed between the two *Gaue.* While Hanover accepted the new policy for the reasons which Hitler had explained at Weimar—the need for the protection against legal action provided by the influence of a parliamentary group—the Göttingen leaders continued to reject completely any participation in elections.[5] At the beginning of 1927, Dincklage wrote to Hitler complaining that the failure of *Gau* Göttingen to follow the party line on this issue might create difficulties for the party in the coming *Landtag* elections in Brunswick.[6] Hitler, however, continued to humour the extreme anti-parliamentary attitude of the Göttingen leaders for another year.

Another problem which dominated the attention of the party leaders during these early years was that of finance.[7] In Hanover the party was burdened with the debts run up by the NSFB during the December 1924 *Reichstag* election campaign. Added to this, payment by the

[1] Röhm, *Die Memoiren des Stabchefs Röhm* (Saarbrücken, 1934), p. 160.
[2] See the reports of the Bremen political police during 1925 in NSAO 136, Nr. 2797 and the correspondence between *Gau* Hanover and Bremen in NSAH Hann. Des. 310 I A, Nr. 11 and 12.
[3] *Gau* Hanover to *Gau* Göttingen, 28 Sept. 1926, NSAH Hann. Des. 310 I A, Nr. 8.   [4] See pp. 67–68 above.
[5] *Gau* Hanover to *Gau* Göttingen, 28 Sept. 1926, NSAH Hann. Des. 310 I A, Nr. 8.
[6] Dincklage to Hitler, 18 Jan. 1927, NSAH Hann. Des. 310 I A, Nr. 19.
[7] Homann to Dincklage, 5 Dec. 1925, NSAH Hann. Des. 310 I A, Nr. 6.

members of their monthly dues (thirty pfennig per member of which ten had to be passed on to Munich) was very irregular. During the first year, the income failed even to cover the day-to-day running expenses and, at the end of December, *Gau* Hanover owed Munich 54,790 RM in unpaid dues.[1]

In November and December 1925, an attempt was made to tap new sources of income. The district organizations of the party were ordered to set up branches of a so-called *Völkisch* Freedom Federation (*Völkischer Freiheitsbund*) to organize financial contributions from wealthy sympathizers who, for various reasons such as fear of repercussions on their businesses, were unable to become members of the party.[2] Furthermore, an approach was made to three leading members of the Right in the Province of Hanover, Graf Hardenberg, von Rheden-Rheden, a leader of the Hanover *Stahlhelm*, and Werner Willikens, like Rheden an important landowner in the Hildesheim district.[3] Hardenberg agreed to contribute 50 RM a month and this was probably matched by the other two, who were shortly to become leading members of the party.[4] These measures failed, however, to make any appreciable difference. Wealthy sympathizers were quickly alienated by the party's hostility to the other right-wing leagues—the *Vaterländische Verbände* —and their opposition to freemasonry.[5] By the end of 1926, the Munich head-quarters had been forced to waive over 2,500 RM which was due to them and an agreement was made between the party treasurer, Schwarz, and Dincklage that *Gau* Hanover would commit itself to paying a lump sump of 100 RM a month and would increase this when its financial situation improved.[6]

Yet this financial weakness did not affect the propaganda activities of the party in Hanover. Writing at the end of 1926, Dincklage rejected the advice that they should not hold meetings if there was no money left:

From the point of view of good economics that is correct and would spare our nerves. But for Hanover–Brunswick it would at the moment be the wrong thing to do. The KDP, which is badly split, offers an opportunity where the

[1] Bouhler to Hanover, 31 Dec. 1925, BA Slg. Schumacher 202 I.

[2] E.g. Hanover to Riecke-Holzminden, 4 Dec. 1925, NSAH Hann. Des. 310 I A, Nr. 6.

[3] A meeting took place on 11 Feb. 1926, see the correspondence between Homann and Willikens in NSAH Hann. Des. 310 I A, Nr. 12.

[4] Hardenberg's contribution is mentioned in Hanover to Dincklage, 13 Aug. 1926, NSAH Hann. Des. 310 I A, Nr. 1.

[5] Dincklage to Excellenz Heinemann (chairman of the Uschla), 30 Nov. 1926, in NSAH Hann. Des. 310 I A, Nr. 8.

[6] See the correspondence between Bouhler and *Gau* Hanover between Feb. and May 1926, in BA Slg. Schumacher 202 I and Schwarz to Hanover, 23 Dec. 1926, in NSAH Hann. Des. 310 I A, Nr. 8.

soil is prepared. . . . In Brunswick we have just held five mass meetings lead-ing to a climax and we are doing the same in Hanover. In eight weeks we have distributed 80,000 leaflets in six different series, not indiscriminately, but carefully aimed at suitable factories and streets.[1]

In effect then, this propaganda was financed out of the contributions which should have gone to Munich.

An important difficulty facing the party in Lower Saxony was the problem of poor communications. It was a predominantly agricultural area with only a few urban districts. A bicycle was often the only means of transport during this early period. Vital to the success of any political party is an efficient network of local contact men or branches, who can organize their own propaganda, supported by only occasional visits from leading party figures. This was particularly true in Lower Saxony.[2] Much would depend on the quality of these local leaders, on their ability to maintain momentum, to keep their members actively engaged, so that they did not lose interest and so that the party re-mained in the public eye, opening the way for new recruits. The im-portance of the period 1925–8 lies largely in the creation of this net-work which was then poised to take advantage of the crisis which began in 1928. What was the character of this local organization and how was it created?

The basic framework had been laid before 1925, in the sense that the party began with a number of supporters who had already been in-volved in the *völkisch* movement either in the DVFP or the NSDAP. It is clear from the histories of local branches which have survived, that a considerable number of those who had been active in the *völkisch* movement before 1925 then abandoned it, and joined organizations such as the *Stahlhelm* or the *Jungdeutscher Orden*, only returning after 1928.[3] Nevertheless, by July 1925 in *Gau* Hanover alone, excluding the state of Oldenburg, there were 1,000 members organized in 121 branches, though many of these 'branches' only consisted of one or two members.[4] It has already been suggested that youth and activism were the most outstanding characteristics of the men who opted in favour of the NSDAP. This fact was of crucial importance in deter-mining the style of Nazi activity at local level. Ludolf Haase, *Gauleiter* of *Gau* Göttingen, has given an exceptionally interesting description of

[1] See footnote 5, p. 94.
[2] 'First it was necessary to find contact men and establish sound bases in the various districts of the *Gau*. Organization at local level therefore preceded propa-ganda.' 'Hitler Fahnen über Osthannover von Gauleiter Otto Telschow' NS, 20 Feb. 1932.
[3] For the histories of a number of local branches in the Hanover area, see NSAH Hann. Des. 310 I A, Nr. 60–92.
[4] Dincklage to Rust, 14 July 1925, in NSAH Hann. Des. 310 I A, Nr. 4.

the atmosphere of an NSDAP local branch in which this emerges very clearly.[1] Haase draws a significant parallel with the army; it would have been even more appropriate to cite the *Freikorps* as a model.

When in the year 1914 our marvellous army went to war, leadership was conferred by rank. . . . But as the years went by, and the period of the great *Materialschlachten* arrived with their incredible spiritual and physical demands, the only real leader as far as his troops were concerned, was the man who proved himself in a crisis. It was the act of setting an example and the willingness to die which for them was the important aspect of the role of an officer, not the uniform. Here in blood, pain and mud National Socialism was born, for which later similar laws applied, though under apparently quite different conditions. But basically in the movement only the true man is leader not the official.

This explains why there was very often tension in the party. The movement wanted to see men at the top who understood how to master conflict and opposition and who would yield to no one. If the leadership was seen to fail, they were soon discontented and, in view of the voluntary character of their obedience, there was the danger of serious disturbance. It need not even be a real failure, only a suspicion was enough and, if there was someone who had personal designs and spread accusations, trying to secure a following, serious damage could be done.

This continual threat of internal unrest in the still immature party increased the quieter things were, since the revolutionary spirits wanted to be kept busy and turned their energy inwards as soon as the external enemy was less active or was attacked less. This hidden yet always operative law of the movement was the death of many a local branch in the early period and more than one *Gauleiter* fell victim to it. The leader of an area grew in the struggle and learned his lessons both from his opponents and from his own troop.

It is clear from the documents that this is an extremely accurate picture of the typical local NSDAP branch during the *Kampfzeit*.[2] Moreover, this 'law' was not simply implicit within the movement but officially encouraged. To a request from Seifert to be reappointed Hanover branch leader the Munich head-quarters replied

that as a matter of principle Herr Hitler does not believe in 'appointing' (*einsetzen*) branch leaders. Herr Hitler believes today more than ever that the

---

[1] Haase, 'Aufstand in Niedersachsen. Der Kampf der NSDAP 1921–1924' (mimeo, 1942), pp. 192–3.

[2] The Sammlung Schumacher in the Bundesarchiv is full of examples of this process. See, for example, the development of the party in Berlin 1925–7. Goebbels was appointed to deal with a typical conflict between the moderate political leadership of Dr. Schlange and the SA—former Free Corps fighters. He solved it by introducing 'a fanatical propaganda drive which was almost entirely limited to aggressiveness, and also the equally unideological dynamic of the organized terror of the Berlin SA with its Free Corps and *Frontbann* tradition.' Cf. Martin Brozsat, 'Die Anfänge der Berliner NSDAP 1926–7' in Vierteljahreshefte für Zeitgeschichte 1960.

most effective fighter in the NS movement is the man who wins respect for himself as leader through his own achievements (*sich auf Grund seiner Leistungen als Führer durchsetzt*).[1]

This 'law' acted as a mechanism for selecting capable branch leaders. An example of it in operation can be seen in the history of the local branch in the city of Osnabrück between 1925 and 1927.[2] On 25 May 1925, the Osnabrück police reported that 'the continued inactivity of the NSDAP appears to be a result of a lack of unity among the leadership. A suitable leader has not yet been found.' By 13 July, the branch had ceased to function altogether although there were still supporters, and this inactivity resulted in a loss of membership. 'The members who left complained . . . everyone wanted to be leader and there was continual change.' By the beginning of November, however, the police were reporting 'greater activity' on the part of the NSDAP and it soon became clear why. A leader—Ernst Gresbrand, a teacher—had succeeded in asserting his will. The result was that, by the middle of December, the branch had increased its membership considerably. At the beginning of November 1926, Gresbrand's success was recognized by his appointment as leader of the Osnabrück district organization of the party and he was replaced as branch leader by Bruno Brasch, a civil servant. The appointment of Brasch soon proved to be an error. During September 1927, disputes broke out again within the branch and Brasch was forced to resign. 'The reason: Brasch did not have the ability (*Schneid*) to settle the disputes.'[3] He was replaced by a dentist, Dr. Otto Marxer, who was a conspicuous success, and propaganda activity revived.

Where there was no suitable leader, the party often refused to appoint one, as occurred in the Hanover and Brunswick branches during the first half of 1927.[4] In these cases, the branch was run by the nearest branch or district leader. This insistence on effective leadership at branch level was of crucial importance to the success of the party. It meant that unlike many other parties, and particularly the rival DVFB, the Nazi organization existed not simply on paper or at election time, but was in continual action.

Rivalry among the membership, however, and between different party organizations, a product of the freebooting character of the Nazi membership, posed serious problems of discipline for the party. These

[1] Amman to Seifert, 27 Oct. 1925; NSDAP Hauptarchiv, Reel 6, Folder 147.
[2] For the following see the weekly reports of the Polizeidirektion Osnabrück in Niedersächsisches Staatsarchiv Osnabrück (in future abbreviated as NSAOsn.). Rep. 116 acc 7/43, vols. i and III
[3] Report of the Polizeidirektion Osnabrück, 28 Sept. 1927, NSAOsn. Rep. 116 acc 7/43, vol. III.
[4] Dincklage to Heinemann, 14 Apr. 1927, NSAH Hann. Des. 310 I A, Nr. 19.

were solved largely by the fact that the basis of legitimacy within the party was loyalty to the charismatic leader.[1] Loyalty to Hitler became the main force of cohesion within the party. And this was, in fact, reinforced by conflict within the organization. For, 'in the bitter rivalries loyalty to the leader became a matter of self-protection against one's competitors and enemies within the movement'.[2]

Although intense rivalry was endemic within the NSDAP, it would be a mistake to underestimate the degree of solidarity within the party which functioned as a vitally important cohesive factor. This sense of solidarity was generated, particularly in the early years, by the feeling that they were a small group, living in a hostile environment, dominated both by active opponents and by an indifferent general public. Those who wrote accounts of the *Kampfzeit* invariably eulogized about the sense of comradeship characteristic of the party and particularly of the SA during these years.[3] They reminisced nostalgically about the lorry journeys through the night to protect or break up meetings, the excitement of the battles, and the return trip when they were tired out, some were wounded, and all would have to be at work the next morning. Yet they all felt a glow of satisfaction that they had proved themselves and done a good deed for Germany, while the comfortable *Bürger* were lying in bed. The party clearly offered these men a feeling of belonging, an element of excitement, and a sense of purpose which was otherwise lacking in their lives.

During the first years after the refounding of the party, organization at the local level was rudimentary. The main burden of party work in the Hanover *Gau* fell on the central office, which was located in the city of Hanover and run by the *Gauleiter*, Bernhard Rust, the deputy *Gauleiter*, Major Karl Dincklage, and the party secretary Otto Homann, who dealt with the correspondence and routine matters. Of the two pre-1923 Hanover leaders, Wenzel was in Spain and Seifert accepted a subordinate role as a propagandist for the party. Born in 1883, Rust had been a schoolmaster since 1909.[4] During the Kapp *putsch*, he had been a company commander of the *Einwohnerwehr* and in 1922, together with his father-in-law, Major Dietlein, a leading figure in the Hanover Right, he had seceded from the DNVP and founded the Hanover branch of the DVFP. He declared his support for Hitler in January 1925. It is clear that Rust possessed considerable

[1] See the important study by J. Nyomarkay, *Charisma and Factionalism in the Nazi Party* (Minneapolis, 1967).

[2] R. Heberle, *Social Movements* (New York, 1951), p. 252.

[3] For examples of such accounts in Lower Saxony see K. Schmalz, *Nationalsozialisten ringen um Braunschweig* (Braunschweig, 1933) and M. Hennigsen, *Niedersachsenland. Du wurdest unser! Zehn Jahre Nationalsozialismus im Gau Ost-Hannover* (Harburg, 1935).

[4] Rust personal files in the BDC.

private means, which must have been of value to the party during this period, and his villa in the Waldhausenstrasse provided a useful centre. During the years 1925–8, however, Rust was absent for long periods through illness; this placed an additional burden on his deputy. Dincklage was born in 1874 and became a career officer.[1] He had a distinguished war record, becoming the first Air Force officer. After the war, he was axed from the army and became secretary of the DNVP branch in Hanover. He joined the secession in 1922 and acted as secretary to the DVFP and NSFB branches, going over to Hitler with Rust in 1925. It would be difficult to overestimate the importance of Dincklage's contribution to the NSDAP in Lower Saxony during these early years. While Rust was absent, he acted as *Gauleiter* and editor of the party paper; he was *Gau* leader of the SA; because of the lack of suitable leaders, he simultaneously ran the local branches in the cities of Hanover and Brunswick; and in addition he undertook long propaganda tours through the *Gau*—often by bicycle or on foot. Dincklage became something of a legend to the National Socialists in Hanover, acquiring the nickname 'the rucksack major'.[2] His energy and obvious commitment and his uncomplicated military manner had great appeal for the NSDAP supporters and attracted new members. In 1928 he was made leader of the SA in North Germany, but he died of a lung disease in 1930. Hitler himself gave the funeral oration. Quite apart from his individual contribution, Dincklage is important as an example of the drive which characterized the NSDAP even during this period of comparative stagnation. Between 1 February 1925 and 1 March 1926, for example, 850 public meetings were held in *Gau* Hanover quite apart from private discussion meetings (*Sprechabende*). Of these Dincklage had held 290, Seifert—who was now active in the Salzgitter–Goslar area—155, while the remainder were divided between nineteen other speakers, eight of whom came from outside the *Gau* and therefore held only a few meetings each.[3] This does not include the party's activities in Oldenburg and East Friesland.

The majority of the local branches in the period before 1930 were founded by these 'wandering speakers'. A typical example was the local branch in the village of Affinghausen in *Kreis* Diepholz. The history of the local branch, written in 1937, records the founding as follows:

In the year 1928–9 the National Socialist speaker, Jan Blankemeyer from Oldenburg came and talked to us about Adolf Hitler and his movement.

[1] Dincklage personal files in the BDC.
[2] In the histories of the local branches in the Hanover area which were founded before 1930, Dincklage is frequently mentioned as the first Nazi speaker to appear in the village or town concerned. See NSAH Hann. Des. 310 I A, 60–80.
[3] Hanover to Hess, 3 Mar. 1926, NSAH Hann. Des. 310 I A, Nr. 8.

Comrade Blankemeyer then came every two months and in winter even more frequently. He was living then in Uenzen, *Kreis* Grafschaft Hoya [a neighbouring *Kreis*]. Comrades from the Uenzen branch ran the meetings here. Then Dincklage came. In October 1929, after a Blankemeyer meeting eleven people joined the party. Then in November 1929 the SA from Borstel near Nienburg [in a neighbouring *Kreis*] held a propaganda march, which was followed by a meeting with comrade Leister from Nienburg and a branch was founded with farmer Hermann Menke as branch leader. Then we carried out propaganda in the surrounding villages.[1]

Much depended on the branch leader—not only, as we have seen, on his organizing ability and his activism, but also on his position with relation to the local community. In the village of Schwarme, *Kreis* Grafschaft Hoya, for example, the first branch leader 'did not have the confidence of our many small farmers, cottagers and artisans. As a so-called big farmer, he was conservative in his attitude.'[2] As a result the branch soon collapsed.

It soon became clear that it would be difficult for the *Gau* headquarters to handle all the correspondence with the local branches and keep an eye on their activities. In the spring of 1925, therefore, the party began creating district organizations (*Bezirksgruppen*), which could handle routine correspondence, such as the collection of membership dues, and oversee the party's progress in their area. The first to be set up, *Bezirk* Garbolzum, under a railway official, Wilhelm Busse, covered the *Kreise* Marienburg, Peine, Hildesheim Land, Ilfeld and Gronau—all in *Regierungsbezirk* Hildesheim, the centre of the party's propaganda activities during this period.[3] There is no evidence before 1928 of whether or how far these district leaders were financed. During 1927 another innovation was introduced, the separation of propaganda activities from the organization, the first step in the process of specialization which from now on was increasingly to characterize the party. In the larger local branches special propaganda cells were established which could concentrate on the details of propaganda, leaving the branch leader to deal with the over-all direction of the organization.[4]

Of vital importance for the party during this early period was the party paper, the *Niedersächsischer Beobachter*.[5] This had originated as

---

[1] Geschichte der Ortsgruppe Affinghausen/Diepholz, NSAH Hann. Des. 310 I A, Nr. 60.

[2] Geschichte der Ortsgruppe Schwarme/Hoya, NSAH Hann. Des. 310 I A, Nr. 87.

[3] Homann to Helmuth Flörke–Hildesheim, 25 Aug. 1925, NSAH Hann. Des. 310 I A, 4.

[4] A propaganda centre was set up in the Hanover city branch on 26 Sept. 1927, see NSAH Hann. Des. 310 I A, Nr. 17.

[5] The *Niedersächsischer Beobachter* (in future abbreviated to *NB*) of 2 Mar. 1929, contains a report on the founding of the paper.

the *Horchposten*, a *völkisch* weekly printed in Bockenem/Harz by Heinrich Rehmann, who had been a member of the *völkisch* movement since before the war. During February 1925, after negotiations with Haase and Rust, he had agreed to put his presses at the disposal of the NSDAP and the new paper appeared as a weekly with four pages on 1 March. Between May and October it increased its circulation from 1,900 to 4,000 and, at Easter 1926, it was sufficiently well established to increase the number of pages to eight. The paper's function was partly to provide propaganda material on current political issues and general party ideology for members to use in canvassing, but above all to keep members informed of the plans of the leadership and to give them an idea of the progress of the party outside their own branch and area. Subscription to it was made compulsory.

(ii) *The emphasis on 'Socialism' in the party's propaganda 1925–1928*

Between 1925 and 1928, the NSDAP in *Gau* Hanover-North concentrated its activities in the industrial area between Hanover and Brunswick and in the mining areas of the northern Harz.[1] The *Gau* head-quarters even advised its supporters in East Friesland, an overwhelmingly agricultural area, to concentrate their propaganda on the few industrial centres such as Emden.[2] They believed that the only way to secure their *völkisch* aims was by winning mass support and at this stage they conceived of this as working-class support. Goebbels and Kaufmann were much in demand as speakers in the industrial towns of the region such as Peine, the centre of the Ilsede steel works, owing to their experience with working-class audiences in the Ruhr; and pamphlets suitable for miners were requested from Elberfeld.[3] At Easter 1927, a course was held to train workers as speakers to enable them to lead the opposition in the meetings of left-wing parties.[4] The titles of the speeches given during this period also demonstrate the attempt to appeal to the workers. Typical were: 'The Struggle Against Capitalism—the Demand of the Hour', 'Down with Capitalism' and 'Capitalism or Socialism? Wall Street or Moscow?'. At three mass meetings in Brunswick on 4 November, which had been banned by the police president, but were permitted by the right-wing Minister of the Interior, Johannes Lieff, Hitler attacked the Majority Socialists for

[1] 'The stronghold of our movement in Lower Saxony and the main centre of attack lies in the largest industrial area in the Province of Hanover, in the Ilseder Hütte.' See Dincklage to Könnecke-Brunswick, 1 Mar. 1926, NSAH Hann. Des. 310 I A, Nr. 12.
[2] Homann to Wagschal, undated c. Feb. 1926, NSAH Hann. Des. 310 I A, Nr. 12.
[3] Homann to Bezirk Rhineland, 3 Dec. 1925, NSAH Hann. Des. 310 I A, Nr. 6.
[4] Dincklage to Rust, 26 Apr. 1927, NSAH Hann. Des. 310 I A Nr. 15.

ORGANIZATION AND PROPAGANDA

betraying the workers.[1] The large dark pink posters advertising the meeting proclaimed:

The socialized railways are now, in the '7th year of the Republic', a capitalist undertaking of the American bank and stock exchange Jews. Workers of the hand and of the brain. You like us are socialists. When are you going to understand?? Today your leaders no longer speak of the *socialist republic*. . . . You don't want alms. You want nothing more and nothing less than your rights, than to live in the Republic a life fit for a human being.[2]

The most important instance of the 'socialist' stance of the party in *Gau* Hanover-North during this period was the policy followed on the question of the expropriation of the royal houses. This was a major political issue in the Hanover-North *Gau* because of the confiscation at the end of the war of the wealth of the Duke of Brunswick.[3] During 1925, the issue of compensation was debated in the Brunswick *Landtag*. The party instructed the single NSDAP deputy in the *Landtag*, Riese, to vote against compensation and attacked the Compensation Law in its paper. Riese, however, who had been won over by the duke in an interview, abstained in the crucial division and the law was passed by two votes. This caused a storm of protest from party members, who feared accusations of double dealing from the left-wing press, and Riese was therefore excluded from the party. But he refused to resign his seat and, in fact, by laying down a policy of opposition to the expropriation campaign, Hitler placed the party in Brunswick in rather a quandary. Rust was forced to call off his campaign against Riese. On 25 February 1926, he wrote to the Brunswick branch: 'the best thing is to counter-attack the Marxist parties for their failure to expropriate the war-inflation-deflation profiteers';[4] and this was indeed the policy followed by the *Niedersächsischer Beobachter* in a series of articles.[5]

It is clear, however, that even at this point when the party was making its greatest effort to appeal to the workers and stress its 'socialist' aspect, its socialism was conceived in very different terms from the Marxist variety. A correction made by Rust to an announcement in the *Niedersächsischer Beobachter* of a speech he was to make illustrates the difference rather well. Rust wrote to the leader of the Brunswick branch:

[1] See the correspondence in NSAW 12 Neu Fb 13h 16185 and Kurt Schmalz. *Nationalsozialisten ringen um Braunschweig* pp. 45 ff., for a précis of his speech.
[2] The reference to the railways referred to the Dawes Plan.
[3] For the following see the correspondence in NSAH Hann. Des. 310 I A, Nr. 5 and 6 and Ernst-August Roloff, *Braunschweig und der Staat von Weimar* (Braunschweig 1964) p. 120.
[4] Rust to the Brunswick branch 25 Feb. 1926 NSAH Hann. Des. 310 I A, Nr. 12.
[5] See two draft articles 'Zur Fürstenenteignung' and 'Völliger Mangel sittlicher Auffassung' in NSAH Hann. Des. 310 I D 1.

102

You have made a most unfortunate printing error in your announcement of the title of my speech for the 14th in Brunswick. The title is: 'The Struggle Against Capitalism—The Demand of the Hour'. To my horror in the paper I read 'The Struggle Against Capital'.[1]

The party, in fact, continued to make the classic *völkisch* distinction between 'creative' capital in the hands of Germans and 'parasitic' capital in the hands of Jews. The theoretical position of the Hanover *Gau* on socialism was summed up in an article in the *Niedersächsischer Beobachter*, published during 1927 and entitled 'Socialism as the Task of the Present Time'.

The main principle of true socialism, is '*Allgemeinnutz geht vor Eigennutz*'. ... The Marxist is a capitalist. He only thinks of himself and is thus as far away from socialism as any bourgeois. . . . The class struggle of the national socialists is not, like that of the Marxists, concerned with material gain, but is the moral commandment, the moral urge of all exploited, productive working people of hand and brain to free work from the yoke of parasitic capital. In other words the struggle of the productive class against the parasitic class. The struggle of the working people against Jewish parasites.[2]

The Nazis believed rightly that the old order, dominated by reactionary Junkers and the solid conservative *Bürgertum* and in which the workers had been alienated from the state, was doomed. Their appreciation of the fact that the mood of the electorate increasingly favoured fundamental change was to give them an incalculable advantage over their bourgeois rivals. The new order, they maintained, would be socialist: 'socialism is the *Weltanschauung* of the future'.[3] But socialism in their sense meant simply the subservience of the individual to the needs of the state, organized and run according to *völkisch* principles. The Nazis saw their concentration on winning the workers—the 'masses'—as the factor which distinguished them from all other nationalist groups. This point was put very well in a letter from an NSDAP contact man (*Vertrauensmann*) in East Friesland as follows:

A permanent conversion of the workers who have been deceived and, through this, the awakening on a large scale of a fanatical determination to fight, can only be achieved if one preaches to the masses the new Epistle of Hitler, national socialism, i.e. socialism *and* nationalism, through socialism to nationalism, for socialism and nationalism determine each other. One without the other is incomplete. But the DVFB is not socialist, but completely reactionary like the *Vaterländische Verbände*.[4]

[1] Rust to Schulz 4 Jan. 1926 NSAH Hann. Des. 310 I A, Nr. 12.
[2] NSAH Hann. Des. 310 I D, Nr. 4.
[3] 'Die Spaltung der Völkischen' Dincklage draft article in the *Niedersächsischer Beobachter*, 12 Aug. 1925 in NSAH Hann. Des. 310 I D, Nr. 1.
[4] Letter of a Verbindungsmann to the 'old Nazis' concerning Norden undated c. Aug. 1926, NSAH Hann. Des. 310 I A, Nr. 13.

Similarly, in a letter to the NSDAP contact men in Bremen, Dinck-lage insisted: 'We can only use 100 per cent socialists. Drum-beaters, we'll-beat-the-French-reactionaries, pure nationalists, *auch Völkische*, are all useless. I hope that under your leadership this distinction will at least be made clear in Bremen.'[1]

The main theme of Nazi propaganda during this period, which could also be used to emphasize the party's socialist stance, was the attack on the Dawes Plan. In the autumn of 1924, the *Reichskommissar für Überwachung der Öffentlichen Ordnung* had reported that the DNVP vote for the Dawes Plan had with one stroke revived the confidence and energy of the *völkisch* groups which had fast been declining.[2] It meant that their position as the exponents of extreme right-wing opposition to the Republic was unchallenged. Their rivals, the DNVP, could from now on be accused of compromise with the Republic. Every NSDAP speech during this period repeated variations on the theme that, by accepting the Dawes Plan, Germany's leaders had made her the slave of international finance capitalism.[3] Two particular aspects of the Dawes Plan were invariably mentioned—the loss of German control over the Reich railways and over the Reich Bank. From now on Nazi propaganda invariably referred to the Reich railways as the Dawes railways.

(iii) *The reorientation of Nazi propaganda—1928*

Yet, despite considerable activity and clever propaganda, by the end of 1927 the NSDAP in Lower Saxony appeared to have reached an impasse. Its membership was stagnating. The monthly membership returns for *Gau* Hanover-North forwarded to Munich—which include figures both for new members and resignations—show that, while during 1925 the party increased its membership comparatively rapidly from 793 on 1 July to 1,860 at the end of December, during 1926 the increase slowed down to only 581 members for the whole year.[4] 1927 was a year of almost total stagnation; there was an increase of only 164. Moreover, these monthly membership returns show there was a great turnover in membership. During 1927, for example, while 542 people joined the party 376 left it.[5] Nor had it succeeded in re-

---

[1] Dincklage to Schulze-Achim/Bremen, 24 May 1927, Hann. Des. 310 I A, Nr. 15.   [2] NSAO 136, Nr. 2915.

[3] This generalization is based on the reports of NSDAP speeches in the files of the *Landespolizeistellen* in Lower Saxony referred to above.

[4] *Gau* Hanover-Nord *Mitgliederstand* 1925-7 and 1927-9 in NSAH Hann. Des. 310 I A Nrs. 8 and 19.

[5] The discrepancy between the over-all increase in members and the difference beween those who joined the party and those who left it during 1927 is a result of the movement of members between *Gaue*. Some moved to Hanover, others left for other *Gaue*.

gaining the electoral support which the Völkisch-Social-Block had secured in May 1924. On 19 November 1927, the party in the city of Oldenburg had only succeeded in winning eighty-five votes for their list of candidates in the city council election.[1] More serious, a week later the party was shown to have insignificant support even in its main centre. At the *Landtag* elections in Brunswick on 27 November, despite speeches by, among others, Hitler, Strasser, Reventlow, Koch, Himmler and Feder, the NSDAP won only 10,358 votes, 3·7 per cent, although in *Amtsbezirk* Salder they did succeed in winning 15·7 per cent.[2]

This impasse, which was not apparently confined to Lower Saxony, was recognized at the highest level in the party. At a meeting of *Gauleiter* in Weimar on 27 November, Hitler conceded that in the next elections it would not be possible to win votes in any numbers away from the left-wing parties.[3] Hitler's solution was explained to a meeting of representatives from *Gau* Hanover-North in December.[4] After reporting an improved financial situation, Rust declared that the main task was 'the carrying out of the tightest organization'. The system of district leaders was abolished and all branches were made directly responsible to the head-quarters in Hanover. The district leaders were replaced by contact men (*Vertrauensmänner*) whose job was 'to keep an eye on the work of the branches, found new branches, and report to the *Gau* on the progress of the organization'. Finally, a new structure of membership dues was introduced, increasing the monthly contributions to 80 pfennigs, 30 pf of which went to the local branch, 30 pf to the *Gau* and 20 pf to the Munich head-quarters. The 10 pf SA tax was retained for non-members of the SA and an additional monthly contribution of 50 pf was introduced for the electoral fund.

More important than these organizational changes, however, was the recognition by the party leadership that there was no chance in the immediate future of winning over the supporters of the left-wing parties. They now realized that they would find more support, in the first place, 'from the small businessman who is the most vigorous opponent of department stores and consumer co-operatives. Further, from the shop assistant who as a member of the DHV is already an anti-Semite.'[5] Above all they switched their emphasis to propaganda among the rural population.

In the period before 1928, the NSDAP had made some attempt to

[1] Oldenburg city police report for Nov. 1927 NSAO 136, Nr. 2858.
[2] Schmalz op. cit., p. 63.
[3] Dincklage to Stöhr, 14 Dec. 1927, NSAH Hann. Des. 310 I A, Nr. 17.
[4] Draft report for the *Niedersächsischer Beobachter* on the *Gauvertretertagung* of Dec. 1927 in NSAH Hann. Des. 310 I D, Nr. 4.
[5] See footnote 3.

win the support of the peasantry, particularly in view of the importance given by the DVFB to agricultural propaganda and its comparative success in rural areas. A key figure in the NSDAP's agricultural
propaganda in Lower Saxony was Werner Willikens, a landowner in
the Hildesheim area who dominated the *Kreislandbund* organization in
Goslar. In January 1927, he organized a 'training week' for peasants,
for the purposes of indoctrination, in his home village.[1] Relations with
the *Landbund* during these early years were good. The *Kreislandbund*
organizations provided the setting for what appears to have been the
main effort in agricultural propaganda during these years—a campaign for agricultural settlement in the East. This was organized by a
Dr. Rosikat from Breslau, who ran a settlement organization, the
Schlesische Landgesellschaft, and was regarded as the leading agricultural expert in the party.[2] The Hanover-North *Gauleitung* founded
a branch of the *Bund für Ostsiedlung*, which was another of Rosikat's
enterprises, and organized a tour by Rosikat who addressed *Landbund*
meetings on 'The problem of second and subsequent peasant sons'
(*nachgeborene Bauernsöhne*).

But although there was a certain amount of propaganda aimed at the
agricultural population, during the years 1925–8 priority was given to
propaganda in industrial areas. The branch in Oldenburg was typical
of this when it reported on 28 September 1928: 'We have now tried
everything to establish ourselves in the rural areas and will of course
continue. But I think our main emphasis will remain on industry.'[3]

On 10 December 1927, however, with a major speech to representatives of North-West German agriculture in Hamburg, Hitler
showed his awareness of new possibilities for propaganda among the
agricultural population.[4] Although it was not publicly admitted and
the NSDAP did not by any means give up its attempts to win over the
workers, this initiated a fundamental reorientation of priorities for
the party's propaganda.[5] On 13 April 1928, Hitler officially 'clarified'

[1] See the correspondence between Hanover and Willikens in NSAH Hann. Des.
310 I A, Nr. 16.
[2] Rosikat was a contributor to the *Nationalsozialistische Briefe* on agricultural
topics. Details of negotiations between *Gau* Hanover-South–Brunswick and Rosikat about speaking tours are scattered through the files Hann. Des. 310 I A, Nrs.
12–16 in NSAH. Rosikat was excluded by Hitler in 1927. See Dincklage to Kerrl,
19 Apr. 1927, in A, Nr. 15.
[3] Oldenburg to Hanover, 28 Sept. 1926, NSAH Hann. Des. 310 I A, Nr. 13.
[4] *VB*, 11 Dec. 1927.
[5] The reorientation became clear with the need to choose a candidate to head the
1928 *Reichstag* list for the electoral district of Hanover-South–Brunswick. *Gau*
Hanover-South informed Munich of their choice of a leading railway employee.
But Rust insisted that if the party wanted to win any votes it was essential to choose
a farmer and Willikens was eventually adopted. See the correspondence between
Rust and Bouhler in Mar. 1928, in NSAH Hann. Des. 310 I A, Nr. 19 and BA
Slg. Schumacher 202 I.

the meaning of the Article 17 of the party's programme—'expropriation of land for communal purposes without compensation'—by declaiming that since the NSDAP accepted the principle of private property, this clause merely referred to property illegally acquired or not run in accordance with the well-being of the community, i.e. 'mainly Jewish speculative companies'.[1]

[1] *Das Programm der NSDAP und seine weltanschaulichen Grundgedanken von Dipl. Ing. Gottfried Feder* (Munich, 1932), pp. 4–5.

VI

THE CRISIS OF THE MITTELSTAND[1] IN LOWER SAXONY 1928–1930

(i) *The protest movement of January–February 1928*

THE reorientation of the party's propaganda towards the *Mittelstand* was occasioned not only by the recognition of their failure to win over the supporters of the 'Marxist' parties, but also by the awareness of growing discontent among the *Mittelstand*. Hitler's Hamburg speech had been designed to exploit the unusual agitation among the peasants of Schleswig-Holstein which had begun in October and which showed no signs of abating.[2] By the end of 1927, this agitation had spread to Lower Saxony. On 15 December, the *Landwirtschaftliches Wochenblatt für Ostfriesland*, the *Landbund* journal for East Friesland, published a call for a mass protest meeting which then took place on 5 January 1928 in Aurich and was attended by over 4,000 people.[3] Simultaneously, the movement had spread to the neighbouring state of Oldenburg, where it began at grass-roots level.[4] Pro-

---

[1] The word *Mittelstand* is used here in preference to 'middle class', partly because it was the term widely used at the time, but also because the word *Stand* implies an archaic status valuation which was crucial to this group during the period and which is not expressed so clearly in the term class, primarily an economic definition. Sociologists at the time subdivided the term into the 'old' *Mittelstand* and the 'new' *Mittelstand*. The old *Mittelstand* referred to artisans, shopkeepers and the self-employed. The peasants were sometimes considered separately and sometimes included within the term as in the following account. Civil servants were also usually included but definitely not by the members of the *Mittelstand* movement described below. This is a good example of the conflicts of interest which in fact existed within the *Mittelstand*. The 'new' *Mittelstand* referred to the new class of *Angestellten*, white-collar workers in industry and commerce, and those in government service who were not in a *Beamtenverhältnis*. For a definition of the term see *Staat und Politik*, hrsg. von Ernst Fraenkel and Karl Dietrich Bracher, Neuausgabe (Frankfurt, 1964), pp. 196–9. And for an excellent contemporary analysis of the *Mittelstand* see T. Geiger, *Die soziale Schichtung des deutschen Volkes* (Stuttgart, 1932).

[2] For the protest movement in Schleswig-Holstein see G. Stoltenberg, *Politische Strömungen im schleswig-holsteinischen Landvolk 1918–1933* (Düsseldorf, 1962), pp. 107 ff.

[3] Regierungspräsident in Aurich to Prussian Minister of the Interior, 14 Jan. 1928, in NSAH Hann. Des. 122a XXXII, Nr. 91a.

[4] For the movement in Oldenburg see the report in *Nachrichten für Stadt und Land*, 26 Jan. 1928, and the police report in NSAO 136 2860.

test meetings in the villages of Cappeln and Essen in the South were followed by a larger meeting in Ahlhorn at the beginning of January, at which a committee was elected to work out specific demands. During January, numerous meetings were held up and down the state, culminating in a mass demonstration of over 20,000 held in the *Pferdemarkt* of the city of Oldenburg on the 26th. From the North West the movement spread rapidly South and East and during February similar protest meetings were held all over Lower Saxony.[1]

The movement was a product of grass-roots economic discontent which was then organized and encouraged by the professional organizations. A series of bad harvests, combined with outbreaks of foot and mouth disease, had aggravated an agricultural crisis for which there were more fundamental causes. At the beginning of 1928, the situation was regarded in agricultural circles as potentially catastrophic.[2] This crisis in agriculture in turn caused a crisis among those economic groups dependent on the prosperity of agriculture. Thus the protest meetings were organized as demonstrations of solidarity between peasants, shopkeepers, house-owners and craftsmen. An analysis of the demands made at these meetings will show how the situation was interpreted by those involved.

The first demand was for protection against 'all surplus imports' and, in particular, the same tariff protection for agriculture as that provided for industry. The election of May 1924 had shown the extent to which post-war imports of dairy and meat products had disillusioned the peasantry of Oldenburg and East Friesland with their traditional support for the liberal parties. The Tariff Act of August 1925 had reintroduced the pre-war tariff rates for the important products; but commercial treaties in 1926–7 had in many cases reduced protection for agricultural produce.[3] At the end of 1927, the Oldenburg *Landwirtschaftskammer* reported that the position in the pig market was catastrophic and 'should be seen as a direct result of tariff-free imports of frozen meat'.[4] The position of the pig market—of vital importance to the numerous small *Geest* farmers of Lower Saxony and of Oldenburg in particular—was further threatened by the negotiations for a trade treaty with Poland which were in progress at this time and, according to which, pigs would be imported into Germany in return

[1] For the movement in Lower Saxony as a whole see the reports of the Regierungspräsidenten to the Prussian Ministry of the Interior in NSAH Hann. Des. 122a XXXII, Nr. 91a.

[2] In Dec. 1927, the Landwirtschaftskammer in Oldenburg reported that an 'agricultural catastrophe' was impending. See Berichte der Landwirtschaftskammer in NSAO 136 151–37 II.

[3] Cf. J. B. Holt, *German Agricultural Policy 1918–1934* (Chapel Hill, 1936), pp. 105 ff.

[4] Berichte der Landwirtschaftskammer NSAO 136 151–37 II.

for advantages for German industrial goods in Poland. The Polish Trade Treaty was a favourite theme of speakers at these meetings.

The second demand was for simplification of the tax system and exemption for peasants, craftsmen and shopkeepers who were in difficulties. Apart from the fact that the tax burden on agriculture, the obligatory membership fees for agricultural organizations, and the insurance premiums had increased since the war, though there was a reduction in 1925, the tax system was also excessively complicated.[1] A peasant was required to pay income tax, turnover tax, property tax, land and buildings tax, extra taxes to the village (*Gemeinde*) and village associations, road tax, vehicle tax, church tax, and social insurance contributions for his employees. The craftsmen had also been complaining for some time about the tax burden. As early as 13 February 1927, for example, the *Niedersächsischer Handwerkerbund* in Oldenburg had organized a protest meeting attended by 1,000 people.[2] They particularly disliked the trade tax (*Gewerbesteuer*), while house-owners objected to the high rates.

The third main demand was for cuts in public expenditure and, in particular, for a reduction in the number of civil servants. An increase in salaries for civil servants which had passed into law on 16 December 1927 had increased the discontent and there was a strong demand for its suspension.

Finally, there was a demand for long-term credit at low interest rates. The credit situation was a major factor in the agricultural crisis. At the end of 1927 the Oldenburg *Landwirtschaftskammer* reported a credit problem such as had not been experienced since the stabilization of the currency in 1924.[3] The annihilation of liquid capital in the inflation, the lack of farm profits and the tax burden had favoured the uneconomic use of credit in the years after 1924.[4] This was encouraged by a government campaign to persuade farmers to intensify and rationalize their farming to make up for the tendency towards extensive farming in the war and inflation period. Farmers did not realize that interest rates would remain roughly twice as high as pre-war. The situation was made worse by the fact that from 1924 onwards the price of land fell and remained below the pre-war figure. Furthermore, apart from mortgages, there was also a large short-term personal debt.[5] By

[1] Holt, *German Agricultural Policy*, pp. 1445 ff.
[2] Oldenburg police report for Feb. 1927 in NSAO 136, Nr. 2858.
[3] Berichte der Landwirtschaftskammer Oldenburg NSAO 136 151–37 II.
[4] Cf. Holt, *German Agricultural Policy*, pp. 132 ff. and E. Topf, *Die Grüne Front* (Berlin, 1933), pp. 32 ff. and 171–5.
[5] The Oldenburg *Landwirtschaftskammer* reported that by the end of 1927 more than 12m RM had been borrowed on a short term personal credit basis and that repayment was being demanded at short notice. This did not include bills of credit for fodder and fertilizer which also had to be paid back. A similar credit situation was described in the reports of the *Regierungspräsidenten*—see p. 109 footnote 1.

1928, however, the sources of credit had dried up and the credit agencies were calling in short-term personal loans. Yet, owing to low prices and increased costs, farm income was often not only inadequate to meet tax and interest demands, but in some cases even the purchase of seed and fertilizer was difficult to finance.

It has, however, been argued that with one exception there was 'no real crisis peculiar to the "old" *Mittelstand*' in the period 1928–33.[1] This may be arguable in terms of their real economic position.[2] But this is perhaps less important for an explanation of their motivation than the fact that they *considered themselves* to be in a crisis in which they were particularly affected. What is certainly true is the fact that this movement was no less important as an expression of resentment at the deterioration in their social status. During the previous half century, rapid economic and social change had to some extent displaced this group from their established position within what was once a static, hierarchical society.[3] Moreover, while under the old regime this process had been partially disguised by the official ideology which emphasized the old values, and by economic measures of protection, the revolution of 1918 laid bare the reality of the situation. The change in the political balance of power had enabled the political representatives of the industrial proletariat to exploit their position by pushing through reforms which weakened both the financial position of the *Mittelstand* and their authority over their employees: taxes were increased; social insurance contributions were raised; and the traditional guild courts were abolished, with the result that craftsmen had to take their disputes to the Labour Courts, where they considered their employees were far better represented and more likely to get a sympathetic hearing. The Eight Hour Day prevented *Mittelstand* employers from working their apprentices and employees for longer hours, and finally, a new Technical Training Law removed from them control over their apprentices' training, by compelling them to allow their apprentices to attend a Technical College for regular instruction.[4]

Although there was something of a reaction after 1924—taxes were slightly reduced and tariffs reintroduced for agricultural products, an alliance between the industrial and urban interests succeeded in taking up once more the Caprivi policy of commercial treaties which had

[1] See T. Geiger, op. cit., pp. 87 ff. Geiger argues that the loss of prestige was of more significance. The exception was the small shopkeeper.

[2] Geiger's argument is confirmed for the small-town *Mittelstand* by the analysis of the situation in Thalburg (Northeim) in W. S. Allen, *The Nazi Seizure of Power*, p. 24. But in his analysis of the economic structure in the state of Brunswick, Roloff produces evidence for a basic structural crisis involving the *Mittelstand*. See Roloff, *Braunschweig und der Staat von Weimar*, pp. 165 ff.

[3] See S. M. Lipset, *Political Man* (London, 1960), pp. 134 ff.

[4] These grievances emerged in the speeches at the protest demonstrations.

previously been thwarted by the political power of Prussian agriculture.[1] These treaties partially undermined the effects of the tariff legislation.

(ii) *Disillusionment with traditional political representatives*

Perhaps the most important aspect of all was the fact that the protest movement reflected the widespread disillusionment of the *Mittelstand* in Lower Saxony with their previous political representatives. This disillusionment had developed steadily during the previous five years and, to analyse it, it is necessary to examine briefly the development of political opinion in Lower Saxony after 1918.

The first years after the war had seen on the surface a considerable amount of continuity with the pre-war period. The *Mittelstand* continued to vote overwhelmingly Liberal in Oldenburg and East Friesland, and Guelph and to a lesser extent Liberal in the Province of Hanover (excluding Aurich).[2] A remarkable feature, however, was the increase in the Guelph vote. Before the war the Guelph vote had been declining. As the former kingdom of Hanover became increasingly integrated into Prussia and the Reich, a new generation had grown up for whom the battle of Langensalza was a matter of history rather than part of their personal experience. What then were the reasons for this sudden increase in the Guelph vote?

Above all the Guelphs benefited from a feeling of alienation from the central government in Berlin, a feeling which was particularly prevalent among the agricultural population—peasants and craftsmen.[3] This had begun with resentment at the restrictive measures imposed by the war economy. It was now accentuated by the knowledge that Berlin was in the hands of the Left—revolutionaries with dangerous ideas of socialization. Furthermore, when the Left took over the government in 1918, they continued wartime policies with the inten-

---

[1] See Holt, *German Agricultural Policy*, pp. 105–7.

[2] In the 1920 election the DVP and DDP won some 40 per cent of the vote in Oldenburg and East Friesland (since 1919 there was a marked swing to the DVP) compared with the Reich average of 22·4 per cent. In the northern and central part of the province of Hanover the Guelphs won an average of 39 per cent, while in the southern part of the province the *Mittelstand* vote was divided between the liberal parties (26 per cent) and the Guelphs (11 per cent). The socialist parties were strongest in this area (Hildesheim), in the industrial part of Hanover district and in Brunswick. The main point was that the trend towards the Right in the 1920 election, which in the rest of the Reich helped the DNVP, was in Lower Saxony absorbed by the traditional representatives of conservatism—the Liberal and the Guelph parties. See Franz, *Die Politischen Wahlen in Niedersachsen 1867 bis 1949*, pp. 27 ff. and also for subsequent election results.

[3] Prilop, *Die Vorabstimmung in Hannover 1924. Untersuchungen zur Vorgeschichte und Geschichte der deutsch-hannoverischen Partei* (Diss., Hamburg, 1954), pp. 207 ff.

tion of protecting the urban consumer, thereby adding concrete economic grievances to the suspicion in which they were already held.[1]
Indeed, it was widely believed in the Province of Hanover that an independent Hanover could survive the economic difficulties of the post-
war period better than Prussia.

The Guelphs, with their programme of a Hanover independent of
Prussia and their tradition of support for the economic interests of the
Mittelstand, were well placed to exploit this widespread sense of alienation and fear. But there was more than purely economic interest involved. The increase in support for the Guelphs was part of a ' Los von
Berlin' movement which manifested itself in many different parts of
the Reich, and of which economic interest was only one of several
motivations. More relevant here than the obvious parallel with the
separatist movements in Bavaria and the Rhineland is a comparison
with post-war developments in the neighbouring province of Schleswig-Holstein. Here the malaise within the *Mittelstand* manifested itself in the rapid growth of a new party—the *Schleswig-Holsteinische
Landespartei*.[2] The *Landespartei* and the Guelphs possessed the same
social basis—peasants, craftsmen and *Akademiker*. They also shared a
similar ideology: a hostility to Prussia, an emphasis on the importance
of local culture, and a belief in the need to protect the *Mittelstand*
from the developments of capitalism and industrialization. A historian's
description of the basic attitude underlying the antipathy of the *Landespartei* to Prussia as 'an expression of a general cultural criticism of the
era of highly developed capitalism from the point of view of a rural-
conservative sensibility'[3] is equally applicable to the Guelphs. For the
main centre of the Guelphs' support was no longer in the original dynastic territories which were now partially industrialized; it had now
shifted northwards to the Stade region, an almost entirely agricultural
area. It continued in the dynastic territories only where agriculture
predominated. The enormous increase in support for the Guelphs in
the Stade region (in the 1920 election they won 62·4 per cent in
Kreis Bremervörde) was of considerable significance because from
1867 until just before the war this area had been a bastion of Liberalism, in other words anti-Guelph. The increase in Guelph support
showed that the main motivation for support of the Guelph party was
no longer dynastic loyalty, though it still played an important role.
More important was the belief, which the Guelphs shared with the
Landespartei, that the period of Prussian rule had represented the
period of 'commercialization and industrialization, the decline of taste

[1] Cf. Holt, *German Agricultural Policy*, pp. 10 ff.
[2] Cf. Rudolf Heberle, *Landbevölkerung und Nationalsozialismus* (Stuttgart,
1963), pp. 139 ff.
[3] Ibid., p. 144.

and the destruction of creative cultural and administrative contributions in the provinces'.[1] For the Guelphs, as for the *Landespartei*, anti-Prussian federalism sprang from a dislike of the modern state as such, the Leviathan which consumed all rooted associations, undermined all organic order, dissolved all regional peculiarities of political life, to replace them with unified institutions.[2]

The main difference between the two parties was only superficially significant. It lay in the fact that the *Landespartei*, as the heir of a tradition of peasant self-government, professed to support liberalism and democracy, while in fact attacking liberalism and democracy in their existing form. The Guelph party, on the other hand, had been founded as a dynastic party and was now deeply divided in its attitude to democracy. Even these differences, however, had been partially obscured by the fact that the new supporters of the Guelphs from the Stade region had a long tradition of peasant freedom and political liberalism. And the similarity represented in the expression of alienation of a section of the population from the government, the political system, indeed the modern world itself, was of more importance, and was to play a significant role in the collapse of that political system.

The election of May 1924 saw for the first time a major break in the continuity of political opinion in Lower Saxony. It had been preceded by a year in which the crisis situation dominating Germany since the Allied break-through in August 1918 threatened to destroy her whole political, economic and social structure. The Ruhr had been occupied in January 1923, paralysing Germany's most important industrial region; partly because of this, inflation had reached fantastic proportions, ruining a section of the middle class; separatism in Bavaria and the Rhineland appeared to threaten the unity of the Reich; and on the Right and Left the opponents of the Republic massed for the kill—in Thuringia and Saxony the Communists were active, in Bavaria right-wing disobedience of the Reich government culminated in the Hitler *putsch*. In this situation, the government, which had declared a state of emergency, was entirely dependent on the army.

Apart from this general background of crisis, the introduction of the *Rentenmark* in the autumn of 1923, which ended the inflation, created a specific crisis in agriculture.[3] The peasants, who had already sold some of the harvest for paper marks, were now forced to dump the rest in order to acquire enough of the new money to buy seed and fertilizer for the new year and to pay their taxes which were, in any case, considerably higher than pre-war. The position was made worse by

[1] Ibid.   [2] Ibid.

[3] For the following see F. Fabian, *Die Verschuldung der Deutschen Landwirtschaft vor und nach dem Kriege* (Diss., Leipzig, 1930), pp. 50 ff.

increasing agricultural imports from abroad. Between November 1923 and June 1924 agricultural prices, particularly for dairy and meat produce which were the main basis for farming in Lower Saxony, collapsed. The result was an enforced remortgaging of the land in short-term, high interest *Rentenmark* credits which wiped out the benefits agriculture had received from the effects of the inflation on their previous mortgages.

In the election of May 1924 the parties supporting the Republic suffered a severe defeat, while the extreme Right made important gains. In Lower Saxony the combined vote of the left-wing parties dropped from 40·3 per cent in 1920 (MSPD + USPD) to 32·3 per cent (SPD + KPD). Even more serious was the decline in the vote of the Liberals, signifying a widespread disenchantment with the Republic among the *Mittelstand* and bourgeoisie. In particular, the DVP vote dropped from 19·1 per cent to 11·8 per cent. This decline was particularly serious in the traditional bastions of Liberalism in Lower Saxony—Oldenburg and East Friesland. In both *Regierungsbezirk* Aurich and the state of Oldenburg the DVP vote was halved from 31 per cent to 15·1 per cent and from 24·8 per cent to 12·2 per cent respectively. This represented little short of a revolution in political opinion. The DVP was obviously suffering from its association with the Republic and identification with the policies of its governments.

Three parties made significant gains in this election and all three were opponents of the Republic. In the first place, the Communists had become a real political force after the amalgamation with the left-wing of the Independent Social Democrats in 1920. In Lower Saxony, however, they won only 7·3 per cent of the vote (Reich average 12·6) and could only reach 10 per cent or over in the few large towns and industrial areas such as Hanover, Brunswick, Emden and Peine.

Secondly, for the first time the DNVP won a significant percentage of the poll, doubling its vote from 7·1 per cent in 1920 to 15·5 per cent. Its rise was most marked in the state of Oldenburg—from 2·4 per cent to 15·8 per cent. If one excludes the two Catholic *Kreise*, the rise was even sharper, from between 1–2 per cent to 25 per cent. It is clear that the motive for supporting left-wing liberalism before the war, namely opposition to the grain tariff policy of the Conservatives, was now overshadowed by other factors. Free trade was no longer so attractive when imports of dairy and meat produce were beginning to flood into the country.[1] Moreover, the DVP had the reputation of being the party of heavy industry, while the DDP tended to represent the urban

---

[1] For example, the Chamber of Agriculture in Oldenburg complained about low butter prices due to foreign competition. See Mar. 1924 Bericht der Landwirtschaftskammer Oldenburg in NSAO 136 151–37 I.

and small town lower middle class. Their leaders had been associated with governments which tolerated or introduced high taxation and social service contributions which had increased by 260 per cent between 1913 and 1924,[1] quite apart from their introduction of the *Rentenmark*. The DNVP, on the other hand, had been in permanent opposition and had consistently opposed policies favouring the industrial workers and urban consumers and had made itself the champion of agriculture in general. Moreover, since the war the DNVP had had considerable success in winning control over the economic-political organization of agriculture in Lower Saxony, through its influence within the *Landbund*.

(iii) *The Landbund*

The *Landbund* was theoretically above party; in fact however, until 1928 at any rate, it was dominated by the DNVP. Before the war, its predecessor the *Bund der Landwirte* had comparatively few branches in Lower Saxony, mainly in the Hildesheim area and in the northern marshes.[2] After 1918, however, the *Landbund* became the leading representative organization for agriculture in Lower Saxony.[3] During 1919, hostility to economic controls and the desire to ensure maximum influence for agriculture in a situation where it appeared as if the interests of the urban consumer would predominate had led to the amalgamation of existing agricultural associations in the *Kreise* into *Kreis* Economic Associations (*Kreiswirtschaftsverbände*). When these proved inadequate, they were replaced by *Kreislandbünde* with individual membership. These *Kreislandbünde* were then organized into provincial *Landbünde* of which there were two in Lower Saxony—Hanover and Oldenburg–East Friesland, and these were then associated with the *Reichslandbund* in Berlin. Only in Oldenburg was the influence of the *Landbund* at first limited by the existence of a rival organization—the *Bauernbund*—which won considerable support as the representative of the small dairy and pig farmers against the influence of the big arable landowners of the East who dominated the *Reichslandbund*. But the *Bauernbund* suffered from its close association with the DDP; from the fact that it could not compete with the resources and influence of the *Landbund*; and from the growing belief that the front was no longer *Junker* versus small farmer, but agriculture and rural society as a whole versus industry and the urban interest.

[1] Fabian, op. cit., p. 55.

[2] Ehrenfeuchter, *Politische Willensbildung in Niedersachsen zur Zeit des Kaiserreiches* (Diss., Göttingen, 1951), pp. 298 ff.

[3] Cf. D. Lohmann, 'Die landwirtschaftlichen Organisationen in Niedersachsen 1764–1964' in *Die Landwirtschaft Niedersachsens 1914–1964* (Hanover, 1964), pp. 28–9.

The success of the *Landbund* in projecting itself as the representative of all types of farming and all sizes of holding may have been an important aspect of and influence on the move to the extreme Right by the agricultural population in Lower Saxony after the war.

(iv) *The electoral success of the Völkisch-Social-Block in May 1924*

The May 1924 *Reichstag* election saw for the first time since the war the participation of the *völkisch* movement in a *Reichstag* election as a specific group—the *Völkisch*-Social-Block. The V-S-B succeeded in winning 154,000 votes in Lower Saxony, 7·5 per cent compared with the Reich average of 6·6 per cent.[1] It was strongest in three main areas: in Brunswick–Wolfenbüttel, where it won support from disillusioned SPD and USPD voters, and further south in the city of Göttingen; in the Lüneburg Heath with support from disillusioned DVP and Guelph supporters; and above all in the *Kreise* Norden, Wittmund and Friesland which form the north and north-east coastal strip of East Friesland. In Friesland the V-S-B won 15·2 per cent of the vote, in Norden 13·1 per cent, and in Wittmund the astonishing figure of 46 per cent. With the exception of Norden, where the conservatives had been strong before the war because of a local notable, Fürst Knyphausen, East Friesland had always been a stronghold of Liberalism. In the elections between 1890 and 1912 the National Liberals and Progressives between them had won an average of 74 per cent of the vote in Amt Jever (Friesland) and 83 per cent in Wittmund. In the previous election of 1920 the two Liberal parties between them had won 49 per cent of the vote in Friesland, 39 per cent in Norden and 59 per cent in Wittmund.

The results of the May 1924 election suggested the vulnerability of some of the rural population in parts of the Lüneburg Heath and East Friesland to *völkisch* propaganda at a time of crisis. *Kreis* Wittmund, for example, was made the main target of an intense election campaign by the V-S-B. It was backed by the local newspaper and totally outclassed that of the other parties.[2] The ground had been prepared by the activities first, of a *völkisch* teacher who lived in the seaside village of Carolinensiel, and secondly, by those of a 'wandering speaker', Jan Blankemeyer, a peasant from Kirchkimmen, a village in the Bremen area. Blankemeyer, who was to become a key figure in the NSDAP's agricultural propaganda in Lower Saxony, spoke and wrote his pamphlets in Low German. He was an extremely effective speaker who mixed

[1] For electoral statistics see Franz, *Die Politischen Wahlen in Niedersachsen 1867 bis 1949.*
[2] For the following see *Anzeiger für Harlingerland* 1923–1924 and Haase, 'Aufstand in Niedersachsen. Der Kampf der NSDAP 1921–1924' (mimeo, 1942), pp. 95–8.

crude racialist themes expressed in popular form—'Why are there so many masculine women and feminine men. So few real men (*ganze Kerle*) and true women?'—with economic questions such as the 'Reasons for the lack of money and the need to break the interest slavery', which could be expected to interest peasants who were short of cash and paying exorbitant interest. In a community whose contacts with the outside world were extremely limited, and who were thus extremely suspicious of strangers, his *Bodenständigkeit* was an invaluable asset and, according to Haase, 'our opponents had nothing comparable'.[1]

(v) *The decline of the DHP*

Finally, 1924 saw the beginning of a fundamental change in political behaviour in Lower Saxony—the decline of the DHP. Two weeks after this *Reichstag* election of 4 May 1924, a referendum (*Volksbegehren*) was carried out in the Province of Hanover (excluding *Reg. Bezirk* Aurich) on whether to hold an official plebiscite (*Volksentscheid*) on the Guelph demand for the separation of Hanover from Prussia. Only 25·5 per cent voted in favour and, since one third of the electorate was necessary, the plebiscite was not carried out.[2] This was a devastating blow to the DHP, putting in question its whole *raison d'être*. In the December 1924 election the party lost 3·2 per cent compared with May and from then on it never recovered.

(vi) *The rise of the Landvolk movement*

In 1924 the DNVP had successfully offered itself to the rural *Mittelstand* in Lower Saxony as a new party of fundamental opposition. By 1928, however, not only had it compromised itself in this role by its participation in government, but also and more important, it had failed to prevent the crisis. The failure of its representatives to satisfy the needs and desires of the *Mittelstand* was brought home to it with full force during the early months of 1928, with a political crisis in Berlin which delayed the carrying out of measures to alleviate the situation.[3] This failure on the part of their traditional representatives—*Landbund*, DNVP, Guelphs and DVP—to produce results led to the alienation of the *Mittelstand* from the political system itself and encouraged fundamental opposition. In the words of Claus Heim, a leading exponent of radicalism within the Schleswig-Holstein movement:

---

[1] Haase, op. cit., p. 94.

[2] Franz, *Die Politischen Wahlen in Niedersachsen 1867 bis 1949*, p. 106.

[3] Cf. Stoltenberg, *Politische Strömungen im schleswig-holsteinischen Landvolk 1918–1933* (Düsseldorf, 1962), p. 114. There was a coalition crisis over a proposed school law.

the fact is that the state, the government, the parties and the agricultural organizations, the chambers of agriculture, and the co-operatives have failed. The fact is that for years the peasant has paid his contributions and for years has heard about all the things that have been done for him and yet sees that his situation is getting worse and worse. The fact is that ... (taxes) have become his sole point of contact with the authorities.[1]

The *Reichstag* election of May 1928 charted the first stage of this disillusionment.[2] Compared with December 1924 the vote of the DNVP was halved from 18·3 per cent to 9·4 per cent, the Guelph vote fell from 16 per cent to 11·4 per cent and the DVP vote dropped from 14·1 per cent to 10·4 per cent. On the other hand, two parties founded specifically to represent the *Mittelstand* as an interest group— the Christian National Agricultural Party (peasants) and the Economic Party (craftsmen and shopkeepers)—won 7 per cent of the vote. The SPD also gained from its years of opposition and from a new agricultural programme orientated towards the small dairy and pig farmers, increasing its vote from 30 per cent to 36·9 per cent.[3]

Apart from the expression of disillusionment with its traditional political representatives and the vigorous assertion of specific economic demands, from the beginning the 1928 protest movement had provided an arena for more fundamental political discontent. At the protest meetings a number of speakers had followed the *völkisch* propaganda by blaming the Dawes plan for the crisis, while according to a newspaper report, Cord Cordes, the general secretary of the Hanover *Landbund*, declared in a speech to a mass meeting in Göttingen that 'the Weimar constitution is the root of all evil. Repeal of the electoral law, abolition of the single chamber system is the most vital need. At a suitable moment one must not shrink from using force.'[4]

This attitude of general opposition to the Republic was encouraged by the spread of the *Landvolk* movement to Lower Saxony from Schleswig-Holstein in the spring of 1929.[5] The *Landvolk* movement had emerged in the autumn of 1928 among the peasants of the west coast and had rapidly spread to the rest of Schleswig-Holstein. Under the leadership of a peasant from Eiderstedt, Wilhelm Hamkens, the movement aimed to encourage passive resistance to taxation and to the expropriation of farms for the non-payment of debt; it also desired the overthrow of the existing political system and its replacement by a

[1] Cf. E. von Salomon, *Der Fragebogen* (Hamburg, 1952), p. 266.
[2] For the election figures see Franz, *Die Politischen Wahlen in Niedersachsen 1867 bis 1949*.
[3] Cf. Stoltenberg, op. cit., p. 116.
[4] Generalstaatsanwalt in Celle to Prussian Minister of the Interior, 31 Mar. 1928, in NSAH Hann. Des. 122a XXXII, Nr. 91a.
[5] For the *Landvolk* movement see Stoltenberg, op. cit., pp. 121 ff. and O. E. Schüddekopf, *Linke Leute von Rechts* (Stuttgart, 1960), pp. 306 ff.

non-parliamentary state friendly to agriculture. In Schleswig-Holstein the movement acquired mass support among the peasantry and, in March 1929, *Landvolk* speakers began to make propaganda in Oldenburg, where they worked with the leaders of the Oldenburg protest movement of the previous year.[1] Apart from their advocacy of resistance to bailiffs, which culminated in a bomb attack on the Oldenburg tax office, they denounced the 'System Parliament', 'international large capital' and 'the Jews'. The *Landvolk* movement soon spread to other parts of Lower Saxony and the finance office in Lüneburg suffered a similar fate.[2] The importance of the movement was the fact that it encouraged radicalism without being able to satisfy the demands which it articulated. It lacked political influence, on the one hand because it avoided representation in the *Reichstag*, and on the other because it was limited to one social group. These were weaknesses which Nazi propaganda was to exploit to the full.

[1] For police reports on the *Landvolk* movement in Oldenburg see NSAO 136 VI–151–48.
[2] For an account of the Lüneburg bombing see NSDAP Hauptarchiv, Reel 44, Folder 895.

VII

THE NSDAP'S MITTELSTAND CAMPAIGN
1928–1930

(i) *The rural Mittelstand campaign*

IN the *Reichstag* election of May 1928 the NSDAP won 4·5 per cent of the vote in Lower Saxony. It would not appear, therefore, as if the NSDAP had won much additional support through the first *Mittelstand* protest movement. This low average vote, however, disguises an important regional variation. For, in the rural *Kreise* of East Friesland and Protestant North Oldenburg, the original source of the movement, the NSDAP won over 10 per cent—and the exceptional *Kreis* Wittmund now with 36 per cent of the vote was joined by the *Kreis* Ammerland in Oldenburg with 28 per cent. How did the NSDAP exploit the *Mittelstand* agitation?

By making a major speech to the representatives of North-West German agriculture as early as December 1927, Hitler had shown his awareness of the opportunity offered by the protest movement. His example was followed by the regional party organization which began at once to exploit the situation. At the mass meeting in Aurich on 5 January, Röver blamed the Dawes plan for the crisis until, after speaking for twelve minutes, he was cut off by the *Landbund* organizers for introducing party political propaganda.[1] At the Oldenburg demonstration no NSDAP representatives were allowed to speak; but the party countered this by organizing three meetings, one in the morning and two in the afternoon which were attended by over 2,000 people in all. A pamphlet was distributed with the words

Peasants! Citizens! Workers [*Schaffende*] of all classes [*Stände*]! Why have your leaders called you to a mass demonstration? Because you have been betrayed by the parties which, on 29 August 1924, accepted the Dawes Plan. That is the Social Democrats, the Democrats, the Centre Party, the Economic Party, the People's Party and the DNVP.[2]

The success of the Oldenburg meetings encouraged the *Gau* headquarters in Hanover to organize meetings at the major *Mittelstand* demonstrations which followed in other parts of Lower Saxony.[3]

[1] *Regierungspräsident* Aurich to Prussian Minister of the Interior, 14 Jan. 1928, NSAH Hann. Des. 122a XXXII, Nr. 91a.
[2] Oldenburg police report of 27 Jan. 1928, in NSAO 136, Nr. 2860.
[3] Hanover to Telschow, 28 Jan. 1928, NSAH Hann. Des. 310 I A, Nr. 21.

The key figure in the party's agricultural propaganda in Oldenburg and East Friesland was a recent recruit, a former clergyman named Ludwig Münchmeyer.[1] In the early 1920s, Münchmeyer had been pastor of the holiday-resort island of Borkum off the coast of East Friesland. Borkum had an anti-Semitic reputation going back to the last decade of the nineteenth century, when an informal ban was imposed on Jewish holidaymakers and a ritual developed of singing a notorious anti-Semitic 'Borkum Song' every day on the beach. After the war, Münchmeyer had made himself the champion of this anti-Semitic tradition which flourished particularly among the small boarding-houses in competition with the hotels. He pursued his opponents with such demagogic virulence that he clashed with the authorities and, after being found guilty of slander, was unfrocked by the church which in future disputed his right to call himself Pastor a.D. (pastor retired). Between 1926 and 1928, Münchmeyer undertook propaganda tours for the DVFB in Oldenburg and East Friesland. At the beginning of 1928, however, he became a member of the NSDAP and such was his reputation that he was immediately made the party's leading *Reichstag* candidate for the Weser-Ems district. It would be difficult to over-estimate the importance of Münchmeyer to the NSDAP in Oldenburg and East Friesland at this period. The success of the party in the *Reichstag* election of 1928 in this area was attributed by both the Bremen and the Oldenburg political police mainly to Münchmeyer 'who for about a year has held meetings in the whole area and has been able to win support for the Hitler movement among the rural population'.[2] The detailed reports of his meetings, which invariably refer to large, enthusiastic and predominantly rural audiences, reinforce this impression.

In view of the success of Münchmeyer's propaganda, it may be worth examining his style in detail. In the first place, he favoured dramatic titles for his announced speeches.[3] Typical examples were— 'He who knoweth the truth and says it not, verily he is a miserable wretch' (Wer die Wahrheit kennet und saget sie nicht, der is fürwahr ein erbärmlicher Wicht), and 'Thunderclouds of ill-foreboding over the year 1928. The last hope of rescue.' The talk would begin with an account of the various court cases in which he was involved owing to his attacks on the Republic and its politicians. By March 1928 he had been involved in forty-two cases, of which he was proud to announce

---

[1] Material on Münchmeyer, particularly legal proceedings in NSAA Rep. 109, Nr. 38, vols. I–III.

[2] Bremen police Lagebericht, 2 June 1928, NSAO 136, Nr. 2799, Oldenburg report, 24 May 1928, in NSAO 136, Nr. 2858.

[3] Press cuttings and police reports of Münchmeyer's speeches can be found in NSAO 136 2860 and NSAOsn. Rep. 116 acc 7/43, No. 1235.

only one had resulted in a conviction. Within the next few years the actions against him more than doubled, with an equal lack of success. He would continue with an unfavourable comparison of the Republic with the Empire, and then begin to spice his talk with sensational revelations: a report of a Jewish trader selling bad meat, an account of Jewish ritual murder, coupled with an announcement that a child in the neighbourhood had mysteriously disappeared, a claim that Schiller had really been poisoned. Next, the politicians and policies of the Republic came under an attack which also included sensational revelations: the Dawes Plan meant the collapse of a flourishing *Kulturvolk*—Dawes was a Jew and a convicted embezzler; Stresemann had been bribed by Jews and had a Jewish son-in-law. The Republic and its politicians would be given colourful descriptions—the Minister-President of Oldenburg was described as a cockchafer to the great amusement of the crowd. Finally, Münchmeyer would produce his patent remedy— the provision of cheap credit by the Post Office through the reserves built up by the Giro system.

An account of the content of Münchmeyer's speeches cannot convey the remarkable effect which they appeared to produce among his audience. The performance would last for four hours, punctuated by an interval in which propaganda was distributed; and, according to the reports, the audience remained enthralled to the end. His combination of crude wit, sentimental recollection of past imperial glories, sensational conspiracy stories, and simple remedies for specific grievances proved irresistible.

Analysing the effects of the election campaign, the *Völkischer Beobachter* reported that

The election results of the rural areas have proved that with a smaller expenditure of energy, money and time, better results can be achieved than in the big cities. In small towns and villages mass meetings with good speakers are events and are often talked about for weeks, while in the big cities the effects of meetings even with 3 or 4,000 people soon disappear. Surprisingly, local successes are almost invariably the result of the activity of the branch leader, or of a few energetic members.[1]

This analysis applied particularly to Münchmeyer but also to other Nazi speakers. In comparatively isolated villages and small towns, apart from anything else, his meetings provided entertainment, an exciting alternative to the cinema.[2] Compared with the rather colourless 'rational' style of the other parties, the Nazis stood out sharply. As the disillusionment of the rural population with their traditional political

[1] *VB*, 31 May 1928.
[2] In conversation with the author, the *Oberkreisdirektor* of Ammerland described how a visit by Münchmeyer caused as much excitement as a visit by the Sarasani circus.

representatives increased, and their economic and social position became more and more precarious, the radical, largely irrational appeal of the NSDAP became increasingly attractive.

The main line followed by the party in its agricultural propaganda had been laid down in an article written by the *Gauleiter* of Schleswig-Holstein for the *NSDAP Jahrbuch* in 1927, whose arguments were expanded in Hitler's Hamburg speech.[1] Apart from attacking the tariff policies of the government which would ruin German agriculture and make Germany a slave of international finance capitalism, the party emphasized that the plight of agriculture could not be viewed in isolation as it was by the traditional representatives of agriculture; only through a movement representing all social groups could the whole system which was responsible be effectively combated, and the NSDAP alone was such a movement. But although the party was opposed to a separate agricultural movement, this did not prevent it from exploiting to the full the concrete grievances of the agricultural population. On 7 March 1930 the party published an official agricultural programme which embodied the experience acquired during the agricultural campaign of 1928–30.[2]

The first part of the programme emphasized the importance of agriculture and the agricultural population. The defeat of 1918 had meant that the country could no longer afford to pay for its food imports with industrial exports; it now had to pay with borrowed money from abroad which made Germany a slave of international finance. An increase in agricultural production, therefore, had become 'a question of life and death' for the German people. Furthermore, they saw in the agricultural population the guarantee of Germany's racial health and the backbone of its military strength. The second part described 'the disregard for the peasantry and neglect of agriculture in the present German state', which was analysed under four headings: taxation, tariff polices, the intolerable high profits of the middle man (Jews), and the exorbitant prices for fertilizers and electricity fixed by mostly Jewish concerns. Because of these factors the peasant was forced more and more into debt until, in the end, he lost his farm to the mainly Jewish owners of loan capital. The third part concerned the party's plans to introduce a new agricultural law which would prevent land speculation by making mortgages illegal and by passing a Law of Entailment. The state would guarantee a supply of credit. Finally, the programme emphasized that

[1] Cf. Heberle, *Landbevolkerung und Nationalsozialismus*, pp. 160–1 and *VB*, 11 Dec. 1927.
[2] 'Parteiamtliche Kundgebung über die Stellung der NSDAP zum Landvolk und zur Landwirtschaft' in *VB*, 7 Mar. 1930. The programme was officially dated 6 Mar.

professional economic organizations cannot effectively help the farmer. Only the political German freedom movement of the NSDAP is capable of this, because the crisis of the agricultural population is one part of the crisis which involves the whole population, and the National Socialist movement is fighting to free the whole country.

This programme formed the basis of the agricultural campaign for the 1930 election. It was probably not intended so much for the electorate as for Nazi speakers and propagandists and in particular to enable the party to deal with opponents who tried to cast doubt on its commitment to the farming population. In fact it would be a mistake to overemphasize the practical content of Nazi propaganda. Although the NSDAP paid considerable attention to the concrete grievances of the agricultural population, indeed of the *Mittelstand* generally, it was not remarkable in this. The DNVP also developed an agricultural programme very similar to that of the NSDAP in its emphasis on the need for autarky and on the importance of the agricultural population to the German economy and to the 'health of the nation'. It was clearly necessary for the NSDAP to take up concrete grievances—necessary but not sufficient. The success of the Nazi party was due to other factors. In their actual speeches Nazi propagandists tended to concentrate more on ideological questions, in Nazi terminology—*Weltanschauung*.[1] These included extreme anti-Semitism and attacks on Liberalism, the previous creed of a large section of the Lower Saxon peasantry, a creed which seemed to have let them down. The Nazis accused Liberalism of producing the 'divisive' party system which had undermined national unity, of exalting the profit motive at the expense of integrative national values, and finally of putting international obligations before national ones. In contrast, they put forward the concept of the *Volksgemeinschaft* which envisaged a society in which the old communal relationships, disrupted by the process of modernization and its liberal ideology, would be restored. It was the combination of these ideological generalities with the activist style of the Nazi party which convinced audiences that the NSDAP was offering something new.

An important question for the party in its agricultural propaganda was relations with the *Landbund*. The *Landbund*, which had been sympathetic to the NSDAP in the early period when it was of no importance, had reacted strongly against the party's attempt to exploit the protest movement. The party retaliated by accusing the *Landbund* of having failed to produce any results from the government and by attacking its close association with the DNVP.[2] There was in fact some

[1] A good selection of speeches by local Nazi propagandists to rural audiences contained in the Oldenburg political police files, e.g. NSAO 136, No. 2860.

[2] E.g. Münchmeyer speech of 8 Mar. 1928, reported in *Der Ammerländer*, 9 Mar. 1928.

disagreement within the party about the attitude which should be adopted towards the *Landbund*. Initially, at any rate, *Gau* Lüneburg-Stade waged open war on the *Landbund* which retaliated in kind. Hanover-North, on the other hand, objected to this policy, preferring a more circumspect tactic of attacking the policies of its leaders but in such a way as not to appear opposed to the *Landbund* as such.[1] Suggestions by members favouring the creation by the party of an alternative organization were opposed on the grounds that 'we want to make use of the work which has already been done, by capturing the existing professional organization from within. With every new peasant member of the party we control the *Landbund* by that much more'.[2]

The *Landbund* had attempted to retain its control over the protest movement with increasing lack of success. In February 1928, the *Reichslandbund* published a declaration that agriculture was no longer prepared to pay taxes out of capital and in future would refuse to pay taxes where there was no income. But the initiative in implementing this policy was soon seized by the *Landvolk* movement. A year later, on 5 April 1929, in a desperate attempt to keep pace with the *Landvolk* and retain its influence, the Hanover *Landbund* declared a 'buyer's strike', advising their members to cease buying commodities.[3]

During the period 1928–30 discontent with the performance of the *Landbund* and the lack of results from the promised emergency programmes increased, and the *Landbund* leaders began to note with alarm the increasing number of members, particularly younger ones, who were joining the NSDAP.[4] An important new recruit for the party at this period was the leader of the *Landbund* district organization in Stade and deputy chairman of the Hanover regional organization, Georg Weidenhöfer, who joined in April 1929.[5] Weidenhöfer, who had been a leading member of the DVFP and then the DVFB, had played a major role in the organization of the 1928 protest movement in Lower Saxony, and his conversion was an important coup for the party. The fact that the younger generation of the peasantry was particularly vulnerable to Nazism was noted by contemporary observ-

[1] Hanover to Telschow, 28 Jan. 1928 and 2 Feb. 1928, in NSAH Hann. Des. 310 I A, Nr. 21 and for continuing disagreement Homan to Dincklage, 22 Dec. 1928, NSAH Hann. Des. 310 I A, Nr. 22.

[2] *NB*, 5 Jan. 1929.

[3] *Oberpräsident* Hanover to the Prussian Minister of the Interior, 5 Apr. 1929, in NSAH Hann. Des. 122a XXXII, Nr. 91a.

[4] E.g. on the 21 Jan. 1929, the *Landrat* of Kehdingen informed the *Reg. präsident* in Stade of 'a certain amount of discontent with the leadership of the *Landbund*' in NSAH Hann. Des. 122a 76f, while on 9 Mar. 1929, at the general meeting of the Göttingen *Landbund* Freiherr von Wangenheim-Haake 'expressed concern that so many *Landbund* members, particularly younger ones, were becoming Nazis', see *NB*, 23 Mar. 1929.

[5] *NB*, 13 Apr. 1929.

ers.[1] The agricultural crisis had interfered with the process of transition within the peasantry from one generation to the next which in Lower Saxony was carefully regulated by the Entailment Law and by custom.[2] The older peasants were unwilling to give up their farms and face penury, while there was not enough cash to pay off the younger sons. Increased competition for employment in the towns meant that surplus youth from the land could no longer be absorbed. Agricultural youth was thus discontented and sought satisfaction and compensation in SA activities, while the settlement propaganda of the party offered younger sons and agricultural labourers the hope of farms of their own. In the countryside National Socialism became the badge of youth in opposition to the Guelph or *Deutschnational* conservatism of the older generation.

(ii) *Other Mittelstand groups*

No less important to the party than its agitation among the peasantry was its propaganda among other *Mittelstand* groups. In his conclusion that the *Mittelstand* was not involved in a fundamental crisis, Theodor Geiger made one exception—the small shopkeepers.[3] In this branch he felt that a 'correction to the excessive overcapacity was inevitable'. After the war too many people had become retailers, although inexperienced or undercapitalized. In the year 1930, for example, nearly 40 per cent of all bankruptcies in Brunswick were small shopkeepers.[4] A key factor in the plight of this group was the increasing competition from department stores, chain stores, and consumer co-operatives which had multiplied during the period of economic recovery 1924–9. Opposition to this competition was an increasingly prominent theme in the meetings of craftsmen and shopkeepers which took place during 1928 and 1929.[5] Opposition to department stores and consumer co-operatives was Point Sixteen in the 1920 NSDAP programme and it was to play a vital role in the attempt to win over these groups. At the

[1] E.g. T. Heuss, *Hitlers Weg, Eine historisch-politische Studie über den National-sozialismus* (Stuttgart–Berlin, 1932), p. 164.
[2] The position in Lower Saxony was similar to that in Schleswig-Holstein, see Heberle, op. cit., pp. 134 ff. and A. Ackermann, *Die wirtschaftlichen und sozialen Verhältnisse des Bremischen Bauerntums 1870–1930* (Diss., Leipzig, 1935), p. 155.
[3] Geiger, *Die soziale Schichtung des deutschen Volkes*, p. 87.
[4] Roloff, *Braunschweig und der Staat von Weimar*, pp. 166–7. Part of the resentment of this group at their plight, and its hostility towards the Republic, may be explained by the fact that before the war they had been extremely prosperous. In Oldenburg, for example, their income had only been exceeded by factory owners and big businessmen. See H. J. Schulze, *Oldenburg's Wirtschaft einst und jetzt* (Oldenburg, 1965), p. 109.
[5] See the newspaper cuttings in the *Mittelstand* file of the Brunswick regional organization of the DVP in the *Stadtarchiv* Braunschweig G x 6, Nr. 35.

beginning of 1928, the *Gauleiter* of Thuringia, Fritz Sauckel, began a tour of Lower Saxony, giving a number of two-hour speeches on 'The Invasion of Department Stores and Consumer Co-operatives.'[1] In conjunction with the tour the party produced a special pamphlet, and the *Gau* head-quarters of Hanover North ordered the local branches, where the meetings were taking place, to begin a campaign 'aimed above all at small shopkeepers and craftsmen'.[2] The party also encouraged and exploited resentment at competition from Jewish shops. At Christmas 1927, for example, the NSDAP ran a campaign with special meetings and stickers urging people to buy at 'Christian' shops.[3] The party also sent members into the meetings of the artisans' and shopkeepers' organizations as discussion speakers to point out that as a single interest group they were powerless and that for ten years the NSDAP had been campaigning against department stores and co-operatives.[4] Finally, in November 1929, a special organization—the *Nationalsozialistischer Deutscher Wirtschaftsbund*—was established to enable the party to organize and direct the discontent of this group.[5] It was founded by an individual party member in Plauen i.V., but branches were soon established throughout the Reich. In Hanover the foundation meeting was held on 4 December.[6] The organizers contrasted the department stores with their 'exaggerated window displays', hairdressing salons, escalators, kindergartens, etc., with the 'German creative *Mittelstand* split up in countless separate groups and branches with, in many cases, Jews at the head of its organizations, Jews who are relations of the department store kings, its mortal enemies'.[7] Not disunity, but amalgamation was necessary, they urged. 'Every worker is prepared to fight for his bread, only the German *Mittelstand* feebly allows its neck to be broken.' The aims of the organization were: to fight against trusts, department stores and consumer co-operatives; the exclusion of Jews and foreigners from public life; the ending of extortionate bank interest rates; a change in the tax system; and the creation of an Economic Parliament. Membership was open both to *Mittelstand* organizations and to individuals.

Finally, the NSDAP did not neglect the 'new' *Mittelstand* of white-collar workers. An article in the *Niedersächsischer Beobachter* drew attention to the factors responsible for the discontentment of this

---

[1] Report of the Hanover political police, 1–31 Jan. 1928, in NSAS G III b 3 Heft III.

[2] Dincklage to Keyser, 16 Jan. 1928, NSAH Hann. Des. 310 I A, Nr. 20.

[3] Osnabrück police report in NSAOsn. Rep. 166 acc 7/43, Nr. 1235, vol. III.

[4] See the article 'Mittelstand auf falscher Bahn' in *NB*, 3 Apr. 1929.

[5] See Mittelungen der Landespolizeistelle Berlin, 15 Mar. 1930, in NSAH Hann. Des. 80 Hann. II, Nr. 771.   [6] *NB*, 7 Dec. 1929.

[7] The 1930 special election number of the *NB* contained a list of Jews in official positions in the Hanover *Mittelstand* organizations.

group.[1] In the first place, the author objected to the loss of the colonies and the effect of Germany's reduced role in the world on the prestige and opportunities for German businessmen. Secondly, in his view, the introduction by the 'Marxists' after the war of the tariff system to cover the salaries of white-collar workers had undermined the 'principle of performance' (*Leistungsprinzip*) and proletarianized German office workers. 'Today it has reached the point where the labourer earns as much as the brain worker.' Thirdly, he objected to the increasing rationalization and mechanization of office work which was making white-collar workers redundant. This was made worse by the increasing employment of women, many of whom—such as civil servants' daughters—had no need of a job. He quoted a figure of 5,837 unemployed male white-collar workers in Lower Saxony. The NSDAP with its extreme nationalism, its contrast between 'personality' and 'the masses', its opposition to the political representatives of the working class without at the same time being reactionary, its anti-Semitism (in this case a form of *Mittelstand* socialism), and its anti-feminism, satisfied both the aspirations and resentments of this class. In his letter to Stöhr of 14 December 1927, Dincklage had drawn attention to the anti-Semitic attitude of the DHV.[2] Now, at a meeting of the North-West *Gau* of the DHV in June 1929, the NSDAP members agreed to form NSDAP groups within the DHV throughout the *Gau* with which to exert pressure on the leadership of the union.[3] The NSDAP was also increasing its support among civil servants. In the summer of 1929, for example, the Wilhelmshaven police reported the existence of a 'National Socialist Civil Service Protection League'.[4]

(iii) *Local government—the NSDAP in opposition*

In October 1929 the Wesermünde police drew attention to the growing support for the NSDAP: 'Their main support comes from peasants and the *Mittelstand*. They are clever at exploiting the crisis of the rural population and the *Mittelstand* for their own interests', and the report continued, 'it may be expected that above all the DNVP and the other representatives of agriculture will lose a large number of votes to the NSDAP'.[5]

This report was written just before the Prussian provincial Diet and local government elections in November 1929. It was the first time the NSDAP had seriously campaigned over a wide front in local elections. The results were a marked improvement on those of the 1928 *Reichstag* election, though not as impressive as those of September

[1] *NB*, 7 Aug. 1929.   [2] See p. 105 above.
[3] Oldenburg police report, 4 Jan. 1930, in NSAO 136, Nr. 2858.
[4] Report of 1 July 1929, in NSAA Rep. 21a, Nr. 9573, Bd. 2.
[5] In NSAS Rep. 80 P 747.

1930. The party succeeded in winning eight seats in the Hanover provincial Diet and it was significant that of these eight members five were peasants.[1] In the town and county council elections the pattern was varied. In the Göttingen city council election, for example, they won eight seats, in Goslar six seats and in Hameln only two.[2]

The NSDAP local government campaign coincided with, indeed exploited, a development within local government of considerable significance—the discrediting of the local bourgeois establishment at a time of growing crisis. The revolution of 1918 had resulted in the abolition of the three-class franchise in Prussia and other restrictions elsewhere, and thereby enabled sections of the community whose demands had hitherto been frustrated by the ruling oligarchy of wealthy citizens to exercise influence through the ballot.[3] The first party to take real advantage of this opportunity was the SPD. The SPD, however, effectively limited itself to championing the claims of the working class and therefore failed to satisfy the claims of the petty bourgeoisie who were now entitled to vote. During the post-war period the bourgeoisie split its local government vote not only between the major bourgeois parties—the DNVP, DVP and DDP, but also among a number of special interest groups—the House and Real Estate Owners' Association, the Tenants' League, the Pensioners' League, the Civil Servants' List etcetera. The presence of the powerful and well-organized SPD, however, forced these parties and groups to unite in some form or other both for electoral purposes and to maximize their influence within the Council chamber. But these 'Bürger blocks' and 'United Bourgeois Lists' were uneasy alliances, combining as they did a wide spectrum of political opinions and economic interests. Moreover, they invariably excluded a number of bourgeois groups and tended to be dominated by the upper middle class.

With the growing crisis in local government which began in 1929, the bourgeoisie became increasingly discontented with the effectiveness of its representatives. In the towns where the bourgeoisie were in power they were forced to introduce measures to deal with the situation which adversely affected bourgeois interests, thereby alienating their own supporters. In towns where the SPD was in control it would have fewer scruples about introducing measures which hurt middle class interests, and in this case the bourgeois element clamoured for more effective representation than could be provided by the mutually hostile parties and fragile alliances of previous years.

[1] Hanover to Richter–Dögerode, 25 Nov. 1929, NSAH Hann. Des. 310 I A, Nr. 27.

[2] See correspondence in NSAH Hann. Des. 310 I A, Nrs. 27 and 28.

[3] See the study of this process in a West German village in G. Wurzbacher and Renate Pflaum, *Das Dorf im Spannungsfeld industrieller Entwicklung* (Stuttgart, 1954), pp. 248–50.

One can see this process, for example, in the town of Göttingen, where the NSDAP succeeded in winning its largest representation in any Council in Germany with the exception of Coburg, where it had a majority.[1] During 1929 the town had begun to experience an economic crisis. The causes were similar to those elsewhere—a burden of debt partly owing to rather extravagant public building in the years 1925–9, declining receipts from taxes and increasing responsibilities with the growth of unemployment. There was a deficit of RM 295,000 for the previous year which had to be met. On 25 August, the *Oberbürgermeister* in a long budget speech pointed out that there were three main sources of income for the city: contributions from the Prussian state taxes, profits from the municipal enterprises such as gas and electricity, and local taxes, and the only possibility of increasing revenue was from the last of these.[2] Contributions from the Prussian treasury were declining, while an attempt to increase the price of gas and electricity would be counterproductive owing to an inevitable cut in consumption. The *Oberbürgermeister*, therefore, suggested a 100 per cent increase in the trade tax (*Gewerbesteuer*) affecting local businesses and an increase of 50 per cent in the real estate tax. With the exception of the DDP, this proposal met with strong opposition from the bourgeois groups on the Council and was defeated. The DNVP, DVP and DHP groups all proposed in place of the increase in the trade tax, which was extremely unpopular among the business community, first, an increase of 100 per cent in the real estate tax which could be paid for by an increase in rents—thus hitting the whole population of the town, and secondly, by cuts in the administration. After five days of negotiations between the *Oberbürgermeister* and the bourgeois majority a compromise was reached whereby the increase in the trade tax was cut from 100 per cent to 50 per cent and the real estate tax was increased from 50 per cent–75 per cent.[3] Yet, although they had forced a compromise, even a 50 per cent increase in the trade tax imposed by their own representatives was sufficient to antagonize small businessmen and shopkeepers. Furthermore, the increase in the real estate tax, though it affected the supporters of the Left most acutely since they could least afford an increase in rents, was a burden on all. Such a large increase in taxation less than three months before the local elections was an unfortunate if necessary move on the part of the bourgeois parties.

In the November election the bourgeois groups saw their main danger as always coming from the Left. On 26 October, therefore, in order to maximize their strength, they formed an 'Above Party

---

[1] Rückblick auf die Geschichte der Ortsgruppe der NSDAP anlässlich des 15 jährigen Bestehens in the *GT*, 6–7 Feb. 1937.
[2] *GT*, 25 Aug. 1929.   [3] *GT*, 30 Aug. 1929.

Group' which contained the DNVP, the DVP and the DHP.[1] But this was by no means inclusive. Apart from the DDP list, there was also a pensioners' list, a civil servants' list and above all the NSDAP list. The election came at a very convenient time for the Nazi party. In the first place, it was already in the public eye as the most active participant in the campaign against the Young Plan and its association with the conservative organizations involved in the campaign helped to confirm its recent attempt to acquire a more respectable image.[2] Secondly, the Sklarek scandal, in which the Berlin SPD *Bürgermeister* had allegedly accepted a fur coat for his wife from the Sklarek brothers who were Jewish businessmen, filled the newspapers and helped to discredit existing local government administrations. Finally, the tax increases and growing economic difficulties of the *Mittelstand* offered fertile soil for propaganda, particularly against their representatives who were in power and who had allowed it to happen. On 9 November 1929, Dr. Hermann Muhs, the leading man on the NSDAP list, addressed a meeting on 'Corruption in Democracy. The Sklareks and we National Socialists'. Apart from the scandal, he attacked the Reich municipalization law of the SPD which facilitated the municipalization of private concerns, and the tax advantages given to department stores and co-operatives. Two days before the election, there was another windfall for the NSDAP in the conviction of a local *Bürgermeister* for embezzlement and fraud.[3] Finally, on the day of the election, the party published a poster appealing to 'Working people of Göttingen of all classes! Don't be led astray by anonymous lists. A Bürgerblock won't help you. Nor will a Pensioners' League or the Communists. Or Sklarek–SPD and Furcoat-Democrats. They will always betray you. But if you want Germany to rise in freedom, then vote for List Twelve of the NSDAP.'[4]

The pattern and style of the party's activity in local government was determined by its aims and by the character of its representatives. The party approached participation in local legislatures in the same way as participation in the *Reichstag*; it used these institutions not in a constructive sense, but as a means of extending its propaganda against those in power. Its candidates were required to sign a form not only declaring that they had no Jewish relations but also that they would 'always act according to the directives of the party leadership, make ruthless use of their legal immunity and energy for the propaganda

---

[1] *GT*, 27 Oct. 1929.

[2] In a report on the first campaign meeting in Göttingen the *Göttinger Tageblatt* noted with satisfaction that 'the most active in this opposition front are the National Socialists who are increasingly taking over the leadership of the great national opposition' *GT*, 28 Sept. 1929.

[3] *GT*, 16 Nov. 1929.

[4] *GT*, 17 Nov. 1929.

struggle in the country, give up half their salaries as deputies to the party, and, should they leave the NSDAP, resign their seats'.[1] Candidates for local government were required to sign a similar declaration. The aim was to win as representatives men who had an established position within the community. There was occasional tension between the local party organization and the local councillors of the party who preferred to co-operate with their bourgeois colleagues rather than pursue a radical course. In Holzminden, for example, there was friction between the district leader and the party's councillors who, by abstaining, had enabled the bourgeois group to bring in extra taxes despite a previous agreement with him to oppose the measure.[2] But this was unusual. The party in fact had difficulty in winning substantial figures as candidates and as a result they tended to be party militants.[3] They were thus predominantly young men or, at any rate, those whose experience of politics was limited to beer-hall demagogy, distributing leaflets and brawling with their opponents. 'Greenhorns' was one of the most frequent taunts of their opponents. They regarded legislative procedures with contempt. Their aim was, as one of them put it, 'to turn every council meeting into a public meeting'.[4] In the town of Hameln, for example, the young white-collar worker and newly elected Nazi councillor, Heinrich Schmidt, seriously embarrassed the rest of the council by demanding an increase in audience space. The other councillors refused until forced to yield by the public gallery.[5] The Nazi councillors brought the activism which they displayed in the streets outside into the chambers themselves. Between 14 September 1930 and 14 September 1931, for example, there were twenty-eight plenary sessions in the Brunswick *Landtag* in which there occurred 8,446 interruptions. Of these, 4,195 came from the nine Nazi members, an average of 406 each, compared with an average for all members of only 211. The Nazis were only outdone by the KPD representatives with 475 each.[6] But the tone of crude brutality which they introduced was unique.[7]

[1] Verpflichtung für die Kandidaten der Braunschweigischen Landtagswahl 1927 in NSAH Hann. Des. 310 I A, Nr. 8.

[2] Kreisleiter Holzminden to Gauleitung Hannover-Süd, 26 June 1931, NSAH Hann. Des. 310 I A, Nr. 43.

[3] Kurt Schmalz, a party leader in Brunswick complained about 'the lack of well-known personalities in the countryside'. See Schmalz, *Nationalsozialisten ringen um Braunschweig*, p. 66.

[4] Article on the Peine town council in *NB*, 25 Jan. 1929.

[5] See 'Aus dem Hamelner Stadtparlament' in *NB*, 9 Jan. 1930.

[6] *Volksfreund* (Brunswick SPD organ), 17 Oct. 1931.

[7] Examples may be seen in the vicious interruptions of the young activists, Albert Schneider from Pattensen in the Brunswick *Landtag* and Otto Herzog in the Oldenburg *Landtag*. See Brunswick Landesversammlung Verhandlungen 1930-3 and Oldenburg Landtagsverhandlungen 1931-3 in NSAO 39.

THE NSDAP'S MITTELSTAND CAMPAIGN

Nazi propaganda in local government used a number of themes which occur so frequently and so widely in Lower Saxony that they may be regarded as typical. A major aim was to discredit the 'system', in this case the local one, by showing that both the authorities and the people's representatives were either incompetent or corrupt, and that only the NSDAP was prepared to bring this to light. This campaign against extravagance and corruption and the clamour to open up local government to public accountability and overthrow the 'cliques' of reactionary *Spiesser* and SPD *Bonzen*, appealed to a bourgeoisie whose anxiety about status made them perhaps more vulnerable to stories of conspiracy and corruption. It was sometimes reinforced by actual cases of corruption such as the Sklarek scandal.

An example of this activity may be seen in the state of Brunswick. Between 1929 and 1930 the NSDAP had only one representative in the Brunswick *Landtag*, Franz Groh, and one in the City Council, Ernst Zörner. But Groh and Zörner pursued a vigorous campaign of harassing the government and city authorities on every possible occasion. In 1928, for example, Zörner had introduced a motion according to which city councillors would be prohibited from placing municipal contracts and followed this up with accusations of corruption against a number of councillors. The councillors sued for slander, but Zörner was found not guilty and, although the court declared at the same time that there was nothing wrong with the way city affairs were run, the publicity value of the affair for the party was of course considerable.[1] Meanwhile, Groh had launched an attack on the management of the Brunswick state bank, criticizing the fact that the city had disposed of its shares to the big *Commerzbank* and had thereby played into the hands of international capital.[2] This was later followed by a major campaign against the chairman of the bank, Stübben, who was accused of corruption.[3] Other examples of the party's activities were criticism of excessive expenditure on a Lessing celebration and of the fact that the *Oberbürgermeister* took a three-week holiday at Easter, although he had only recently been appointed.[4] During the same period 1928–30, the NSDAP leader in Oldenburg, Röver, who was a city councillor, waged a campaign with meetings and pamphlets against the *Oberbürgermeister* for turning the municipal power station into a private company, on the grounds both that it would result in a loss and that the shares would be acquired by international finance capital.[5] In Wesermünde

[1] *NB*, 28 May 1929.
[2] Ibid.
[3] Cf. E. A. Roloff, *Bürgertum und Nationalsozialismus 1930–1933. Braunschweig Weg ins Dritte Reich* (Hanover, 1961), p. 83.
[4] *NB*, 3 May 1930. The *NB* contains numerous examples of these tactics employed in a number of towns.
[5] See reports of the Oldenburg city police, e.g. Mar. 1928 in NSAO 136 2858.

the party was apparently successful in bringing about the conviction of an SPD *Bürgermeister* for the misuse of funds.[1] But even where they were unsuccessful in proving anything, they evidently counted on the effectiveness of the belief of 'no smoke without fire' to discredit the authorities and give themselves the reputation of courageous exposers of corruption and mismanagement.

One of the reasons why the NSDAP had gone into local government was their belief that 'the strong position of the SPD comes less from its ideological basis and more from the fact that the SPD early on seized all the positions of power in the villages and towns and, by using all its opportunities to help its supporters, keeps them loyal'.[2] One of the important areas which the SPD controlled was the Health Insurance Offices; and the NSDAP mounted a major campaign to attempt to discredit the way these were run. A special pamphlet was published with the title 'The Dangerous Policy of the Health Insurance Offices' and the party press carried frequent reports of the extravagance and corruption of the Health Insurance administration.[3]

Another favourite target of the party's local government propaganda was the municipal theatre administrations. In 1929, for example, the NSDAP representatives on the Hanover city council brought in a motion demanding a guarantee that the city theatre would resist 'moral, religious and racial corruption'.[4] A year later an article in the *Niedersächsischer Beobachter* criticized the director of the Brunswick theatre for running up a deficit and for putting on the 'Threepenny Opera' and 'Mahagonny'.[5]

The attempt to win the support of the *Mittelstand* was one of the main features of Nazi local government activity. This took two forms. In the first place, the NSDAP representatives introduced a number of motions designed to assist the *Mittelstand*. Thus they would invariably introduce a motion calling for special taxes for department stores or chain stores and for the subjection of the consumer co-operatives to the trade tax. Their attitude to the financial crisis which overtook the *Kreise* and municipalities as unemployment increased was also aimed at the *Mittelstand*. In October 1930, the Brüning government passed an emergency regulation enabling the local government authorities to increase taxation. The NSDAP strongly objected to these increases, which were often passed by bourgeois majorities. Instead of raising taxes, they insisted on economy measures, in particular the reduction in the number of local government officials and in the salaries of the

[1] Niedersachsen–Stürmer report of 5 Sept. 1931.
[2] Willikens article in *NB*, 9 Mar. 1929.
[3] E.g. reports in *NB* of 13 Apr. 1929, 4 May 1929, 5 Oct. 1929, 29 Mar. 1930.
[4] *NB*, 6 Apr. 1929.
[5] *NB*, 9 Apr. 1930.

higher officials.[1] They also maintained that the crisis was the result of reparations and the irresponsible financial policies of the 'system'.

The second form of *Mittelstand* propaganda derived from local government activity was a continual attack on the performance of its representatives. The aim was to show that the Economic Party, the DVP and the other local *Mittelstand* representatives were failing to assert its interests, either by their opposition to NSDAP motions, or by their support for the SPD, whose admitted, ideologically-based hostility to the *Mittelstand* was continually emphasized. In May 1929, for example, the *Niedersächsischer Beobachter* carried an article entitled 'The Crooked Game of the So-called Representatives of the Mittelstand'. The article described how the votes of the *Mittelstand* group in the Brunswick *Landtag*, the '*Gemeinschaft der Mitte*', had helped to save the SPD government's budget, which meant higher taxation for the *Mittelstand*, while the SPD-governed consumer co-operatives were still exempt from the trade tax. With characteristic skill the NSDAP made the group's initials GdM in future stand for '*Gefolgschaft der Marxisten*' (followers of the Marxists).

With its vicious attacks on the 'Marxists', the NSDAP actively took the lead in the class conflict at local level, a conflict which was being intensified by the depression. With this tactic the NSDAP won over a large number of the middle class who no longer felt capable of mastering the situation and feared the coming of Bolshevism.[2] The NSDAP thus established in effect another united Bourgeois Front, but with the difference that this time the old establishment had had to give up control to the petty bourgeoisie, as represented by the local leadership of the NSDAP.

(iv) *The Stadtwächter Affair*

The vulnerability of the *Mittelstand* at this period to a local government campaign composed largely of scandal and anti-Semitism is shown by a significant development which occurred in the city of Osnabrück during 1929 and 1930.[3] On 28 April 1929 a herbal doctor in Osnabrück, named Dr. Heinrich Schierbaum, founded a daily paper, the *Stadtwächter*, as a protest against the refusal of the city's press to accept notices advertising his practice. The paper became a platform for his attack on academic medicine and on the

[1] See the reports on the local government activity of the branches in their monthly propaganda reports to *Gau* head-quarters in NSAH Hann. Des. 310 I B, Nr. 9.

[2] For a study of this process see Allen, *The Nazi Seizure of Power*, p. 24.

[3] For the following see Karl Kühling, *Osnabrück 1925–1933* (Osnabrück, 1963), pp. 91 ff. The files of the *Stadtwächter* are in the Niedersächsisches Statsarchiv Osnabrück. Sammlungen B XIII 6.

authorities generally. It was characterized by cranky views and a very extreme but journalistically effective style. Typical of its contents were articles with titles such as 'A Gigantic Swindle with the Knowledge of the Reich Finance Minister' or 'Warning Notice: Experiments on Babies'. The paper began as a 'politically and confessionally neutral' organ, but it very soon took on a strong anti-Semitic bias. And although a fortnight after its founding, it described the NSDAP as 'a right-wing radical party, about whose methods one may have different opinions', in fact, articles soon began to appear signed by the NSDAP local branch, though the paper maintained its independence.

The *Stadtwächter* described itself as the organ of the *Mittelstand* and, significantly, it aimed at exactly the same targets and with the same arguments as the NSDAP. In the first place, it attacked the alleged secrecy of local government: 'Why are the citizens' affairs dealt with in so many secret sessions? Why not in open sessions? We will fight against all secret dealings.'[1] Secondly, there was a populist hostility against the Establishment: 'We want to strive to ensure that the excessive class pride, this stupid pride which is unfortunately so prevalent in our city decreases. Let us take our hats off to all who do their duty. They are just as important as the highest official, the richest patrician.'[2] Finally, individual targets were identical with those of the NSDAP: the department stores, health insurance offices, the extravagance of the administration, reparations and the iniquity of international finance capitalism. A particular target was the local housing office which was responsible for distributing rented accommodation. It was attacked for the extravagance and unfairness with which it operated and the blame was put on 'the system and on the complete failure of the so-called tenants group on the city council'.[3] The attitude of its subscribers was well expressed in the following letter to its editor: 'I have read your paper with interest, and I am convinced that with the publication of this organ you have at last made possible the enlightenment of the public about all intrigues and conspiratorial and secret dealings. We are not there simply to pay our taxes. No! We have also a right to know about all the goings on in certain circles and in government offices.'[4]

The success of the *Stadtwächter* was such that Schierbaum decided to put up a *Stadtwächter* list of candidates for the municipal election on 17 November 1929. He was only able to persuade five candidates to stand, but the *Stadtwächter* list won 5,447 votes which entitled it to seven seats on the Council. It seems clear from the votes of the other lists that the *Stadtwächter* list won its support primarily from the lower middle class non-party groups—the Tenants' Defence League,

[1] *Stadtwächter*, 17 Nov. 1929.　　[2] Ibid.
[3] *Stadtwächter*, 3 Nov. 1929.　　[4] *Stadtwächter*, 19 May 1929.

for example, lost over 5,000 votes, so that the *Stadtwächter* tenants' campaign appears to have paid off.

During 1930, the extremism and anti-Semitism of the paper increased and so did the circulation. But in September legal proceedings began against a *Stadtwächter* editor who, it was revealed, had a criminal past, and the paper was discredited. In October it began appearing only twice weekly and from then on the paper declined.

Although the NSDAP began by using the *Stadtwächter*, the decision by the paper to put up a separate list in the municipal election alienated the party and clearly cost it some votes. The NSDAP list in fact won only 1,114 votes and thereby failed to win a seat. The paper, however, continued for a time to give indirect support to the NSDAP and produced a leaflet for the 1930 *Reichstag* election urging people to support the only anti-Semitic party. Relations were finally broken off in June 1931 after the paper had begun criticizing Hitler.[1]

The *Stadtwächter* affair is important because it shows that a significant section of the electorate—predominantly tenants, artisans, small shopkeepers and clerks, to judge by the groups at which the paper was aimed—were sufficiently alienated from the bourgeois city establishment and from their own representatives[2] to prove vulnerable to a populist-type campaign based on a combination of conspiracy stories, appeals to their economic interest and resentment at the authorities expressed through a scandal sheet. This was exactly the same group to which the NSDAP appeal—couched in similar terms—was directed during these years 1928–30. And it is significant that just as the supporters of the *Stadtwächter* were non-party men, supporters of interest groups, the most alienated from the highly politicized field of post-war local government, so it was, as we shall see, to the former non-voters that the NSDAP's 1930 electoral success was most clearly attributable. In Osnabrück the *Stadtwächter* had served the useful purpose of preparing the soil from which after its demise the NSDAP could reap the fruits.

[1] See Osnabrück police report in NSAOsn. Rep. 116 acc. 7/43 1235, vol. IV.

[2] It is significant that the *Stadtwächter* list had not been recommended by the *Niedersächsischer Handwerkerbund*, the main professional body for artisans in Lower Saxony. See the *Osnabrücker Zeitung*, 16 Nov. 1929, for a list of the parties that were recommended.

VIII

DEVELOPMENTS IN ORGANIZATION
1928–1930

APART from a concentration on *Mittelstand* propaganda and the change of emphasis from urban to rural areas, the year 1928 was notable for a major reorganization of the party.[1] The *Gaue* were now reorganized so that they corresponded to the *Reichstag* electoral districts from which in future they were to take their names. The decision of whether or not to subdivide the *Gaue* into districts or *Kreis* organizations, or subdivide large branches into sections was left to individual *Gauleiter*. The minimum size of a branch was deemed to be fifteen members; a smaller group of members could form a cell, but they would be directly subordinate to the *Gau* head-quarters. It was laid down that the deputy must be confirmed by the Reich head-quarters. Further, branch leaders should be elected by acclamation at membership meetings and then be confirmed by the *Gauleiter*. A year later, however, this directive was cancelled and in future branch leaders were appointed by the *Gau* authorities directly.[2] The new directives also extended the control of the party head-quarters over disciplinary procedure. Each branch was ordered to establish a committee of investigation (Uschla) which would be subordinate in turn to the *Gau* and the Reich Uschla.[3] These committees had the function of arbitrating in the frequent conflicts between members and dealing with breaches of party discipline.

These directives were aimed both at strengthening the control of the party head-quarters and at ensuring that the party was better organized to fight *Reichstag* election campaigns. They necessitated a complete reorganization of the party in Lower Saxony. In the Weser-Ems region, the separate district within *Gau* Hanover-North which had been created the year before now became a separate '*Gau* Weser-Ems' under its leader, Röver. The new *Gau* included the city of Bremen but retained its head-quarters in Oldenburg. But while *Gau* Hanover-North lost its Weser-Ems district, at the same time it acquired the area

[1] For the following see Richtlinien für die Untergliederungen der NSDAP, 15 Sept. 1928, in National Archives T-81, Reel 164, Frames 303350.
[2] A decision of the 1929 party congress; see Maul to Klagges (district leader Harz), 4 Dec. 1929, in NSAH Hann. Des. 310 I A, Nr. 26.
[3] 'Richtlinien für den Uschla der NSDAP', ibid., frames 303395–303402.

round Göttingen which had existed as *Gau* Hanover-South and hence-forward adopted the name *Gau* Hanover-South–Brunswick, corresponding to the *Reichstag* electoral district of the same name. From now on therefore the NSDAP in Lower Saxony was divided into three *Gaue*: Hanover-South–Brunswick, covering the states of Schaumburg-Lippe,[1] and Brunswick, and the Prussian districts of Hanover and Hildesheim; *Gau* Hanover-East covering the Prussian districts of Lüneburg and Stade; and *Gau* Weser-Ems covering the state of Oldenburg, the city of Bremen, and the Prussian districts of Aurich and Osnabrück.

The reorganization of the party following the directives of September 1928 was continued in 1929 and given increasing importance. In the words of the secretary of *Gau* Hanover-South: 'Hitherto we have emphasized propaganda work. This will also happen in the future; but at the same time, from now on we will have to devote the same attention to organization, otherwise the propaganda is wasted.'[2] The party went back to its original district (*Bezirk*) system of organization. *Gau* South-Hanover–Brunswick, for example, was divided into fifteen districts; and the district leaders were responsible to the *Gauleiter* for party work in their area, though the branches still dealt directly with the *Gau* head-quarters. These district leaders were invariably men who had joined the party shortly after its refounding in 1925 and had already proved themselves as branch leaders. They were financed by collections. At the end of 1929, however, a new network of smaller *Kreis* organizations modelled on the existing official administrative division began to be introduced between the local branches and the district leaders with the aim of eventually replacing the latter.[3] This encouragement of smaller organizations was an important aspect of the party's organization. The NSDAP believed in granting independence to its smallest units as soon as possible on the grounds that 'a smaller group which must work independently and on its own responsibility inevitably develops much greater activity than if it is directly dependent on another branch'.[4] The *Gau* head-quarters rewarded the efficient branches by assigning to them the most popular speakers. This was important in view of the tremendous competition among the branches to get the 'big guns' of the party to speak in their district.[5]

One stimulus for these organizational developments was the rise in membership figures which began in 1928. By 31 December 1928

[1] In Jan. 1931, Schaumburg-Lippe was reapportioned to *Gau* Westphalia-North.
[2] Hanover to Richter, branch leader in Dögerode, 27 Dec. 1929, NSAH Hann. Des. 310 I A, Nr. 27.
[3] Richtlinien für die Ortsgruppen und Stützpunkte des Gaues H-S-B, 1 Jan. 1930, NSAH Hann. Des. 310 I E, Nr. 30.
[4] Maul (*Gau* secretary S-H-B) to Lehre branch, 28 Mar. 1930, NSAH Hann. Des. 310 I A, Nr. 80.   [5] See footnote 3 above.

Gau South-Hanover–Brunswick had a membership of 2,268 compared with 1,761 in January.[1] But the figures were distorted by the reorganization and the real increase was more like 1,000 members. By 31 May 1929, the last figure we have, the *Gau* had 3,210 members, an increase of 1,000 in five months. And apparently, at the end of the year, applications to join were coming in at the rate of 500 a month.[2] The same development was occurring in Weser-Ems. Between January and August 1928 the Weser-Ems district increased its membership from 150 to 800.[3]

Who were these members of the party who joined before the *Reichstag* election of 1930?[4] In the predominantly agricultural *Gaue* of Weser-Ems and Hanover-East peasants formed the largest occupational group with 27 per cent and 30 per cent respectively, with larger peasants predominating in Hanover-East and smaller peasants in Weser-Ems. Next came workers from both industry and agriculture with 22 per cent in Weser-Ems and 20 per cent in Hanover-East. These were closely followed by the self-employed (artisans, shopkeepers and small businessmen and the professions) with 18 per cent and 19 per cent respectively. White collar workers formed 18 per cent of the membership in Weser-Ems and 14 per cent in Hanover-East. The residue was formed by civil servants (4 per cent) and others (7–8 per cent). In the more industrial *Gau* Hanover-South–Brunswick a smaller proportion of the membership were peasants (20·7 per cent) and the membership was split fairly evenly between the self-employed (22 per cent), the workers (21 per cent) and the white-collar workers (20 per cent). The residue was again made up of civil servants (5 per cent) and others (9 per cent). Two thirds of the membership during these years was under forty, with slightly more falling in the age group twenty-one–thirty than the group thirty-one–forty; 37 per cent of the members were ex-servicemen.

These membership figures confirm what has been suggested above, namely that up to 1930 what success the party had had was based primarily on the support of some members of the younger generation of the *Mittelstand*—peasants, artisans, shopkeepers and small businessmen and white-collar workers.

In November 1929 the DNVP *Kreisleiter* in Bersenbrück complained to his *Landesverband* in Osnabrück that 'the National Socialists are making big gains in this *Kreis* because they hold meetings with

[1] Mitgliederstand 1927–9 NSAH Hann. Des. 310 I A, Nrs. 19 and 24.
[2] Maul to Kerrl, branch leader in Peine NSAH Hann. Des. 310 B, Nr. 4.
[3] Oldenburg to Hanover, 18 Aug. 1928, NSAH Hann. Des. 310 I A, Nr. 22.
[4] By 14 June 1930, membership figures had reached 5,562 in *Gau* Hanover-South, 3,552 in *Gau* Weser-Ems, and 2,296 in Hanover-East. It is to these members that the following statistics are applicable. See *Parteistatistik*, Stand 1 Jan. 1935. Herausgeber, Der Reichsorganisationsleiter der NSDAP, Bd I, pp. 86 ff.

good speakers in almost every village'.[1] Phenomenal propaganda activity continued to be the most striking feature of the NSDAP. In the last four weeks of 1928 and the first four weeks of 1929, for example, 160 meetings were held in *Gau* Weser-Ems, excluding the routine weekly branch meetings.[2] The other *Gaue* showed similar activity. From 3–31 May 1929, for example, two of the main speakers in Hanover-East, Hölzke and Lütt, addressed forty-six meetings between them.[3] It should be emphasized that these were normal periods —there was no election in the offing. In the autumn of 1929 *Gau* South-Hanover–Brunswick introduced a new propaganda technique, whereby all the leading speakers of the *Gau* would descend on a single *Kreis* over the week-end and hold six meetings each. On 8–9 February 1930, for example, twenty-four meetings were held in the Göttingen area in twenty-eight hours with a total audience of 1,500. As a result four new branches and nineteen cells were founded and 150 new subscribers won for the *Niedersächsischer Beobachter*.[4] Most of the burden of speaking in public meetings at this period fell on relatively few speakers within a *Gau*. For this reason, in June 1929, the party started its own school for speakers in Herrsching am Ammersee and *Gauleiter* were ordered to encourage suitable members to attend the course.[5] For the majority who could not afford to attend, Fritz Reinhardt, the director of the school, sent out material for speakers every fortnight. Branches also began holding their own 'training courses' to educate their members in Nazi ideology.[6]

But activism was not limited to the speakers; it was also demonstrated by the SA men who distributed propaganda or undertook frequent marches, 'mostly young people, under twenty-five, who devote themselves with real fanaticism to the efforts of the party'.[7] This aspect of 'fanaticism' is of crucial importance in understanding the NSDAP of the *Kampfzeit*. Here were young peasants, artisans, apprentices and white-collar workers with no previous political experience, who in normal circumstances would be unlikely to have participated in politics, suddenly devoting all their spare time and often travelling some distance in order to take part in party activities. One SA man described the effect on him after joining the SA group in Harzburg as follows:

[1] NSAOsn. Erwerbung II, No. 74.
[2] 'Unser Vormarsch in Gau Weser-Ems' in *NS*, 2 Feb. 1929.
[3] *NS*, 24 May 1929.
[4] 'Grosspropaganda im Bezirk Göttingen, 12 Feb. 1930', in NSAH Hann. Des. 310 I B, 43.
[5] Reichspropagandaabteilung München Rundschreiben, 6 May 1929, gez. Himmler NSAH Hann. Des. 310 I A, Nr. 24.
[6] E.g. in Osnabrück in Jan. 1929, see police report NSAOsn. Rep. 116, acc 7/43, Nr. 1235, vol. II.
[7] Oct. 1929, report of the Wesermünde political police in NSAS Rep. 80, p. 747.

Now a completely new life began for me. There was only one thing in the world for me and that was service in the movement. All my thoughts were devoted to the movement. I could only talk about politics. I didn't know anything else any more. At that time I was a promising sportsman and was very fond of sport which was going to be my career. But I had to give this up as well. The only thing I was interested in was agitation and propaganda.[1]

The party also increased the activism of its members by financial and other incentives. By laying down a fee of RM 7 per speech, together with free board and lodging and travel, members were encouraged to become speakers and to make as many speeches as possible.[2] As unemployment increased this was to become increasingly important since for many members their income from public speaking became their only means of support. For example, in May 1932 after the tremendous efforts of the presidential campaigns and the Prussian Diet election, the party justified its continuation of the propaganda drive because of the need 'to employ those *Gau* speakers who, because of their activity for the party have lost their jobs. . . . We must keep them going so that they are ready for the next election.'[3] By then there were thirty-two such unemployed speakers in *Gau* Hanover-South–Brunswick alone. The fact that an entrance fee was charged was also an incentive for branch leaders to ensure that their meetings were organized efficiently with adequate advance propaganda. The financial incentives were not limited to meetings. At the beginning of 1930, for example, *Gau* Hanover-South–Brunswick began a campaign to sell the *Niedersachsischer Beobachter* and offered a prize of a holiday in the Alps for the largest number of new subscriptions. It was won by Blankemeyer with 600 new orders.[4]

The problem of finance remained serious during this period 1928–30. The increase in the membership fee and introduction of an election contribution at the end of 1927 had aroused strong protests from the membership and it was not always possible to enforce it.[5] The election campaign of 1928 plunged *Gau* Hanover-South–Brunswick once more into debt and the Reich head-quarters was once more forced to waive arrears, this time over 700 RM, and Rust was compelled to promise to set up a special check to ensure that expenditure did not

[1] Geschichte der Ortsgruppe Harlingerode/Bad Harzburg NSAH Hann. Des. 310 I A, Nr. 69.

[2] The fee was laid down in Richtlinien für die Ortsgruppen und Stützpunkte des Gaues Hanover-Süd–Braunchsweig, 1 Jan. 1930, NSAH Hann. Des. 310 I E, Nr. 30.

[3] Gaupropagandaleitung Süd-Hannover–Braunschweig Monatliches Rundschreiben, 24 May 1932, NSAH Hann. Des. 310 I E, Nr. 30.

[4] Gaupropagandaleitung Hannover-Süd–Braunschweig Rundschreiben, Jan. 1930, NSAH Hann. Des. 310 I B, Nr. 4.

[5] Könnecke-Braunschweig to Hanover, 8 Jan. 1928, NSAH Hann. Des. 310 I A, Nr. 18.

exceed income and that the Reich head-quarters received its contributions (increased to 30 pf per member in 1929 at the expense of the *Gau*
and local branches) as a matter of priority.[1] A speech by Hitler in
Hanover in January 1929 helped out by producing a profit of RM
1500.[2] But in November 1929 the *Gau* was still in difficulties; and the
party was forced to found another 'subscribers' club' for sympathizers.[3]

These financial difficulties were shared by its main bourgeois rivals
—the DVP and DNVP.[4] But with these parties financial difficulties
were both a symptom and a cause of more fundamental weaknesses in
organization. They were suffering from the effects of participation in
government in terms both of disillusioned supporters and splits within
the party. The DNVP, during the period 1925–8 at any rate, was
affected by 'a general weariness'. Its machine 'worked ponderously
and functioned inadequately'; its members lacked idealism and were
not prepared to make sacrifices or play an active role in party activities.
Furthermore, the organization was bedevilled by decentralization and
lack of discipline on the part of the lower echelons. For example, they
overwhelmed the party head-quarters in Berlin with mail, completely
bypassing the intermediate party authorities. The result was that letters were not answered and consequently the branches felt neglected.
Regional organizations often refused to supply the party head-quarters
with speakers for election propaganda in other areas and also felt free
to make public declarations which contradicted the party line.

The DVP was also in difficulties. Thus the attempt on the part of
the Brunswick *Landesverband* of the DVP to 'put new drive into the
membership, so that there were no longer more people who died off
than who joined, was defeated by the general discontent and the fact
that they wanted new aims for which they could work with renewed
energy'.[5] Moreover, in some areas the NSDAP was already calling
the tune. A report of a DVP meeting in the village of Schandelah near
Brunswick at the end of April 1928 throws an interesting light on the
deterioration in the party's position and on Nazi tactics.[6] According to
the speaker, despite the distribution of 200 invitations to the meeting

[1] Rust to Schwarz, 29 Apr. 1929, NSAH Hann. Des. 310 I A, Nr. 24.

[2] Rechnung für die Hitlerversammlung, 28 Jan. 1929, NSAH Hann. Des. 310
I A, Nr. 25.

[3] Abteilung Opferring Rundschreiben an alle Ortsgruppen, 1 Nov. 1929,
NSAH Hann. Des. 310 I E, Nr. 30.

[4] For the following see U. Schelm-Spangenberg, *Die Deutsche Volkspartei im
Lande Braunschweig* (Braunschweig, 1964), pp. 106 ff. and M. Dörr, *Die Deutschnationale Volkspartei 1925–1928* (Diss., Marburg, 1964), pp. 431 ff.

[5] A remark of the DVP secretary in Brunswick, Bretschneider, quoted in
Schelm-Spangenberg, op. cit., p. 118.

[6] In SAB GX 6, Nr. 1031.

only twelve people had turned up and all were members of the NSDAP. 'It was', wrote the speaker, 'the most unedifying meeting that I have ever experienced because every time I began to speak someone interrupted me. The meeting became quite excited because I lost my temper and accused them of having the manners of Jews. There wasn't a single person there from our lot—they are scared of the national socialist methods.' Schandelah was one of five villages in the rural *Kreis* of Brunswick in which the NSDAP had won the largest number of votes in the 1928 *Reichstag* election; and there were eighteen out of seventy-nine villages in which they were the largest party with the exception of the SPD.[1]

Compared with the bourgeois parties, the NSDAP had enthusiasm and by 1930 it was beginning to acquire an effective administrative machine. The local branches communicated only with their *Kreis* or *Gau* head-quarters; and the *Gau* head-quarters were obliged to put their speakers at the disposal of the Reich head-quarters at every general and state election, to be used to the best advantage. Branches were occasionally paralysed by internal conflict and cases of embezzlement or sheer financial incompetence were not infrequent, but on the whole the party administration operated fairly effectively. Comparing the NSDAP in this connexion with other Right radical movements, it is clear that the party's achievement in combining a charismatic type relationship between leader and follower with a bureaucratic structure was of crucial importance to its success. A student of the extreme Right in America during the 1940s and early 1950s, for example noted that 'their local followership and indeed even their remote followership have been based largely on a direct unilateral personal relationship between the leader and the group' and attributed their failure to the fact that there was 'no hierarchical structure of the sort which is absolutely necessary if the actions of large numbers of people are to be co-ordinated. Public meetings are often conducted in an informal unplanned manner'.[2] The NSDAP by contrast was able to rely on a large number of petty functionaries who were eager to carry out the relatively simple bureaucratic routines necessary for the functioning of an increasingly complex organization.

Furthermore, unlike its rivals, the NSDAP never allowed financial difficulties to cripple its propaganda which, in *Gau* Hanover-South–Brunswick, expanded not only in extent but also in range. The *Gaue* Weser-Ems and Hanover-East were less developed in terms of organization, but extremely active among an increasingly sympathetic rural

[1] Election figures for Braunschweig-Land in NSAW 126 Neu vorl., Nr. 6367.
[2] Cf. E. A. Shils: 'Authoritarianism "Right" and "Left"' in R. Christie and M. Jahoda, eds., *Studies in the Scope and Method of 'The Authoritarian Personality'* (Glencoe, Ill., 1954), pp. 42–9.

population. By 1930, the party in *Gau* Hanover-South–Brunswick had built up a corps of speakers with which it could appeal to almost any type of audience. Apart from the numerous good *Mittelstand* speakers—peasants, artisans, white-collar workers, and even a few civil servants who braved the threat of disciplinary action, the party had also gained an important new recruit in Berthold Karwahne, formerly a leading member of the KPD, who from now on played a key role in the renewed attempt to win over the workers.[1] In May, a *Gau* propaganda director was appointed; and another innovation introduced during 1930 helped the party to exploit its varied propaganda talent to the full and is a good illustration of the efficiency of the propaganda machine even before the party became a mass movement: standard application forms were printed for requesting speakers, in which branches had to state whether they wished the speaker to address 'an area with a predominantly peasant population' or 'an area with a strongly Marxist population', thereby enabling head-quarters to use its speakers with maximum efficiency.[2] Furthermore, the party had begun to widen the scope of its propaganda to include the performance of plays, films and special 'Hermann Löns evenings', 'to catch those who are impossible to win with political meetings'.[3] Löns was a popular poet of the Lüneburg Heath. The evenings were organized by his brother, who was a member of the NSDAP, and they were apparently very successful.

[1] Personal file BDC.
[2] Redner-Anforderungsformulare in NSAH Hann. Des. 310 I B, Nr. 4.
[3] See Richtlinien für Hermann Löns Abende NSAH Hann. Des. 310 I B, Nr. 4.

IX

THE REICHSTAG ELECTION OF
14 SEPTEMBER 1930

(i) *The 1929 Young Plan Plebiscite*

URING 1929, the party's main propaganda effort occurred
during the autumn and winter months when the Prussian
Diet and local government elections coincided with the plebiscite against the Young Plan. Propaganda against the Young Plan was
undertaken under the combined auspices of the DNVP, the *Stahlhelm*, the *Landbund* and the NSDAP. While the campaign was financed by the DNVP, it is clear from the police reports that most of the
actual propaganda work was carried out by the *Stahlhelm* and the
NSDAP, with important help in agricultural areas from the *Landbund*. The NSDAP met complaints from its members about its willingness to co-operate with these groups with a promise that 'our
struggle against the DNVP will not ease off one bit'.[1] And in fact the
party did keep its co-operation with the plebiscite committees to a
minimum. Reporting on the considerable propaganda activity of the
NSDAP during October 1929, for example, the Osnabrück police
emphasized that the party had 'concentrated more on winning party
members than on the plebiscite. The committee members of the
NSDAP have not attended any committee meetings during the last
few weeks'.[2] The plebiscite was a failure in Lower Saxony as elsewhere. But compared with the Reich average of 13·8 per cent, the
19·3 per cent participation in Lower Saxony represented a considerable
success.[3] The districts of Stade with 29·2 per cent, Aurich with 29·9
per cent, the state of Oldenburg with 25 per cent and the district of
Lüneburg with 23·5 per cent were particularly remarkable as evidence
of right-wing discontent. It had already been remarked that the vague
völkisch propaganda undertaken by the *Stahlhelm* during the previous
years had provided fertile soil for Nazi political propaganda.[4] The

[1] Hanover to Elligsen–Stöckheim, 25 July 1929, NSAH Hann. Des. 310 I A,
Nr. 29.
[2] Report of Osnabrück police, 28 Oct. 1929, NAOsn. Rep. 116, acc. 7/43, No.
1235, vol. II.
[3] Figures for the plebiscite in Franz, *Die Politischen Wahlen in Niedersachsen
1867 bid 1949*, p. 58.
[4] By the Brunswick SPD after the 1928 election, cf. Schelm-Spangenberg, op.
cit., p. 114.

same thing was now true of the plebiscite. In the first place, the plebiscite had helped to persuade the peasantry that a relationship existed between the international position of Germany—the 'tribute payments' and the domestic situation. From now on, the deteriorating economic situation appeared to give renewed proof of the correctness of this analysis. The NSDAP was in a far better position to exploit this development than its rivals because the attack on the Dawes Plan had formed one of its main propaganda themes since 1924, whereas half the DNVP had voted for the Plan and since then, in its attempts to join a government, the party had apparently shown itself ready to accept the basis of Stresemann's foreign policy.[1] Secondly, the alliance of the NSDAP with the leading conservative groups not only helped to define the party in the public mind as a serious proposition, but also helped to remove the 'labour' image which the party had so assiduously cultivated between 1925 and 1928, but which had now become a serious barrier in its recent attempts to win over the *Mittelstand*.[2]

(ii) *The Reichstag Election Campaign*

For the *Reichstag* election of September 1930 the party's propaganda throughout the Reich was centrally directed from Munich by Goebbels, the propaganda chief. This central direction applied not only to general themes, but also to details such as the provision of a choice of draft standard pamphlets and posters. The campaign began from where the anti-Young Plan plebiscite had left off. It was fought under the slogan—'For or Against Young' and the *Gaue* were instructed to ensure that 'the acceptance of the Young Plan and the resulting economic collapse is continually emphasized'.[3] The attitude to be adopted to the various parties was also laid down by Goebbels in a series of memoranda and, since these provided the foundation for much of the campaign, it may be worth examining them in some detail.[4]

(1) *The DNVP.* The attack was concentrated on the opponents of the Hugenberg wing and it was emphasized that the collapse of the party was inevitable. Significantly, Goebbels insisted that 'for tactical reasons' Hugenberg should not be attacked personally, but the Hugen-

[1] Cf. Dörr, op. cit., p. 251.

[2] The opponents of the NSDAP made great capital out of this, e.g. a branch leader complained that the *Landvolk* party was alleging that 'we wanted to socialize everything like the SPD and were really a "workers' party"'. Richter-Dögerode to Hanover, 21 Nov. 1929, NSAH Hann. Des. 310 I A, Nr. 27.

[3] Rundschreiben of Gau Gross–Berlin Propagandaabteilung, 5 Aug. 1930, copy in Mitteilungen der Landeskriminalpolizeistelle Berlin NSAH Hann. Des. 80 Hann II, Nr. 846.

[4] See Reichspropagandaabteilung Monatliche Rundschreiben, June–July 1930, gez. Goebbels NSAH Hann. Des. 310 I B, Nr. 1.

berg group should be described as 'capitalist' in contrast to the 'social-ist' NSDAP.

(2) *The DVP.* The DVP was described as 'the faithful valet of the SPD which in the last few months has attempted to shift the burdens resulting from its "Fulfilment policy" onto the shoulders of the broad masses'. 'It must be ruthlessly moved from the battlefield if the main confrontation between National Socialism and Marxism is to take place.'

(3) *The Economic Party.* It was accused of becoming a 'Young Party' through its participation in the Brüning government and had thereby betrayed the interests of the *Mittelstand.* The previous *Mittelstand* propaganda line of the need for a change in the political situation if the economic situation was to improve was also emphasized.

(4) *The Landbund.* The *Landbund* was accused of treason to the national idea through its co-operation with the 'Young government', and its agrarian programme and plan to help East German agriculture were described as 'miserable'. It was compared to the trade unions as a '*Bonzenapparat*' which had an interest in making the crisis permanent in order to prove its own importance.

(5) *The SPD.* The SPD was attacked on two fronts: first, on the grounds of the contrast between its foreign policy promises and ex-pectations (a reasonable peace, fraternity and humanity) and the facts of the post-war period (the squandering of German hard work and the pawning of German bread). Secondly, it was attacked on the grounds that it had destroyed the so-called gains of the revolution because of its support for deflation, and had failed completely to solve the unemploy-ment and housing questions.

(6) *The Guelph Party.* The attitude to be adopted towards the Guelph party was not included in these memoranda of Goebbels, be-cause of course it was peculiar to Lower Saxony. Since the failure of its referendum in 1924, the Guelph party, despite desperate efforts to retain the support of its *Mittelstand* base, had been unable to avoid a steady decline.[1] In the 1928 election it had succeeded in regaining a little of the ground lost in December 1924 in its main centres—Lüneburg and Stade—but its over-all vote in the province of Hanover declined from 16 per cent to 11·4 per cent.[2] By 1930 the party was in a serious situation. Its financial position was precarious and on 20 April its main organ, the *Hannoversche Landeszeitung* was forced to cease publica-tion.[3] There were a number of reasons for this.[4] In the first place, ever

[1] The party created a number of economic committees to press the interests of the *Mittelstand*, see Hanover police report, Feb. 1927, NSAS G III 103.

[2] Franz, op. cit., p. 50.

[3] Prilop, *Die Vorabstimmung in Hannover 1924*, p. 352.   [4] Ibid., pp. 351 ff.

since 1918 the party had been split on the one hand between those who clung to its monarchist traditions and those who wished to come to terms with the new Republic and merely press for greater autonomy within it; on the other hand, between a 'radical' wing which wished to win support from workers, settlers and small tenant farmers and a 'moderate' wing which aligned itself with the DNVP. While the first conflict remained undecided, the second conflict was won by the 'moderates' with the result that the image of the party became blurred and indistinguishable from the DNVP. Hence voters switched to the larger and more effective party.

Secondly, the party failed to attract young people. An attempt was made to exploit the general post-war trend towards paramilitary organizations with the foundation of the 'moderate' *Deutsche Legion* and the 'radical' *Grossdeutscher Orden Heinrich der Löwe*, which had some success, particularly in rural areas. But the Guelph ideology of an archaic, rural conservatism failed to attract a young generation whose conservatism, after the experience of war and revolution, was of a revolutionary rather than a reactionary nature.

Finally, and most important of all, the economic crisis demonstrated with devastating force the irrelevance of the Guelph programme to the problems of the *Mittelstand*. After the revolution the *Mittelstand* had voted Guelph in large numbers because of a belief that an independent Hanover would offer a framework in which their problems could be solved more easily. The failure of the referendum in 1924 had shown the impossibility of independence in the near future and therefore removed the *raison d'être* of the party. Faced now with urgent problems the *Mittelstand* looked elsewhere for salvation—to a party which not only understood their problems but which also, because it was not limited to one province, offered the possibility of solving them effectively at Reich level, where experience had shown that real power lay. To a group which was breaking with long-standing political ties, a completely new party was more attractive than parties which had previously been rivals and which had also shown no success in solving problems. This factor applied also to those breaking their long tradition of Liberalism owing to disillusionment and anxiety. In its propaganda the NSDAP emphasized this theme of the irrelevance of the Guelphs to the contemporary situation, while at the same time paying lip-service to the sentiments of local loyalty and tradition which remained strong among the rural population. As the *Niedersachsen-Stürmer* put it,

The NSDAP is aware of the injustice of 1866 and is also in favour of a greater Germany. But in the present crisis of the Fatherland it is not important to accept the wishes of small parties. Instead we must defend ourselves in a united front against the present system of robbery.[1]

[1] Quoted in Prilop, op. cit., p. 358.

Apart from specific attacks on its opponents, the NSDAP could also reap the benefit of its previous prophecies of economic crisis. At the beginning of 1929, for example, the *Niedersächsischer Beobachter* in a headline had prophesied with uncanny accuracy:

1929, the last step towards chaos. The index of economic prosperity, Parker Gilbert's Yearly Report, i.e. the basis for a more ruthless reparations *diktat*. In depression and sharper social and political conflicts the German people is beginning the crisis year 1929, a year which will have much similarity with the terrible times of the year 1923.[1]

Their prophecy had been fulfilled and, as the economic situation deteriorated, the party exploited its advantage to the full.[2] During 1929, the price of pork remained stable, but the price of beef was depressed owing to foreign competition.[3] Between December 1929 and January 1930, the price of butter collapsed as Denmark flooded the market and increasing unemployment in the cities cut consumption. In April and May 1930 the price of milk and eggs fell and the price of pork plunged disastrously. The *Niedersachsen-Stürmer* forecast that 'it will not be possible to halt the decline in the price of pork because there is over-production and, owing to the trade treaty with Poland, a million live and dead pigs will be imported'.[4] In August and September, the harvest was devastated by atrocious weather, and a plague of mice affected grazing so badly that peasants were forced to sell their livestock before they had been fattened, with a corresponding loss.

It is perhaps easy to overestimate the effectiveness of the NSDAP campaign by judging it simply on the basis of Nazi correspondence. The party was still comparatively small in terms of membership and there were many areas where it possessed only a skeleton organization. Nevertheless, many observers agreed that of all the parties the NSDAP had shown the greatest activity.[5] And the directives from *Gau* Hanover-South–Brunswick give the impression of a formidable propaganda machine and a campaign of exceptional skill. The NSDAP in fact had the advantage that it could simply increase the tempo of its already well-oiled machine, while the other bourgeois parties had to improvise a campaign specifically for the election.

---

[1] *NB*, 5 Jan. 1929.

[2] *Schadenfreude* at the contrast between Stresemann's vision of a 'silver lining' and the actual course of events was much in evidence in Nazi propaganda.

[3] See Berichte der Landwirtschaftskammer Oldenburg 1929–30 in NSAO 136 151–37 II.

[4] *NS*, 4 May 1930.

[5] The local police observers held this view. See the reports referred to above. From 15 Aug. to 14 Sept., the NSDAP in *Gau* Hanover-South–Brunswick held between 300 and 400 meetings a week, in all approximately 1,500, including two torchlight parades through the city of Hanover with 2–2,500 people. See *NB*, 20 Sept. 1930.

The first directive to the branches relating to the election went out on 25 July.[1] It fixed the beginning of the campaign for 15 August and laid down that from then on the *Gau* would control the use of speakers centrally. Branches were expected to have ordered their speakers by 2 August on a special form and the same deadline was fixed for the submission of candidates by the *Kreisleiter*, candidates whose relative merits would be decided by the *Gau* head-quarters, and who would then be submitted to Reich head-quarters for approval. Branch leaders were ordered to equip themselves with a new brochure produced by Reich head-quarters entitled 'Modern Political Propaganda' and were threatened with dismissal if they published pamphlets without approval from the *Gau*. From then on each week the *Gau* propaganda department sent out a detailed directive to all branches.[2] A special 120-page handbook '*Reichstag* Election 1930' was produced by the Reich head-quarters with details of the activity of the NSDAP *Reichstag* deputies and excerpts from speeches and details of the party line on important current issues; speakers were kept up to date with regular reports on day-to-day events as they happened. Special propaganda methods were developed such as aluminium coins with the head of Hitler on one side and on the other 'Vote NSDAP on 14 September'. These were then thrown into the crowd from SA lorries—a technique which had apparently paid off in the preceding Baden election. The effect of the propaganda was judged to a nicety. Those in charge of propaganda were ordered 'to make absolutely sure that the posters are put up on the specified day and at the specified intervals'. Special green stickers were produced with which to cover up opponents' posters, since 'green had proved to be the most effective colour'. For the day before the election, branches were ordered to keep a printer in readiness to rush out answers to opposition 'lies', and to engage a sympathetic district judge who could serve a writ immediately.

The economic crisis and the hectic propaganda campaign had caused an unprecedented politicization of the electorate.[3] The NSDAP increased its vote in Lower Saxony from 4·5 per cent in 1928 to 23 per cent, compared with the Reich average of 18·3 per cent.[4]

[1] Gauleitung Hannover-Süd–Braunschweig Reichstagswahl Anordnung Nr. 1, 25 July 1930, NSAH Hann. Des. 310 I E, Nr. 13.
[2] See the weekly *Gaupropagandaleitung Rundschreiben* from 1 Aug. 1930, in ibid.
[3] The election saw a larger popular vote than ever before recorded in Germany, see J. K. Pollock, 'The German Reichstag Election of 1930', *American Political Science Review*, vol. 24 (1930). In Lower Saxony there was an increase of 5·8 per cent in the total vote compared with 1928. See Franz, op. cit., p. 96.
[4] Franz, op. cit., p. 96. *Gau* Hanover-South–Brunswick won the highest NSDAP *Gau* vote in Germany. Cf. *NB*, 20 Sept. 1930.

Two other parties increased their vote: the KPD from 2·9 per cent to 5·6 per cent, and the Centre from 8 per cent to 8·6 per cent. All other parties lost votes: the SPD 4·9 per cent, the DVP 4·4 per cent, the DNVP 3·1 per cent, the Guelphs 2·9 per cent, the DDP 1·1 per cent and the minor parties 2·8 per cent. It has been suggested that a larger proportion of the new NSDAP support came from those who had not voted in 1928 because of ineligibility, apathy or alienation from the previous bourgeois-party voters.[1] This is confirmed by the figures for Lower Saxony. The NSDAP won 458,298 more votes than in 1928. The combined loss of the bourgeois parties (i.e. excluding the SPD) was 214,887 votes of which a few at least may be assumed to have gone to the Centre. Thus over half of the increase in the NSDAP vote came from new voters. An analysis of the figures for the *Kreise* show that the correlation between the rise in the NSDAP vote and the decline of one or more parties varied markedly from *Kreis* to *Kreis*. In the north of *Regierungsbezirk* Hanover, for example, where the NSDAP made very big gains, the DNVP suffered very heavily in *Kreis* Diepholz losing over 1,000 votes, whereas in the neighbouring *Kreise* Syke and Hoya it actually increased its vote slightly. Here the most devastating losses were suffered by the DVP and the Guelphs.[2]

Although the trend was general, the NSDAP remained strongest in north Oldenburg and East Friesland where it had made big gains in 1928.[3] In this election, however, the party extended its influence south-eastwards into the neighbouring *Kreise* Diepholz (44 per cent) and Hoya (37·5 per cent). These *Kreise* had much in common with Oldenburg and East Friesland. They were overwhelmingly agricultural and had bad communications. Their soil was poor—*Geest* and moor—and was worked by small to medium-sized peasants who were heavily dependent on pig and cattle farming.[4] Their political traditions, however, were different. Before and even after the war, they had been bastions of the Guelph party, though in 1924 the DNVP had made serious inroads. It was clear, then, that in this election, political traditions were finally being broken down by the economic crisis and that the NSDAP was seen to provide the most suitable vehicle for solving all problems. Indeed, although north-west Lower Saxony proved most vulnerable to Nazism, the election result showed that the party could succeed under very different conditions. In the south of Lower

[1] Cf. H. Striefler, *Deutsche Wahlen in Bildern und Zahlen. Eine soziographische Studie über die Reichstagswahlen der Weimarer Republik* (Düsseldorf, 1946), p. 63.

[2] For detailed figures on Diepholz, Syke and Hoya see *Diepholz Kreiszeitung*, 16 Sept. 1930.

[3] In Wittmund and Ammerland the party secured an absolute majority.

[4] *Die Wirtschaftsstruktur im Bezirk des Landesarbeitsamtes Niedersachsen.* hrsg. Wirtschaftswissenschaftliche Gesellschaft zum Studium Niedersachsens C.V. Reihe A. Heft 14 (Hanover, 1930), p. 51.

Saxony, round Göttingen, for example, a region of small and medium-sized holdings but with good soil producing grain, root crops and sugar beet, the NSDAP was also successful in making big gains.[1] In *Kreis* Einbeck, for example, where previously they had had no success whatever and where the first branch was only founded in February 1930,[2] the NSDAP won 30·7 per cent of the vote. Significantly, even the largest cities showed Nazi gains above the Reich average: Hanover 20·6 per cent, Brunswick 24·5 per cent, Emden 23·4 per cent and Wilhelmshaven 24·4 per cent.

There were two main areas where the NSDAP vote was below average. The first was districts in which there was a predominance or high proportion of Roman Catholics. This was most strikingly evident in South Oldenburg and in the Catholic parts of *Regierungsbezirk* Osnabrück. In *Kreis* Vechta in Oldenburg, for example, the NSDAP won only 2·1 per cent compared with a Centre party vote of 81·7 per cent, while in *Kreis* Aschendorf-Hümmling in Osnabrück the NSDAP vote was 1·9 per cent compared with 80·6 per cent for the Centre. This pattern was also reflected, though to a lesser extent, in parts of *Regierungsbezirk* Hildesheim, for example in the predominantly Catholic *Kreis* Duderstadt, the NSDAP was only 12·8 per cent compared with the Centre party's 64·9 per cent. The figures for Oldenburg and Osnabrück are particularly important in view of the fact that in terms of social and economic structure these areas were more or less identical with the NSDAP strongholds to the North. The 1928 protest movement in Oldenburg had been initiated from the Catholic South. It is clear that in these rather remote agricultural areas religious loyalties were strong enough to withstand even the severest economic crisis.

The second area where the NSDAP failed to reach the average for Lower Saxony was the *Regierungsbezirke* Lüneburg (16·6 per cent) and Stade (19·7 per cent). The main reason for this appears to be that despite the fact that the Guelphs had suffered devastating losses—13·5 per cent in Lüneburg and 11 per cent in Stade—their vote in these areas remained well above the 8·5 per cent average for the province of Hanover as a whole, Lüneburg with 18·2 per cent and Stade with 17 per cent. Thus it is clear that although the Guelph supporters in general were proving vulnerable to the appeal of Nazism, there remained a hard core in the traditional centres of the party whose loyalty to the Guelph cause was sufficiently deep-rooted to resist the first pressure of economic crisis. These deeply conservative peasants were still suspicious of the radicalism and novelty of the NSDAP. The

[1] Ibid., p. 73–4.
[2] Hanover Gau Propagandaleitung to Meyer–Einbeck, 20 Feb. 1830, in NSAH Hann. Des. 310 I B.

question was: what effect would a long period of economic crisis have on their political attitude—given the obvious impotence of their traditional representatives together with a skilfully conducted campaign by the NSDAP, which was exploiting their economic grievances and promising a restoration of the values of the old agrarian society which they had found embodied in the programme of the Guelph party?

X

DEVELOPMENTS IN ORGANIZATION
1930–1933

I n his chapter 'Propaganda and Organization' in volume II of
Mein Kampf, Hitler summed up his views on the relations between
organization and propaganda in a political movement in the following epigram: 'The task of propaganda is to attract followers; the task
of organization is to win members. A follower of a movement is one
who declares himself in agreement with its aims; a member is one who
fights for it.'[1] This statement was written in 1925 when the party was
nothing if not a band of fighters. However, the vast influx of new
members which followed the victory of September 1930, created an
entirely new situation. Hitler had foreseen the danger if the party grew
too big too quickly:

> The greatest danger which can threaten a movement is a membership that has
> abnormally increased by too rapid successes. For, as much as a movement—as
> long as it has to fight hard—is avoided by all cowardly and egoistic people, as
> rapidly will the latter usually acquire membership if, in its development, a
> great success of the party has become probable or is already a fact.[2]

In *Mein Kampf*, Hitler had suggested the limitation of membership as
a solution. Yet once an organization is winning new members, and particularly when it depends to a considerable extent on subscriptions for
financing its growth and development, this solution is not attractive;
indeed it only became feasible after the *Machtergreifung*, apart from
temporary halts to the admission of new members owing to administrative pressure. Thus after 1930 there appeared a very real danger of
bureaucratization, and of a loss of impetus owing to the dilution of the
enthusiasm of the original hard core by opportunists. The important
fact about the NSDAP was that, despite the enormous growth in the
membership and bureaucracy after 1930, the party retained its original
élan. A study of the development of the NSDAP organization in
Lower Saxony between 1930 and 1933 may help to provide an explanation for this.

Secondly, the development of a whole range of specialist organizations which contributed to the effectiveness of the party's propaganda
will be examined.

---

[1] See Hitler, *Mein Kampf*, p. 849.   [2] Ibid., p. 853.

Finally, another problem facing the NSDAP after 1930 was that of resolving the tension and conflicts which existed within the party. We have seen that the reverse side of the *élan* of the NSDAP was the intense rivalry of the membership and the permanent tension of a revolutionary party following constitutional methods of winning power. This had been accentuated since the reorientation of the party in 1928 towards the winning of the *Mittelstand*. After 1930 this rivalry and tension continued and found expression in conflict between the SA and the political organization. This conflict will be analysed as it affected the party in Lower Saxony.

(i) *The danger of a loss of impetus*

In the September 1930 *Reichstag* election the NSDAP had demonstrated the success of its propaganda. The next task of the party was, in the words of a directive from *Gau* Hanover-South–Brunswick, 'to make National Socialists of the 284,000 voters in our *Gau*, to activate this mass of voters and recruit from it as many fellow-fighters as possible'.[1] The NSDAP electoral success was followed by a flood of new applications for membership which put a considerable strain on the party's organization. During 1931, there were frequent complaints from the lower echelons that people were leaving the party because of the failure of head-quarters to supply them with membership cards.[2] But quite apart from the purely administrative aspect, there was also the problem of 'activating' this mass of new members. Those who had joined the party in its period of relative obscurity before 1930 could be expected to be dedicated activists. After the September election, however, the new members were suspected of jumping on the band wagon. Commenting, for example, on a report of tension between the members of long-standing and the new recruits in the Clausthal-Zellerfeld branch, the *Gau* secretary wrote to the district leader in Goslar as follows:

I cannot of course form an opinion from here, but I have the feeling as if our fine old party comrades have some reason for talking about the new bourgeois line (*Richtung der Spiesser*). It is probably slightly exaggerated, but I can believe that the new 'bourgeois-decent' behaviour is rejected by our old comrades.[3]

In August 1931, the *Kreisleiter* of Clausthal–Zellerfeld, a very old member of the party, complained that a member of this new group

[1] Gaupropagandaleitung Rundschreiben, 17 Sept. 1930, NSAH Hann. Des. 310 I E, Nr. 13.
[2] E.g. Bezirk Mittelweser-Nord to Gauleitung, 9 June 1931, complaining about a member who had joined in Feb. and still had not received a card, NSAH Hann. Des. 310 I A, Nr. 45.
[3] Maul to Bezirksleiter Goslar, 17 Oct. 1930, NSAH Hann. Des. 310 I A, Nr. 41.

who had become a branch leader had failed hopelessly to deal with an attack by the KPD on the branch head-quarters:

In the struggle for National Socialism I have unfortunately had to learn that it is impossible to make fighters out of bourgeois (*Spiesser*) and salon-socialists. Herr Riese is suited for keeping the party books, but in a real fight he will always fail.[1]

In view of this problem, the party felt the need to take measures against the possibility of a loss of impetus and of fossilization. At the beginning of 1931, therefore, the party in Hanover-South–Brunswick introduced monthly 'activity reports' in which the branches were compelled to report on their own activity and that of their opponents. Branches which failed to report that they had held a public meeting during the month were sent a special reprimand form which ordered them to give reasons and told them that if they failed to start preparations for a meeting the *Gauleiter* would be informed.[2] In November 1931, the *Gau* introduced the 'performance principle', whereby each branch leader had to keep a record of the performance of every member. A meeting of all functionaries was planned for the beginning of January 1932, at which the branch leaders were to be 'called out in order of their performance. Those who are not good enough must make way for the more efficient'.[3] Furthermore, the *Gauleiter* appointed a number of tried officials as 'inspectors' to control the performance of the branches.[4] In 1932, members who joined the party in *Kreis* Goslar received the following letter:

Dear Comrade, You now belong to the NSDAP and realize that this membership brings with it duties. Since we wish to save the German people, we must demand from every individual member that he take on some job. You can choose one and send your declaration of agreement by return. You can be (1) an SA man or SA Reserve man; (2) an SS man; (3) in the women's department; (4) a political functionary; or (5) take on special duties.

Everyone must take on a job, otherwise they should not have become National Socialists. The only excuses accepted are illness or age. Under (5) special duties is understood:—to provide a private car twice a month; to win a new member every month; to win a new subscriber to an NS paper every month; to donate RM 10 per month to party funds; to sell a certain number of tickets for party meetings; to canvass etc.[5]

[1] Kreisleiter Clausthal–Zellerfeld to Maul, 23 Aug. 1931, NSAH Hann. Des. 310 I A, Nr. 47.
[2] Gaupropagandaleiter to Ortsgruppe Kirchbrak, 21 Apr. 1931, NSAH Hann. Des. 310 I A, Nr. 76.
[3] Gauleitung Rundschreiben, 20 Nov. 1931, NSAH Hann. Des. 310 I E, Nr. 30. There is, however, no evidence on whether this meeting took place.
[4] Ibid., Gauleiter, 'Die Parole für den Winter 1931–1932', 20 Nov. 1931.
[5] Draft letter in NSAH Hann. Des. 310 I E, Nr. 27.

There is no evidence of how widespread these formal demands were, but there is no doubt that members were expected to involve themselves actively in the work of the party.[1] For example, unemployed members who could not afford the subscription were required to sell *Bausteine* (contribution stamps) of equivalent value.[2]

It is questionable, however, how necessary these measures were. Many of the new members were young activists little different in their background and attitudes to those who joined before 1930. Indeed the party statistics for the three Lower Saxon *Gaue* show that just over two-thirds of the new members who joined before 30 January 1933 were under forty with nearly twice as many coming from the age group twenty-one–thirty as from the group thirty-one–forty.[3] In terms of their occupations, the new membership had undergone a slight shift away from the *Mittelstand* towards the working class. Whereas the workers had made up only between 20 per cent and 22 per cent of those who joined before 14 September 1930, of those who joined during the whole period before 30 January 1933, 28 per cent in Hanover-South–Brunswick, 29 per cent in Weser-Ems and 29 per cent in Hanover-East were workers. This percentage increase in working class membership was largely at the expense of the peasantry who dropped from 30 per cent to 22 per cent in Weser-Ems, and from 20 per cent to 17 per cent in Hanover-South–Brunswick, considering the period between 1925 and 1933 as a whole. Only in Hanover-East did they continue to hold their own with 27 per cent before 1930 and 27 per cent from 1925–33. The self-employed group also dropped slightly in all three *Gaue*.

One should be wary of making generalizations on the evidence of such a small shift, but it appears as if the party's rapid numerical expansion during the period 1930–3 also represented a very slight broadening of its social base, while the average age of its recruits went down still further. This influx of young men caused a certain amount of friction. In Clausthal–Zellerfeld, for example, conflict continued during 1932. The *Kreisleiter*, Preiss, had been one of the first members to join the party in the *Gau* after 1925. He was a road worker and already in 1930 during the dispute with the bourgeois group, the party secretary had admitted 'that Preiss is not the ideal man to lead a branch

[1] In Sept. 1931, in order to counteract the 'laxity' of the membership, the Harburg branch made its weekly evenings compulsory and imposed a fine of 50 pf for those who did not turn up, the money to be used to pay the subscriptions of unemployed members. See Harburg police report, 5 Sept. 1931, NSAS G VII 65.
[2] Gauleiting Hannover-Süd–Braunschweig Kasse Rundschreiben, 10 Sept. 1931, NSAH Hann. Des. 310 I E, Nr. 30.
[3] For the following see *Parteistatistik*, Stand I, Jan. 1935. Herausgeber, Der Reichsorganisationsleiter den NSDAP Bd. I, pp. 202–4 and pp. 146–8.

of the size which Clausthal now is'.[1] At the time, however, he had emphasized that he still preferred Preiss to a 'solid bourgeois member'.[2] During 1932, however, a member reported his annoyance at developments within the Clausthal organization to the Reich head-quarters as follows:

For officials we were presented with comrades Dr. Hagemann and Dipl. Ing. Schneider, two other Dipl. Ing. and other young comrades. . . . I saw in the first few weeks that they wanted to take over the *Kreis* and get rid of the old *Kreisleiter* Preiss. . . . Wherever one looks there are young members in official positions and these young people bring in still younger friends as functionaries and officials. People who have hardly left school are made leaders over the older ones who have longer experience of life and push them out of the movement. I am attacked by these members because I have the confidence of the workers. In general I must say that things looked damned bad in the subordinate organizations. Wherever one goes there are the same complaints.[3]

Some of these men who were disillusioned by the new orientation towards the *Mittelstand* and by the rise of young men, a number of whom were *Akademiker*,[4] to positions of influence within the party, helped to fill the ranks of Otto Strasser's left-wing opposition. The majority, however, swallowed their pride and disillusionment and continued as simple party members, probably trying to win prestige after 1933 with their early party membership.[5]

(ii) *The Gauleiter*

The rapid growth in the number of branches meant that the *Gau* head-quarters could no longer control the work of the party at local level.[6] At a special meeting of functionaries on 21 February 1931, therefore, the *Kreis* organization was established for *Gau* Hanover-South–Brunswick by which every administrative *Kreis* unit would

[1] Maul to the Bezirksleitung Goslar, 17 Oct. 1930, NSAH Hann. Des. 310 I A, Nr. 41.
[2] Ibid.
[3] H. Kratzin to the Reichsleitung der NSDAP, NSAH Hann. Des. 310 I A, Nr. 117.
[4] In Göttingen too the old branch leader Uhlendorff, a train driver, was superceded by a young lawyer Dr. Muhs, who was a fairly recent recruit (1929). See Uhlendorff's letter of complaint to Strasser, 21 Sept. 1931, in BA NS 22 vorl. 369 and Muhs Personal files in BDC.
[5] A good example of one who evidently swallowed his pride and annoyance but felt strongly on this issue was a co-founder of the Hanover branch in 1921—Karl Schiebeck. See Schiebeck to Hitler, 12 Sept. 1931, and further correspondence in NSAH Hann. Des. 310 I A, Nr. 118.
[6] On 1 Jan. 1931 there were 368 branches in *Gau* Hanover-South–Brunswick compared with 60 on 1 Jan. 1930. See Landespolizeistelle Hanover Report for Feb. 1931, in NSAH Hann. Des. 80 II, Nr. 723.

have a corresponding NSDAP *Kreis* organization.[1] These *Kreisleiter* had considerable responsibility, particularly since they had the power of recommending branch leaders to the *Gau* head-quarters. It is significant that they were appointed largely from those who had made their name before 1930 who could be guaranteed to recommend only those who were both loyal and activist, and who would maintain the party's pre-1930 style.

Yet the relationship between the *Kreis* and branch leaders was carefully balanced. On the one hand, the *Kreisleiter* acted as the representative of the *Gauleiter*, as his 'commissar' or organ of control over the branches in the *Kreis*.[2] On the other hand, however, his executive authority did not go so far as to enable him to take fundamental organizational measures such as dismissal without the approval of the *Gauleiter*. Furthermore, the *Gau* head-quarters still communicated directly with the local branches, except in the matter of the distribution of speakers which was handled by the *Kreis* organization. Finally, the *Kreisleiter* had no independent source of income. All the *Gau* head-quarters was prepared to offer was the belief that 'the branches will gladly make a monthly contribution provided, in the first place, it does not overburden their treasuries and secondly, that they are convinced the *Kreisleiter* are really working for them'.[3] In fact, the *Kreis* organizations financed themselves largely with collections. This was a typical example of the confused lines of responsibility which characterized Nazi organization.

The *Führerprinzip* established the *Gauleiter* as the key figure in the NSDAP's regional organization.[4] His position was defined by the 'Regulations for local branches in *Gau* Hanover-East' as follows:

The *Gauleiter* is the representative of the party leader and does not need as, for example, democratic principles dictate, the 'confidence' of his *Gau*; he is responsible to the party leader alone. The *Gauleiter* lays down for the area of his *Gau* the tactics of political activity, the line to be taken, the holding of meetings in the individual *Kreise* and branches, and the construction of the organization. He nominates the *Kreisleiter* and branch leaders who must be men who are in his confidence.[5]

Given the internecine rivalry within the subordinate organization, the dominant position of the *Gauleiter* was vital to the efficient functioning of the *Apparat*. During the first years after 1925, even *Gauleiter*

[1] Organisationsleitung I Anordnung für die Grenzen des Kreises Gandersheim, 3 July 1931, NSAH Hann. Des. 310 I A, Nr. 48.
[2] Maul to Kreisleiter Münden, 14 Dec. 1931, NSAH Hann. Des. 310 I A, Nr. 47.
[3] Ibid.
[4] On the Gauleiter in general see Peter Hüttenberger, *Die Gauleiter. Studie zum Wandel des Machtgefüges in der NSDAP* (Stuttgart, 1969).
[5] BA NS 22 vorl. 369. Undated, but probably 1931.

on occasion fell victim to this rivalry. But later, as the party structure became more formalized, the party leadership was extremely unwilling to permit the overthrow of a *Gauleiter*, with the disorganization and undermining of discipline which would result. Members who rebelled against the *Gau* head-quarters were ruthlessly excluded. A good example of this unwillingness to sacrifice a *Gauleiter* even when he had proved to be incompetent occurred in *Gau* Hanover-East during 1931.[1] During 1930 and 1931, Telschow was at odds with a considerable number of his subordinates. There were a whole variety of reasons for this. The party organization in Harburg, for example, objected to the fact that the *Gauleiter* preferred to work from his small-town base of Buchholz and to concentrate on agricultural propaganda, which meant that, in their view, he neglected Harburg. In Bremerhaven there was a more fundamental conflict involving the SA.[2] In Celle there had been a long conflict within the branch involving the *Gauleiter*. Apart from the particular reasons for the individual cases, part of the trouble was that Telschow was a crude man who lacked flair in his dealings with subordinates. By the autumn of 1931 these conflicts had weakened the organization to such an extent that Munich was obliged to despatch Ley, the deputy head of the Reich party organization on a tour of inspection. Ley reported that the organization in Hanover-East corresponded to that of one-and-a-half to two years before in most other *Gaue*, but that every *Gau* had had to go through 'a period of backbiting' and that there had been an improvement in recent weeks. Rather than appoint a new *Gauleiter*, he suggested that Telschow should be given a trial period of three months in which to prove himself.[3] He evidently passed the test.

It would be difficult to overestimate the importance of the *Gauleiter* to the NSDAP in the period before 1933. Though they were backed up by the Reich head-quarters, it was they who assumed the main burden of organization and supervision of party propaganda activities. It is not easy to estimate their degree of independence from the Munich head-quarters from the documentary material available. Between 1930 and 1933 it was probably rather less than after 1933 when the central party machine became less important.

(iii) *Specialized Nazi organizations*

Apart from the political organization, the party had of course, ever since 1925, developed a number of separate organizations. The SA

[1] See the correspondence relating to this affair, ibid.
[2] For details see below p. 184.
[3] Ley, Bericht über die Inspektion im Gau Hannover-Ost der NSDAP, 2 Dez. 1931, in BA *NS* 22 vorl. 369.

and the SS had been followed in 1926 by the Hitler Youth and by the students' organization. Furthermore, a number of organizations were established for members of specific professions—the NS Teachers' League and the NS Lawyers' League were the first of these.

These specialized organizations offer an important insight into the development of the Nazi party organization. They were almost invariably founded not by the central party organization, but by individuals in various parts of the Reich—the *Hitlerjugend* by Kurt Gruber in Plauen im Vogtland, the teachers' organization by Hans Schemm, the lawyers' by Hans Frank, etc., who then persuaded the party to give their organizations official recognition. The party organization treated these new bodies with considerable reserve. In his justification for the banning of membership of the *NS Wirtschaftsbund* Strasser argued—rather as Hitler had in opposition to the formation of a party trade union—that these organizations weakened the party by concentrating on the economic or professional aims of specific groups, to the detriment of the general interests of the party.[1] Specialized sections within a party to organize the appeal to specific interests were, however, by no means unique to the NSDAP. They were a response to the way in which interest groups permeated the political parties during the Weimar period.[2] By 1930, with the decline in faith in the traditional parties, with the increasing economic pressure caused by the depression and with the growing tension between interests which this produced, individuals were acutely conscious of their immediate economic or professional interests and the NSDAP was forced to respond to this situation by developing these specialized organizations. It did so to a degree hardly paralleled even by the SPD and KPD; and these groups played an important role in facilitating the party's rise to power.

The propaganda organized by these specialist groups concentrated above all on trying to win control of the professional organizations from below by converting their membership. This not only helped to remove from the bourgeois parties their social and financial basis;[3] it also was to simplify the establishment of totalitarian control over German social and economic life after 1933. Secondly, specialized groups provided expert information for the party. This was useful in the fight to win control of the state. For example, the *Gau* legal expert and his colleagues provided counsel for large numbers of party members who were prosecuted, and SA doctors patched up wounds. They had another function too. At the 1929 party congress, the committee dealing

---

[1] Anordnung 2 der ROL I v. 16 Jan. 1930, Punkt 3.
[2] Cf. K. D. Bracher, *Die Auflösung der Weimarer Republik* (Villingen, 1960), pp. 199 ff.
[3] E. A. Roloff, *Bürgertum und Nationalsozialismus 1930–1933*, p. 106.

with questions of organization recommended that a second organization department should be set up to deal with preparations for the construction of the future national socialist state. On 22 October Hitler issued a directive concerning 'the intellectual preparations for the future structure of the National Socialist state' in which he emphasized that 'when the rotten shell of the present state collapses, the foundations of the National Socialist state must be ready. The intellectual material for the new building and the trained builders must be prepared'.[1] Experts were encouraged to send in memoranda to the department and to give lectures to small groups of party members and sympathizers. It was suggested they should begin with a discussion of Fascist economic and trade union policy. It is doubtful whether these blue prints had much significance for the Third Reich; they did, however, provide a field of activity for unemployed specialists and thus helped to commit potentially useful recruits to the party.

By the beginning of 1931, the *Gauleitung* of Hanover-South–Brunswick consisted of nineteen departmental heads:[2]

> The *Gauleiter*
> The *Gau* Secretary
> The *Gau* Treasurer
> The *Gau* Propaganda director
> The *Gau* Press Officer
> The chairman of the *Gau* party court

The director of the *Gau* Department of Organization I and the following specialists:	Director of Organization II and the following specialists:
NSBO (Factory Cell Organization)	Agriculture
War disabled and war dependants	Financial and economic policy
Civil servants questions	Cultural policy
Mittlestand questions (excluding agriculture)	Local government
	Medicine
	Legal questions
	Youth questions

A list of members of the *Gauleitung* Hanover-East of the same date shows that, although there were slight variations—*Gau* Hanover-East had no specialist on civil servants but a representative for mining—the organizational structure was basically the same.[3] And this is not sur-

---

[1] Reichsleitung Org. Abteilung II Anordnung betr. Geistige Vorbereitung des zukünftigen nationalsozialistischen Staatsaufbaues, 22 Oct. 1929, gez. Adolf Hitler in NSAH Hann. Des. 310 I E, Nr. 33.

[2] Abtleilungsleiter der hiesigen Gauleitung, 9 Mar. 1931, in BA NS 22 vorl. 369. In Aug. 1931 the *Gau* established a party school for training the various functionaries from branch leader and branch specialist upwards, see Tätigkeitsbericht Aug. 1931, NSAH Hann. Des. 310 I B, Nr. 13.

[3] Gauleitung Hannover-Ost, 27 Mar. 1931, BA *NS* 22 vorl. 369.

prising since those departments were set up on instructions from Munich. The distinction between the Department of Organization I, which was supposed to deal with the operation of winning power within the existing state, and the Department of Organization II, which was established to lay the foundations of the future Nazi state, was in fact mainly theoretical. Thus the agricultural section within Department II was as much involved in the current political struggle as, for example, the factory cell organization, NSBO; even the cultural department was responsible for putting on propaganda plays.

The device of developing separate organizations within the party to represent and appeal to specific interests was a response to the importance of interest groups in Weimar politics, but it posed the problem of competing jurisdictions which, given the numerous conflicting interests within the party, could have resulted in chaos. The specialist functionaries were responsible both to their political leadership and to their departmental superiors. At the beginning of 1931, Rust had insisted on a definite statement from Strasser defining the power structure within the *Gau* with reference to these departments.[1] Strasser replied reaffirming the superiority of the *Gauleiter* over the various departments within his *Gau* and, in particular, the power of appointment, dismissal and discipline.[2]

(iv) *The Agrarpolitischer Apparat*

Perhaps the most successful of all the party's professional organizations was the agricultural department—the *Agrarpolitischer Apparat* (ApA).[3] Although individual *Gaue* such as those in Schleswig-Holstein and Lower Saxony had pursued an active propaganda campaign among the peasantry between 1928 and 1930, it was not until March 1930 that the central party organization made a serious attempt to organize agricultural propaganda with the publication of an official agricultural programme.[4] Soon after this, in May, R. W. Darré was appointed agricultural adviser to the party head-quarters in Munich. But although Darré at once began planning an agricultural organization for the party, it was not until after the September election that the ApA really began to operate. During November, in a series of important directives, Darré defined its aims and tactics.[5] The aim of the ApA was, in his view, not to create a separate National Socialist

[1] Rust to Strasser, 5 Jan. 1931; in BA *NS* 22 vorl. 369.
[2] Strasser to Rust, 19 Jan. 1931, ibid.
[3] For a detailed study of the ApA see H. Gies, 'NSDAP und landwirtschaftliche Organisationen in der Endphase der Weimarer Republik' in *Vjhfzg*, 15. Jg. 1967.
[4] See above pp. 121–5.
[5] See NSDAP Hauptarchiv, Reel 46, Folder 953.

peasant organization to rival the *Landbund* for which they did not have the resources. Nor was it advisable to launch a frontal attack on the *Landbund* as the party had previously tended to do. This was now considered a mistake because it simply united the *Landbund* against the NSDAP. Furthermore, they needed the '*Apparat* of the *Landbund* as the preparatory organization for the self-governing corporate body of farmers in the Third *Reich*'.[1] The new tactic advocated was 'to conquer the existing agricultural organizations from within by a form of factory cell technique'.[2] To this, it was believed, the *Landbünde* would prove vulnerable because 'in general, the German Nationalists would now rather work with us than with the Landvolk'; and also because 'the officials of the *Landbund* (directors, etc.) are scared of losing their jobs and are trying to cover themselves as far as we are concerned'.[3]

The new organization was initially subdivided into *Gau*, district (*Bezirk*) and *Kreis* agricultural advisers; in the summer of 1932 branch advisers were also appointed.[4] The role of these advisers was to act as experts for their political leaders; to act as a liaison between the political leadership and their professional colleagues; to be the eyes and ears of the Reich head-quarters; and above all 'to organize the conquest of every non-National Socialist agricultural organization'.[5]

At the end of 1930, the Lower Saxon *Gaue* were among the fifteen which reported to head-quarters that the organization of district and *Kreis* leaders had been carried out.[6] In its Activity Report for January 1931, *Gau* Hanover-South–Brunswick reported that relations with the *Landbund* were excellent thanks to the liaison of Werner Willikens.[7] The previous twelve months had seen the recruitment of two important figures in agriculture in the area of the *Gau*. On 1 April 1930 Hartwig von Rheden-Rheden had been won for the party by Willikens.[8] Apart from being a leading landowner and *Landbund* figure in the Hildesheim district, von Rheden was also a leader of the *Stahlhelm* regional organization in Hanover. Even more important, at the end of 1930 the NSDAP recruited Hermann Deumeland, who had been a co-founder of the *Bund der Landwirte*, had founded the Lower Saxony *Landbund* after 1918 and was now the vice-chairman

[1] Darré Rundschreiben, 16 Dec. 1930, ibid.

[2] Darré Rundschreiben, 20 Nov. 1930, ibid.

[3] See footnote 1.

[4] Kreisleitung Alfeld to Ortsgruppe Gronau, 19 May 1932, NSAH Hann. Des. 310 I A, Nr. 67.

[5] Der Nationalsozialistische landwirtschaftliche Fachberater, 18 Nov. 1930; in NSDAP Hauptarchiv, Reel 46, Folder 949.

[6] Undated report, c. Dec. 1930, ibid.

[7] Tätigkeitsbericht für den Monat Januar 1931, NSAH Hann. Des. 310 I B, Nr. 13.

[8] H. von Rheden-Rheden Lebenslauf, NSAH Hann. Des. 310 I B, Nr. 8.

of the Brunswick *Landbund*.[1] Deumeland had made an important contribution to the previous success of the DVP among the agricultural population in Brunswick and now flung himself into agricultural propaganda for the NSDAP. In *Gau* Hanover-East, where Weidenhöfer was the *Gau* expert, the party could report that 'the *Landbund* now has an understanding attitude towards us'.[2] The support at such an early stage of such important figures in Lower Saxon agriculture as von Rheden-Rheden, Deumeland and Weidenhöfer, in addition to Werner Willikens, made a significant contribution to the campaign among a social group which was notoriously suspicious of outsiders.

Nevertheless, although the *Landbund* now had to tread warily in its attitude to the NSDAP, at the beginning of 1931 there was still a large number of hostile *Kreislandbünde* and even in 1932 relations with the Hanover regional organization remained tense owing to the opposition of its general secretary, Cord Cordes.[3] During 1931, the ApA kept up its pressure by holding meetings and demonstrations to coincide with the general meetings of the *Kreislandbünde*.[4] In some cases they were successful in turning the *Landbund* meeting into a demonstration of support for the NSDAP.[5] By the beginning of 1932, the DNVP regional organization for East Friesland was complaining that 'more and more of the committees (of the *Kreilsandbünde*) are composed of Nazis'.[6] Once a *Kreislandbund* was in the hands of the NSDAP, it could be used as a forum for a much wider audience than would attend a normal party meeting. Above all it could be used to push Nazis into leading positions in the regional organizations.[7]

During 1931 the agricultural situation deteriorated still further and it was reported from the Stade region, for example, that many parents could no longer afford the school money for their children.[8] With this situation extremism in the countryside increased and, during 1931,

[1] Hermann Deumeland Lebenslauf, ibid.

[2] *NS*, 27 June 1931.

[3] In Apr. 1932, the ApA organized a letter campaign against Cordes after he had attacked 'socialism', implying the NSDAP, in the Hanover *Landbund* organ. See Rheden Rundschreiben an alle Herren des ApA, 22 Apr. 1932, in NSAH Hann. Des. 310 I B, Nr. 44.

[4] E.g. on 21 Nov. 1931, at the time of the *Landbund* general meeting in Stolzenau. See Willikens and Weidenhöfer correspondence with *Gaupropagandaleitung* H-S-B in NSAH Hann. Des. 310 I B, Nr. 35.

[5] See the description of the meeting in Gifhorn in *NS*, 21 Nov. 1931.

[6] Protokoll der Vorstandssitzungen vom 23 Nov. 1932, in Emden and 7 July 1932 in Aurich der DNVP Landesverband Ostfriesland in NSAA Dep. L I, Bd. 2.

[7] After pressure from the Nazi dominated *Kreis* organizations in Brunswick, a leading Nazi peasant, Giesecke-Lobmachtersen was appointed vice-chairman of the Brunswick *Landbund*. See Roloff, *Bürgertum und Nationalsozialismus*, pp. 104–5 and Schmalz, *Nationalsozialisten ringen um Braunschweig*, pp. 149 and 196.

[8] Landwirtschaftlicher Hauptverein für den Reg. Bez. Stade e.V an die Landwirtschaftskammer für die Provinz Hannover in NSAS Rep. 80, p. 831.

the NSDAP had to compete for support among the agricultural population with the *Landvolk* movement whose radicalism at times threatened to outpace it, and which tempted peasant members of the party to
co-operate in its activities. In the autumn of 1931, the threat was so
acute in the Hildesheim area that Strasser himself intervened and persuaded Rust to appoint von Rheden, who was a leading landowner in
the area as *Gau* agricultural expert.[1] Perhaps as another counterweight
to the activities of the *Landvolk*, a meeting of *Gau* agricultural experts
in the Brown House on 10–11 August 1931 demanded from the
government a series of emergency measures which were widely publi-
cized by the party.[2] They included a year's moratorium on all agricultural debts; a cut in interest rates to not more than 2 per cent above
bank rate; a reduction in the price of fertilizer; the cutting-off of surplus imports through the establishment of cheap harvest credit to flour
mills; and co-operatives to get round the 'parasitic middlemen'.
Another form of propaganda undertaken by the ApA was to counteract the exploitation of Article 17 of the 1920 programme by opponents, who accused the party of 'socialism'.[3] Despite the fact that Hitler
had already made an official 'clarification' of the article, it remained
very dangerous ground for the party.

The major test for the ApA came with the elections for the Chambers of Agriculture in the winter of 1931–2. The ApA defied the
demands of the Hanover *Landbund* that the elections should be non-
political and put up a separate NSDAP list. The result was a striking
demonstration of support for the party among the peasantry. Of the
thirty-six seats in the Hanover Chamber of Agriculture the NSDAP
won twenty-six compared with only six for the *Landbund*.[4] Out of
twenty-six *Kreise*, the *Landbund* was only victorious in three—Hanover, Diepholz and Stolzenau—and von Rheden became vice-chairman of the Chamber. In Oldenburg the result was nearly as decisive.
Here, significantly, the *Landbund* had given its members instructions
to vote for the NSDAP list against the Catholic *Bauernverein*.[5] The
NSDAP won twenty-three out of thirty-six seats and overthrew the
ruling *Praesidium*.[6] The Protestant Nazis of the North revelled in

[1] Strasser to Rust, 27 Oct. 1931, BA *NS* vorl. 369. Under von Rheden the party
competed with the *Landvolk* not by resisting the actual foreclosures, which would
have been illegal, but by ensuring that the auction rooms were so packed with party
members that bids were effectively prevented.

[2] Die landwirtschaftliche Hilfsforderungen in *NS*, 22 Aug. 1931.

[3] Article 17: 'We demand land reform adapted to our national needs. The creation of a law for the expropriation of land for communal purposes without compensation. The abolition of interest on land and the prevention of speculation in
land.' See A. Rosenberg, *Das Parteiprogramm. Wesen, Grundsätze und Ziele der
NSDAP* (21 Auflage, München, 1941), p. 15.

[4] *NTZ*, 13 Jan. 1932.   [5] *NS*, 21 Nov. 1931.

[6] *Nachrichten für Stadt und Land*, 12 Nov. 1931.

their triumph over the Catholics of the South who had dominated the Chamber for so long. In reply to a demand for consideration for the South, Hobbie, the NSDAP leader, replied: 'You can go home. You have nothing more to say. We shall enjoy our revenge coldly but intelligently . . . and we shall neutralize your party from top to bottom. (. . . *und werden Sie kaltstellen und zwar von oben bis unten in Ihrer Partei*).'[1]

Success in the elections to the Chambers of Agriculture enabled the NSDAP to increase its pressure on the *Landbund* for recognition as the leading political representative of German agriculture. At the end of 1931 the NSDAP succeeded in placing Werner Willikens as a vice-chairman of the *Reichslandbund*.[2] Since another top *Reichslandbund* official, Director von Sybel, became a member of the NSDAP at the same time, it meant that during 1932 the NSDAP had an important influence on the *Reichslandbund*, which in turn had an important influence on Reich politics.[3]

Apart from its major function of organizing agricultural propaganda in co-operation with the propaganda department and infiltrating the *Landbund* and Chambers of Agriculture, the ApA had two other minor tasks. In the first place, it was responsible for organizing the collection of food-stuffs from sympathetic peasants to supply the SA kitchens.[4] Secondly, within the ApA was set up a special department *Ostland* which had branches throughout the Reich.[5] This department may have been of some importance for the development of SS foreign policy.[6] Its function was to prepare and propagate policies based on Chapter 14 of *Mein Kampf*, volume II ('Eastern Orientation or Eastern Policy'), and to observe the attitudes of the authorities, the parties, the churches, other organizations and leading personalities to *Ostraumpolitik*.

The ApA was, of course, operating among a social group which was in any case extremely sympathetic to the NSDAP, so that it is not easy to assess its contribution to the growth in the party's support among the

[1] Ibid., 17 Dec. 1931.

[2] R. W. Darré, *Um Blut und Boden* (München, 1941), p. 377.

[3] *Nachrichten für Stadt und Land*, 17 Dec. 1931. For the influence of the Reichslandbund on Reich politics see Bracher, *Die Auflösung der Weimarer Republik*, pp. 511 ff. and 697 ff.

[4] See LGF v.d. Decken Rundschreiben an alle Bez.—Kreis—Ortsgruppenleiter, SA, SS, und LBF und LKF, 30 Sept. 1931, NSAH Hann. Des. 310 I A, Nr. 120.

[5] Reichsleitung Abteilung Landwirtschaft. Unterabteilung: Ostland Rundschreiben, 5 Jan. 1932, NSAH Hann. Des. 310 I A, Nr. 37.

[6] In view of the close links between the ApA and the SS, see E. Neusüss-Hunkel, *Die SS* (Frankfurt, 1955), pp. 72–3. Rauschning describes a long lecture by Darré to party leaders on *Ostraumpolitik* at this period. See Rauschning, *Hitler Speaks* (London, 1939), pp. 39 ff.

agricultural population. What is clear is that it provided the party with a superb organization through which it could make maximum use of this support. Moreover, by its successful organization of the conquest from below of the *Landbund* and the Chambers of Agriculture before 1933, the ApA thereby helped to facilitate the *Gleichschaltung* of agriculture after 1933.[1]

(v) *The Mittelstand department*

Another example of an extremely effective professional organization within the party was the department for the *Mittelstand* (interpreted as artisans, shopkeepers and house owners). As we have seen, in 1929, an *NS-Wirtschaftsbund* had been founded to organize those sympathetic to the party within this social group.[2] But this organization was a private operation by its founder, Albert Steingrüber of Plauen i.V. and, by allowing *Mittelstand* associations to join *en bloc* instead of as individual members of the party, went directly against the standard practice of the NSDAP, quite apart from the fact that at this stage the Munich head-quarters was opposed to party organizations for interest groups. On 16 January 1930, therefore, Strasser banned membership of this organization.[3]

Significantly, however, this did not put an end to the matter. Artisans and shopkeepers within the party were evidently anxious to have their own representative group and, almost at once, the banned NS *Wirtschaftsbund* was replaced by another *Mittelstand* organization which had emerged *within* the party, known as the 'Artisans and Traders Group of the NSDAP', which consisted simply of individual members of the party who followed these specific trades.[4] By the beginning of 1931, a special *Mittelstand* department had been established within the *Gau* head-quarters, and during the following months a subordinate organization of *Kreis* and branch specialists was built up. These specialists controlled within their area a large number of special groups which had emerged simultaneously and which represented different trades (such as butchers), each with its own leader (*Obmann*). By July 1932 there were sixty such groups in the city and *Landkreis* of Hanover alone, in which more than 1,000 *Mittelstand* members were organized.[5] The *Mittelstand* department was able to use as functionaries and speakers men who already had positions of influence within

[1] Darré refers to this, op. cit., p. 377 ff.
[2] See above, p. 128.
[3] Anordnung der ROL I v. 16 Feb. 1930, Punkt 3.
[4] Maul to Schmalz, 5 June 1930, NSAH Hann. Des. 310 I A, Nr. 33.
[5] Gaureferent für Mittelstandsfragen an die Kreisfachberater, 15 July 1932, NSAH 310 I A, Nr. 122.

the professional organizations, notably Schrader of Hanover who was a senior official in the Chamber of Trade (*Handwerkskammer*), Schmidt-Nordstemmen, a top official in the North-West German Guild of Young Butchers, Wilhelm Sturm, deputy chairman of the North-West Association of Young Bakers; furthermore, the party succeeded in recruiting Paul Hey, the former *Gauleiter* of the Economic Party in the Hanover area.[1]

The role of these functionaries was virtually identical with those of the ApA. A propaganda device peculiar to the *Mittelstand* department, however, was the compilation and publication of a special directory of artisans and shopkeepers who were party members. The *Gauleiter* then authorized the department to threaten members or their wives who shopped in department stores or co-operatives with expulsion.[2] In this way, the party recruited customers for the *Mittelstand*. The NSDAP promised the *Mittelstand* full representation in a future Chamber of Estates, 'the return of the economy to individual firms', and above all the closing of the department stores: 'the millions of Marks profit now made by department stores will, in itself, give thousands of members of the *Mittelstand* the means of existence'.[3] The *Mittelstand* department received important support from the Reich head-quarters of the party's department of economics, whose director, Wagener, gave definite preference to the *Mittelstand* over big industry.[4] In a directive of 14 January 1932, for example, he declared that 1932 would be 'devoted to the conquest of the *Mittelstand*' and ordered his *Gau* departments to co-operate with the *Mittelstand* experts.[5]

The main aim of the *Mittelstand* department was to take over control of the professional organizations and they were successful. Their biggest coup in Lower Saxony was the conquest of the main professional organizations of artisans in North-West Germany—the *Nordwestdeutscher Handwekerbund*, a classic demonstration of the NSDAP technique of conquest from below.

In the 1930 election the *Handwerkerbund* had recommended that its members vote for bourgeois parties which would use their influence

[1] Gaurednerverzeichnis, 1 Oct. 1931, NSAH Hann. Des. 310 I E, Nr. 33.

[2] Aufbau—Organisation der Fachgruppen gez. Schlottmann, NSAH Hann. Des. 310 I A, Nr. 122 and Rust to Schlottmann, 25 Jan. 1932, NSAH Hann. Des. I A, Nr. 35.

[3] G. Schrader, 'Die NSDAP und der Mittelstand', NSAH Hann. Des. 310 I A, No. 122.

[4] This is clear from Wagener to the Brunswick Branch, 28 Jan. 1932, ibid., in which he asks to speak to representatives of the *Mittelstand* rather than leaders of industry.

[5] Reichsorganisationsabteilung II Wirtschaftspolitische Abteilung Anordnung 6, 14 Jan. 1932, NSAH Hann. Des. 310 I A, Nr. 35.

to support a strong government of the Centre.[1] The result of the election, however, showed only too clearly that many of their members had failed to follow their advice. During 1931, the NSDAP rapidly increased its support among the artisans, but it was not until the beginning of February 1932, at the meeting of delegates from the *Kreishandwerkerbünde*, that it was possible to make a bid for power within the organization.

The campaign began with negotiations between Rust and the *Praesidium* of the *Handwerkerbund*. It soon became clear that although the legal adviser (*Syndikus*) was sympathetic towards the NSDAP, the president, an Economic Party man, was totally opposed to it; it was therefore necessary to apply pressure from below if the party was to win control.[2] Four weeks before the meeting, Rust circularized his *Kreis* officials with instructions to find out: (a) the politics and general quality of the chairman and secretary of their local *Handwerkerbund* branch; (b) whether any artisan member or sympathizer was suitable for a position in the *Praesidium*; (c) which members of the NSDAP were organized in the *Handwerkerbund*, and therefore 'what influence could be thrown into the scales'.[3] A meeting of the relevant *Kreis* officials with the *Gauleiter* was fixed for 14 January. On 16 January, Rust contacted the other *Gauleiter* in North-West Germany and emphasized the need to exert political pressure on the regional representatives of the *Handwerkerbund* and the need for agreement between themselves on candidates for the *Praesidium*. A meeting of *Gauleiter* took place on 21 January to settle this issue. During the two weeks preceding the delegates' meeting, special meetings of artisans were held throughout *Gau* Hanover-South–Brunswick and presumably in the other *Gaue*, and pressure was exerted on the *Kreishandwerkerbünde* to instruct their delegates to vote for the NSDAP candidates. As a result, at the meeting, the *Kreis* delegates replaced the president with an NSDAP sympathizer and appointed two party members as vice-presidents.

The take-over of the *Nord-Westdeutscher Handwerkerbund* was not only important from the point of view of the added propaganda opportunities it offered; it also played a significant part in altering the internal political balance in Brunswick. In July 1932, after the *Bund* had called on its members to vote for the NSDAP in the *Reichstag* election, the two representatives of the *Vereinigter Mittelstand* in the Brunswick *Landtag* felt compelled to leave the bourgeois *Fraktion*, the

---

[1] Report in 'Der Ammerländer', 15 Aug. 1930.
[2] The following account is based on documents in NSAH 310 I A, Nr. 35.
[3] Eiliges Rundschreiben an die Herren Kreisleiter und Kreisfachberater für Mittelstandsfragen des Gaues Süd-Hannover–Braunschweig gez. Rust, NSAH Hann. Des. 310 I A, Nr. 35.

Bürgerliche Einheitsliste and join the NSDAP group. The result was that the relative strength of the two groups in the governing coalition (DNVP and NSDAP) was reversed from 11–9 to 9–11.[1]

(vi) *Other NSDAP professional departments*

The technique of infiltration and conquest from below was applied in every conceivable sphere. In February–March 1932, for example, the NSDAP Reich Department for Race and Culture planned an attempt to take over the 'German Stage Employees Co-operative', using this method;[2] and in June 1932, the NSDAP put up a list for the Hanover Parents' Council Election, for which all NSDAP parents were instructed to vote.[3] Perhaps the most important of the other professional party organizations, however, was the Department for Civil Servants. For the majority of civil servants, especially those in Prussia, membership of the NSDAP was officially frowned upon and activity for the party was liable to result in dismissal. As a result, the organization was composed of loose groups (*Arbeitsgemeinschaften*) to which sympathizers could be attached.[4] The aim was to establish contacts in all the government offices in the particular area, to get members on the candidate lists of the professional organizations and prevent them from making hostile statements about the party. The department had some success. At the end of 1931, for example, the Police President in Hanover reported that in the main Post Office, in the Welfare Office and in the *Landesdirektorium* Nazi agitators had spread the rumour that Hitler would come to power in January and that all civil servants who were not by then members of the NSDAP would be dismissed.[5] An example of the department's attention to detail is provided by a poster advertising NSDAP meetings for civil servants in Brunswick early in 1932.[6] Between 29 January and 5 February the NSDAP held six meetings: one each specifically for postal and customs officials, officials and employees of the state authorities, the municipal officials

---

[1] See E. A. Roloff, *Bürgertum und Nationalsozialismus*, op. cit., pp. 111–12.

[2] Reichsorganisationsleiter II Abteilung Rasse und Kultur. Rundschreiben 31, 8 Feb. 1932. NSAH Hann. Des. 310 I A, Nr. 37.

[3] NSDAP Bezirk Gross-Hannover, 29 Apr. 1932, Rundschreiben an sämtlichen Ortsgruppen, 29 Apr. 1932, NSAH Hann. Des. 310 I E, Nr. 33.

[4] See Verordnungsblatt der Reichsleitung, 30 Apr. 1932, and Gau Süd-Hannover–Braunschweig Abteilungsleiter für Beamtenfragen, 8 June 1932, NSAH Hann. Des. 310 I E, Nr. 2.

[5] Der Polizeipräsident to Regierungspräsident Hannover, 17 Dec. 1931, NSAH Hann. Des. 122a XI, Nr. 80. The most useful civil servant recruit was a Kriminalsekretär in the Hanover Polizeipräsidium who kept the party fully informed of police intentions, see H. Bohm, *Hitler-Jugend in einem Jahrzehut* (Braunschweig, 1938), p. 170.

[6] BSA H XVII.

and employees, financial officials, officials and employees of the Reich and state railways and finally, officials and employees of the state and private banks.

Another party organization which illustrates the NSDAP's awareness and exploitation of all areas of possible support was the war-disabled department. On 1 October 1930, following a directive from Reich head-quarters, *Gau* South-Hanover–Brunswick established a department for advising the war-disabled and war-widows, in particular by providing assistance with their claims to the welfare offices.[1] The party was inspired to do this by the belief that the majority of these people belonged to welfare organizations which were close to the SPD and by the realization that this section of the community was one of the most discontented. Thus the *Gau* war-victims department advised the *Gau* propaganda department to concentrate on this group on the grounds that 'the war victims are fearfully embittered with the present system owing to their monstrous treatment by the Emergency Laws'.[2] Furthermore, they estimated the number of war victims in *Gau* Hanover-South–Brunswick alone at 120,000. The Reich organization was run by a war-disabled man, Oberlindober, who produced a special paper—*Der Dank des Vaterlandes*—and eventually arranged alternative insurance facilities for members who were war victims. By the summer of 1932 *Kreis* specialists had been appointed.[3]

The existence of specialized groups may have helped to minimize friction between different interests. We have seen that even within the *Mittelstand* interest diverged—for example, those of the civil servants from those of the peasantry. This was even more the case between the interests of the *Mittelstand* and those of the workers. The NSDAP, therefore, met this problem with yet another separate organization.

(vii) *The Nazi factory cell organization (NSBO)*

Although the years 1928–30 had seen a change of emphasis in the party's propaganda away the workers and towards the *Mittelstand*, the NSDAP did not give up its attempts to win over the industrial workers even in *Gaue* such as those in Lower Saxony, where they formed only a minority of the population. The idea of substituting National Socialism for Marxism was one of its main ideological tenets, and the traditional political representatives of the workers were its most tenacious and bitter opponents. Above all, Nazism was a totali-

[1] Gau Süd-Hannover–Braunschweig Rundschreiben, 30 Oct. 1930, NSAH Hann. Des. 310 I E, Nr. 13.

[2] Gau Süd-Hannover–Braunschweig Abteilung Kriegsopferversorgung to Gaupropagandaleitung, 26 Feb. 1932, NSAH Hann. Des. 310 I A, Nr. 122.

[3] Kreisleitung Bad Pyrmont to Ortsgruppe Polle, 21 June 1932, NSAH 310 I A, Nr. 35.

tarian movement which could not tolerate the idea of any social group remaining outside its influence. The NSDAP therefore felt compelled to continue to try to increase its support among the industrial working class. The initiative for concentrated activity among industrial workers after 1928 came from *Gau* Berlin where the need to win support among the proletariat was of more obvious importance. During 1929, the NSDAP in Berlin formed cells in various branches of economic activity, by no means limited to industry.[1] These cells were then organized into so-called 'rings' with one ring for each type of economic activity. From the start no distinction was made between blue- and white-collar workers.

The first evidence for this activity in Lower Saxony comes from the city of Osnabrück where, in September 1929, the police reported the founding of factory cells of which the first was in the municipal corporation and called itself 'Gas and Water'.[2] In February 1930 the leader of the factory cell organization in Berlin, Engel, addressed a meeting of the Osnabrück branch on factory cells and it was agreed to take part in the Factory Council elections which were coming up. It appears, however, that the party was only able to put up one list—for the municipal corporation's works council election—and declared that the list should also be valid for white-collar workers, presumably because they feared insufficient support from the manual workers. This, however, was rejected by the municipal authorities with the result that they failed to put up a list. The party was more successful in Göttingen where they won 189 votes and two seats in the municipal corporation works council election.[3] It appears that municipal corporations were a favoured target of the Nazi factory cell organization, possibly because of the fact that these employees tended to claim for themselves a rather higher, quasi-civil servant status than the average industrial worker and were less likely to be organized in the Free Trade Unions. The first real challenge to the party in Lower Saxony in its relations with the workers came in December 1930 when there was a metal-workers' strike in Hanover. The Hanover branch declared its solidarity with the strike, threatened blacklegs with exclusion from the party, and agreed to pay RM 5 per day to married strikers and RM 3 to the unmarried plus food and clothing for those in real need.[4] The necessary funds were raised by a compulsory contribution of RM 1 from all the membership, and large branches were ordered to hold meetings with

[1] See A. Krebs, *Tendenzen und Gestalten der NSDAP* (Stuttgart, 1959), pp. 71 ff.
[2] For the following see the reports of the Osnabrück police in NSAOsn. Rep. 116 acc 7/43, Nr. 1235, vol. II.
[3] *NB*, 24 May 1930.
[4] *Gau* Hannover-Süd–Braunschweig Propagandaabteilung. Monatliches Rundschreiben, Nr. 1, 15 Dec. 1930, BA Slg. Schumacher 202 I.

speeches on 'The Attitude of the NSDAP to the Hanover Metal-workers' Strike'.

The election victory of 1930 gave added impetus to the factory cell movement. The NSDAP had shown that it could smash the middle-class parties but it still made little impression on the 'Marxist' parties. The party found it difficult to reach the workers who tended to stay away from its meetings. On 1 January 1931, therefore, an official fac-tory cell organization was established for the party as a whole—the *Nationalsozialistische Betriebszellenorganisation* (NSBO), otherwise known as the *Reichsbetriebszellen Abteilung*.[1] Beneath the head-quar-ters of the NSBO, which for a time was in Berlin, there were depart-ments in the *Gaue* and a representative in each branch who was responsible for the work of the factory cells in his area. A more elabor-ate organizational framework envisaging industrial and specialized sections was postponed. The aim of the NSBO was defined as purely political as opposed to the economic activities of the trade unions. The NSDAP did not have the resources to run a proper trade union and believed that conventional trade union activities would dissipate ener-gies which should be devoted to political activity.[2] The NSBO had two primary tasks:

first, the propagation of the national socialist *Weltanschauung* in factories and the winning of the valuable sections of the working class for the party (where-by the NSBO simply operates as a transit-station); and secondly, the education of the most valuable groups of the recruited workers of hand and brain as leader-types of a future German working class.[3]

The NSBO was distinguished from the previous organizations of the party by the fact that those who sympathized with the NSDAP but were not yet members could join.

The factory cell leaders were given very specific instructions as to the style and content of the propaganda which was their main func-tion. They were ordered not 'to concentrate on individual employers as objects of hate, but only on employers as the inevitable product of the liberal-capitalist economic system'.[4] They should not attack trade unions as such, but only the leadership and their use of trade unions for

---

[1] Organisation der National-sozialistischen Betriebszellen von Reinhold Mu-chow, 1 Jan. 1931, NSDAP Hauptarchiv, Reel 15, Folder 283. On 28 June 1932, it became Hauptabteilung VI of the Reichsleitung, see NSBO Rundschreiben, 1 July 1932; in NSDAP Hauptarchiv, Reel 15, Folder 283.

[2] NSBO Rundschreiben an alle Gau-Betriebszellenleiter, 8 Aug. 1931, in NSDAP Hauptarchiv, Reel 15, Folder 283.

[3] Ibid.

[4] Organisation der Nationalsozialistischen Betriebszellen v.R. Muchow, ibid. Folder 283.

the class war. 'The point of National Socialists remaining in the trade unions is to penetrate and conquer them'; the NSDAP could not provide equivalent services. As far as the style of the propaganda was concerned, they were advised always to generalize from concrete instances to keep it clear, unromantic and to the point—very different from the party's usual style. Indeed, they were told that their propaganda should 'not completely turn its back on the forms of speech of the Marxist propaganda methods which the masses have been used to for years'. To facilitate propaganda and control, the NSBO established its own weekly paper, *Arbeitertum* at 10 pf a copy for members; the proceeds went to the *Gau* NSBO departments, although they were then obliged to contribute fixed sums to NSBO head-quarters depending on the number of copies they ordered.[1] The aim was to help the *Gau* organizations to establish a current balance and to encourage them to sell the paper which cost 20 pf to non-members. Backing the newspaper, the NSBO ran a special press service, composed of press officers in the branches who were also responsible for feeding the local cell papers with material and ensuring that they maintained the party line.[2]

Although initially the NSBO had planned to concentrate entirely on political propaganda, the nature of its activities in a time of economic crisis inevitably involved it in economic matters. In order to compete with the Free Trade Unions who immediately branded it a 'yellow' organization, the NSBO had to show that it was both sympathetic and responsive to the needs and demands of the workers. This became particularly important in the summer and autumn of 1932 when the NSDAP was accused by the left-wing parties of being sympathetic to the Papen government. The first directive of the organization had laid down that blacklegs, members of 'yellow' organizations and those who joined the *Technische Nothilfe* (a state emergency organization for ensuring essential services during strikes) would be excluded.[3] But the NSBO was soon compelled to work out its attitude to strikes. In fact, they accepted strikes, provided they were *economically* motivated, and agreed to give strike pay to all those who had been members of the NSBO for at least three months and had paid their dues. The amount was determined by the standard rate of the Free Trade Unions for the particular area; and the money was drawn from the funds of the Reich and *Gau* NSBO head-quarters strike collections and sometimes grants from the political treasury of the *Gau*. Participation of the NSBO in strikes had to have the approval of the

[1] NSBO Rundschreiben, 28 Feb. 1931, ibid.
[2] Tätigkeit der NSBO-Pressewarte und die Organisation des *Arbeitertumnachrichtendienstes*, ibid. Folder 278.
[3] Organisation der NS Betriebszellen v.R. Muchow, 1 Jan. 1931, NSDAP Hauptarchiv, Reel 15, Folder 293.

Reich NSBO head-quarters.[1] By 7 November 1932, the NSBO claimed to have participated in over twenty-six large and small strikes.[2] Furthermore, the NSBO also provided free legal advice in all cases arising from employment and concerning social insurance.[3]

How successful was the NSBO? The first challenge for the organization came with the Works Committee elections in the spring of 1931. In the Reich as a whole the NSBO claimed 12 per cent of the workers' vote and 25 per cent of the white-collar workers' vote in those elections for which they put up lists.[4] The NSBO also entered for the Works Committee elections in the civil service industries—the Post Office and the Railways. For the election to the main Post Office Works Committee in May, the NSBO, lacking an adequate organization of its own, made an agreement with the *Deutsche Postgewerkschaft*, according to which NSBO members received the second and fifth places on their list and 45 per cent of all the places on the list.[5] In the Railway Committee elections, the NSBO won 3·5 per cent of all the votes, but significantly, in the offices of the regional head-quarters (*Direktionsbüros*) they won 20 per cent.[6] In *Gau* Hanover-South–Brunswick the NSBO won only a handful of seats. There were only two firms where it won more than one seat—Continentalgummi in Hanover, where the white-collar workers' list won two seats (there was no workers' list), and Ilseder Hütte-Bergbau in Lengede where they also won two seats. In *Gau* Weser-Ems, despite the fact that the party had been trying to found factory cells in Osnabrück for over a year, they apparently ordered their supporters there to support the Christian trade unions because their organization was inadequate for putting up separate lists. Only in the municipal works election did they manage to win one seat.[7] In *Gau* Hanover-East the NSBO was not started until July 1931.[8]

The year 1932 saw a considerable expansion of NSBO activities. In January a special department was set up to deal with the unemployed with the aim of training propagandists and supplying the party's

---

[1] Streikunterstützungbestimmungen der NSBO; in NSDAP Hauptarchiv, Reel 15, Folder 278.

[2] NSBO Rundschreiben, 7 Nov. 1932, ibid., Folder 283.

[3] NSBO Gau Hannover-Süd–Braunschweig Auszug aus dem Merkblatt, ibid., Folder 280.

[4] Details of the NSBO performance in 'Erfolge der NS Betriebszellen bei den Betriebsrätewahlen im Frühjahr 1931' in *Arbeitertum*. Sonderheft, Nr. 1, ibid., Folder 283.

[5] NSBO Rundschreiben, 15 May 1931, ibid.

[6] Mitteilungen der Landespolizeistelle Berlin, 15 Mar. 1930, in NSAH Hann. Des. 80 Hann. II, Nr. 775.

[7] 23 Mar. 1931, report of Osnabrück police, NSAOsn. Rep. 116 acc 7/43, Nr. 1235, vol. IV.

[8] Telschow to Schumann, 10 Sept. 1931 in BA *NS* 22 vorl. 369.

press with relevant material.[1] By the 1st of May the NSBO claimed 100,000 members;[2] and in August a new layer of functionaries was added to the organization with the introduction of *Kreis* NSBO departments.[3] *Gau* Hanover-South–Brunswick was evidently ahead of the Reich organization on this because it had introduced NSBO *Kreisleiter* as early as January.[4] There is further evidence for the seriousness with which the *Gau* took its factory cell organization. Already in 1931 for example, it had started producing its own biweekly NSBO newspaper for functionaries—*Der Betriebspionier*; the branch in Brunswick produced a regular broadsheet—*NSBO-Signale*,[5] while a regular NSBO section appeared in the *Gau*'s daily paper, the *Niedersächsische Tageszeitung*. Furthermore, in April 1932, after the banning of the SA, the *Gauleitung* turned a former SA training school in Kreiensen over to the NSBO as a camp for training functionaries and canvassers.[6] Ten courses of ten days' duration were planned with 100–120 participants on each course. The apparent enterprise of the NSBO in *Gau* Hanover-South–Brunswick was partly due to the fact that an extremely energetic former KPD man, Berthold Karwahne, was based in Hanover as 'Inspector' of the north-western region of the NSBO.[7]

What were the problems facing the NSBO? The most obvious was finance. In November 1931 a crisis meeting of the *Gau* NSBO leaders was held in Munich which was informed that *Arbeitertum* was running a deficit of RM 20,000. And although Hitler agreed to pay RM 1,000 out of the political funds, in future the *Gaue* were forced to meet themselves the cost of printing the numerous forms which were used for correspondence.[8]

[1] NSBO Rundschreiben, 12 Jan. 1932, NSDAP Hauptarchiv, Reel 15, Folder 283. According to Krebs, op. cit., p. 74, the section for the unemployed was the most effective branch of the NSBO. Geiger, *Die soziale Schichtung des deutschen Volkes*, p. 111 writing at the time (1931–2) confirmed this and noted that the latest tactic was 'to win the factories by making agreements with employers to employ unemployed NSDAP members'. This also worked with the railways where as we have seen the staff in the regional offices were increasingly sympathetic to the NSDAP. For an example of the tactic in operation in Lower Saxony see the description of events in Northeim in Allen, *The Nazi Seizure of Power*, pp. 110–11.
[2] NSBO Rundschreiben, 1 May 1932, NSDAP Hauptarchiv, Reel 15, Folder 283.
[3] Gau Hannover-Süd–Braunschweig NSBO an alle Kreisleiter und Ortgruppenleiter, 30 Aug. 1932, NSAH Hann. Des. 310 I B, 14.
[4] Der Betriebspionier, Nr. 15, Ende Jan. 1932, NSDAP Hauptarchiv, Reel 15, Folder 280.
[5] Copies in BSA H VII, Nr. 142a.
[6] Der Betriebspionier, Nr. 18, 29 Apr. 1932. Only 60 NSBO members took part in the first course, see NSDAP Hauptarchiv, Reel 15, Folder 280.
[7] See NSBO Rundschreiben, 7 Nov. 1932, in NSDAP Hauptarchiv, Reel 15, Folder 283.   [8] NSBO Rundschreiben, 21 Nov., ibid.

DEVELOPMENTS IN ORGANIZATION

There were, however, more fundamental problems. In the first place, there was a lack of co-operation from other sections of the party.[1] On at least one occasion branch leaders were reprimanded for their failure to co-operate with the NSBO.[2] Furthermore, after an incident in which the SA had acted as blacklegs in a strike involving the NSBO, Röhm was forced to issue a ban on similar activities in the future.[3] Apart from bureaucratic rivalry, it is not perhaps surprising that the *mittelständisch* branch leaders were suspicious of an organization which was specifically intended for employees.

Secondly, there was the delicate problem of NSBO propaganda which, in order that it should not alienate potential supporters from the upper and middle classes or endanger important negotiations with political and business leaders, had to be kept on a tight rein. This became increasingly difficult during the winter of 1932.

Thirdly, the organization was bedevilled by confusion with regard both to membership and structure. Initially, as we have seen, even civil servants could be members.[4] Furthermore, plans were continually mooted for subdividing the organization on the basis of different economic sections with special groups for each trade or industry.[5] During 1932, many of these special groups were set up, particularly at local level, and, significantly, they included both employers and employees. The NSBO leadership made frequent attempts to clarify the situation and return to the principle of membership being limited to employees.[6] But apparently with little effect. The disastrous results of this proliferation of special groups as seen by the NSBO leadership were described with great lucidity in an extremely interesting memorandum, dated 31 January 1933, i.e. before Hitler's chancellorship had had time to influence developments.[7] For a picture of the NSBO in the period before the *Machtergreifung* it is worth quoting at some length. The memorandum began,

The past year has shown that here and there people have tended to deviate from the basic direction of NSBO organizational policy.... Above all, in the

[1] See Der Betriebspionier, Nr. 19, 6 May 1932, NSAH Hann. Des. 310 I B, Nr. 14.
[2] NSBO Rundschreiben, Apr. 1932, an alle Ortsgruppenleiter National Archives T-81, Reel 176, Frames 318222–3.
[3] NSBO Rundschreiben, 26 Aug. 1932, containing Röhm Verfügung NSDAP Hauptarchiv, Reel 15, Folder 283.
[4] They were excluded and passed over to the expert for civil servants on 27 July 1931. See National Archives T-81, Reel 175, Frames 317760.
[5] E.g. Anlagen zum Organisationsplan der NSBO Jan. 1932, in NSDAP Hauptarchiv, Reel 15, Folder 283.
[6] E.g. Verordnungsblatt der Reichsleitung, 15 July 1932, NSAH Hann. Des. 310 I B, Nr. 44.
[7] NSBO Rundschreiben, 31 Jan. 1933, NSDAP Hauptarchiv, Reel 15, Folder 283.

last few months there has been a desire to found all sorts of specialist groups (*Fachgruppen*). . . . Almost the entire work of internal organization was expended on keeping these structures going. . . . Often inflated specialist group administrations began to concentrate not so much on propaganda and canvassing for members which would have been all right, but in composing 'memoranda' about corporate reconstruction, wage questions, international economic policy(!), the apprentice system etc. . . . Furthermore, these specialist groups used a lot of money but did not bring anything in. Many *Gau* NSBO leaders were surrounded by dozens of specialist group functionaries. . . . Fantastic structures emerged (e.g. a specialist group for 'cattle dealers', an industrial group for 'hairdressers' etc.) . . . in other words a process of gradual bureaucratization.

The memorandum went on to emphasize that, although a subdivision of the NSBO was envisaged for the future,

the beginning and end of all our work is the *factory* (*Betrieb*). . . . Therefore the slogan must always be: 'Conquer the factories!' Conquer the *real* factory workers and employees. . . . In other words we must not make things easy for ourselves by organizing only those who come to us more or less of their own accord. *Instead we must really smash the red strongholds.* . . . Back to the old NSBO method of attack of 1930–31.

The memorandum banned the founding of further specialist groups and insisted that those already in existence must limit themselves to propaganda and canvassing for membership.

Next, the memorandum referred to the overburdening of the organization with the work of representing members' claims at the Work Courts; it warned against entering into commitments which could not be fulfilled, emphasizing that they did not intend to become an 'economic association'. Furthermore, it reported the 'mountain of debts' which almost all the *Gau* NSBO organizations had built up. In the words of the author—'it is a mystery to me how we are ever going to collect these sums'.

Finally, the memorandum noted that

we are continually noticing that some factory papers contain statements which in no way reflect National Socialist policy, and which, therefore, put the NSBO and its aims in a completely false light. . . . It must, therefore, be repeated that every *Gau* NSBO director should keep a strict control through his press officer of all the NSBO factory papers in his area.

One may conclude that the NSBO had only very limited success in fulfilling its original function. It became stifled by a proliferation of minute, mainly *Mittelständisch* economic interest groups pressing their particular aims and in general advocating the idea of a 'corporate state', which would reflect their interests. Yet the balance was not entirely negative. At the beginning of 1931, the Osnabrück police had doubted the ability of the NSBO to found a cell in the big copper works in the city on the grounds that 'there are no suitable people belonging to the NSDAP who have experience of trade union affairs'.[1] The construction of a network of functionaries specializing in the problems of the workers helped to fill this gap, though after 1933 many of these NSBO functionaries proved to be too radical for the taste of the Nazi government.[2]

(viii) *The SA*

The problem of competing jurisdictions was even more urgent in the relationship of the political organization to the SA than between the different groups within the political organization. According to an SA directive of 2 November 1926, which was then incorporated in GRUSA (Basic SA directive) III of 3 June 1927, the political leader assigned tasks to the SA leader, but the actual carrying out of those tasks was in the hands of the SA and it was up to the SA leader to decide whether they were capable of performing the task.[3] Furthermore, the SA leader was responsible for 'organization, recruitment and exclusion, the appointment and dismissal of leaders, punishments, uniform, badges and logistics'. The independence of the SA was further emphasized by the fact that it did not come within the jurisdiction of the party court apparatus, the *Uschla*. If there was a dispute between an SA and a party official the matter was dealt with by negotiation between the party and SA superiors of the disputants.

The semi-independent status of the SA was regarded by many political leaders as a thorn in their flesh; but it was vigorously defended by the SA. Conflict between the two organizations was endemic within the NSDAP. It could take the form of a simple conflict over jurisdiction—for example over whether or not the branch leader could ban the taking of a flag to a meeting.[4] But the most common form was a struggle over finance. Initially, the SA was financed by a tax which was paid by the *Gaue* to Munich and then redistributed to the *Gaue* SA. But, in 1930, this tax was suspended and the SA became financially dependent on the political organization, which was not always cooperative. As the economic situation deteriorated, the position of the SA membership became worse. They already had an additional burden of insurance contributions. In December 1928, the voluntary

---

[1] Report of the Osnabrück police, 2 Mar. 1931, in NSAOsn. Rep 116 acc 7/43, Nr. 1235, vol. IV.

[2] See Krebs, op. cit., p. 77.

[3] For the following see Bennecke, *Hitler und die SA*, pp. 131 ff. and 247–8. Bennecke includes a copy of GRUSA III.

[4] See the dispute between the Brunswick branch and SA leaders during May 1927, in NSAH Hann. Des. 310 I A, Nr. 14.

insurance system which the NSDAP had introduced for the SA in 1926 was reorganized and a so-called *Hilfskasse* established under Martin Bormann to which all SA members were compelled to belong, paying a monthly contribution of 30 pf.[1] This provided insurance against possible injury or death in the service of the party.

In March 1930, the SA leader in North Germany tried to improve the situation by striking a bargain with the district party leaders.[2] He insisted that, in future, when political leaders wished to order the SA band for a meeting, the proceeds of the meeting must be divided fifty-fifty between the *Bezirks-* or *Kreisleiter* and the SA. He pointed out that this would give the *Kreisleiter* an independent source of income. But this was only an expedient. The crisis came to a head with the Stennes rebellion of August 1930, in which finance was one of the factors involved.[3] On 2 September, Hitler gave way to the pressure and introduced a compulsory SA tax for all party members of 20 pf per month. The entrance fee was increased from RM 1 to RM 2, of which RM 1 went to the local SA head-quarters; it was also laid down that 50 per cent of all contributions collected at party meetings should go to the SA. This did not, however, put an end to conflict over finance and, until 1933, there were complaints from *Kreis* and branch leaders about the SA collecting money and provisions without permission, which meant there was nothing left for the party.[4] Equally, the SA complained about the failure of the political leadership to fulfil their obligations.[5] For this reason, the SA tried to develop independent sources of income. They had already set up a 'Quartermaster' organization in 1928, producing uniforms and equipment, which had the double advantage of standardizing the equipment and collecting the proceeds from the purchase of uniforms by members.[6] They also undertook a directly commercial operation by establishing an SA cigarette firm, marketing 'Sturm' cigarettes, the profits of which were distributed to the *Gau* head-quarters according to their sales.[7]

These conflicts over jurisdiction and finance reflected a struggle for prestige within the NSDAP. The SA with its quasi-military structure developed a definite *esprit de corps* and it resented having to do most of

---

[1] Bennecke, op. cit., pp. 148 and 252.

[2] Osaf-Nord Rundschreiben am alle Kreis und Bezirksleiter, 24 Mar. 1930, NSAH Hann. Des. 310 I E, Nr. 33.

[3] See Report of the Reichskommissar für Überwachung der Öffentlichen Ordnung, 17 Feb. 1929, in NSAH Hann. Des. 80 Hann II, Nr. 720.

[4] For examples see NSAH Hann. Des. 310 I A, Nr. 120 among other files.

[5] Vierteljahresberichte der OSAF, 8 Dec. 1931, NSDAP Hauptarchiv, Reel 16, Folder 306.

[6] Bekanntmachung gez. Adolf Hitler, 21 Nov. 1928, NSAH Hann. Des. 310 I A. Nr. 120.

[7] For details see National Archives T-81, Reel 175, e.g. Frame 317736.

the dirty work while being subordinate to the political section. This resentment emerged in criticism of party *Bonzen* and could quickly explode if the political leadership failed to act decisively and show quick results. After the electoral victory of 1930, new problems arose. Hitherto, the whole party had consisted of activists in total opposition to the existing order. Many members were in the SA. After 1930, however, with the proliferation of departments the party bureaucracy increased at a phenomenal rate. Furthermore, after 1930, the party had acquired political influence within the existing system which, if it was to be used to maximum effect, required tactical compromises which were liable to be interpreted as a 'sell-out' by the ordinary party militants, the majority of whom were in the SA.

The most striking example of this problem in Lower Saxony occurred in the Unterweser district in *Gau* Hanover-East during 1930–1.[1] The struggle within the party here lasted for just over a year and was fought with unparalleled bitterness. On two separate occasions branches had to be dissolved by the *Gau* head-quarters with Hitler's consent. In November 1930, the rival groups put up two separate lists for the Bremerhaven city council election. And finally, in August 1931, the SA physically attacked a meeting of members called by the *Gauleiter*. The exact motives of the participants are not clear. One motive was rivalry between the *Gauleiter* and Bruns, the leader of one of the groups, over their respective newspapers. Bruns was a printer who had started a National Socialist newspaper for the Unterweser area— *Die Sturmwelle*—to help himself out of financial difficulties. This paper, however, threatened to take subscriptions away from the official *Gau* paper—*Der Niedersachsen-Stürmer*—which was owned by the *Gauleiter*. Personal rivalries also played a major part. Nonetheless, the language used by the group opposing the *Gauleiter* indicated a more fundamental conflict of attitudes. Thus a pamphlet produced by this group, who appear to have been in the majority, maintained that

for a long time there has been a bitter struggle between the *petit bourgeois* element which pushed its way into the party after the electoral success of 14 September and the old activists. The future dynamic of the party depends on the outcome of this struggle.[2]

Three weeks later, on 10 September 1931, having been expelled from the party, the group gave full vent to its feelings in an open letter to Hitler as follows:

For years our SA has worked hard for you and the NSDAP; for years the party membership have undergone the severest sacrifices. Comrades have been thrown into prison because of their National Socialist beliefs—and no party

[1] Documents on this conflict in BA NS 22 vorl. 369 and the reports of the Wesermünde police department in NSAS Rep. 8, Op. 758.
[2] BA *NS* 22 vorl. 369.

leaders have shown concern for them. Unemployment among the SA men is catastrophic and yet their contributions have been ruthlessly squeezed out of them. Anyone who could not pay was thrown out. . . . While the *Reich* headquarters refused to pay a Wesermünde man, who had been badly injured in a fight at a meeting, RM 200 to enable him to buy false teeth, they built a million mark palace in Munich [the Brown House]. . . . Through your striving after ministerial posts, you provoke the opposition of all true National Socialists, as is proved by the attitude of Groh and Franzen in Brunswick. We do not dream of supporting you in your plan to join a Brüning government. . . . It will be our task to open the eyes of all SA men so that they recognize that Germany cannot be saved by a parliamentary party, but only through revolutionary action. . . .[1]

The problem was to retain the revolutionary *élan* of the SA for propaganda purposes, while preventing it from erupting into violence against the established order which would jeopardize top-level political negotiations, alienate potential supporters from the bourgeoisie, and possibly even bring about the prohibition of the party.

The party dealt with this problem in a number of ways. In the first place, strict instructions were given and continually reiterated banning the carrying of firearms and the performance of military exercises, in order to discourage ideas of a *putsch*.[2] Secondly, ordinary SA men were officially discouraged from concerning themselves with detailed political questions (but not with *Weltanschauung*), though this was unlikely to have much effect.[3] In the spring of 1932, the SA leadership itself tightened its control over discipline by introducing special training squads for new members who henceforward began as SA probationers.[4] Most important of all, however, the extremism of the SA was canalized into frenetic propaganda activity, which in itself provided sufficient scope for the expression of violence. It was here that the contribution of the SA by far outweighed its negative aspect as a disruptive force. In the first place, in the words of Theodor Heuss, in the SA 'the party possessed a human reserve which was always ready for the small change of political activity, distributors of pamphlets, poster stickers, cheer leaders and so on'.[5] By January 1932, there were 27,714 of them in Lower Saxony alone.[6] Such work was given added attraction by the

---

[1] *Nachrichten für Stadt und Land*, 10 Sept. 1931.

[2] E.g. Parteibefehl in *VB*, 5 Dec. 1928.

[3] See Article 'Aufgabe der SA' by *Gau* H-S-B secretary Erich Maul in *NB*, 14 Sept. 1929.

[4] OSAF Rundschreiben, 7 Mar. 1932, NSDAP Hauptarchiv, Reel 15, Fold 307.

[5] Theodor Heuss, *Hitler's Weg. Eine historisch-politische Studie über den Nationalsozialismus* (Stuttgart, 1932), p. 123.

[6] 14,586 in H-S-B, 5,238 in H-E and 7,880 in W-E, see OSAF Betr. Stand der SA nach dem Stande des letzten Stärkemeldung, 27 Feb. 1932, NSDAP Hauptarchiv, Reel 17, Folder 307.

fact that it was carried out in uniform and in a disciplined group. Above all the propaganda marches were an exceptionally effective weapon in a society which valued military symbols so highly. The aim was to give a 'powerful impression of our unity, strength and discipline, and thereby to drive home to the German people by suggestion that the NSDAP has the strength, the will and the ability to create order again in Germany'.[1] These marches were regarded by the propaganda department in Hanover-South–Brunswick as *the* most effective propaganda technique.[2]

The second important task of the SA was violence in the service of the party, either to protect its functions or to intimidate opponents. The SA was by no means alone in indulging in political violence. A list of injuries received in political fights during 1931 in the Hanover *Regierungsbezirk* shows that seventy-one NSDAP, six *Stahlhelm*, forty-seven *Reichsbanner* and seven KPD members were injured and one *Reichsbanner* man was killed.[3] Nevertheless, the SA played a full part in the encouragement of political extremism and violence. In the words of the *Kreisleiter* of Hameln, referring to an SA march: 'Disturbance is the main thing—never mind how it arises.'[4] In its monthly progress report to the Reich head-quarters for June 1931, *Gau* Hanover-South–Brunswick described how the SA had beaten their left-wing opponents by tying their chairs together so that they could not be used as weapons and then locking the doors so that they could not escape. The battle had then spread from the hall into the centre of Hanover to the annoyance and horror of the shopkeepers. 'Such events', commented the *Gauleitung*

are very useful for increasing discontent with the political situation and a subsequent collection from the frightened shopkeepers was very successful. Perhaps head-quarters knows of ways and means whereby other *Gau* propaganda departments can be informed of our experiences.[5]

Special instructions were drawn up for the work of the lower echelons, including minute details on the initiation of new recruits and

[1] Gau Osthannover Propagandaleitung Rundschreiben, 14 July 1932, NSAH Hann. Des. 310 I E, Nr. 2.
[2] Gau H-S-B Richtlinien der Propagandaabteilung gez. Rust and Gutterer, 1 June 1931, in NSAH Hann. Des. 310 I B, Nr. 5.
[3] Übersicht, 1 Jan. 1931 to 30 Dec. 1931, Reg. Bez. Hannover NSAH Hann. Des. 80 Hann II, Nr. 722.
[4] H. Schmidt to Rust, 15 May 1931, NSAH Hann. Des. 310 I A, Nr. 46.
[5] Tatigkeitsbericht, June 1931, NSAH Hann. Des. 310 I B, Nr. 13. It is interesting to note that by the beginning of 1932 the owners of the two largest cafés in Hanover (Café Kröpke and the Wiener Café), the director of the *Herrenhausen* brewery, who was also chairman of the Brewers' Association, and Firma Ahrberg, a large Hanover firm, were all regularly paying substantial sums to the SA. See Gutterer to *Gauleiting* H-S-B, 5 Jan. 1932, NSAH Hann. Des. 310 I A, 120.

suggested programmes for the regular SA evenings.[1] Training courses were organized for SA leaders. At the end of 1931, *Gau* Hanover-South–Brunswick rented three disused factories in Kreiensen near Göttingen for an SA and SS school which held monthly courses.[2] The first, which was held in November, was attended by 100 SA leaders who came from as far away as the Rhineland. *Gau* Hanover-East held intensive week-end courses at an inn in the Lüneburg Heath.[3] Apart from lectures on ideology and matters of organization, the week-end also included physical exercises and the measurement of the participants.

The attempt by the authorities to deal with the SA met with mixed success. The ban on the wearing of the uniform which was introduced in Prussia in June 1930 had little effect but helped party propaganda.[4] The SA got round it by wearing white shirts as an alternative uniform and the ban proved unenforceable in the courts.[5] The ban of April 1932, on the other hand, was completely effective at any rate from the point of view of the obedience of the NSDAP. The party did not wish to run the risk of a total ban and therefore ordered the SA to dissolve itself and be reabsorbed by the political organization.[6] It may not be purely imaginative to detect a certain relish in the tone of the *Gauleiter* in declaring that the former SA leaders had no special rights in the political section.[7] To what extent the party suffered from the ban is difficult to estimate since it lasted for so short a time.[8]

(ix) *The SS*

The SS was re-established in September 1925—before the *formal* reorganization of the SA.[9] It was clear from the first directive that it was intended to be an élite in the particular service of Hitler.[10] Thus,

[1] SA Dienstvorschrift für die Untergruppe (Gausturm) Hannover-Ost in NSAH Hann. Des. 310 I E, Nr. 3.

[2] Der Polizeipräsident Hannover to Oberpräsident Hannover, 8 Jan. 1932, NSAH Hann. Des. Hann. 80 Hann II, Nr. 722.

[3] See report of Harburg political police, 20 Dec. 1931, for the following. NSAS Rep. 8, Op. 758.   [4] See Bennecke, op. cit., pp. 146–7.

[5] The courts either used procedural points to avoid conviction or showed blatant prejudice. See examples in NSAH Hann. Des. 122a. XI 79.

[6] Gau H-S-B Rundschreiben an alle Ortsgruppen- und Kreisleiter, 3 May 1932, NSAH Hann. Des. 310 I A, Nr. 120.

[7] See Gauleiter Ost-Hannover Rundschreiben, 16 Apr. 1932, NSAH Hann. Des. 310 I E, Nr. 2.

[8] Bennecke, op. cit., pp. 180 ff., suggests that the ban had little effect. The Harburg police, however, reported a definite loss of dramatic effect in the party meetings. See report of 12 May 1932, in NSAS Rep. 80, p. 758.

[9] See Heinz Höhne, *Der Orden unter dem Totenkopf. Die Geschichte der SS* (Gütersloh, 1960), pp. 27 ff.

[10] Richtlinien der 'Schutzstaffeln' der NSDAP undated (1925); in NSAH Hann. Des. 310 I A, Nr. 8.

although it was given many of the same tasks as the SA, such as the protection of meetings and propaganda, its members were to be men 'on whom Adolf Hitler can rely completely', and they were to provide his personal bodyguard at meetings. There were special rules for membership. Members had to belong to the NSDAP and be between the ages of twenty-three and thirty-five (compared with only a minimum age of eighteen for the SA), though exceptions could be made by headquarters. All new applicants were obliged to supply two referees who were party members. The SS organization was made independent of the SA and of the political section and was directly responsible to Hitler. This was reinforced by independent financial arrangements. Each member had to pay a monthly contribution of 50 pf to the SS headquarters and, to strengthen this independence, a system of 'supporting members' (*Fördernde Mitglieder*) was introduced, that is sympathizers who were not members of the party but who agreed to give a regular contribution to the SS.

Initially, the North German party leaders objected to the new organization. They saw it as interference from Munich in the running of their affairs. Rust informed Munich in November 1925 that he would 'of course follow the instructions for the creation of *Schutzstaffel*', but 'only when the party and SA organization is so far advanced that *Schutzstaffel* can be formed from it'.[1] In the autumn of 1926, in order to win the co-operation of Pfeffer in running the SA, Hitler was compelled to agree to the subordination of the SS to the SA head-quarters. The SA could now keep a careful control over its rival and indeed limited the number of SS men in any area to one-tenth of the SA.[2] Nevertheless, it is clear that the SS continued to regard itself and was regarded by others as an élite organization. Its membership qualifications were increased to include at least a year's membership of the party and a height of 1 metre 70 centimetres (except for former servicemen).[3] Furthermore, its tasks were extended to include the gathering of information on the activities of opponents and details of known freemasons and Jewish leaders. Leaders of the SS were expected to be of higher calibre than those of the SA. In November 1926, for example, the branch leader in Brunswick carefully avoided making the SA leader, leader of the SS because 'he lacks the necessary intellectual qualities'.[4] The man he chose as SS leader was a former army lieutenant, an employee of a transport firm. This élite reputa-

[1] Rust to Munich, 16 Nov. 1925, *ibid.*

[2] Höhne, op. cit., p. 107.

[3] Vorläufige Dienstordnung der SS, 29 June 1928, NSAH Hann. Des. 122a XI 76f.

[4] Ortsgruppe Braunschweig to Rust, 11 Nov. 1926, NSAH Hann. Des. 310 I A, Nr. 9.

tion had its drawbacks, however, particularly for relations with the SA. Thus, according to a police report, at the end of 1927 an attempt to establish an SS group in Hanover proved abortive because the whole SA at once volunteered.[1] This was to be a continuing source of annoyance to the SA. In January 1932, for example, the SA in Hanover-East underwent medical examination to find out those who were physically and racially suitable for membership of the SS. Apparently, this aroused expectations among the SA men who qualified, and they had to be informed that the predicate 'suitable for the SS' by no means meant that they were to be accepted as members of the SS.[2]

The chance for the SS to regain their independence came with the Stennes rebellion of August 1930, in which they had proved their worth to Hitler by defending the Berlin *Gau* head-quarters against the SA.[3] Hitler used the opportunity offered by the resignation of Pfeffer to redefine the relationship between the SA and the SS. In a directive dated 7 November 1930 Hitler insisted that 'their tasks are completely different. The task of the SS is, in the first place, to perform a police role within the party.'[4] He laid down that no SA leader was permitted to give orders to an SS leader and vice versa. Furthermore, although the SS was banned from actually recruiting from the SA, the 10 per cent clause was dropped. Also, in order to reinforce this independence and build up the organization as quickly as possible, Hitler ordered an increase in the contributions of the 'supporter members' from 1 April 1931, and laid down that the ordinary SS contributions should be paid to the local SS head-quarters instead of to its Munich head-quarters.[5]

These measures inevitably increased the rivalry between the SA and the SS.[6] In December 1931, Röhm was forced to inform his SA leaders that he did not agree with their reports opposing the increase of the SS to 22,000 men.[7] The political organization also resented the independence of the SS. There were frequent complaints from *Kreisleiter* about the SS arranging meetings or collecting money and provisions without permission.[8] It is interesting, however, that one such complaint

[1] Polizeipräsident Hannover to Reg-präsident Hannover, 25 May 1929, NSAH Hann. Des. 80 Hann II, Nr. 749.

[2] Gausturm Hannover-Ost Rundschreiben, 20 Jan. 1932, gez. Hasse NSAH Hann. Des. 310 I E, Nr. 3.

[3] See the report of the Berlin police on the Stennes rebellion in NSAH Hann. Des. 80 Hann II, Nr. 773.

[4] Adolf Hitler Befehl, 7 Nov. 1930, in National Archives T-81, Reel 90, Frame 10276.

[5] SS Befehl, Nr. 24, 20 Mar. 1931 (copy), in NSAH Hann. Des. 80 Hann II, Nr. 775.

[6] A struggle which culminated in the purge of 30 June 1934.

[7] OSAF an sämtliche Gruppenführer und den Reichsführer SS, 2 Dec. 1931, in NSDAP Hauptarchiv, Reel 16, Folder 306.

[8] For examples see NSAH Hann. Des. 310 I A, Nr. 120.

from the *Kreisleiter* in Eutin was answered by his *Gauleiter* to the effect that the SS were permitted to canvass for 'supporter members' and that many members of the *Gauleitung* contributed to the SS.[1]

(x) *The Hitler-Jugend and its associated organizations*

Unlike the SS, the Hitler Youth (HJ) was not founded on the initiative of NSDAP head-quarters.[2] Initially, indeed, Munich was indifferent to the activities of those who were too young to be party members or voters. But during 1925–6 groups of young National Socialist supporters began to form throughout the Reich; in Lower Saxony the initiative was taken by a group in Peine.[3] The most important of these groups was the *Grossdeutsche Jugendbewegung* established in Saxony by Kurt Gruber from Plauen i.V, which received official recognition from Hitler in October 1925. At the party congress in Weimar in July 1926 Gruber's organization was renamed 'Hitler Youth, League of German Workers' Youth' and was recognized as the official party youth organization with Gruber as Reich leader.

The party in Lower Saxony was not entirely happy about this centralization under Gruber's leadership.[4] At the beginning of 1927, therefore, in order to provide a North German alternative to the 'mode of operation of the Saxons and south Germans', they united with the *Gau* HJ leaders in Berlin–Brandenburg, Hamburg, Anhalt Saxony North and the Ruhr to form an independent organization under the leadership of Berlin.[5] Significantly, 'for tactical reasons' they dropped the name Hitler Youth and left only the name 'League of German Workers' Youth'. It is clear from their manifesto that the group wanted to adopt a more 'socialist' stance:

We call upon all activist revolutionary elements among German youth to free themselves at last from the tutelage of reactionary and Marxist organizations. Your place is in the ranks of those who are involved in a passionate struggle for the reorganization of the German people and state in a nationalist and socialist spirit. Break the fetters of bourgeois cowardice and Marxist mendacity. Join the LGWY.[6]

[1] Gaugeschäftsführer Schleswig-Holstein to Wolf, 15 Dec. 1932, National Archives T-81, Reel 104, Frame 302883.
[2] For the following see Hans Christian Brandenburg, *Die Geschichte der HJ* (Köln, 1968), pp. 22 ff. and A. Klönne, *Hitlerjugend. Die Jugend und ihre Organisationen im Dritten Reich* (Hannover/Frankfurt, 1960), pp. 9–12.
[3] Betr. NSDAP Jugend (undated) c. June 1925, NSAH Hann. Des. 310 I A, Nr. 5.
[4] Rust to Hitler, 28 Oct. 1926, NSAH Hann. Des. 310 I A, Nr. 8.
[5] Bressel-Brunswick to Dincklage, 13 Feb. 1927, NSAH Hann. Des. 310 I A, Nr. 16.
[6] Quoted in Brandenburg, op. cit., p. 32.

This move is particularly interesting in that it was clearly under-taken with the sanction of the *Gauleiter* concerned. The organization was subject to final control by the *Gauleiter* and *Gau* directives required their counter-signature. Yet it was not approved by the party head-quarters in Munich. Indeed it represented a serious blow to the Hitler Youth organization, which still existed only in embryonic form.

At the end of 1927, the Reich head-quarters decided to reassert its control over the youth organization and insisted therefore that Gru-ber's Hitler Youth was the only youth organization recognized by the party and, in particular, that the 'League of German Workers' Youth' was no longer acceptable.[1] It was during 1928, then, that the first official Hitler Youth branches were established in Lower Saxony, and on 1 December an HJ *Gau* head-quarters was established in Han-over-South–Brunswick, though an office was not acquired for several months.[2] The *Gau* head-quarters consisted of a *Gau* leader, a secre-tary, the head of the *Gau* hiking department (in fact a form of SA), and the head of the *Gaufahrtenamt*, which handled traditional youth move-ment activities. By May 1929, a sports department had been added; in September, a special Hitler Youth paper was founded for *Gau* Han-over-South–Brunswick—*Die Zukunft*; and in November, the *Bund deutscher Mädel* (BdM) was established for girls who helped out with first aid, sewing, etc.

On 21 March 1930, a new *Gau* HJ leader was appointed—Hart-mann Lauterbacher, who, after being made HJ branch leader in Brunswick in November 1929, had quickly shown his ability.[3] Lau-terbacher is in fact a good example of rapid promotion on the basis of performance. The former HJ *Gauleitung* in Hanover was ruthlessly discarded.

After the 1930 election campaign, in which the HJ played a full part, Lauterbacher concentrated on tightening up the organization: new district leaders were appointed; the *Gauleitung* was staffed by people who could work full-time for the organization; monthly *Führerbriefe* were composed to keep the branch leaders in touch, and these were backed by regular meetings between the district leaders and the *Gau* leader. A major problem as with the rest of the organization

[1] Reichsleitung Abteilung Jugend to *Gau* Hanover-South, 14 Dec. 1927, NSAH Hann. Des. 310 I A, Nr. 19.
[2] For the following see H. Bolm, *Hitler-Jugend in einem Jahrzehnt. Ein Glau-bensweg der niedersächsischen Jugend* (Braunschweig, 1938), pp. 64 ff.
[3] Hartmann Lauterbacher born 1900, educated at a Gymnasium and 1929–30 at a Pharmaceutical college. As a member of the 'Junge Gemeinschaft' of the Kuf-steiner Gymnasium played an active part in the 1923 Ruhr resistance; then led an NS youth group with thirty members which he amalgamated with the HJ in 1927. He was later appointed deputy Reichsjugendführer, and then took over *Gau* Han-over-South–Brunswick, see BDC files.

was finance. In November 1930 the *Gau* treasurer had agreed to provide a subsidy of RM 200 a month to be provided from the salaries of the *Gau*'s parliamentary deputies.[1] Two months later, however, he was having to apologize to Lauterbacher for his failure to pay the money, explaining that the deputies had not yet paid up.[2] Lauterbacher described the resulting financial situation as 'catastrophic', owing to the fact that only about 50 per cent of the members paid their dues, while he was expected regularly to forward the share of the Reich head-quarters to Munich.[3] He was forced to use such expedients as holding lotteries at meetings.

Nevertheless, the HJ in *Gau* Hanover-South–Brunswick grew fairly rapidly. In March 1930, there were only seven branches with ninety-eight members; by August 1931, there were fifteen districts with 115 branches, containing 2,000 members; and by the end of January 1932, there were 3,000 members.[4] According to statistics for the Reich as a whole, of the HJ membership 69 per cent were workers and apprentices, 10 per cent were in business and 12 per cent were secondary school pupils. A large percentage were unemployed.[5] An analysis of the social background of HJ leaders maintained that 38 per cent were workers including agricultural workers, 18 per cent were artisans, 14 per cent were in business, 16 per cent were from secondary schools and 14 per cent were in other professions.[6]

Between 1930 and 1933 the HJ emulated the incessant propaganda activity of the party. When there was no election on which to concentrate their efforts, a '1,000 man plan', i.e. a target of 1,000 new members, was set up for a specific period for members to aim at.[7] At the end of 1931, the HJ copied the party's training courses for speakers by introducing a scheme for training 'ten-minute speakers'. HJ activities appear to have been integrated fairly closely with those of the party, particularly the SA. In terms of its relationship to the other party organizations, the HJ occupied a rather indeterminate position. On the one hand, it was closely linked with the political section.[8] HJ leaders were obliged to obey orders from the political leaders, and to take part in propaganda activities, so far as it was within their strength; the HJ required their permission to hold large public functions. In return, the HJ leaders were permitted to take part in meetings of party leaders so far as they were relevant.

On the other hand, the HJ was also subordinate to the SA leader-

[1] Schmalz to Wittenberg, 7 Nov. 1930, NSAH Hann. Des. 310 I A, Nr. 33.
[2] Gaukasse to Lauterbacher, 15 Jan. 1931; NSAH Hann. Des. 310 I A, Nr. 112.
[3] Lauterbacher to Wittenberg, 4 Feb. 1930 [*sic*], ibid.
[4] Bolm, op. cit., pp. 155 and 172.
[5] Klönne, op. cit., p. 11.   [6] Bolm, op. cit., p. 134.   [7] Ibid., p. 154.
[8] Richtlinien zwischen HJ und Partei, 3 Apr. 1929 (copy), in NSAH Hann. Des. 80 Hann II, Nr. 770.

ship.[1] This meant that initially it was subject to the ban of April 1932. The authorities, however, soon allowed the party to establish a 'non-paramilitary' youth movement and Munich therefore gave orders for the founding of the *Nationalsozialistische Jugendbewegung*. This did not affect the HJ organization; it simply meant new membership cards and new stamps.[2]

By June 1932, the HJ *Gauführung* had developed into a formidable *Apparat*.[3] There was now a Gauführer, a secretary, a treasurer, a director of the *Gauscharamt* (the organization department), a propaganda director, a press director, a director of social affairs, a director of training and a director of military sport. There was also the director of the '*Bund deutsches Jungvolk*', an organization for boys up to the age of fifteen which had been integrated with the HJ in March 1931.[4] Furthermore, from 1 April 1932, the party rented Burg Campen, an old castle outside Brunswick as a HJ training school.

One further department was added to the HJ during the summer which requires special emphasis—the NS *Schülerbund*. It had soon been recognized within the party that senior pupils at grammar schools provided particularly fertile soil for Nazi propaganda. In May 1929, therefore, *Gau* Berlin had established a special department for directing propaganda at this group under Dr. Adrian von Renteln.[5] After a battle lasting several months between the HJ and the NS *Studentenbund* for control of the department, which was imitated in other *Gaue*, Hitler decided in November 1929 to allow it to exist as an independent organization and to found branches throughout the Reich, though its leaders were required to be 'passive' members of the HJ. The aim of the organization was primarily to recruit members for the HJ within the schools, since the HJ itself tended to concentrate on those who had left school early and were either working or unemployed. It worked, above all, by personal 'mouth to mouth' propaganda; by establishing cells in schools and classes; and then, when the ground had been prepared, by holding public discussion evenings and, in the cities, big public meetings. Members paid 50 pf per month and the organization published its own newspaper—*Aufmarsch*, the proceeds of which helped to finance the local organization.[6]

The NSDAP in Lower Saxony was quick to exploit the opportunities offered by right radicalism within the schools. In August 1929, for example, pupils of the secondary school in Goslar had caused a sensation throughout Germany by removing the black-red-and-gold

[1] OSAF Verfügung, 5 Nov. 1931 (copy), NSAH Hann. Des. 80 Hann II, Nr. 779.   [2] Bolm, op. cit., p. 197.
[3] Ibid., pp. 191 and 206.   [4] Bolm, op. cit., pp. 199–204.
[5] Landeskriminalpolizeiamt Berlin report of 15 Jan. 1930, NSAH Hann. Des. 80 Hann II, Nr. 844.
[6] NS Schülerbund Richtlinien, 10 Jan. 1931 (copy), in ibid., Nr. 775.

(Republican) ribbons from the wreaths at a big sports occasion. An investigating commission appointed by the Prussian Ministry of Culture decided that the pupils should not be allowed to take the *Abitur* at the Goslar school, thereby enabling the local NSDAP branch in Goslar to make big capital out of the scandal of the interference of 'Marxist' officials in Goslar's affairs.[1] In Weser-Ems, the NS *Schülerbund* was founded on 30 August 1930.[2] During the next few months they were so overwhelmed by new recruits that, during January 1931, the Bremen district organization was temporarily forced to close the membership list.[3] The effects of their activity soon became apparent. In November 1930, for example, the *Reichsbanner* branch in Oldenburg complained to the Oldenburg Ministry for Churches and Schools that, owing to the agitation of the NS *Schülerbund*, the children of Republican parents were bullied and their satchels smeared with swastikas.[4] 'Since', the letter added, 'the children of Republicans are in the minority at the grammar schools, they cannot defend themselves against the united attacks'. The result was that the children could not work properly and were then often, in addition, victimized by their teachers. Indeed, because of the additional activities of the NS *Lehrerbund*, many schools were riven by faction.

The attitude of the authorities to Nazi activity in the schools varied. In the province of Hanover, Noske had forbidden schoolchildren to belong to the NSDAP and its associated organizations as early as January 1930.[5] In Oldenburg, on the other hand, the *Evangelisches Oberschulkollegium* claimed that, 'since the aims of the NSDAP are not directed against the state or morality', there was no justification for banning the NS *Schülerbund*.[6] They based their argument on Hitler's 1931 speech to the Reich court in Leipzig in which he had promised to work within the constitution.

An important factor in the National Socialist youth movement was the nature of the relationship between the HJ and the bourgeois *Jugendbewegung*.[7] In certain respects there were similarities. The HJ

[1] See the Aug. and Sept. 1929 issues of the *NB*.
[2] Police report Osnabrück, 30 June 1930, NSAOsn. Rep. 116 acc. 7/43, Nr. 1235, vol. II.
[3] Report of an article in the *Gau* Weser-Ems paper of 31 Jan. 1931, in Bremen police report, 4 Feb. 1931, NSAO 136, Nr. 2799.
[4] Reichsbanner Ortsverein Oldenburg to the Ministerium der Kirchen und Schulen NSAO 131, 1207.
[5] Provinzialschulkollegium der Provinz Hannover gez. Noske an alle Leiter und Leiterinnen sämtlicher uns unterstellten Schulen unseres Amtsbereiches, 2 Jan. 1930, NSAH Hann. Des. 80 Hann. II, Nr. 879.
[6] Evangelisches Oberschulkollegium to the Staatsministerium der Kirchen und Schulen, 3 June 1931, NSAO 131.
[7] For the following see E. M. Jovy, *Deutsche Jugendbewegung und Nationalsozialismus* (Diss., Köln, 1952) and W. Laqueur, *Young Germany* (London, 1962)

imitated the uniforms and the rituals of the youth movement—the log fires and Midsummer Eve ceremonies. Its organization appeared similar to the Orden character of the *Bund*, with its charismatic *Führer-Gefolgschaft* structure of authority. There was also a common dislike of the 'system'—of parliamentarism and parties—and a common sense of mission for the younger generation to break down the 'corrupt and decadent' liberal-capitalist order. In its place would come the Third Reich; leaders of a new type would replace the party functionaries, leaders who would stand above the conflicting interests and arbitrate between them; and a corporate state would replace the parliamentary system.

Yet there were important differences of interpretation between the two groups. Thus the *Bündische* conceived the Third Reich largely in metaphysical, the HJ in political, pseudo-biological terms. The *Bund* was conceived as an élite group, and the NSDAP, as a mass movement, offended against the 'good taste' of the *Bündischen*.[1] They disliked its bureaucratization of the charismatic principle. They criticized its Roman-fascist tendencies and agreed with Otto Strasser in his criticism of its essentially bourgeois, indeed, Wilhelminian character. While the HJ concentrated almost entirely on party propaganda, and its members saw themselves as merely preparing for their future role as members of the party, the *Bund* was an end in itself. It represented in the eyes of its members the smallest cell of the future state, whose principles must become generally applicable through the penetration of official life by the *Bündischen*.

The success with which the Nazis manipulated the jargon and symbols of the *Jugendbewegung* nevertheless confused a large number of people into accepting as *echt* what was in fact *ersatz*. This was particularly true at the time of the national 'uprising' in the first weeks after the 'seizure of power'. One reason for the failure of the youth movement to resist this development was the fact that their ideas and organization were not relevant to the political and economic needs created by such a crisis as that which struck Germany in 1929. An example is the failure of the *Jungdeutscher Orden*, which one might describe as an adult youth movement, when it tried to enter politics; its manifesto of December 1927, for example, hardly mentioned economic questions.[2] To this extent the Nazis were correct in their criticism of the youth movement for its social exclusiveness and its ivory tower intellectualism. The vacuum, created by lack of understanding of politics was filled by the machine and the crude but effective propaganda of the NSDAP.

While the *NS Schülerbund* was absorbed within the HJ in the

---

[1] Jovy, op. cit., p. 133.
[2] Cf. K. Hornung, *Der Jungdeutsche Orden* (Düsseldorf, 1958), pp. 92 and 106.

summer of 1932, the other major Nazi youth organization—the National Socialist Student League (NSDSt.B)—retained its organizational independence except at the highest level, where it too was subordinate to its old leader, Schirach, now Reich Youth Leader. The NSDSt.B had been established at the end of 1925 by two law students.[1] They concentrated on trying to win support among the so-called work students, that is those who had to earn money to pay for their studies. They also tried to bring workers and students together. But in February 1928, at a meeting attended by representatives from twenty NSDSt.B organizations from throughout the Reich, Hitler made a speech attacking the 'socialist' aims of the NSDSt.B. In July of the same year Baldur von Schirach was appointed leader and the headquarters was transferred to Munich where it could be kept under the eye of the party leadership. In place of the previous newspaper—*Der Junge Revolutionär* (The Young Revolutionary)—the *Akademischer Beobachter* was introduced.[2] But it was not until 1929 that the organization began to show results in terms of winning votes and seats in the student council (ASt.A) elections. From that year onwards, however, its progress was rapid.

The student population proved peculiarly vulnerable to the appeal of Nazism. An article in the *Vossische Zeitung* in July 1930 suggested that the so-called 'free' students—those who did not belong to a corporation—were especially liable to fall for Nazi propaganda.[3] This group was particularly badly affected by the crisis situation. In many cases their parents could no longer afford to subsidize them which meant they had to finance their studies themselves at a time when work was almost impossible to get. More important than this economic pressure, however, were

the overcrowding of the professions, the threat continually repeated from all sides to introduce the *numerus clausus*, the hopelessness of the most desperate efforts when the protective hand of a father (the war) or of good 'connections' are lacking. . . . As a result, thousands of young academics who come from poor or ruined families see themselves faced with a precarious future despite talent and hard work, and therefore have no faith in themselves or in their environment.

These students, and middle-class school leavers in general, lacked the jobs for which they had been prepared and therefore were forced to enter employment—if they could get it—in which their training

---

[1] For the following see Brandenburg, op. cit., pp. 46–8.

[2] *Akademischer Beobachter* Schriftleitung an alle *Gaue*, Dec. 1926, NSAH Hann. Des. 310 I A, Nr. 21.

[3] 'Der Freistudent als Hitler-Beute' in Vossiche Zeiting, 13 July 1920, quoted in an official memorandum 'Über den Nationalsozialistischen Deutschen Studentenbund' in NSAO 134 1207.

would be wasted and above all their sense of status affronted.[1] Many of them turned to an organization which offered employment in an alternative bureaucracy, status in terms of titles and uniforms, and the vision of a future state in which their various emotional and economic needs would be satisfied.

But if the 'free' students were vulnerable, the statistics for the university elections in Göttingen appear to show that the Corps students were even more so. Between 1929 and 1930 the list of the Göttingen student associations (*Verbindungen*) lost four seats, while the NSDSt.B gained four and the free students retained their single seat.[2] These Corps students were already part of the *völkisch* movement. At the 1920 *Burschenschaft* meeting at Eisenach it had been decided to ban membership for Jews and the individual *Burschenschaften* were encouraged to educate their members so that 'marriage with a Jewish or coloured woman is unthinkable'. Other corporations followed their example. During the 1920s demonstrations and boycotts were organized by these groups against Jewish or politically suspect professors. In 1925, for example, 200 students at the Technical University (TH) in Hanover broke up a lecture by a Professor Lessing.[3] When the university authorities disciplined eleven of the students, 1,200 students out of the 1,500 at the university transferred to the neighbouring TH in Brunswick. Yet the student corps were to some extent insulated from National Socialism by an unwillingness to become involved in party politics, an attitude typical of the German upper middle-class from which they came. They also continued the old-fashioned nationalist style of their fathers, celebrating events such as the foundation of the Reich in their caps and colours with excessive beer drinking and patriotic songs. This was a long way from the street marches and beer-hall fights of the Nazis. With the growing economic and political crisis, however, this tradition came under increasing strain as students felt the inadequacy of previous attitudes and modes of behaviour to deal with the situation. The spread of unemployment to middle-class professions brought home the significance of the crisis in a very immediate way. In 1931 Eduard Stadtler, the well-known right wing publicist, described the feelings of the average student who 'no longer believes in a solution of the crisis through his own education or through the enlightenment of others, but only through activity in common, through action. He knows that the chaos can no longer be

---

[1] See Geiger, op. cit., p. 100.

[2] For the following see Peter Melcher, 'In Couleur und Braunhemd. Die Studentenschaft in der Weimarer Republik', *Politikon*. Göttinger Studentenzeitschrift für Niedersachsen. On this general point see also H. P. Bleuel and E. Klinnert *Deutsche Studenten auf dem Weg ins Dritte Reich* (Gütersloh, 1968).

[3] Brandenburg, op. cit., p. 107.

overcome by intellectual education, but only through the native forces of body and soul.'[1] This activism and irrationalism made students vulnerable to the appeal of Nazism, a movement in which action had priority over thought and which played on the guilt feelings of upper middle-class youth for their social isolation and appealed to their idealism by its claim to a socialist policy and a close relationship with the workers as opposed to what increasingly appeared to be the anti-social exclusiveness of the Corporations. The Nazis offered middle class students the opportunity to indulge their social concern, while remaining true to their nationalst and *völkisch* values which the alternative idealism of the Left repudiated.

In its propaganda, the NSDSt.B concentrated on broad ideological themes:[2] the decadence of liberalism and its responsibility for the decline and defeat of Germany; the need for a combination of nationalism and socialism to bring about the revival of Germany, in particular contrasting the concern of the NSDAP for the workers with their neglect by the old regime and by the bourgeois parties. With these ideological statements went an appeal to the concrete interests of the students in the form of a demand for the introduction of a *numerus clausus* for Jews of all professions. An idea of the quality of thought of these students may be gained from quoting from a speech by the leader of the Göttingen NSDSt.B, Hugo Rönck, a theology student.[3] The speech, which was entitled 'The Bases of the National Socialist *Weltanschauung*', illustrates albeit in an extreme form, the combination of quasi-religious fervour and sentimentality which was characteristic of much of Nazi propaganda and which gave the party an appeal not unlike some of the American religious sects.

The speaker began by declaring: 'Today we live in a state which is threatened from all sides', on the one side was communism, on the other side the ordinary citizen who did not concern himself with politics. Then Hitler appeared and gathered round him a group of men who demonstrated national ideals. 'Just as Christ helped his fellow men, so the National Socialist wishes to help his fellow men and fellow Germans. Therefore we say "Love your neighbour as yourself".'

Hitler did not wish to create a party, he wanted to show us a way, a way according to which we, the people, can live. We consider him to be a prophet who will lead us into a new Reich. The way is rough and many obstacles lie before us. As a parable for our movement let us take the fairy tale Sleeping

[1] Quoted in Melcher, op. cit., p. 10.
[2] For examples of NSDSt.B speeches see the Göttingen police files; in SAG XVIII 156, No. 4.
[3] For the following see the Bericht über den Verlauf der öffentlichen Versammlung des Nationalsozialistischen Deutschen Studentenbundes vom 1 May 1931, ibid.

Beauty. Many brave men and kings' sons were unable to penetrate through the thick thorn hedge to free the king's daughter. At last there came a prince who broke down the hedge and brushed away all obstacles. He freed the princess. So Nazism will one day break down the thorn hedge and found a new Third Reich.

In Lower Saxony the position of the NSDSt.B corresponded largely with that in the rest of Germany. At the Brunswick *Technische Hochschule* (TH) and at Göttingen University it was very successful. In 1929, the NSDSt.B list for the student committee (ASt.A) elections in Brunswick won 103 votes and 3 seats out of 20; in 1930 it won 195 votes and 5 seats and its leader was elected ASt.A chairman;[1] and in 1931 it won 379 votes and 9 seats, compared with 8 for the Corporations' list and 3 for the SPD.[2] The NSDSt.B in Brunswick made use of its influence within the university and exploited the fact that, from October 1930, the Education department within the state government was in the hands of a Nazi. It mounted vicious attacks on the TH authorities who attempted to remain neutral.[3] At Göttingen University they were no less successful—in 1929 they won 2 seats out of 20; in 1930, 6 out of 20; and in 1931, 11 out of 20.[4] Apart from breaking up the lectures of Jewish professors, the NSDSt.B attempted as in Brunswick to browbeat the university authorities.[5] In 1930, at the anniversary celebration of the university, they ignored a ban by the rector and stationed themselves at the entrance of the Assembly Hall so that the professors had to walk through a cordon of brownshirts. They were protected from disciplinary action by a friendly proctor and by the end of 1931 even the rector shielded them. At the Hanover TH the NSDSt.B was slightly less successful, at least initially. In 1929, they won only 5 per cent of the votes and in 1930 15 per cent.

Despite the electoral success of the NSDSt.B, membership of the organization remained small. In Hanover, according to an estimate of the political police, even by February 1932 the TH branch had only eighty-five members out of a student population of 1,800.[6] And in December 1931 the Göttingen police estimated the membership of the university branch at approximately fifty with twenty-five female

---

[1] See the official memorandum 'Über den Nationalsozialistischen Deutschen Studentenbund'. Footnote 3, p. 196.

[2] *NTZ*, 8 Feb. 1931.

[3] See Roloff, *Bürgertum und Nationalsozialismus 1930–1933*, pp. 86–8 and pp. 122 ff. for a detailed description of these events.

[4] Peter Melcher, 'In Couleur und Braunhemd. Die Studentenschaft in der Weimarer Republik', *Politikon*, Nr. 9.

[5] Ibid.

[6] Bracher, *Die Auflosung der Weimarer Republik*, p. 148 and Polizeipräsident Hannover to Oberpräsident Hannover, 25 Feb. 1932, NSAH Hann. Des. 80 Hann. II, Nr. 742.

students.[1] These estimates are unlikely to be wide of the mark for they receive some support from the party's official statistics. According to these, in *Gau* Hanover-South–Brunswick the combined number of students and secondary school pupils who joined before 1933 was 642.[2] This would include all schoolboys over eighteen, a comparatively large number in Germany, and all institutes of higher education. Apart from these actual members, however, there were a considerable number of sympathizers.[3]

Conclusion

The specialization within the NSDAP organization fulfilled a number of functions: it facilitated the propaganda appeals to specific groups; it enabled the party to stage-manage the conquest of professional organizations from below and thereby prepared the way for the post-30 January 1933 process of *Gleichschaltung*; finally, it succeeded in integrating within the party numerous conflicting interests.

Yet the apparent success of the party in performing this function of integration disguised the conflicts which existed between the various organizations and interests. At this stage, before 1933, those conflicts were hidden to some extent by the concentration on intensive propaganda activity and by the eclecticism of the party's propaganda. After 1933, when priorities had to be set in every field, the conflicts were to come out into the open.

[1] Göttingen Polizeidirektion Bericht an den Polizeipräsident Hannover, 18 Dec. 1931, in SAG XXVII 156, No. 3, Bd. 2.
[2] *Parteistatistik*, I, p. 134.
[3] See footnote 1 above.

XI

TECHNIQUES AND THEMES OF
PROPAGANDA 1930–1932

ONE of the most complicated questions in considering Nazi propaganda is the extent to which particular themes and techniques contributed towards the success of the party. How important, for example, was foreign policy as an issue? To what extent was the success of National Socialist propaganda due to rational or to irrational appeals? Since it is impossible to quantify the use of topics and techniques over such a wide area, as for example was possible for the small town of 'Thalburg',[1] and since there were no opinion polls, the following account concentrates on describing the development of the themes and techniques used by the party in the campaigns of 1931 and 1932 in Lower Saxony and particularly Hanover-South–Brunswick. This can be reconstructed from the propaganda directives and propaganda reports of the Reich and *Gau* head-quarters and the local branches.

(i) *Propaganda activity during 1931*

Three days after the *Reichstag* election of Sunday, 14 September 1930, the *Gau* propaganda head-quarters in Hanover-South–Brunswick emphasized in a directive to its branches the need to continue the struggle without any let-up: 'Adolf Hitler said in conclusion: the *Reichstag* electoral campaign finished on the 14th but the 15th will see us once more in the fight.'[2] As we have seen, during the period after the election the party was engaged in constructing in a very few months a fairly sophisticated *Apparat*. This included a reorganization of the propaganda department. At the beginning of 1931, all branches were ordered to appoint propaganda directors.[3] In April, the Reich propaganda head-quarters began producing a monthly pamphlet—*Wille und Weg*—which contained both directives and articles by party leaders. The paper had an initial circulation of 11,000 and because it went to all branches, it was considered more effective than the

---

[1] Allen, *The Nazi Seizure of Power*, p. 297.
[2] Gaupropagandaleitung Rundschreiben, 17 Sept. 1930, NSAH Hann. Des. 310 I E, Nr. 13.
[3] Gaupropagandaleitung Rundschreiben, 25 Jan. 1931, NSAH Hann. Des. 310 I E, Nr. 33.

directives to the *Gaue* which they often failed to pass on. Above all it ensured that 'any unauthorized moves by subordinate sections are completely excluded'.[1]

The major reorganization which took place after the election did not, however, mean that the party neglected the propaganda side of its activities. One of the impressive features of the NSDAP's propaganda machine was its success in mobilizing its resources and in concentrating on priority tasks. At the end of November 1930, for example, the Bremen City Council election was to be held and in the September election the NSDAP had failed to win as big a percentage of the votes there as its average for the Reich as a whole. The party, therefore, launched a full-scale propaganda drive which involved not only *Gau* Weser-Ems, but many outside speakers as well, and culminated in a big Hitler rally on 28 November.[2] The result of the campaign was astonishing. In the twelve weeks between the September *Reichstag* election and the Council election the NSDAP had doubled its vote from 25,045 to 51,324 votes. It was clear that with its success in the September *Reichstag* election the party had become a serious alternative for a wider section of the politically disaffected.

The Bremen election was followed by the next immediate task in Lower Saxony—the *Kreistag* elections in the state of Brunswick on 1 March 1931. In January and February, the party held 600 meetings within the state, of which during February alone 100 were held by outside speakers, although the Reich head-quarters had not declared the election to be a priority.[3] Activity in Brunswick was of course made easier by the fact that the NSDAP was now in the government coalition and could therefore operate unhindered by hostile police which was not the case in Prussia.

After striking gains in this election (for example nine seats in Brunswick-City compared with none in 1928), the party moved on to the Oldenburg *Landtag* election of 29 May. For this, the resources of the whole Reich organization was mobilized, and although the hoped-for majority did not materialize, the NSDAP increased its vote from 17,000 in 1928 and 76,216 in 1930 to 97,287, and its seats from three in 1928 to nineteen.[4]

During the summer of 1931, the NSDAP maintained its propaganda activity. The *Stahlhelm* plebiscite for the dissolution of the Prussian *Landtag* provided a focus for activity, although the NSDAP adopted a rather ambiguous attitude towards it. Even during the har-

---

[1] Reichspropagandaleitung Monatsbericht, Nov. 1931, NSDAP Hauptarchiv, Reel 15, 284.
[2] Bremen police report, 3 Dec. 1930, NSAO 136, Nr. 2800.
[3] Tätigkeitsberichte for Jan. and Feb. 1931, NSAH Hann. Des. 310 I B, Nr. 13.
[4] Oldenburg police report for May 1931, NSAO 136, Nr. 2860.

vest month of September, *Gau* Hanover-South–Brunswick held eleven big rallies, 400 public meetings, 400 indoctrination and discussion evenings and fifty other functions (such as SA concerts and 'German Evenings').[1]

(ii) *Propaganda techniques*

Because of signs of a surfeit on the part of audiences who became more demanding in their choice of speakers, the party endeavoured to diversify its propaganda.[2] The Lower Saxony NS Theatre Company, for example, was active, performing 'Poison Gas 506' and the *Gau* joined a film library. A booklet published in July 1931 by *Gau* Hanover-South–Brunswick for the information of branch propaganda directors detailed all the propaganda techniques available and placed particular emphasis on simple 'mouth to mouth' propaganda.[3] The party also developed a ritual of seasonal celebrations, beginning with Hitler's birthday on 20 April, followed by Midsummer's Eve, 9 November ('the day of mourning of the movement'), and ending with Christmas.

For the reasons already outlined, there was no problem of lack of speakers and indeed the party was able to impose strict standards. From 1 February 1931 all speakers who wished to speak outside their own *Kreis* or *Gau* were required to possess a special *Gau* or Reich certificate.[4] To acquire these, they were obliged to provide a personal history, references, a police declaration that they had no police record, and to pass an examination.[5] In August 1931, of twenty-five candidates for the *Gau* certificate in Hanover-South–Brunswick only seven passed.[6] The *Gau* set up a special school for speakers but, by October 1931, despite the high standard required the *Gau* was forced to cease granting certificates 'because already only a small number of our official speakers can find employment'.[7] The speakers' certificates also performed a useful function of facilitating doctrinal control.

Another form of propaganda which the NSDAP expanded during this period was the press. From 1 October 1930, the *Niedersächsischer Beobachter* was published twice weekly, and from 1 February 1931 a

---

[1] Tätigkeitsbericht, Sept. 1931, NSAH Hann. Des. 310 I B, Nr. 13.

[2] For signs of surfeit see Leister-Nienburg to Gauleitung H-S-B, 24 June 1931, NSAH Hann. Des. 310 I B, Nr. 35.

[3] NSAH Hann. Des. 310 I B, Nr. 5.

[4] Gaupropagandaleitung Rundschreiben, 25 Jan. 1931, NSAH Hann. Des. 310 I E, Nr. 33.

[5] Even old party members such as Seifert were required to pass; see Seifert-Rust correspondence in NSAH Hann. Des. 310 I B, Nr. 35.

[6] Tätigkeitsbericht, Aug. 1931, NSAH Hann. Des. 310 I B, Nr. 13.

[7] Gaupropagandaleitung H-S-B to Schierholz-Osterde NSAH Hann. Des. 310 I B, Nr. 3.

new *Gau* daily was started in Hanover-South–Brunswick—the *Niedersächsische Tageszeitung*—with a guaranteed circulation of 14,000 under the editorship of Dr. Joachim Haupt.[1] Almost immediately, however, the paper ran into difficulties. On 20 March, it was banned for nineteen days by *Oberpräsident* Noske and was faced with bankruptcy. An urgent directive was sent out to all branches by the *Gauleiter*, insisting that discussion about the quality of the paper must cease and that all members should not only subscribe to the paper themselves but, in addition, should win two new readers each.[2] Furthermore, the party treasurer sent out share certificates in the paper valued at RM 5, 10, 20, 50 and 100, of which each branch was ordered to take RM 10 per member.[3] The paper was not yet out of trouble, however. On 29 June, it was banned for six days; on 20 July, for a month; and on 16 October, for seventeen days.[4] As a result, by the beginning of November, with one exception, all the editorial staff had been dismissed. The exception was the local correspondent and the rest of the paper—the political, economic and entertainment sections—were supplied by another NS publishing house.[5]

The poor quality of the *Niedersächsische Tageszeitung* and its relatively high price, encouraged local party organizations to produce their own papers which they could tailor to the needs and interests of the local readership. Such local papers, moreover, provided a useful source of income for the branch as well as prestige for the leader. As a result, a considerable number of local party papers sprang up all over Lower Saxony—*Fanfare* (Göttingen), *Hört Hört* (Northeim), *Wächter vom Leinetal* (Einbeck), *Blatt der Niedersachsen* (Harburg) and *NS-Front* (Osnabrück) are examples. These local papers took circulation away from the official *Gau* papers and as such were a direct threat to the financial and political interests of the *Gau* head-quarters.[6] There were innumerable conflicts between the *Gauleiter* and local leaders over

---

[1] See the correspondence in NSAH Hann. Des. 310 I A, Nr. 34. Haupt was born in 1900, attended Cadet schools; joined the Free Corps; while at university took numerous labouring jobs; appointed to post at Staatliche Bildungsanstalt Plön; activist in the NSDAP since 1921, see Ch. 3. III; in 1930 dismissed from his post because of Nazi activity; from 1931 also headed Organization Department II in the *Gauleitung*. Haupt was an important figure among the pro-Nazi academic youth in North Germany. See personal files BDC and A. Krebs, *Tendenzen und Gestalten der NSDAP*, pp. 207–8.

[2] Copy of Rust's directive in report of Landespolizeistelle Hannover, 6 June 1931, in NSAH Hann. Des. 80 Hann. II, Nr. 720.

[3] Kassenverwaltung Rundschreiben, 27 Mar. 1931, NSAH Hann. Des. 310 I E, Nr. 30.

[4] For dates when the paper was banned see NSDAP Hauptarchiv, Reel 48, Folder 1076.

[5] Report on the early difficulties of the *NTZ* in *NTZ*, 1 Feb. 1934, ibid.

[6] Krebs gives an account of the difficulties in Hamburg in op. cit., pp. 78 ff.

these issues. During 1930, for example, there was a major row between the *Gauleiter* of Weser-Ems and Dr. Marxer, head of the important Osnabrück district organization, over the latter's publication of *NS-Front*.[1] Attempts by the NTZ management to suppress their local rivals were unavailing, until eventually *Gauleiter* Rust decided that the propaganda advantages of vigorous local newspapers were outweighed by the disadvantages of weakening the *Gau* paper and his control over the party press, and he banned all local party newspapers from 1 October 1932.[2]

Another rival, this time to the party press in general, was the local bourgeois press. From 1930 onwards, the local press came under increasing financial pressure. Many small towns had two rival bourgeois papers, quite apart from the inevitable SPD paper. The economic crisis intensified rivalry for subscribers, while their source of income from advertisements dried up.[3] In this situation, many papers turned more and more towards support for the NSDAP as a means of acquiring new subscribers, though this was also of course an adaptation on the part of the paper to the changed views of its readership.[4] By the summer of 1932, a large number, in fact probably a large majority, of the bourgeois papers in Lower Saxony were, if not entirely committed to the NSDAP, at least very sympathetic to it.[5] Perhaps the most notable example of this trend was the old-established *Hannoversche Kurier*, which before 1918 had been the leading National Liberal paper in the province of Hanover. By 1932, the paper was in serious financial difficulties and, after negotiations at the highest level involving Hess, Keppler and Rust, it agreed to follow an NSDAP line in future and presumably received some sort of financial guarantee in return.[6] Although this development was of course of tremendous assistance to the party's propaganda campaign, it did limit the success of its own press.[7]

[1] See the Osnabrück police reports for 1930 NSA Osn. Rep. 116 acc 7/43, Nr. 1235, vols. II and IV.

[2] Gauleiter Rundschreiben an sämtliche Kreisleiter, Ortsgruppenleiter etc., 28 Sept. 1932, NSAH Hann. Des. 310 I B, Nr. 14.

[3] An entertaining fictional account of the difficulties of local newspapers during this period is contained in Hans Fallada, *Bauern, Bonzen und Bomben* (Rowohlt Taschenbuchausgabe Hamburg, 1964).

[4] For example the Hoyaer Wochenblatt and the Hoyaer Zeitung competed with one another during 1932 for the favour of the party. See correspondence in NSAH Hann. Des. 310 I A, Nr. 117.

[5] Examples of papers sympathetic or totally committed to the NSDAP: *Osnabrücker Zeitung, Goslarsche Zeitung, Einbecker Tageblatt, Butjadinger Zeitung, Die Schaumburg*.

[6] For correspondence relating to the *Hannoversche Kurier* see NSAH Hann. Des. 310 I A, Nrs. 37 and 117.

[7] The Gauleitung in Hanover-East for this reason rejected any co-operation with these papers, see Rundschreiben, Betr. Presse, 3 May 1932, NSAH Hann. Des. 310 I E, Nr. 30.

TECHNIQUES AND THEMES OF PROPAGANDA

During the winter campaign, the party developed new techniques of propaganda. There was a slight trend away from ordinary public meetings. In the words of *Gauleiter* Rust: 'We must finish with the idea that a public meeting with a well-known speaker will always work miracles and ensure, for example, the conquest of a Red area at one blow.'[1] Instead, he emphasized that

personal canvassing (*Kleinarbeit*) is the movement's most effective weapon. Branch leaders must therefore at once examine the relationship of individual members to relations and colleagues, of the employee to his employer and vice versa and set them suitable canvassing tasks.

Furthermore, where there was obviously no desire for a general public meeting, branches should hold specialist meetings or meetings with invited guests instead. The NSBO and the ApA were particularly involved with the campaign.[2]

One technique developed by *Gau* South-Hanover–Brunswick received particular mention from Goebbels in his November 1931 report and other *Gaue* were urged to imitate it.[3] This method involved holding big rallies with the most famous speakers in the *Gau*, the proceeds of which helped to finance a 'shock troop', composed of a few speakers from different occupations, who would spend a fortnight in a *Kreis* in which the party was backward and saturate it with meetings. In December, after a 'shock troop' had worked in *Kreis* Alfeld, the *Gau* reported the creation of several new branches and 221 new members.[4]

(iii) *Propaganda targets and themes*

During 1931, the directives from the Reich propaganda headquarters asserted that the bourgeois parties were finished and that the main effort should be directed against the political parties which had resisted the Nazi onslaught—the Catholic Centre and 'Marxism'.[5] Instructions for the struggle against the Centre party were precise: attacks 'must never extend to religion or church institutions. Continually repeat that National Socialism is not a religious *Weltanschauung*.'[6] The attack was concentrated on the claim that the Centre party misused religion for political purposes.

[1] Gauleiter, 'Die Parole für den Winter 1931–1932', 20 Nov. 1931, NSAH Hann. Des. 310 I E, Nr. 26.
[2] The party in Lower Saxony was disturbed by the success of the KPD in agricultural areas. See Monatsberichte der Reichspropagandaleitung for Nov. and Dec. NSDAP Hauptarchiv, Reel 15, Folder 284.
[3] Ibid.
[4] Tätigkeitsbericht, Dec. 1931, NSAH Hann. Des. 310 I B, Nr. 13.
[5] See NSAH Hann. Des. 310 I B, Nr. 1.
[6] Reichspropagandaleitung Rundschreiben März 1931 gez. Goebbels, ibid.

This attack on the Centre could be expected to evoke sympathy from bourgeois Protestants, particularly in areas where the denominations were mixed and where there had long existed a certain amount of tension between them—for example in Oldenburg and Osnabrück. Moreover, the NSDAP made other attempts to exploit the religious sentiments of the Protestant bourgeoisie. In the first place, they championed the cause of religion against 'atheistic socialism'. In practical terms this meant that they supported the opponents of the SPD's attempts to lessen the influence of religion on education. The question of religious influence in education had become a very live political issue after the revolution of 1918 had placed the Ministries of Culture in many states, including Prussia, in the hands of the SPD. The conflict was particularly acute in Brunswick where Socialist and bourgeois governments had alternated during the 1920s. The SPD government of 1927–30 had caused particular resentment among the bourgeoisie because of the activities of the Minister of Culture, Sievers, who had pursued a rather extreme policy of appointing a considerable number of SPD members and agnostics to posts in the education system, and of encouraging agnostic propaganda within the schools. The Nazi exploitation of this issue in the 1930 *Landtag* election campaign may well have played no small part in the result.[1] By making themselves the champions of religious education, the NSDAP exploited an issue which was of great importance to bourgeois Protestant parents and furthered their aim of being accepted as a party for which conservative bourgeois citizens need not be afraid or ashamed of voting.[2]

A classic example of the way in which the NSDAP manipulated religious and nationalist symbols can be seen in the ritual of their *Gau* congresses and flag dedication ceremonies. These followed a standard procedure which invariably included a march through the town, a wreath-laying ceremony at the War Memorial and a military church service attended by all SA and party members at which the sermon would be given by a pastor sympathetic to the party.[3] Such a ritual was of course calculated to impress the bourgeois citizenry with their conservative-nationalist-militarist outlook and helped offset the revolutionary impression which the party tended to convey.

It was not difficult to find pastors prepared to give sympathetic sermons, for the NSDAP acquired a considerable number of supporters

---

[1] For this issue see Roloff, *Braunschweig und der Staat von Weimar*, p. 141 ff.

[2] An example of the way in which the NSDAP made themselves acceptable to the bourgeoisie by leading the opposition to the SPD on the religious issue is provided by W. S. Allen's account of the events in Northeim when the SPD tried to challenge the bourgeois control of the Church Elders. See *The Nazi Seizure of Power*, pp. 40–1.

[3] See virtually any account of the early history of the party, e.g. Hans Hennigsen, *Niedersachsenland du wurdest unser!* (Harburg-Wilhelmsburg, 1935).

within the Protestant church. Not only was there sympathy for the nationalism and anti-bolshevism of Nazism, but also some became committed to the new cause from a sense of guilt at the social isolation of the church.[1] The church had been frequently criticized for its failure to emerge from its upper and middle class social background and culture and for its inability to establish contact with the people. With the emergence of the NSDAP as a mass movement, some were prepared to overlook its anti-Christian aspects in return for a sense of participating in what they saw as a *Volksbewegung* engaged in a national revival.

Individual pastors had belonged to the NSDAP from its earliest years. But the first official attempt to organize pastors within the party in Lower Saxony occurred on 7 May 1931 when, at a meeting in Bremen, it was agreed to found a 'Lower Saxony Group of Protestant Pastors' within the NS Teachers' League.[2] The group included the three Lower Saxony *Gaue* and Hamburg and was led by Pastor Hahn of Elmslohe, an ex-Free Corps man who was elected to the Prussian *Landtag* in 1932.[3] Other important figures within the group were Pastor Meyer who was simultaneously NSDAP branch leader in Aurich, Pastor Voss, a former member of the DVFP and DVFB and Prussian *Landtag* member, and in *Gau* Hanover-South–Brunswick Pastor Jakobshagen of the *Gartenkirche* in Hanover and Pastor von Lintig. In the autumn of 1931 *Gau* Hanover-South–Brunswick founded its own section which by May 1932 contained thirty-two members, of whom seventeen were members of the NSDAP.[4] The functions of the group were to watch the non-party press and write articles answering attacks on the non-Christian character of the NSDAP, to speak at party meetings, and to hold party church services.[5] Under the direction of Wilhelm Kube, the leader of the NSDAP Prussian *Landtag* group, the party took part in the Protestant Church Elder elections in 1932 with a separate list of 'Protestant National Socialists'.[6] And finally, during 1932, the party expanded its church organization by appointing *Gau* specialists who in turn ordered all branches to appoint their own specialists.[7] Both *Gau* and branch specialists were usually laymen involved in church affairs.

[1] See E. Klügel, *Die Lutherische Landeskirche Hannover und ihr Bischof 1933–1945* (Berlin and Hamburg, 1964), p. 16.

[2] *NS*, 30 May 1931, and correspondence in NSAH Hann. Des. 310 I A, Nr. 34.

[3] Not by Pastor Meyer as maintained by Klügel, op. cit., p. 16.

[4] von Lintig to Gauleitung H-S-B, 23 May 1932, in NSAH Hann. Des. 310 I A, Nr. 117.

[5] *NS*, 7 Nov, 1931.

[6] Strasser to Kube, 17 Dec. 1931. Strasser told Kube to keep the official involvement of the party to a minimum and make it appear as if the initiative came from the membership. NSAH Hann. Des. 310 I A, Nr. 34.

[7] Gau Weser-Ems to all branch leaders, 13 May 1932, National Archives Reel 164 303312.

The main target for propaganda, however, was 'Marxism'. For the winter of 1931, the Reich propaganda head-quarters planned a major three-month campaign under the slogan 'Fight Hunger'.[1] This was directed in the first place against the KPD, which appeared to be gaining ground, and secondly against the SPD. The campaign was preceded by and included special anti-Marxist indoctrination courses organized by Meier-Benneckenstein/Harz, who used material prepared in collaboration with his former colleague, Dietrich Klagges—now Minister of the Interior in Brunswick.[2] These courses were given throughout the Reich, but in *Gau* Hanover-South–Brunswick the propaganda department organized its own courses in addition, with the intention of training special anti-Marxist agitators.[3]

Finally, anti-Semitism was of course a constant theme in Nazi propaganda. Although it is impossible to quantify over such a wide area as Lower Saxony, anti-Semitism appears to have been a major theme between 1925 and 1930, particularly during the *Mittelstand* campaign of 1928–30. After 1930, however, while remaining an important theme, it was used more as a background to appeals to economic interest and general political propaganda. In other words, the party had to adjust its propaganda from that of a small anti-Semitic sect to that suitable for a mass party bidding for wide voting support among a population in which anti-Semitism was endemic, but which was more interested in economic and political matters than racial ideology. It remained, however, a major theme in the campaign to win peasants, artisans and small shopkeepers, and was important for the SA and the party rank and file, many of whom were drawn from these groups.

Anti-Semitism, as articulated by the NSDAP, was in the first place an appeal to economic interest. There were thousands of small shopkeepers who were threatened by department stores of which a considerable number were in Jewish hands, quite apart from the rivalry of ordinary Jewish shopkeepers.[4] Equally, the peasantry paid high interest to banks, of which a considerable number were owned by Jews and, even where this was not the case, the widely held conviction of the predominant influence of Jews in financial matters was sufficient for

[1] Reichspropagandaleitung Rundschreiben an alle Gauleitungen, 4 Nov. 1931, NSAH Hann. Des. 310 I B, Nr. 1.
[2] Gaupropagandaleitung H-S-B Rundschreiben, 23 Nov. 1931, NSAH Hann. Des. 310 I E, Nr. 30 and Reichspropagandaleitung Rundschreiben NSAH Hann. Des. 310 I A, Nr. 37.
[3] Gauleiter, 'Die Parole für den Winter 1931–1932', 20 Nov. 1931, NSAH Hann. Des. 310 I E, Nr. 26.
[4] In 1932 Jewish department stores were responsible for 79 per cent of the turnover in department stores in Germany. The Jews were also strong in the textile and groceries trades. See E. Bennathan, 'Die Demographische und wirtschaftliche Struktur der Juden', in *Entscheidungsjahr 1932. Zur Judenfrage in der Endphase der Weimarer Republik*. Hrsg. von Werner, E. Mosse (Tübingen, 1965), p. 114.

propaganda to work upon.[1] There were also a large number of Jewish cattle dealers whom the peasantry were unlikely to hold in great affection in a period of economic crisis.[2] But it would be a mistake to over-emphasize the economic aspect.

At another level anti-Semitism was an expression of general resentment at the encroachment of modern economic methods and modern social and cultural ideas on a society which still had not come to terms with the modern world. The Jews, who in the countryside tended to represent the forces of the market in the flesh and who were rightly seen as pioneers of modern ideas and forms in culture, were made scapegoats for the dislike of modern developments in general.

Finally, there was another and totally irrational level. Just as in the Middle Ages natural disasters were sometimes followed by pogroms, now under the influence of a long period of first *völkisch* and then Nazi propaganda, the rural *Mittelstand* may well have come to see the Jew as a figure of absolute evil and a scapegoat for the crisis in which they found themselves. The extreme tone and lurid fantasy of much of the anti-Semitism aimed at these groups, for example in Münchmeyer's speeches, could only have been acceptable on this assumption.

(iv) *The Presidential campaigns of March–April 1932*

Over Christmas 1931, Brüning imposed a ban on all political meetings. The ban ended on 1 January 1932 and the propaganda department in *Gau* Hanover-South–Brunswick ordered a 'barrage' to begin on that date.[3] By the end of the month, the *Gau* could report to Munich that its organization in the city of Hanover was now so efficient that within four hours it could distribute 138,000 pamphlets to all the households in the city.[4]

This efficiency was soon to be put to the test in the Reich presidential elections of March and April 1932. On 20 February, Goebbels

---

[1] Jews owned 45 per cent of all private banks in Germany, ibid., p. 118.

[2] A list of 266 cattle dealers in the big Oldenburg market contains 57 Jewish-sounding names; but this proportion does not show the importance of big Jewish dealers such as de Levie and de Beer. See Verzeichnis der Mitglieder des Vereins der Viehhändler vom Freistaat Oldenburg und Umgegend 1929, in Stadtarchiv Oldenburg. An incident which occurred in 1926 suggests that there was little love lost between the peasantry and the Jewish dealers. Two youths wearing swastikas annoyed Jewish dealers at the cattle market in Aurich and were about to be beaten up when peasants intervened to protect them. The peasant witnesses at the subsequent trial alleged that one of the Jewish dealers had said that the peasants could not live a day without them (the dealers) because 'we have the power and the money'. For reports of the trial see NSAA Rep. 109, Nr. 45.

[3] Gaupropagandaleitung Rundschreiben, 19 Dec. 1931, NSAH Hann. Des. 310 I E, Nr. 33.

[4] Tätigkeitsbericht Jan. 1932, NSAH Hann. Des. 310 I B, Nr. 13.

sent out the first directive for the election.[1] The slogan for the campaign was: 'Put an end to it now. Everyone vote for X' (*Schluss jetzt. Alles wählt X*).[2] Goebbels explained

The theme of our slogan is roughly as follows: the mass of the German electorate must be clearly shown through posters and pamphlets that the National Socialist movement is determined to use the Presidential election to put an end to the whole post-1919 system.

Nine days later, he expressed this in another suggested slogan: 'Those who want everything to stay as it is vote for Hindenburg: those who want everything changed vote for Hitler', a powerful slogan given the conditions then existing within Germany.[3] As far as their other opponents were concerned, the party was ordered to describe Düsterberg as the candidate of those who wished to split the nationalist cause, since he had no chance of success, while Thälmann intended the destruction of Germany. Goebbels concluded:

The basic sentence which must be continually repeated goes: 'Adolf Hitler is not only our candidate, Adolf Hitler is the future President'. We shall win because we want to win. The conviction of victory held by the whole party must be raised to blind faith. . . . Every party member must be clear that if we lose, the party will have received the severest blow, that if we win, we shall be masters of Germany.[4]

The campaign demonstrated once again the party's energy, efficiency and virtuosity. Between 1–12 March alone there were 625 public meetings and rallies in *Gau* Hanover-South–Brunswick.[5] Moreover, for the first time, discussion was banned at all public meetings, thereby giving them in future the appearance of rallies.[6] A list of nine suggestions for raising voter participation sent by the *Kreis* leader in Nienburg to his branch leaders, which urged a careful control through the voters' list and a transport service to the polls, suggest an efficient local organization.[7] And finally, there was the usual careful attention to the details of display. For example, the party produced a special poster

with a fascinating portrait of Hitler's head on a completely black background. The caption in white on black reads 'Hitler'. It is the wish of the Führer

[1] Reichspropagandaleitung Sonderrundschreiben, 20 Feb. 1932, NSAH Hann. Des. 310 I B, Nr. 1.

[2] Hitler's candidature had not yet been publicly announced.

[3] Reichspropagandaleitung Rundschreiben, 29 Feb. 1932, in NSAH Hann. Des. 310 I B, Nr. 1.

[4] Reichspropagandaleitung Rundschreiben, Feb. 1932, NSAH Hann. Des. 310 I B, Nr. 1.

[5] Tätigkeitsbericht, Mar. 1932, NSAH Hann. Des. 310 I B, Nr. 13.

[6] Gau Ost-Hannover Rundschreiben, 20 Feb. 1932, NSAH Hann. Des. 310 I E, Nr. 2.

[7] In NSAH Hann. Des. 310 I A, Nr. 50.

that this poster should not be put up until the last few days. For experience has shown that, over the last few days, the poster columns scintillate with bright colours and this poster, because of its completely black background, will stand out from all the bright posters and thus produce a tremendous effect on the masses.[1]

In this first election Hitler won 36·9 per cent of the vote in Lower Saxony (Reich average 30·1 per cent).[2] He only managed to secure an absolute majority in East Friesland. But Hindenburg too only secured an absolute majority in one area—Osnabrück—which he owed to the support of the Centre. The Communist vote was well below the Reich average, while in Hanover-South at any rate 30–40 per cent of the *Stahlhelm* voted for Hitler rather than Düsterberg.[3]

The task facing the party in the second presidential election was a formidable one. The first election had clearly shown that Hitler had virtually no chance of defeating Hindenburg and yet the party was forced to wage the campaign as if this were a serious possibility. It was in this situation that the organization could really prove itself.

The main tasks in the second election were seen as first, to persuade the Düsterberg voters to ignore Hugenberg's advice to call off the struggle and therefore, by implication, to abstain. And secondly, and more important, to persuade those who, 'for reasons of fear or sentimentality', voted for Hindenburg.[4]

As regards the first task, the party was advised to ignore the DNVP and the *Stahlhelm*, in order to prevent the appearance of a divided nationalist opposition, but also to urge Düsterberg voters that a vote for Hitler would be a warning both to the government and to foreign opinion, particularly France.[5]

Some idea of the views of the *Stahlhelm* on the election may be gained from the notes for a speech made by the *Stahlhelm* leader in the Hildesheim district on 3 April 1932. Since they are of considerable interest in illuminating the ambivalent attitude adopted towards the NSDAP by the *Stahlhelm* leadership and probably by many DNVP voters, it is worth quoting from them at some length:

NSDAP. *Disadvantages*: Arrogance. Wanting to do everything themselves. Promises which can't be kept. Tragedy of the party: no peaceful, steady development. Few leader-personalities. They accept everyone. Not well-drilled.

[1] Reichspropagandaleitung Rundschreiben, 29 Feb. 1932, NSAH Hann. Des. 310 I B, Nr. 1.

[2] Franz, *Die Politischen Wahlen in Niedersachsen 1867 bis 1949*, p. 60.

[3] Der Stahlhelm B.d.F Der Salzgau, 'Politischer Stimmungsbericht für das I/1932', 31 Mar. 1932, BA R 72/5.

[4] Gaupropagandaleitung H-S-B Rundschreiben, 20 Mar. 1932, NSAH Hann. Des. 310 I E, Nr. 30.

[5] Ibid.

Party egoism. Danger of *Bonzentum* [political self-seeking]. Personality of Hitler: clever, strong, great influence on the masses, big drummer, statesman? His associates. *Advantages*: Mass movement. Youth. Enemy of Marxism. Strong, perhaps strongest element for the recovery of the nation. Those who are well-intentioned towards the party, as I am, must watch out for certain opposition elements within it, ensure that its development is steady [i.e. not radical].

2. Election. . . . Hitler has no chance. Necessary to give him here a third warning. So that he is ready for an alliance, to the greater good of the national movement. . . . The watchword is: the *Stahlhelm* as such has no interest [in the election]. Individuals are not bound by instructions. Obviously not a vote for the system. The fewer votes Hitler gets for his hopeless candidature the better for the NSDAP, national front, and Fatherland. . . . Every vote is valuable? No, valueless, Hitler won't win anyway. Anyone who is plagued by conscience should vote for Hitler. But to stop the NSDAP from making bad mistakes, it is logical not to flock to it, but to place another strong party at its side.[1]

To achieve the second task of winning Hindenburg voters it was first of all necessary to establish who these Hindenburg voters were. Branch leaders, therefore, were ordered to 'find out at bakers, butchers, grocers and in public houses who voted for Hindenburg for the reasons noted above'.[2] Once this had been achieved, intensive canvassing had to begin. Speakers were discouraged from making personal attacks on Hindenburg since they simply resulted in the closing of the meeting by the police. The record of his presidency should be the subject of the attack. A particularly effective form of anti-Hindenburg propaganda was apparently statements published in the press by 'representative' citizens in support of Hitler.[3] The signatories ranged from professors and retired generals to factory workers and war widows.

Particular emphasis was placed on individual appeals to specific social groups. Special pamphlets were printed directed at particular occupations, and branches were ordered, for example, to concentrate on canvassing women since they were 'the largest reserve' of votes, particularly women in employment. Pamphlets were printed in an effort to remove the anti-feminist image which the party's opponents had been quick to exploit.[4] The party was also warned not to drive off the workers 'through speakers threatening the Marxists in general terms'. 'We should only attack the *Oberbonzen*' and the SA 'should

[1] Stichworte für den Vortrag des Landesführers am 3 Apr. 1932, BA R 72–5.
[2] Gaupropagandaleitung S-H-B Sonderrundschreiben betr. Osterfrieden, 18 Mar. 1932, NSAH Hann. Des. 310 I E, Nr. 30.
[3] Schmalz, *Nationalsozialisten ringen um Braunschweig*, p. 195. With the intention, of course, of removing the 'party political' image from Hitler's candidature.
[4] Richtlinien für die zweite Reichspräsidentenwahl von der Reichsleitung (copy), NSAH Hann. Des. 310 I B, Nr. 44.

TECHNIQUES AND THEMES OF PROPAGANDA

not adopt an aggressive attitude when German workers want enlighten-ment'.[1] The election showed the party desperately trying to win votes from even the most unlikely quarters.

As regards general propaganda, the party was ordered to combat the accusation that their policies were inflationary—'one of the most effective electoral lies of the System parties',[2] for memories of 1923 were still fresh in people's minds and financial orthodoxy reigned supreme. Finally, speakers were advised to

emphasize above all *foreign policy questions*, for example Lithuania and the threat from Poland, the sufferings of the Germans in Czechoslovakia, the French encirclement policy through the attempt to form a Danubian League against Germany which will rob Germany of her last reasonably fruitful in-dustrial export market and *put more German workers on the streets*.[3]

The management of the Reich campaign reached a new level of sophistication. Apart from the famous air campaign, more effective use was made of the party press. All party newspapers were ordered to treble their circulation for the period 29 March to 10 April and to put two-thirds of the copies at the disposal of the *Gau* head-quarters for free distribution.[4] The press was then used for a massive build-up of Hitler. On 29 March, all papers were required to carry an article on 'Hitler as a man' with pictures of Hitler with babies and dogs; on the 30th, on 'Hitler as a comrade' '(loyalty, attitude of social responsibility etc.)', on the 31st on 'Hitler as a fighter' '(tremendous achievement through his strength of will, etc.)', and finally, on 1 April 'Hitler as a statesman' with pictures of Hitler in statesmanlike poses. This was a build-up to Hitler's air campaign in which, once more, the press was closely involved. Wherever Hitler spoke there was a fully equipped press office linked to four communications centres in various parts of the Reich which passed on information to the newspapers in their area; and every day all party papers carried front page accounts of Hitler's activities the day before.

The second presidential election resulted in an absolute majority of 53 per cent for Hindenburg in Lower Saxony.[5] But Hitler had in-creased his vote to 44 per cent (Reich average 36·8 per cent) and this time he won an absolute majority in both Oldenburg and East Fries-land. Clearly many Düsterberg voters had supported him.

[1] Ibid.
[2] Reichspropagandaleitung No. 3/4 Rednerinformation 1932–1 Apr. 1932.
[3] Italics in the original, ibid. There is, however, no evidence of foreign policy as an important theme in Nazi propaganda in Lower Saxony beyond the usual refer-ences to reparations. In border areas such as East Prussia, it may have been of more significance.
[4] Anordnung für die Werbeaktion der nationalsozialistische Presse für den 2. Wahlgang zur Reichspräsidentenwahl, 23 Mar. 1932, gez. Goebbels NSAH Hann. Des. 310 I B, Nr. 1.   [5] See Franz, op. cit., p. 60.

After the election, the NSDAP had no time to become depressed by the result for, ten days later, on 23 April, the Prussian *Landtag* election took place. The party could therefore maintain its momentum and, in *Gau* Hanover-South–Brunswick, for example, in the period between the two elections 595 meetings and rallies were held in the Prussian part of the *Gau* alone.[1] The emphasis this time was on attacking the SPD and the Centre, in particular by criticizing the failure of the Prussian emergency policies to provide work and by publicizing the NSDAP work programme.[2] The party was careful to counteract propaganda from their opponents that they were opposed to social insurance and were in favour of euthanasia for old people and cripples. Those in homes for old people and cripples were sent personal letters, while the blind even received pamphlets in Braille.

At the end of April 1932 in its report to the Reich propaganda headquarters, *Gau* Hanover-South–Brunswick drew some conclusions from its experiences during these three months of unprecedented propaganda activity.[3] In the first place, the *Gau* asked for a measure of decentralization so that *Gaue* which contained people of the same race (*Volksstamm*) could combine to provide suitable posters for their particular area. Decentralization would also avoid delays in supply which had been causing considerable annoyance. Secondly, they urged that the posters should in future contain 'more about our plans for the future and less about the miseries of the present'. Finally, the *Gau* reported that

Better than ten meetings, 1000 posters and 10,000 pamphlets are mass rallies in the open air. This propaganda weapon, which up till now was used almost solely by the Marxists, must in future be made use of in a completely different way. For example, in Hanover, we got hundreds of thousands out. This rally was of a size which has only been paralleled during the revolution days of 1918. On the day of the election its effect showed in the marked increase in votes at the polls near the site of the rally.

(v) *The Reichstag election of 31 July 1932*

This new emphasis on mass rallies was a significant development in Nazi propaganda for it reflected a growing disillusionment within the party about the effectiveness of a plethora of meetings. During the second presidential election, the branch leader in Göttingen had reported a feeling of exhaustion among audiences.[4] During May, this

[1] Tätigkeitsbericht, Apr. 1932, NSAH Hann. Des. 310 I B, Nr. 13.
[2] Reichspropagandaleitung No. 5 Rednerinformation 1932, 15 Apr. 1932.
[3] Ergänzung zum Propagandabericht, Feb./März/Apr., 28 Apr. 1932, in NSAH Hann. Des. 310 I B, Nr. 13.
[4] Zuchold-Göttingen to Gaupropagandaleitung, 9 Apr. 1932, NSAH Hann. Des. 310 I B, Nr. 37.

feeling had become general throughout the *Gau* and the party had to order branches to hold a specific number of meetings in order to provide employment for their eighty-two *Gau* speakers.[1] In this situation, the party had to revive people's jaded appetites with something special and so the trend was more to mass rallies, entertainment evenings (*Deutsche Abende*) and military display evenings (*Armeemarschabende*).[2] On 1 May, for example, the Hanover district branch held a long procession through the city with floats for the representation of the various occupations, with the intention of demonstrating that the NSDAP was already a microcosm of the future *Volksgemeinschaft*.[3] This trend reached its height in the *Reichstag* election of 31 July, in which Goebbels ordered the *Gaue* 'to place the main emphasis of the whole propaganda campaign on mass demonstrations and big SA marches'.[4] Furthermore, greater stress was placed on film propaganda, loudspeaker vans and—a technique developed in the presidential elections —personal letters sent to all voters who were not members of the party appealing to their particular interests.[5]

In this election the NSDAP had to face far more sophisticated competition than hitherto from their left-wing opponents. For the Left had recognized the effectiveness of the Nazi propaganda techniques by copying them. Thus, after the shock of the 1930 *Reichstag* election result the *Reichsbanner* had been forced to transform its propaganda on the principle of 'learning from the opponent'.[6] Under the direction of a professor of psychology and former assistant of Pavlov, who had gained his experiences of propaganda in the Russian revolution, the Left began to reject their traditional 'rational' style in favour of 'mobilizing against moods, excitement, and passion equivalent moods, excitement and passion'.[7] The principles of Professor Tschachotin with

[1] Gaupropagandaleitung S-H-B Monatliches Rundschreiben, 24 May 1932, NSAH Hann. Des. 310 I E, Nr. 30 and list of 82 *Gau* Redner of, 20 May 1932, in NSAH Hann. Des. 310 I D, Nr, 10.

[2] Tätigkeitsbericht, Mai 1932, NSAH Hann. Des. 310 I B, Nr. 13.

[3] Ibid. These processions became a regular May Day ritual throughout the Reich after 1933.

[4] Reichspropagandaleitung an alle Gauleiter gez. Goebbels, 1 July 1932, NSAH Hann. Des. I B, Nr. 15.

[5] Tätigkeitsbericht, Juni/Juli 1932, NSAH Hann. Des. 310 I B, Nr. 13, e.g.: special letters were addressed to civil servants, white-collar workers, women, agricultural labourers, etc. One branch leader pointed out, however, that it was important to make sure that 'a letter meant for left-wing people is not sent to a right-winger' [!], Kirchrode branch to Gaupropagandaleiter, 15 Mar. 1932, NSAH Hann. Des. 310 I A, Nr. 69.

[6] See K. Rohe, *Das Reichsbanner Schwarz-Rot-Gold* (Düsseldorf, 1966) p. 364 and pp. 404 ff.

[7] See the Rundschreiben Nr. 9/1932 des Reichsbannergauvorstandes Hannover of 23 Mar. 1932, an alle Ortsgruppen in Gau Hannover printed in Matthias and Morsey, eds., *Das Ende der Parteien 1933* (Düsseldorf, 1960), pp. 217 ff.

their emphasis on mass intimidation, the use of symbols, and the importance of emotion in the reactions of the masses read very like those enunciated by Hitler in *Mein Kampf*. They were implemented for the first time on a large scale in this election, and *Gau* Hanover-South–Brunswick was forced to admit the effectiveness of the three arrows sign which had been introduced by the Iron Front as a counter symbol to the swastika.[1]

The election was also harder fought because, for the first time, the NSDAP was forced to some extent on to the defensive. The Left succeeded in making the attitude of the NSDAP to the Papen government a key issue in the election. They fought with the slogan 'Iron Front against Hitler barons', a slogan which, according to the report of *Gau* Hanover-South–Brunswick, had 'a devastating effect'.[2] For, the NSDAP was in an awkward position *vis-à-vis* the Papen government. They did not wish to ruin the possibility of future influence with Papen or Hindenburg by appearing too hostile, but they could not afford to be in any way identified with his reactionary and unpopular government. In the first directive for the election which appeared on 4 June 1932, that is before Papen had lifted the ban on the SA, the first consideration was uppermost in the party's mind.[3] Goebbels ordered speakers to attack the record of the previous governments and the parties which had held office in them and insisted: 'All discussion about von Papen's cabinet by the party in this election is forbidden, and all attempts to raise this issue by our opponents must be blunted.' But the NSDAP found itself forced more and more to attack the Papen government in order to demonstrate that, despite Papen's lifting of the SA ban, they were not committed to him in any way.[4]

To avoid being branded as reactionaries, and because audiences were increasingly anxious to hear positive proposals as well as negative criticism, the NSDAP made particular efforts in this election to emphasize its plans for the provision of work.[5] The party blamed the collapse of the social insurance system on the deflationary measures of 1931–2, and insisted that the provision of work alone could preserve the system since contributions would then begin to come in again. It

[1] Tätigkeitsbericht, Juni/Juli 1932, NSAH Hann. Des. 310 I B, Nr. 13.

[2] Ibid.

[3] Reichspropagandaleitung zur vertraulichen Kenntnisahme an alle Parteistellen 4 June 1932, NSAH Hann. Des. 310 I A, Nr. 37.

[4] Reichspropagandaleitung an alle Gauleiter, 1 July 1932 NSAH Hann. Des. 310 I B, Nr. 15.

[5] See ibid., and Reichspropagandaleitung der NSDAP No. 8 Rednerinformation 1932, 15 July 1932. Already in the Presidential election the branch leader in Göttingen had reported that 'people are no longer interested in barrages of insults. They are interested in the following questions: work, bread, war and inflation.' See Zuchold-Göttingen to the Gaupropagandaleitung, 14 Mar. 1932, NSAH Hann. Des. 310 I B, Nr. 37.

accused the government of having sacrificed the German economy to the international economic system through its acceptance of reparations and its liberal import policies. The economy could only be revived by a policy of autarky based on a healthy agricultural sector protected from foreign competition. Much use was made of Strasser's *Reichstag* speech of 10 May in which he had offered to work with the trade unions to solve the unemployment problem. An attempt was made to exploit what the party alleged was a growing divergence between the trade unions and the SPD on the question of measures to deal with unemployment.

Although the main emphasis of the NSDAP campaign appears to have been on trying to break in at last to the SPD voting reserves, the party did not neglect the bourgeois voters. The party was ordered to point out to the bourgeoisie the increased danger of civil war owing to the emergent united front of the *Reichsbanner* and the KPD.[1] And, as an aspect of this tactic, the party press was ordered to concentrate for a whole week on the street fight in Altona as a symptom of the growing danger.[2] In this situation, the NSDAP pointed out that the bourgeois parties were simply not strong enough to have any effect on the issue and votes for them would therefore be wasted.[3]

The result of the election showed a marked increase in the NSDAP vote in Lower Saxony. With 45·2 per cent of the vote (Reich average 37·2 per cent), the NSDAP had slightly increased the percentage of its vote compared with the vote for Hitler in the second presidential election, despite the fact that this time the DNVP had its own list.[4] The party was strongest in the areas where it had made such large gains in 1930—North Oldenburg and East Friesland,[5] though these had now also been joined by many rural *Kreise* in other areas. All other parties, except the KPD, lost votes, though in many towns and industrial areas the SPD and KPD vote kept the NSDAP vote below the average.[6] The Centre party performed a similar role in Catholic areas. An interesting example of the contrast between the NSDAP vote in Protestant and Catholic areas is provided by the results in the neighbouring *Kreise* of Leer (Protestant) and Aschendorf-Hümmling (Catholic). Aschendorf was wholly agricultural, Leer less so because

---

[1] See footnote 4, p. 217

[2] Reichspropagandaleitung Rundschreiben, 19 July 1932; NSDAP Hauptarchiv, Reel 15, Folder 284.

[3] Denkschrift der Reichspropagandaleitung zur Reichstagswahl, July 1932, ibid.

[4] For a detailed break-down of the NSDAP vote see Franz, op. cit., pp. 60–5.

[5] Ammerland (77·8 per cent) and Wittmund (68·8 per cent) were the *Kreise* with the highest percentages in Lower Saxony, ibid., pp. 262 and 236.

[6] Even in some towns in rural areas such as Celle (NSDAP vote 40·4 per cent) and Lüneburg (39·2 per cent), ibid., pp. 172 and 174.

of its medium-sized town and port. Yet in Leer, the NSDAP succeeded in winning 55 per cent of the vote; in Aschendorf-Hümmling only 8·3 per cent, compared with the Centre party's 79·5 per cent.[1]

The period 1930–2 confirmed the impression created in the 1930 election of the resourcefulness of the Nazi propaganda machine: its willingness to experiment with different media and techniques—for example, the aeroplane tour and films; its adaptability to changes in the mood of its audiences—for example, the switch from ordinary meetings to entertainment and rallies; and its efficiency in employing its resources with maximum effect and in mobilizing the membership. This flexibility and sheer administrative efficiency was the result of the excellent channels of communication between the local branches, the *Gau* head-quarters and the Reich leadership. This was achieved through the creation of a separate propaganda department with representatives at all three levels which could concentrate entirely on propaganda, and also through the co-ordination of the *Kreisleiter*. Speakers were trained and given financial incentives; the technical aspects of propaganda were explained in an easily comprehensible form in manuals and directives; above all, the local departments were kept constantly up-to-date about the various themes and techniques which required particular emphasis. They not only felt fully involved in the party's activities and in its successes and failures, but were also able to keep the membership fully informed. Finally, the NSDAP's propaganda organization was distinguished from all its rivals, with the exception of the KPD, by its open-mindedness and freedom from the inhibitions of tradition. Local leaders were encouraged to report on their experiences and to experiment with new techniques (though not with content) which, if successful, would be recommended by the *Gau* or Reich leadership.

With the development of the mass rallies, the style of the NSDAP's propaganda had become even more irrational than before. It has been shown in the description of Münchmeyer's success that certain sections of the population in Lower Saxony were particularly vulnerable to irrational propaganda. A contemporary observer has noted that the Hanoverian peasantry, although generally characterized by a down-to-earth attitude, were also liable to political irrationality.[2] In earlier times they had believed in the 'rider on the white horse who comes from Celle'; this had been followed by a romantic loyalty to the Guelph dynasty; and now, this observer has suggested, the tendency re-emerged in 'secularized eschatology' born of crisis and despair.[3] It

[1] Ibid., pp. 232 and 212.
[2] See P. Fleisch, *Erlebte Kirchengeschichte in und mit der hannoverschen Landeskirche* (Hanover, 1952), pp. 150 ff.
[3] Ibid., p. 150.

is also interesting in this context that Ludendorff's Tannenberg League which propagated Nordic mythology combined with anti-Semitic, anti-Catholic and anti-Freemasonry propaganda had considerable success in the rural areas of Lower Saxony; so much so indeed that the party in Hanover East was forced to outdo it in its anti-Semitism and hostility to Freemasonry.[1]

Sociological reasons have been put forward to explain this tendency. It has been shown that the Nazi movement won votes in the Province of Hanover particularly from those 'whose basic value orientation and organizational experience had been of a *Gemeinschaft*, primary, folk, or familistic nature and whose formal, contractual, bureaucratic obligations and affiliations had been insignificant', and from 'individuals with limited experience and obligations as active members of dynamic large-scale political or religious social structures'.[2] In other words, Nazism succeeded best among those, like the rural *Mittelstand* in the Province of Hanover, who had least experience of modern economic and social organization. This almost certainly applied equally to Oldenburg and East Friesland, particularly the *Geest* areas, where the NSDAP secured its highest vote.[3] For, the Nazi movement was among other things 'a rebellion against the institution, against the programme, against paper, against the *neue Sachlichkeit*', although paradoxically its own organization was in one sense extremely bureaucratic.[4]

On the other hand, the party continued to root its propaganda to a considerable extent in an appeal to economic interest, as for example with the unemployment programme. A good example of the complexity of the appeal of Nazi propaganda which could act simultaneously at different levels, is provided by the party's anti-Semitism. Above all, through the vagueness and eclecticism of its propaganda, the party, unlike its opponents, did not limit itself to any particular social group or programme. With its ideal of the *Volksgemeinschaft* and the evidence of the classlessness of its own organization, it offered itself as the ideal vehicle for overcoming the social and political divisions which had bedevilled Weimar. Finally, by emphasizing the bankruptcy of the 'system' and by its own activism, the party projected itself as the creator of the future Germany at a time when the population was bewildered and disillusioned by the evident failure of the Weimar

[1] See, for example, the contents of the *NS*.

[2] See C. P. Loomis and J. A. Beagle, 'The Spread of German Nazism in Rural Areas', *American Sociological Review* (1946), pp. 752 ff.

[3] For the successes of the NSDAP in the *Geest* areas of Schleswig-Holstein see R. Heberle, *Landbevölkerung und Nationalsozialismus* (Stuttgart, 1963), pp. 92 ff.

[4] Heuss, *Hitler's Weg*, p. 166. On Nazism as in part a reaction by traditional elements against the process of rationalization, a reaction sharpened by *anomie*, see also the essay 'Some sociological Aspects of the Fascist Movements' in Talcott Parsons, *Essays in Sociological Theory*, revised edn. (New York, 1964), pp. 124 ff.

politicians to solve the crisis. The Nazis were assisted in this by the fact that the sense of disillusionment with democratic politics as practised under Weimar had spread to the supporters of democracy themselves, sapping their self-confidence and will to resist. It was only in July 1932 that the Left staged something of a recovery and by then it was too late.

XII

THE NSDAP IN POWER
—THE NAZI GOVERNMENTS IN
BRUNSWICK AND OLDENBURG

LOWER Saxony was remarkable for containing two of the five states in which the NSDAP held office in the period 1930–3 —Brunswick and Oldenburg.[1] It would be unwise to draw too many conclusions about the exercise of power by the NSDAP from a study of these two instances. The influence of the party's ministers was limited by the fact that it did not control the Reich government, and in Brunswick additionally by the need to maintain the coalition with the two bourgeois parties. Yet it may be argued that these limitations in fact form an interesting framework in which to study the style of the NSDAP in power through its reaction to them.

The winning of office in Brunswick and Oldenburg simultaneously presented the NSDAP with great opportunities and serious problems. The opportunities were for greater freedom in propaganda both from interference by hostile authorities and to introduce measures which would bring popularity. Above all, there was the chance to appoint party members and sympathizers to positions of influence within the state. The problems sprang from the fact that, by taking part in the government, the party could no longer exploit the opposition role which had proved so fruitful in the past: it was now burdened with the responsibility for a situation which was desperate, while its power to change things was severely limited.

In both Brunswick and Oldenburg the party exploited its advantage to the full.[2] In the first place, while its opponents were hindered by bans on marches and newspapers, the NSDAP was given full support

---

[1] In Brunswick in a coalition with the DNVP and DVP from 1 Oct. 1930, with a short break between 27 July and 15 Sept. 1931; in Oldenburg with an absolute majority from 16 June 1932. The other three states were Thuringia, Mecklenburg and Anhalt.

[2] The most famous benefit which the NSDAP received from participation in state government was, of course, the acquiring of German citizenship by Hitler through his appointment as an official of the Brunswick delegation to the *Reichsrat* in Berlin. The circumstances of this affair have been described at length in Roloff, *Bürgertum und Nationalsozialismus 1930–1933*, pp. 89 ff., and R. Morsey, 'Hitler als braunschweigischer Regierungsrat', in *Vjhfzg* 1960.

even when it took the law into its own hands.[1] Secondly, it introduced measures such as a ban on Jewish ritual slaughter, a tax on consumer co-operatives and an increase in the tax on department and chain stores, and a cut in the salaries of ministers to RM 12,000, which were calculated to have direct electoral or party appeal.[2] But finally, and most important of all, it made good use of its power of appointment and dismissal within the state civil service.

The basis of the attempt to purge the state administration was provided by three points in the Nazi programme for reform of state government: first, 'the cleansing of the state administration from civil servants and employers who, without any special training or suitability, have penetrated the civil service simply on the basis of their party card'; secondly, 'the simplification of and economies within the state and education administrations'; and finally, 'the banning of the Marxist spirit from education and its replacement by the awakening of a strong will of German self-assertion'.[3]

Education provided, in fact, the most obvious field to which the NSDAP could turn its attention because the party could expect to win sympathy from the bourgeoisie for its aim of rooting out 'Marxism' from the schools. In Brunswick, for example, the first few months of the new government saw a major purge of the education administration: seven school inspectors were dismissed; forty-six teachers were retired and twenty-six agnostic teachers who were not yet officially appointed were dismissed.[4] The ruthlessness of these measures was facilitated by the consensus among the bourgeoisie that the former SPD Minister of Education, Sievers, had allowed party political motives to dominate his appointments. In Oldenburg, too, the Nazi government took steps to purge the education system. Two school inspectors were dismissed on the grounds that 'because of their *Weltanschauung* they are incapable of carrying out the inspection of schools in the way and in the spirit desired by the ministry'.[5] In Oldenburg, however, the government was limited by the fact that the school system was partially controlled by two *Oberschulkollegien* run by the Protestant and Catholic churches respectively. In order to get round this control, the government therefore published an emergency decree on

[1] For examples in Brunswick see NSAW 12 A Neu Fb 13h 16041–2, and 16047–8; in Oldenburg the *Landtag* debates in Dec. 1932–Jan. 1933, in which the NSDAP showed amused satisfaction at the complaints of its opponents. See NSAO 39 VII Landtag.
[2] For Nazi motions in Brunswick see Landesversammlung Verhandlungen, Niederschriften und Sitzungsberichte 1930–3. Druckschriften; in Oldenburg NSAO 39 VII Landtag.
[3] See Schmalz, *Nationalsozialisten ringen um Braunschweig*, p. 126.
[4] Roloff, *Bürgertum und Nationalsozialismus*, pp. 29–33 and 39.
[5] Deutscher Beamtenbund to Staatsministerium 3 Oct. 1932 in NSAO 131–627.

19 September 1932 whereby, on the grounds of 'economy and efficiency', the *Oberschulkollegien* were abolished and their responsibilities transferred to the ministry. But this measure resulted in strong pressure from the two churches, and the government was forced to compromise by creating separate Protestant and Catholic departments within the ministry, whose members would only be appointed after consultation with the president of the *Evangelischer Oberkirchenrat* and the *Offizial* of the Bishop of Münster.[1]

The police were another department which the NSDAP was anxious to control. In Brunswick the process of *Gleichschaltung* was begun in January 1931 with the dismissal of the SPD commander of the constabulary *(Schutzpolizei)*.[2] It was continued by Klagges who forbade the police to belong to the Republican Brunswick Police Federation *(Polizeibeamtenverband)* and applied pressure on them to join a new Nazi police organization.[3] In Oldenburg too, there was a reorganization of the police department.[4] On 27 July, the government appointed 230 SA men as temporary auxiliary police on the grounds that public disorder and the possibility of a communist rebellion necessitated a strengthening of the police. Pressure from the Reich Ministry of the Interior ensured that the appointments were only temporary—until 11 August; but the affair had permanent results in a reorganization of the police department. Major v.d. Hellen, who had asked awkward questions about the SA auxiliaries, and *Oberst* Wandtke, the commander of the combined police *(Ordnungspolizei)*, were honourably retired and replaced by *Polizei-Hauptmann* Dr. Lankenau, a Nazi, and *Polizei-Major* Sassenberg, a right-wing sympathizer. Although Sassenberg was made commander of the *Ordnungspolizei*, the key figure was Lankenau, who acted as liaison between the Ministry of the Interior and the police, and was made directly responsible to the Ministry. He was later the Oldenburg Gestapo chief.

A major propaganda theme of the NSDAP in its years of opposition had been its attack on corruption in the financial administration. As early as 1929, the party had campaigned against the director of the Brunswick state bank, Stübben, while in Oldenburg the party had complained about the fact that private bankers sat on the board responsible for the financial institutions of the state, and therefore could con-

---

[1] For the above see NSAO 39 VII Landtag 1. Versammlung. Gesetze IV.

[2] Roloff *Bürgertum und Nationalsozialismus*, p. 33.

[3] Ibid. pp. 80–2. An amendment to the law on police officers was also passed making it easier to dismiss policemen after ten years' service—a useful weapon against those who were unco-operative particularly those appointed in the period of SPD–USPD government 1919–24. See Landesversammlung 1930–3 Drucksache 163.

[4] For the following, see the correspondence in NSAO 205 and the reports in *Nachrichten für Stadt und Land* 27 July–11 Aug. 1932.

trol their activities and use secret information for their own advantage.[1] Once in power, the party seized the opportunity to intimidate the bourgeoisie, to maintain its reputation as a broom which would sweep clean the Augean stables of the 'system', and to increase its own influence in the financial sphere. In Brunswick, the campaign against Stübben both within and outside the *Landtag* was stepped up until he was replaced.[2] In Oldenburg the government published an emergency decree, reorganizing the financial institutions, banning those who had private banking interests from sitting on the boards, and increasing the powers of the State Commissar who was replaced by a Nazi.[3] Protests from the Chambers of Commerce and Trades, which in future were only allowed to suggest names instead of being allowed to elect their representatives to the boards of the financial institutions, were ignored; and when they refused to co-operate, the government published a new decree enabling it to appoint representatives without consultation with the Chambers.

Although the acquisition of power in Brunswick and Oldenburg offered the NSDAP very considerable advantages, it also created problems by involving the party in responsibility at a time of crisis while its hands were tied by emergency laws passed by a Reich government which it did not control.

On 27 July 1931, after a series of Reich emergency laws, the Nazi Minister in Brunswick, Franzen, resigned on the grounds that, by continuing in office, the party would be countenancing Brunswick's loss of independence and 'the anti-social policies of the Brüning dictatorship'.[4] Initially, he was supported in his action by the party leadership. Within a week, however, Hitler had realized that the resignation of the Nazi minister in Brunswick would mean that the party no longer held power anywhere in the Reich—except in local government—and the loss of influence which that would entail. Furthermore, he appreciated that while the emergency laws took away much of the independence of the states, they also thereby lessened the responsibility of the state ministers. Indeed, by applying the emergency laws with excessive rigour while laying the blame on the Reich government, it

---

[1] See articles in the *NB* during 1929 and NSAO 39 VI Landtag 1. Verslg. 5 *Sitzung*, 23 June 1931, Röver Antrag.

[2] Roloff *Bürgertum und Nationalsozialismus*, pp. 82 ff.

[3] For the following see NSAO 39 VII Landtag 1. Verslg. Gesetze III Nr. 1–18.

[4] For a detailed account of the resignation of Franzen see Roloff *Bürtertum und Nationalsozialismus*, pp. 50 ff. According to Krebs, *Tendenzen und Gestalten der NSDAP*, p. 255. Röver also objected to becoming Minister-President, but in his case because he felt himself unsuitable. 'For six years I have attacked *Bonzen*. Now they will point at me saying: "Look Karlchen Röver has become a Bonze himself. Wants to achieve something which he doesn't understand and which he hasn't learnt."'

might be possible to increase discontent with the 'system'. This was in fact to be the policy to be followed by the party's new minister, Dietrich Klagges.[1]

In Oldenburg too the Nazi government took advantage of the Reich emergency legislation, but in a rather different way. Although the emergency laws limited the powers of the states in many fields, they did enable the state governments to pass financial measures by decree which then only required subsequent confirmation by the *Landtag*. On 6 July, therefore, the NSDAP used its absolute majority to adjourn the *Landtag* indefinitely—in fact until December—and to rule by decree, thereby effectively stifling opposition criticism.[2]

Yet freedom from the need to rely on a coalition soon proved to be a double-edged weapon. For, while in Brunswick the DNVP minister was responsible for financial policy, leaving the Nazis with police and education, in Oldenburg the NSDAP was forced to deal with the economic situation on its own. The excuse that the state government's hands were tied by the Reich had already been used by the previous government. The NSDAP had to show that it could do better. Furthermore, previously, Nazi speakers had frequently complained that the Oldenburg government had not offered sufficiently energetic opposition to the policies of the Reich government. They insisted that it was 'both obsequious and tyrannical to force the population to pay more and more taxes'.[3] As a result, when it came into office in June 1932, the party found itself burdened with prior promises of militant action against Berlin.

It soon became clear that the Nazi government had no intention of challenging Berlin directly. Thus, although the first government statement proudly declared that the 'independence of Oldenburg must be defended to the last drop of blood', at the same time it insisted that 'unless in a very short time national socialist policies are introduced *by the Reich* in all spheres of life, the recovery of the Free State of Oldenburg from its difficult situation will be just as impossible as that of the German people as a whole'.[4]

---

[1] See Roloff *Bürgertum und Nationalsozialismus*, p. 56. Dietrich Klagges, born 1891, was a teacher in *Mittelschulen* until dismissed from his post as Assistant Headmaster in Benneckenstein on 8 Dec. 1930, because of his membership of the NSDAP. Before joining the NSDAP in 1925, he had been a member of several *völkisch* organizations, e.g. Hammerbund, Deutschbund, Pan-German League, etc. Within the party he had established a reputation for himself as an 'expert' on Marxism and an effective organizer in the Harz area. After his dismissal as a teacher he was given a post as *Regierungsrat* in the Brunswick Ministry of Education on 30 Dec. 1930, and in the Third Reich became a senior SS official. See files on Dietrich Klagges in NSDAP Hauptarchiv, Reel B, Folder 1408 and BDC.

[2] See NSAO 39 VII Landtagsverhandlungen.

[3] Böhmcker speech reported in *NfSL*, 16 Jan. 1932.

[4] *NfSL*, 8 July 1932. Italic in the original.

The government began its activity with measures calculated to confirm its popularity among its main supporters—peasants and artisans.[1] In the first place, it introduced an arrangement whereby peasants were allowed to pay tax arrears in kind, a measure which, however, proved impossible to administer. Secondly, it adopted a suggestion from the 'Working group of the Oldenburg *Mittelstand*' to give householders tax rebates for money spent on house repairs, which clearly encouraged the employment of artisans. Finally, they announced a reduction in the salary of ministers from RM 18,000 to RM 12,000. Although the opposition attacked these measures as basically fraudulent—the real reduction in salaries, they maintained, was only from RM 13,800 to RM 14,000–RM 12,000, and the payment of tax arrears in kind was, they argued, irresponsible favouritism towards the peasantry and would prove impossible to administer[2]—the measures were a clever move. Instead of a negative policy of introducing taxes, the government was apparently being constructive by economizing and by helping people to pay their taxes while simultaneously providing work.

This impression was reinforced by a clever public relations exercise which they organized for 8 July. This was a meeting of all the leading figures in public life within the state (excluding the trade union leaders) which was addressed by the three Nazi ministers—Röver, the Minister-President, Pauly, the Minister of Finance,[3] and Spangemacher, the Minister of Education and Culture. The emphasis was on constructive co-operation. Röver assured his audience that the interests of the state and its people, and not those of any single party, were the sole concern of his government. He declared that he did not believe in attacks on his predecessors, and emphasized the necessity for all to rally round the government.[4]

Yet the true face of the government had already shown itself in the indefinite adjournment of the *Landtag* two days previously and was to become increasingly apparent in the succeeding months. The tax concessions to the peasants and houseowners were paid for in part by a cut in the salaries of civil servants, and ministers in their public speeches embarked on what was almost a campaign of vilification of the civil service.[5] Although this lost them support in the city of Oldenburg itself, which had a large civil service population, they could be sure of a

---

[1] *NfSL*, 7 July 1932 and NSAO 39 VII Landtag. Dokumente.

[2] The opposition were right about the payment of taxes in kind. This proved impossible to administer and was not renewed.

[3] Julius Pauly, born 16 Feb. 1901, studied law, becoming a Gerichtsrat. He joined the party late, in 1931.   [4] See the report in *NfSL*, 9 July 1932.

[5] Announcement of cut in civil service salaries from 1 Oct. in *NfSL*, 16 Sept. 1932.

sympathetic audience in the countryside. In any case they were aware
that many of the civil servants in Oldenburg supported the *Staatspartei*.[1]

The few economic measures of the government, however, were
soon dwarfed in the public mind by a series of incidents which illustrate
very clearly the nature and style of the new movement and in particular its complete contrast with anything which had gone before. The
first occurred in September when a coloured Lutheran preacher from
German Togoland, Kwame, was invited to preach to children at the
St. Lamberti church in the city of Oldenburg. The department for
public instruction in the *Gau* head-quarters at once protested to the
(Nazi) Ministry of Culture about this *Kulturschande* and maintained
that 'a circus would be a more suitable place to show a negro'.[2] The
Ministry of Culture replied by announcing that it did not wish to interfere in the internal affairs of the Church, but it was soon clear from
public speeches by Röver and others that this was window-dressing and
that the intention was to bully the authorities into cancelling the en-
gagement.

The reaction of the Church authorities to this affront is of considerable interest. The vicar of St. Lamberti began by replying in a
conciliatory tone. He praised the Nazi campaign against 'cultural decadence' as represented in the cult for negro art such as jazz, but at the
same time insisted that Kwame, as a loyal spokesman for the German
national cause in South West Africa, was in an entirely different category. Throughout the ensuing controversy the Church continued to
base its arguments on the importance of Kwame's mission as a representative of German *Kultur* and therefore the importance of not
offending him, a fact which is perhaps as illuminating about the climate
of the time as about the attitudes of the Protestant church. It represents one of the first examples of those pathetic attempts by groups such
as the Jewish Old Soldiers League to satisfy the Nazis by an assertion
of their national loyalties. Despite adverse publicity throughout the
Reich, the Nazi authorities refused to be impressed. Röver publicly insisted that a negro was a negro and that it was the racial aspect that was
important. He boasted, moreover, that they knew what to do with
those where were not aware of this. The Church, however, refused to
be bullied into submission. Kwame held his sermon and after this
Röver speech, the *Oberkirchenrat*, the senior Protestant Church council in Oldenburg, sued Röver on the grounds that he had publicly

[1] Joel, the Nazi President of the *Landtag* informed Ehlermann, the Staatspartei
Landtag deputy in a letter that 'I as a civil servant know that here in Oldenburg the
remnants of the Staatspartei electorate are recruited from middle-ranking civil
servants.' See *NfSL*, 2 Nov. 1932.

[2] For the Kwame affair see *NfSL* from 14 Sept. 1932.

threatened their liberty. The action was shelved, however, when Röver produced a transcript of his speech in which the offending passage had been carefully excised, thus enabling him to deny the charge.

The second example of the style of Nazi government occurred in October in the province of Birkenfeld.[1] The aim here was to replace the *Regierungspräsident*, Dörr, a Centre Party man, with a Nazi. The campaign began on 7 October 1932 with a statement from the government press office declaring that 'the greater part of the population in the province of Birkenfeld regard the *Regierungspräsident* with the greatest mistrust'—because of his alleged separatist activities in the early period of the Republic. The statement continued that, since no suitable *Beamte* was available, he would be replaced by an *Angestellte*. This accusation caused a sensation in the province and even the Nazi deputies there, including Wild, the *Angestellte* with whom the Nazis intended to replace Dörr, were obliged to deny the charge. However, the furore raised by the announcement provided the Oldenburg government with the excuse to begin a disciplinary enquiry 'to establish once and for all whether or not the rumours going around about *Regierungspräsident* Dörr are true'. Meanwhile, the government maintained, because of the friction created by the affair, it was impossible for Dörr to work satisfactorily and therefore he should be employed elsewhere. In his place Wild was appointed Commissar. Two weeks later, on 26 October, Minister Pauly publicly retracted his suspicions about Dörr, but by then, of course, the object of the exercise had been achieved.

The final example of the ruthlessness of the party and its stubbornness in the face of stiff opposition occurred in the province of Lübeck. During the autumn of 1932, conflict developed between the DNVP *Oberbürgermeister* of Eutin, Dr. Stoffregen, and the Nazi *Regierungspräsident* of Lübeck, Böhmcker.[2] Stoffregen had increasingly resented the aggressiveness and interference of the Nazi majority on the city council, in particular of the deputy *Oberbürgermeister*, Kahl. The conflict came to a head, however, over a series of bomb attacks on consumer co-operatives. It was suspected that the explosives used had been taken from the police stores by the SA when they were acting as auxiliaries. Böhmcker ordered the arrest of the Prussian detectives who entered Lübeck to investigate the affair, and when they were

[1] For the Dörr affair see *NfSL* during Oct. 1932.

[2] For the Stoffregen affair see *NfSL*, Nov. 1932 and NSAO 39 VII Landtag Verhandlungen 5. Sitzung and I. Verslg. A. Eingaben. Böhmcker was another typical young academic recruit to the NSDAP. According to an Oldenburg DVP leader, *Oberlandesgerichtsrat* Florin, Böhmcker had twice failed his law examinations and had been turned down for the civil service. See the report of Florin's speech of 12 Nov. 1931 in *NfSL*, 13 Nov. 1931.

released by a local police official dismissed him. Finally, when Dr. Stoffregen refused to allow him to look at documents concerned with the case, Böhmcker dismissed him too on the basis of a number of trumped-up charges worked out in collaboration with the Nazi city councillors. Stoffregen, however, refused to obey on the grounds that the *Regierungspräsident* had no legal right to dismiss him; he had to be removed from his office by the police. Böhmcker's action was un-doubtedly illegal—only the *Staatsministerium* had the power of dismissal—and Stoffregen brought an action against him. Böhmcker, however, had committed the prestige of the party by announcing in a public meeting that Stoffregen would never return, so that although the *Staatsministerium* was forced to put the legal position in order by cancelling the dismissal, it simultaneously suspended Stoffregen pending a disciplinary enquiry into the charges against him. Furthermore, the Nazi majority in the *Landtag* refused to agree to the lifting of Böhmcker's immunity as a member of the *Landtag*, with the result that the case against him was unable to proceed.[1]

The failure of the government's policies to bring quick results—it had even been forced to introduce the slaughter tax which was ex-tremely unpopular among the agricultural population—together with its erratic and arbitrary behaviour must have contributed to make the fall in the NSDAP vote (8·3 per cent) in the November *Reichstag* election in Oldenburg double the Reich average of 4·1 per cent.[2] In the city of Oldenburg the fall was 15·8 per cent, probably in part the revenge of the civil servants, but even in the Protestant countryside it was between 6·7 per cent (Friesland) and 9·6 per cent (Oldenburg-Land). It is not surprising, therefore, that discontent flourished in the party organization. On the 5th of December, the party organization in *Kreis* Cloppenburg wrote to the NSDAP *Landtag* group complain-ing that the main reason for the loss of votes was 'that so far there had been no vigorous measures from the governments in the states with Nazi majorities'.[3] It urged the government to put into effect the twenty-five points of the party's programme and pointed out that if Reich laws were thereby infringed and, as a result, a Reich Commissar was ordered into the state to take over, then 'the responsibility falls on the Reich and the party has its opposition posture back again'.

The Cloppenburg organization was justified in complaining that the government had not attempted seriously to challenge the Reich. Hit-ler's policy was one of coming to power legally and therefore, his state

---

[1] The government delayed the enquiry on Stoffregen until, after 30 Jan. 1933, it was of no more significance.

[2] NSAO 39 VII Landtag. Petitionen.

[3] In Brunswick, on the other hand, the fall was only 4·7 per cent; see Franz, *Die Politischen Wahlen in Niedersachsen 1867 bis 1949*, p. 56 and pp. 256 ff.

governments had the task of sitting it out until things changed at Reich level. Yet, the record of the NSDAP in power in Brunswick and Oldenburg gives the impression of considerable activity within the given limits. Indeed the characteristic style of the Nazi government which emerges is of a ruthlessness and a self-confidence which are remarkable given the limitations within which the party worked. This had little to do with efficiency. In Oldenburg the party's acts were often unplanned and unco-ordinated. Pauly's accusation against Dörr was a colossal blunder. The campaign against Kwame was totally unnecessary in political terms and calculated to alienate a large number of potential sympathizers. The Stoffregen affair was Böhmcker's private war in which he involved the state government in an extremely embarrassing way. The main lesson to be drawn from the experience of the Nazi governments of Brunswick and Oldenburg was first, the lack of co-ordination among the Nazi leaders in authority; and second that the NSDAP had no respect for established rights and conventions of whatever kind and that, in the pursuit of power and ideological principles, it would ruthlessly eliminate those who stood in its way. Perhaps the most interesting question, therefore, is why the bourgeoisie failed to profit from this lesson.

In Brunswick, as in many other parts of the Reich, the experience of the bitter struggle with the socialist parties since 1918 ensured that, in view of the nationalist and anti-Marxist aspects of the NSDAP, the bourgeois parties were prepared to overlook the strong-arm methods and extremism of the party as temporary aberrations due to the crisis situation.[1] This tolerance of violence by the bourgeoisie is also partly explicable in terms of the fact that for a generation which had gone through the First World War, the 1918 revolution, the Free Corps, and the 1923 *putsches*, political violence was not a new phenomenon, but one to which they had become to some extent conditioned. Many were prepared to rationalize the violence of the Nazis with the excuse that violence had been—and still was—practised by their opponents on the Left. Secondly, the increasing loss of members and votes to the NSDAP between 1930 and 1933 totally undermined the self-confidence of the bourgeois parties, who felt resigned in face of the greater dynamism of the Nazis. In the words of the honorary chairman of the Brunswick DVP, who joined the NSDAP in 1933: 'We are all involved in a life and death struggle against Bolshevism . . . the party has done its best to fulfil its historic task and it is now fulfilled.'[2] Finally,

---

[1] For a detailed study of the relations between the NSDAP and the bourgeois parties in Brunswick see Roloff, *Bürgertum und Nationalsozialismus 1930–1933*, and for the DVP, Schelm-Spangenberg, *Die Deutsche Volkspartei im Lande Braunschweig* (Braunschweig, 1964), pp. 133 ff.

[2] Quoted in Roloff, *Bürgertum und Nationalsozialismus*, p. 16.

by working with those who they considered moderates in the party, of whom Hitler in their view was one, they thought they could neutralize 'radicals' such as Goebbels.[1] An important part of this policy was the idea of forcing the NSDAP to share the responsibility of government. In short, they believed that 'in the national socialist movement there were valuable elements with healthy national feelings with whom political co-operation was possible'.[2]

In Oldenburg, unlike Brunswick, there was no history of political extremism and the bourgeois parties were rather more critical of the NSDAP. In 1931, for example, the DVP refused to support the NSDAP candidate for the post of Minister-President.[3] Furthermore, during the period of Nazi government, the DNVP *Landtag* deputy, Bunnemann, publicly criticized the party-political nature of NSDAP appointments and even compared the policy unfavourably with that of the former DDP Minister-President, Tantzen.[4] Yet, even in Oldenburg, and even after the Stoffregen affair, the dislike of the democratic and Republican parties by the DNVP was sufficient to prevent them from making a common front against the NSDAP. Thus, on 13 December 1939, when the *Landtag* met for the first time since its adjournment in July and the policies of the Nazi government came under strong attack, Bunnemann declared for the DNVP that 'today we have little or nothing to add to this government statement. It corresponds completely with our view. We have already informed the government in a letter of the things which we object to about the measures of the present government.'[5]

---

[1] It must be remembered that during this period Hitler in private speeches made a great effort to win over the nationalist bourgeoisie, e.g. his speech to the Ruhr Industry Club in Düsseldorf in Jan. 1932, whereas Goebbels and others were far less inhibited.

[2] Roloff, *Bürgertum und Nationalsozialismus*, p. 44.

[3] *NfSL*, 13 Nov. 1931.

[4] *NfSL*, 10 Oct. 1932.

[5] NSAO 39 VII Landtag 1 Verslg. 5 Sitzung.

XIII

THE CRISIS MONTHS:
AUGUST 1932–JANUARY 1933

(i) *Crisis within the NSDAP*

ALTHOUGH the July 1932 *Reichstag* election had resulted in an increase in votes for the NSDAP, it had not brought them an over-all majority. In any case, with the appointment of Papen as Chancellor, who could only count on the votes of the DNVP in the *Reichstag*, it had become even clearer than with Brüning that the size of a party's electoral or parliamentary support was of less immediate importance than winning the confidence of the President. The failure of Hitler to persuade Hindenburg to appoint him as Chancellor at the interview on 13 August was a crushing blow to the NSDAP.[1] In desperation, the party tried to form a coalition with the Centre, but given the existing power situation the famous vote of no-confidence which they achieved with the help of the Centre and their other previous opponents was a futile gesture. Moreover, the DNVP was quick to exploit the rather ludicrous situation of the NSDAP uniting with its old opponent to defend their parliamentary rights against a right-wing dictatorship.[2] The political tactic which the party had followed since 1925 of trying to win power by parliamentary means appeared to have led to a cul-de-sac. Furthermore, the Papen government could be expected to appeal to a large section of the bourgeoisie which hitherto had supported the NSDAP. Opposition to Papen would alienate this group and thus aggravate the crisis within the party caused by the failure of 13 August. On the other hand, the alternative—a toleration of Papen—was inconceivable for a party bent on winning absolute power, quite apart from the loss of popularity among other social groups which would result.

These major political developments which occurred during August were observed with growing concern by the NSDAP membership. In its August report to the Reich head-quarters *Gau* Hanover-South–Brunswick observed that

---

[1] See Bullock, *Hitler. A Study in Tyranny*, pp. 218–22.
[2] The party had to warn against this danger in its propaganda directives for it became an important theme in the November election. See Denkschrift zur Reichstagswahl am 6 Nov. 1932, NSAH Hann. Des. 310 I E, Nr. 23.

among the *Mittelstand* generally, among the peasantry, and even among those workers who support us, there was a very depressed, pessimistic mood. Everywhere people are saying that there would be a noticeable fall in our vote if an election were held now.[1]

At the end of September, the *Gau* reported that, while only eighty-four had joined the party during the month, 330 had left it and 155 had been excluded.[2]

This exodus was motivated for some by political disagreement, for others by financial hardship or simply disillusionment. As the party moved to the 'left' with the build-up of the anti-Papen campaign, complaints began to come in from bourgeois supporters. Typical was a letter from the leader (*Obmann*) of the *Gau* special group for shoemakers who complained:

The measures which the NSDAP is now adopting are crassly opposed to the interests of employers. I am therefore compelled to resign my post as *Obmann*. . . . I welcome any wages cut which helps us return to normal conditions and deeply regret that, as well as me, many other master craftsmen are being alienated from the NSDAP because it calls on German workers to strike.[3]

Another group, however, was disgruntled because of the failure of the party to win power and produce results in return for their contributions. Describing a conflict within the Hanover-City branch, the police reported that

the circles who are discontented with the NSDAP are mostly disgruntled shopkeepers who had bargained on an improvement in their business if the NSDAP came to power. Since an improvement has not occurred, they accuse the party of extravagance and above all complain that they pay too high salaries to the functionaries.[4]

They also accused the local *Kreisleiter* of nepotism.

Finance was another serious problem. During the autumn and winter months a serious financial crisis developed which threatened to undermine the whole party organization. An audit undertaken by the *Gau* Hanover-South–Brunswick treasury at the end of October revealed that the branches owed large sums in arrears to the *Gau*, quite apart from money owed to creditors in their areas for such things as

[1] Tätigkeitsbericht, Aug. 1932, NSAH Hann. Des. 310 I B, Nr. 13.
[2] *Gau* Mitgliederstand per 30 Sept. 1932. Total *Gau* membership was 39,336, NSAH Hann. Des. 310 I A, Nr. 38.
[3] Heinrich Belling (Königlicher Lieferant für elegante Schuhe nach Mass) to Abtlg. IV Gau Hannover-Süd–Braunschweig, 10 Oct. 1932, NSAH Hann. Des. 310 I A, Nr. 35.
[4] Polizei-Präsident Hannover to Reg-Präsident Hannover, 24 Sept. 1932, NSAH Hann. Des. 80 Hann. II, Nr. 742.

rent, telephone, the hiring of halls, posters, etc.[1] The indebtedness of the local branches in turn undermined the position of the *Gauleitung* whose expenses were considerable. Even during 1931, there were seven members of the *Gauleitung* in Hanover-South–Brunswick in full-time employment in the service of the party, earning sums of up to RM 250 a month, and during 1932 the number almost certainly increased.[2] Apart from this, there were the office expenses for rent, telephone, office quipment and correspondence.

The crisis involved all the methods hitherto used to finance the party. The first problem was a decline in the payment of members' subscriptions. On 29 November, the *Gau* treasurer reported to the Reich treasurer that only about 50 per cent of the branches had paid their contributions for October, despite the fact that the November contributions were now due.[3] Apart from disillusionment, unemployment among the membership was also responsible. On 12 December, for example, the Nienburg branch wrote begging for its arrears to be waived on the grounds that 104 out of 240 members were unemployed.[4] Another factor was that the proliferation of departments during 1931 and 1932, nearly all of which imposed their own dues, put increased pressure on members who may well have preferred to pay the dues to their own interest department rather than to the political organization. The second problem was that falling attendances at party meetings meant that they no longer showed a profit, a serious matter when the branches were forced not only to pay for the hiring of the hall and advertising, but also the speakers' fee.[5] Finally, and most important of all, it was becoming more and more difficult to use the party's traditional method of overcoming debts, namely collecting donations from sympathizers.[6] There were a number of reasons for

[1] The sums owing to the Gau ranged from RM 700 from *Kreis* Ilfeld to over RM 13,000 from Brunswick-City. The treasury was forced to waive a large proportion of these debts, see NSAH Hann. Des. 310 I A, Nr. 51.

[2] There are no details on the number who were in full employment but seven members of the *Gauleitung* were insured with the Barmer Ersatzkasse in 1931 by the party and Wittenberg, the party treasurer, received RM 250 per month, see NSAH Hann. Des. 310 I A, Nr. 112.

[3] NSAH Hann. Des. 310 I A, Nr. 38. Compared with 90 per cent in the first months of the year.

[4] NSAH Hann. Des. 310 I E, Nr. 18.

[5] Kassenbericht Kreisleitung Hannover-Stadt, 7 Oct. 1932, NSAH Hann. Des. 310 I A, Nr. 50.

[6] This occurred through the sympathizers' organizations (Opferringe), through the sale of special stamps—so-called 'bricks' (*Bausteine*), and through the collection of agricultural produce. It is difficult to estimate the contribution of these collections to the party, both to the *Gauleitung* and to the individual branches, but it was clearly very large indeed. See for example the emphasis on the importance of rich benefactors in the history of the small branch of Grasdorf near Hanover—NSAH Hann. Des. 310 I A, Nr. 67.

this. In the first place, in agricultural areas other organizations were also collecting for the Winter Emergency Programme (*Winter-hilfe*); secondly, the party had collected too ruthlessly in the past and was getting a bad name as a 'beggars club',[1] and finally, and most important, was the problem that, as the *Kreisleiter* of Hildesheim reported, 'contributions have become very scarce since our clean break with the DNVP'.[2] In desperation, therefore, and in order to finance the November *Reichstag* election, the party started street collections in tin boxes.[3]

The financial crisis aggravated tension between the political organization and the SA. The SA men were unwilling to pay their membership dues,[4] and antagonized the political section with their unauthorized collections. The SA had been particularly disgruntled by the failure to take over power after the July election. By September, the situation had become sufficiently disturbing for the SA headquarters to ask for reports from all *Gruppen* and *Untergruppen*. The reports from the Lower Saxony SA varied in their estimates of the situation.[5] The majority tended to play down the seriousness of the position and reported that, with a few exceptions, they had a good relationship with the political section. But all were forced to admit that the number of members joining the SA had fallen off substantially, while quite a proportion had left, though this was explained as a result of a weeding out of the poor elements among those who had joined during the mass influx at the beginning of the year. One *Untergruppe*, however—Brunswick—failed to agree with the fairly cheerful picture painted by the other groups. 'It cannot be denied', they reported,

that because of the continual postponement of the political decision a clearly discernible discontent has arisen among the troops and, in view of the completely opaque situation which once again exists, it is more likely to increase than to diminish. Despite all the extra activities which have been laid on, such as shooting, camping etc., the troop is slowly but surely becoming apathetic. The most active elements (the best) came to the movement and joined the SA to bring about a decision. This motive has inspired them for years, and now there is the prospect that even after in some cases 5 or 6 years of marching they may not break through. . . . The carrying of unemployed men, which we have managed up till now with some effort, is becoming so difficult in view of the economic situation, that it is difficult to provide for even the most necessary

[1] Kreisleitung Sulingen to Gaukasse, 3 Oct. 1932, NSAH Hann. Des. 310 I A, Nr. 53.

[2] Kreisleitung Hildesheim-Land to Gaukasse, 14 Nov. 1932, ibid.

[3] In one such collection in Hanover they got RM 2,100. See Gaukasse to Reichsleitung, 24 Oct. 1932, NSAH Hann. Des. 310 I A, Nr. 36.

[4] See Gauschatzmeister H-S-B to the Reichsschatzmeister, 22 Sept. 1932, in NSAH Hann. Des. 310 I A, Nr. 38.

[5] National Archives T-81, Reels 91–2, Frame Nos. 105074–218.

expenses. . . . As a last straw, there is so much paper work that it is impossible to expect SA leaders to cope with it. In my opinion, in view of all this, unless a decisive change occurs with the coming election, a considerable upheaval may be expected, particularly since a difficult winter period lies ahead.[1]

Furthermore, the report complained of the 'arrogant behaviour of even the lowest political functionaries', which occurred from time to time, and reported that

the tutelage of the SA by the political section and the lack of understanding for the financial requirements of the subordinate groups have always produced a certain tension between the political sections and the SA. The nomination of the last *Reichstag* candidates helped to emphasize these differences. The mood was not rosy, but has got a good deal worse since the introduction of uniforms for the political functionaries. . . . Furthermore, there is the fact that these sometimes quite young comrades think they can act as the superiors of the SA.

How true this picture was of the relations between the SA and the political section in other parts of Lower Saxony is difficult to say. But certainly during October relations deteriorated. Hitler had attempted to pacify the SA first, by reducing their membership dues which was paid for by increasing those of members in full employment;[2] and secondly, by laying down that 50 per cent of the *Reichstag* candidates, lists should be made up of SA and SS men.[3] But these measures appear to have had little effect. For, on 24 October, the *Gauleiter* of Hanover-South–Brunswick was forced to write to the *Gau* SA leader complaining that

not only is the propaganda work of the SA not functioning in several parts of the *Gau*, but in some cases it has not even begun, and a number of SA leaders have refused to take part in any propaganda and are opposing the activities of the political section.[4]

During September, the political section had been completely reorganized.[5] In the first place, the Reich organization Departments I

[1] SA Untergruppe Braunschweig an die OSAF, 22 Sept. 1932, National Archives T-81, Reel 91, Frames 105171–2.
[2] Gau S-H-B Kassenabteilung Rundschreiben, 12 Sept. 1932, NSAH Hann. Des. 310 I E, Nr. 29. But this measure antagonized a number of branch leaders; see Kreisleitung Sulingen to Gaukasse, 3 Oct. 1932, NSAH Hann. Des. 310 I A, Nr. 53.
[3] Muhs to Ahrens, 22 Oct. 1932, NSAH Hann. Des. 310 I A, Nr. 116.
[4] Muhs to Korsemann, 24 Oct. 1932, NSAH Hann. Des. 310 I A, Nr. 120.
[5] This reorganization had originally been announced in the Verordnungsblatt der Reichsleitung Folge 25, 2 Jahrgang, 17 June 1932, NSAH Hann. Des. 310 I B, Nr. 44 but was not actually carried out until Sept. Originally, Section III had been planned to include all special departments except economics and agriculture, but on 17 Sept. Strasser turned it into a research department and made various sections within it independent. See Anordnung Nr. 7 des Reichsorganisationsleiters, NSAH Hann. Des. 310 I A, Nr. 37.

and II were replaced by a single department with a number of sections: the Reich Inspectorates I and II, each of which controlled approximately half the *Gaue*; Section III, a research section planning policy in the domestic field for the future Nazi government; Section IV, economics; Section V, agriculture, etc. Secondly, a new regional organization of *Landesinspektionen* was created between the Reich head-quarters and the *Gauleitungen*. A *Landesinspektion* was established for Lower Saxony containing the *Gaue* Westphalia-North, Westphalia-South, Weser-Ems, Hanover-East and Hanover-South–Brunswick and Rust was appointed to head it.[1] He was replaced as *Gauleiter* of Hanover-South–Brunswick by Dr. Muhs, the Göttingen leader.[2] Thirdly, the subordinate organization was subdivided into units of uniform size: local branches were in future to contain between fifty and 500 members and these were subdivided into cells of ten–fifty members, and finally into blocks of up to ten members.[3] As an example of what the new organization looked like, the city of Hanover which had previously been divided into a few large branches with subsections, now consisted of thirty-three branches.[4] The *Lutherkirche* branch, for example, covered twenty-two streets and was subdivided into three cells, containing in all seventeen blocks. Each cell was under its own cell leader, but the block leaders were each responsible for two or three blocks.

(ii) *The Reichstag election of 6 November 1932*

The aims of the reorganization were described by Strasser as—uniformity throughout the Reich, simplicity, strength, flexibility and easier control.[5] But, as far as the November election was concerned, it is probable that the upheaval created by the reorganization outweighed these benefits. After four elections already in one year the organization was in any case very tired and 'very tense'.[6] In this situation, Goebbels believed that 'if we want to keep the party together we must appeal again to the most primitive mass instincts'.[7] He

[1] Verordnungsblatt Folge 30, 2 Jahrgang, 31 Aug. 1932, in NSAH Hann. Des. 310 I A, Nr. 37.

[2] Dr. Hermann Muhs. Born 1894. Became a lawyer 1927. Joined the party winter 1929. Joined the SS 1931. In the Third *Reich* became Regierungspräsident in Hildesheim. Typical of the young *Akademiker* who saw in the NSDAP the main chance. See personal files in BDC.

[3] Originally branches were to have a minimum membership of 300, but this was subsequently altered, see Kreisleitung Blankenburg Rundschreiben Nr. 10, 2 Sept. 1932, NSAH Hann. Des. 310 I A, Nr. 73.

[4] Neuorganisation in Gau Süd-Hannover–Braunschweig, 22 Sept. 1932, in NSAH Hann. Des. 310 I B, Nr. 24.

[5] See footnote 5, p. 237.

[6] J. Goebbels, *Vom Kaiserhof zur Reichskanzlei* (Munich, 1937), p. 181.

[7] J. Goebbels, ibid., p. 158.

ordered a 'ruthless' campaign against the Papen government 'which must only be limited by the laws and not by any tactical considerations'.[1] And on 7 September he told his Berlin functionaries that the slogan was 'Against the Barons'.[2]

This extreme propaganda policy, however, played straight into the hands of Papen and the DNVP who at once accused the NSDAP of preaching class warfare.[3] Because of this, Hess, presumably acting for Hitler, was forced to intervene in the propaganda campaign to prevent attacks on the aristocratic composition of the Papen cabinet, on the grounds that they would alienate the voters coming from the Right, while those on whom they made an impression would support the party which preached class warfare most uncompromisingly, namely the KPD.[4] Hess pointed out that

in this election we are faced with a government which has succeeded in giving the impression to a number of voters and undoubtedly to a number of those who have hitherto voted for us that it is carrying out, and in some cases has already carried out, the things which the National Socialists aimed for but which they themselves are not in a position to carry out.

Although the campaign continued to attack the reactionary nature of the Papen government—'Against reaction, the power to Hitler' was the first official party slogan[5]—the tone became slightly more moderate after this memorandum. Indeed, on 24 September, the Reich propaganda head-quarters was forced to tone down some of its pamphlets. For example, in the phrase 'His aristocratic clique wishes to ... the people', the word 'aristocratic' was struck out, and in the sentence 'He is trying to set up an unconstitutional dictatorship with the Black-White-and-Red property-owning bourgeoisie and money-bags people' (*Geldsacktum*) the words 'Black-White-and-Red' were removed.[6] Furthermore, even while supporting strikes, the party was warned not to treat all employers as alike, but 'only to attack the anti-social employers'.[7]

[1] Reichspropagandaleitung Rundschreiben, 12 Sept. 1932, NSAH Hann. Des. 310 I B, Nr. 15.
[2] J. Goebbels, *Vom Kaiserhof*, p. 158.
[3] E.g. in a broadcast speech by Papen on 12 Sept. National Archives T-81, Reel 1, Frame 11424.
[4] Hess, 'Bemerkungen zur Propaganda für den Reichstagswahlkampf' (undated), ibid., Fr. 11427–32.
[5] Anlage zum 2. Wahlrundschreiben der Gaupropagandaleitung H-S-B, NSAH Hann. Des. 310 I E, Nr. 3.
[6] Reichspropagandaleitung an alle Gauleitungen und Gaupropagandaleitungen, 24 Sept. 1932, NSAH Hann. Des. 310 I B, Nr. 15. They tried to explain the changes as due to mistakes over the telephone.
[7] Reichspropagandaleitung Rundschreiben, 20 Sept. 1932, NSAH Hann. Des. 310 I A, Nr. 37.

Nevertheless, despite the slight toning down of the propaganda, Papen, his government, and his bourgeois supporters were made the main object of the party's attacks, almost to the exclusion of other groups. In reply to a complaint from the branch leader of Stadtoldendorf that there was very little propaganda against Marxism in Brunswick, the *Gauleiter* replied that they had not changed their attitude to Marxism, but that

at this time, it is tactically clever, and therefore necessary, that we should not attack the personality of the Marxist opponent, particularly if he is a worker, but only Marxism in general. For, at this time, an emphasis on the common interest in the struggle against the reactionary opponent will make it easier to win over the Marxist to National Socialism.[1]

The main point in the propaganda aimed at SPD supporters was summed up in the slogan—'Without the SPD no Hindenburg, without Hindenburg no Papen cabinet.'[2] The KPD was attacked through a campaign to enlighten the workers on the real conditions existing in Soviet Russia.[3] As for the other main opponent—the Centre—the *Gau* authorities in Hanover-South–Brunswick advised their speakers that 'this time we do not expect such a sharp struggle against us as before. We are no longer treated as enemies of the Church, which previously influenced good Catholics against us.'[4] The party was still toying with the idea of a coalition with the Centre.

Apart from criticism of its reactionary nature, the Papen government was attacked for the failure of its policies: its isolation in foreign affairs through its reliance on France and the trade war with Italy; the defeat of its Prussian policy through the decision of the Reich Court that the former Prussian government was still the legal authority; and, above all, the alleged failure of its economic policies and the increase in unemployment.[5] An anti-Semitic twist was given to this criticism by the accusation that Papen had prepared his economic programme in consultation with the Jewish banker, Jakob Goldschmidt. The NSDAP wished to convince the bourgeoisie that the Papen government was *not* an alternative to Hitler. They tried to twist round the DNVP accusations of their encouraging class war, by pointing out that the reactionary policies of Papen were leading to an increase in Communist support, and therefore, to the danger of civil war. The

[1] Gauleiter to Dr. Bahrs, 20 Sept. 1932, NSAH Hann. Des. 310 I A, Nr. 94.
[2] Gaupropagandaleitung S-H-B, 10 Oct. 1932, Kurzbericht über die Rednertrgung in Hannover am 2 Oct. 1932; NSAH Hann. Des. 310 I E, Nr. 23.
[3] A 'League of Soviet Opponents' had been formed in *Gau* Essen a few months earlier by Germans who had worked in Russia and come back disillusioned. See Denkschrift zur Reichstagswahl am 6 Nov. 1932, ibid.
[4] See footnote 2.
[5] See footnote 3. Denkschrift.

only alternatives now facing the German people were the 'swastika and the Soviet star'.

The techniques used in this campaign were determined to a great extent by the resources at the disposal of the party. As we have seen, the party was hindered by a serious financial crisis, which Goebbels described as 'perhaps the most difficult question which we have had to solve during these weeks'.[1] As a result of the lack of money, the main emphasis was on personal canvassing, agitators in the streets and *Sprechchöre*. Propaganda with symbols was strongly emphasized, but not through massive demonstrations, for which there was no money and for which the weather was no longer suitable. Instead flags and badges were used. All party members were ordered to hang out a flag and to wear a badge.[2]

(ii) *The Strasser affair*

On 5 November, the eve of the election day, Goebbels wrote in his diary: 'We are all glad that this election is over.'[3] But the result—a loss of 5·7 per cent of the vote in Lower Saxony (compared with an average loss in the Reich as a whole of 4·1 per cent)—brought no comfort to the party and no solution to its problems.[4] Indeed the fall in the vote had removed from the party that 'aura of invincibility' in the eyes of both the electorate and the membership which was so crucial to its success.[5] Goebbels, for one, realized 'The party must always be kept on the move. If one lets such a large fighting organization come to a stop, the strongest men become weak. The wildest fanatics then become petty mischief-makers.'[6] The difficulty was to know in what direction the party should move; for what end was it possible to fight given the fact that revolution had been excluded and parliamentary methods had failed? This impasse created the most serious crisis within the NSDAP since its refounding in 1925. Divisions emerged within the leadership over the correct tactics to be followed. The tactic advocated by Hitler was to move 'sharply against the KPD, otherwise splendid isolation'.[7] He hoped to win back the sympathy of the *haute*

[1] Goebbels, *Vom Kaiserhof*, p. 167. 20 Sept. 1932.
[2] Denkschrift zur Reichstagswahl am 6 Nov. 1932, NSAH Hann. Des. 310 I E, Nr. 23.
[3] Goebbels, op. cit., p. 196.
[4] Franz, *Die Politischen Wahlen in Niedersachsen 1867 bis 1949*, p. 65.
[5] Before the election the Gauleiter of H-S-B had urged his *Kreisleiter* to work for success so that the party would be 'surrounded by the aura of invincibility'; see Gauleiter an alle Kreisleiter, 29 Oct. 1932, NSAH Hann. Des. 310 I E, Nr. 23.
[6] Goebbels, op. cit., p. 202. 14 Nov. 1932.
[7] This was Goebbels' directive to the party press on 15 Nov., see ibid., p. 203. It was also the line adopted by Hitler until the negotiations with Papen.

bourgeoisie, and that the collapse of the Papen and the Schleicher governments would force the authorities to realize that no other nationalist group possessed sufficient mass support. Gregor Strasser, however, was of another opinion. At a meeting of *Landesinspektoren* which he held on 8 December, he announced his resignation because of disagreement with Hitler on the proper course for the party to follow.[1] He believed that there was no sign of Hitler being made Chancellor for a long time to come and that, as a result of his refusal to compromise, 'the movement is faced with serious stresses which will shake its determination and possibly even result in splits and collapse'. According to Lohse, the *Gauleiter* of Schleswig-Holstein, however, Strasser made no attempt to win over his audience to join him in resignation, but rather urged them 'not to draw any conclusions about your own position from my actions, but rather to continue to do your work and perform your duty'. The *Landesinspektoren* reacted sentimentally, urging Strasser at least to talk the matter over with Hitler. Rust then arranged a meeting of the *Landesinspektoren* with Hitler. They went with considerable reservations about the *Führer*'s policy, but Hitler gave one of his masterly monologues, and, through a combination of emotional appeal and rational analysis of the situation, succeeded in winning them over completely.

The Strasser affair poses two questions for any study of the NSDAP's local organization: first, how far was Strasser correct in his belief that the party was in danger of breaking up because of its continued failure to come to power? Secondly, what were the effects of his resignation on the party.

There is no doubt that the unsuccessful outcome of the November election aggravated the crisis within the NSDAP in Lower Saxony. Thus the Police President in Hanover reported that

the unfavourable outcome of the November election for the NSDAP has increased the signs of division and led to the founding of new political organizations out of the splinter groups. Thus on 19 and 20 November the German Socialist Workers Party was founded in Hanover which wishes to fight corruption within the National Socialist movement, but otherwise to uphold the old aims of the NSDAP.[2]

Also a purely paramilitary organization—*Kampfbund Oberland*—was founded by disillusioned SA men to support the aims of Ludendorff. The police in Harburg also reported an aggravation in the crisis which originated from

[1] For the following see 'Der Fall Strasser' by Heinrich Lohse. Typewritten, in the Forschungstelle für die Geschichte des Nationalsozialismus in Hamburg.
[2] Der Polizeipräsident Hannover to Regierungs präsident Hannover, 14 Dec. 1932, NSAH Hann. Des. 80 Hann II, Nr. 723.

a strong mistrust and jealousy of one another by the leaders of all ranks and all organizations down to the most unimportant functionaries. . . . This results in the individual formations cutting themselves off from one another and in many places going their own way with their leaders. Discipline suffers and individuals give orders and carry out measures independently.[1]

The party documents for *Gau* Hanover-South–Brunswick also show a considerable amount of discontent. Most important, were the continuing disagreements between the political section and the SA and SS.[2] In an attempt to overcome these, the *Gauleiter* and the *Gau* SA and SS leaders signed an agreement on 1 December defining once more the relationship between their organizations.[3] There was little new in the document except a requirement for the political leader to define in *writing* the exact tasks he was giving to the SA and SS and a ban on 'self-help or aggressive disputes' if there were disagreement.

Secondly, the financial situation remained abysmal. On 5 December, for example, the town of Hameln branch wrote desperately to the *Gau* treasury for help because its creditors were becoming so pressing.[4] And, at the beginning of the month, the Reich treasurer ordered all subordinate organizations to reach agreements with their creditors on the payment of debts in order to avoid foreclosures.[5] In desperation, the *Gau* opened a lottery with 100,000 tickets at 50 pf, of which each member was obliged to take two.[6]

Finally, there was a considerable amount of discontent among artisans and shopkeepers within the party about the advertisement policy of the party's press, which ignored the NSDAP programme by taking advertisements from chain stores.[7] They also objected to the monopolistic position of the SA Quartermaster organization in the supply of uniforms and equipment.[8] The party tried to counter this discontent and to win new support by planning a large exhibition of *German* goods to be held in Hanover at the end of January.[9]

---

[1] Der Polizeipräsident Harburg to Regierungspräsident Stade, 16 Dec. 1932, NSAS Rep. 80p 798.

[2] For examples see NSAH Hann. Des. 310 I A, Nr. 120.

[3] An die Hoheitsträger der PO. An die SA und SS-Führer, 1 Dec. 1932, ibid.

[4] Kreisleitung Hameln-Stadt to Kasse, 5 Dec. 1932, NSAH Hann. Des. 310 I A, Nr. 52.

[5] Reichsschatzmeister, Leiter der Rechtsabteilung & Geschäftsführer Anordnung, 2 Dec. 1932, NSAH Hann. Des. 310 I A, Nr. 37.

[6] Abteilung Kasse Rundschreiben, 26 Nov. 1932, NSAH Hann. Des. 310 I E, Nr. 22.

[7] Muhs an die Reichsleitung Hauptabteilung IV, Dec. 1932, NSAH Hann. Des. 310 I A, Nr. 35.

[8] Muhs to Zeugmeisterei-Nord, 14 Dec. 1932, NSAH Hann. Des. 310 I A, Nr. 120.

[9] Gau Abteilung IV Rundschreiben, 11 Nov. 1932, NSAH Hann. Des. 310 I E, Nr. 3.

The resignation of Strasser undoubtedly increased the crisis of confidence within the party. Party functionaries were particularly resent-
ful of the fact that they first heard the news through the hostile press.[1]
The Lippe election success helped to some extent to restore confidence,
but on 21 January 1933 the *Gauleiter* of Hanover-South–Brunswick
still felt it necessary to tour the *Gau*, holding meetings of all the party
functionaries and party members, in order to enlighten them about
'the political situation and developments within the party'.[2] Yet,
despite serious disquiet, there was no question of a revolt in favour of
Strasser. The party's activity continued.[3] Why was this?

In the first place, Strasser not only made no attempt to take the lead
in such a revolt, but even emphasized the personal nature of his decision. He gave as one of his reasons Hitler's growing coolness towards
him and the intrigues of other party leaders against him.[4] It appeared
as if that peculiar relationship with Hitler compounded of a sense of
both loyalty and inferiority which had paralysed the 1925–6 North-
West German *Arbeitsgemeinschaft* continued to prevent Strasser from
making a real challenge.

Secondly, once Hitler had won over the *Gauleiter*, he had complete
control over the party's power structure.[5] The subordinate functionaries, even if they had been prepared for rebellion, had no means of co-
ordinating their actions, for the whole organization operated through
the head-quarters of the *Gaue*. In any case, the district and branch
leaders were completely unprepared for what happened as is indicated
by the fact that many first learned about it from their opponents. Their
reaction as expressed in their requests to the *Gau* head-quarters for information was a mixture of bewilderment and anger at what they regarded as a betrayal of the party and treason against the Führer.

Thus although the evidence shows that a considerable amount of
discontent and rivalry existed, it did not yet add up to a serious threat
to the party's unity. Too many people had too much invested in the
party in terms of hopes and energy, and received too much from the
party in terms of position, prestige, and even in some cases money,
readily to risk the wilderness of opposition, particularly at such an in-

[1] E.g. Kreisleitung Hildesheim Stadt to Gaugeschäftsführer, 15 Dec. 1932,
NSAH Hann. Des. 310 I A, Nr. 50.

[2] Der Gauleiter Rundschreiben, 21 Jan. 1933, NSAH Hann. Des. 310 I E, Nr.
29. For a report on one of these meetings in which the Gauleiter spoke of 'examples
of an infinite disloyalty' see *NTZ*, 31 Jan. 1933.

[3] The activity report of Gau H-S-B for Dec. reported forty-six film and nine
theatre evenings, 426 members' meetings and 400–500 Christmas celebrations, see
NSAH Hann. Des. 310 I B, Nr. 13.

[4] Lohse Denkschrift, 'Der Fall Strasser', in FGN, pp. 21–2.

[5] Hitler immediately reorganized Strasser's organization department taking it
over himself with Ley as his deputy. See ibid., pp. 30–1.

hospitable time. The example of those who had tried it in the past was not encouraging. The opposition groups, including Otto Strasser's Revolutionary National Socialists, were insignificant and powerless. But continuing in the party meant continuing with Hitler as leader. The deification of Hitler which had developed since 1925, and which was partly a result of his conscious policy and partly a result of the membership's need for such a leader, had linked the party indissolubly with his charisma. The *Landesinspektoren* who, after their meeting with Hitler, 'once more sealed the old alliance with a handshake',[1] were not alone in sensing that the NSDAP had already entered a *Schicksalsgemeinschaft* with its leader. The appointment of Hitler as Chancellor less than two months later appeared to justify their confidence in the Führer.

[1] Ibid.

CONCLUSION

THIS account of the development of the NSDAP from 1925–33 has tried to show that the NSDAP made its break-through in Lower Saxony in the period between 1928–30 by integrating the *Mittelstand*. Its concentration on winning over the workers before 1928 had been in vain and had led the party into an impasse. It was only after 1930 that members and voters were won from the working class in any numbers and even then these remained proportionately few and probably largely confined to the younger generation. This was despite the fact that after 1930 the party concentrated its propaganda more and more on winning the workers from 'Marxism'.

There are at least two important questions concerning this development which the second part of this book has attempted to answer: first, why had it become possible by the end of the 1920s for a movement to perform this function of political integration for the *Mittelstand* when this had hitherto proved impossible? And secondly, in what ways did the propaganda and the organization of the NSDAP contribute to this successful process of integration which eventually embraced industrial workers? In short, how was it possible for the NSDAP to become a quasi-*Volkspartei*, a political phenomenon of which the Centre Party, with Catholicism as its bond, was the only previous example in German history?[1]

Lower Saxony, a predominantly rural area whose economic structure was dominated by small and medium-sized concerns, had a large *Mittelstand* population. Since the middle of the previous century, the social groups which composed the *Mittelstand* in Lower Saxony had been divided in their political allegiance among several different parties: before 1918, between Free Conservatives, the Guelphs, the National Liberals, the Progressives, and the *Bund der Landwirte*; after 1918, between the DNVP, DVP, DDP and Guelphs. These different parties to some extent reflected different interests—for example, the Progressives and their heirs, the DDP, championed Free Trade in the cause of the small farmer in Oldenburg, who needed cheap imported barley, and against the Prussian Conservatives, who desired protection for their corn, and against their allies the National Liberals. They also reflected different *Weltanschauungen* formed by regional traditions, social and economic position, and historical experiences. The DHP, for example, was formed round and inspired by the experi-

[1] Bracher refers to this characteristic of the NSDAP in *Die Auflösung der Weimarer Republik*, pp. 98–9.

ence of resentment felt by the Hanoverian aristocracy and the rural *Mittelstand* in parts of the Province of Hanover at the conquest of the Kingdom of Hanover by Prussia in 1866.

After 1918, these different representations of *Mittelstand* interests remained. But the important fact was that the interests and experiences which had previously sustained them were becoming less and less relevant in the new situation created by the economic developments following from the war, the revolution and the post-war period. The policy of Free Trade which had been championed by the Progressives and was taken up by the DDP had the reverse effect of that intended when it resulted in imports of cheap pigs from Poland and dairy products from Denmark and Holland flooding the German market.

Because the DVP was clearly dominated by industrialists it no longer satisfied the rural backbone of National Liberal support in Lower Saxony. The industrialists were prepared to sacrifice the interests of agriculture in their desire for guaranteed export markets through trade agreements with neighbouring agricultural countries. More important than these economic aspects, however, was the fact that both the Liberal parties were indissolubly linked with the Republic and its fortunes. The failure of the Republic to establish its legitimacy in the minds of the *Mittelstand* meant that these parties too failed to retain their support. Liberalism, from being the creed through which the *Mittelstand* in Lower Saxony asserted, if rather feebly, its independence from reactionary Prussian Junkers, and its pride in belonging to a new nation state, now became identified in their minds with a bankrupt political system and a bankrupt economic and social order. The monarchist basis of the Guelph cause also looked increasingly less viable in Republican Germany—even the policy of a state of Hanover independent of Prussia was no longer realistic after its defeat in the 1924 referendum—while, as a representative of *Mittelstand* interests, the party provided no political *strength* at Reich level with which to compete against the massive and well-organized industrial and consumer interests. Finally, no party adequately represented the interests and the combination of nationalist and 'socialist' attitudes of the new class of white-collar workers which had multiplied during the 1920s and which had hitherto only found expression through the DHV.

During the 1920s, this growing discontent with their political representatives had caused different groups within the *Mittelstand* to form their own interest parties. In 1924, the Economic Party was established to represent the interests of artisans and small shopkeepers; in 1928, the *Landvolk* party was founded as a party specifically for the peasantry of Central and North-West Germany.[1] The weakness of

---

[1] Its full name was 'Christlich-nationale Bauern und Landvolk Partei' not to be confused with the *Landvolk* movement from Schleswig-Holstein.

CONCLUSION

these organizations derived first, from the fact that they were simply
economic pressure groups of limited political influence; and second,
that they represented the interests of only one group in what was increasingly felt to be a fundamental political, economic and social crisis
affecting the *Mittelstand* as a whole. It was a crisis involving a sense of
declining status, of acute economic pressure, and of alienation from the
political system in particular and, on the part of the 'old' *Mittelstand*,
from modern social and cultural developments in general.

The sense of disorientation created by this crisis, which found expression in the protest movement of 1928, provided a political vacuum
into which the NSDAP could move. Through its propaganda, it appealed to the ideals and interests of the *Mittelstand* groups. It was not
burdened by the limitations created by historical experiences and commitments; it offered an ideology which reaffirmed the traditional
status, symbols and values of the 'old' *Mittelstand*; it provided the
'new' *Mittelstand* with an ideology which was nationalist without
being reactionary and socialist without being Marxist; through its exploitation of the reparations issue and the evils of 'international finance
capitalism' it provided an easily comprehensible explanation for the
economic crisis, while its programme of autarky provided an apparently
simple solution. Finally, its propaganda hammered away at the weakness of any political representation, such as the Economic Party, which
was limited to one specific group. Through its organization the
NSDAP provided a solution to this weakness of the interest parties, by
creating an integrative framework in which all social and economic
groups could find individual representation and expression in their own
department or *Fachgruppe*. The problem of conflicting interests,
which had bedevilled other parties, was avoided by its tight discipline,
by its refusal to participate in a Reich government of which Hitler was
not the head, and by its vague vision of the Third Reich in which all
were encouraged to expect the fulfilment of their demands. In the
meantime these demands could simply be fed into the propaganda
machine where they were processed into effective slogans; meanwhile
the various professional organizations were infiltrated and taken over,
thereby facilitating the process of *Gleichschaltung* after 1933.

Above all, however, the NSDAP offered an all-embracing *Weltanschauung* with which to fill the vacuum left by a discredited liberalism.
Nazi propaganda successfully portrayed liberalism as the ideology of
selfish individuals and selfish parties which, by undermining the unity
of the nation, had already helped destroy the Second Empire and was
now responsible for the present crisis. In the place of liberalism and the
'divisive' party system, the Nazis promised to substitute the *Volksgemeinschaft* in which the common weal would take precedence over
individual gain, and in which the class barriers of the old society would

248

CONCLUSION

be overcome. In a situation in which capitalism had clearly broken down and in which the individualism which was the basis of liberalism had been simplified to the point of catch-as-catch-can, a creed which condemned such a system as selfish and emphasized the importance of community values had a great attraction, particularly to a society which had never really absorbed the liberal ethos, but remained attached to archaic *Gemeinschaft* values.

There was, however, a second aspect to this process of integration. Although in its propaganda, the NSDAP portrayed itself as the party best able to overcome the divisions within German society, one of its most effective techniques for integrating the *Mittelstand* was to emphasize and exploit the division in Germany between the politically organized working class and the bourgeoisie. This was particularly effective in local government. The problem originated, of course, in the Bismarckian era or even earlier. By excluding the working class from effective political influence and by appropriating the idea of patriotism for an extreme form of nationalism, the authorities and the great majority of the middle class in the second Reich had themselves helped to ensure that the German working class would be '*Vaterlandslose Gesellen*', bitterly opposed to the ideology and symbols of that society and forced to establish what was virtually a separate SPD community. This division was then exacerbated by the revolution of 1918. Significantly, immediately after 1918, the bourgeoisie was successful in uniting for a political purpose by creating *Bürgerblöcke* in local government with which to resist the SPD.[1] In a similar way, the Nazis exploited the fear and resentment of the Left which increased in intensity as the economic crisis deepened and social conflict sharpened. They created a sense of obligation in the minds of the bourgeoisie by continual emphasis on the sacrifice which young SA men were making on their behalf in the front line.[2] After 1929 the NSDAP succeeded in convincing the middle class of its indispensability and in creating what was virtually another *Bürgerblöck*.

Yet, there was an important difference between the *Bürgerblöck* created by the NSDAP and those formed after the revolution. The latter were clearly counter-revolutionary. The NSDAP, however, although the reactionary aspects of its ideology and its opposition to the political results of the revolution conveniently disguised the fact, was a revolutionary movement. It was revolutionary in two senses: in the first place, the cadres which it created contained 'new' men from the lower middle class who wished to overthrow the *status quo*. In the

[1] For example in Brunswick see Roloff, *Bürgertum und Nationalsozialismus 1930-1933*, pp. 42-3. The DDP however remained outside.
[2] The party always made great propaganda out of the funeral services and deaths of its 'martyrs'.

second place, its organization and *Weltanschauung* were totalitarian, and would not only transform the political structure, but would also disrupt the traditional patterns of German social life.[1]

One key to this revolutionary aspect of the party was the way the NSDAP was able to exploit the deep rift which existed between the generations in the Weimar period.[2] During its first years, the party succeeded in creating a political style which could appeal to the younger generation, its desire for charismatic leadership, personal commitment, and a sense of *Gemeinschaft* through a quasi-military organization; its contempt for the institutions and processes of the Weimar political system; its desire to escape from social convention—*Spiessertum*—and the rigidities of the class structure. Above all, the organization of the NSDAP provided an effective instrument for exploiting the energies of this group while retaining control in the hands of the leadership. Young activists could make it to a considerable extent *their* party as opposed to the other parties which, with the significant exception of the KPD, were staffed with ageing functionaries who treated politics in purely 'rational' terms and who viewed experiments with undisguised suspicion.[3] Promotion was rapid for those who proved effective; communications between the local leadership and *Gau* head-quarters were good—a stream of directives from the *Reichsleitung* were passed on by the *Gauleitung* to local leaders, keeping them informed of party tactics and propaganda techniques; and, above all, every member was provided with an active role in the party's work.

The organization in some ways was tightly disciplined. Through its use of the *Führerprinzip* and bureaucratic rules such as speakers' passes and signed declarations of loyalty by their deputies, the party leadership kept a close control over all important aspects of party activity—the content of propaganda, appointments, relations with outside groups and individuals. Yet the party's discipline was subject to permanent strain. The lines of jurisdiction within the party often overlapped, and conflict was continually breaking out between

---

[1] See Dahrendorf, *Gesellschaft und Demokratie in Deutschland* (Munich, 1965), pp. 432 ff.

[2] E.g. an article in the *Niedersächsische Beobachter* of 4 May 1929, maintained that 'the rebuilding of Germany is not the task of the generation whose best representatives were already by 1914 formed and completed personalities. All the acts and measures of these politicians and leaders become reactionary at the decisive moment. As the generation of the 30-year-olds, in other words, those who were formed by war, revolution, and the post-war period without ever being able to become torpid or to age seriously, enters politics, the contrast to the pre-war generation will become sharper.'

[3] S. Neumann, *Die deutschen Parteien. Wesen und Wandel nach dem Kriege* (Berlin, 1932), pp. 100 ff. Rohe describes the opposition of the SPD functionaries to the attempts to transform its propaganda style after 1930 in *Das Reichsbanner Schwarz-Rot-Gold*, p. 409.

CONCLUSION

individuals and sections of the party at different levels within the organization. This tension was the reverse side of the remarkable activism of the party. Conflict, however, tended to reinforce the position of Hitler. For, by 1927, he had established his absolute authority and, from then on, the charge of disloyalty to Hitler was an important weapon in the internecine rivalries which continued; no member or leader, therefore, dared question that authority. This authority could, in turn, be used to support the *Gauleiter* and other leaders in their struggles with rival groups and individuals. In short, recognition and promotion within the NSDAP depended first, on absolute loyalty to the *Führer*, and secondly, on performance, as measured by the degree of activism shown by the member or functionary. Members were, therefore, obliged to compete with one another both in loyalty and activism. This competition, which was encouraged by Hitlers's refusal to define clearer lines of jurisdiction between its organizations, helped to sustain the dynamic of the Party.

Through its authoritarian structure, then, of which the charismatic *Führerprinzip* was the core, the NSDAP maintained the discipline which, given the heterogeneous and radical nature of the membership, was essential to its effectiveness, particularly in the crisis months after July 1932. In the period of the Nazi electoral successes, however, it was the skill of the party in retaining and exploiting the radical commitment of its members and cadres for the purposes of propaganda which was decisive. For, the youth and commitment of the party's membership created that *élan* and sense of destiny—expressed, for example, through the sheer number of party meetings and in the SA marches—which proved such a magnetic attraction to a society which had lost its sense of direction. It was this impression of representing the future—the chiliastic vision—which the party was able to project, with Hitler as its prophet, which was perhaps, in the last analysis, crucial to the success of Nazism.[1] In this sense, the revolutionary style and organization of the NSDAP provided the final impetus to integration; and it is in this context that the pre-1927 period in the party's development, during which its style and structure had been formed, and the leadership of Hitler established, acquires its real significance.

[1] For a discussion of the chiliastic features of the Nazi movement, see Heuss, *Hitler's Weg*, pp. 166 ff. and N. Cohn, *The Pursuit of the Millennium* (London, 1962), pp. 307 ff.

BIBLIOGRAPHY

A note on sources

This book is based primarily on Nazi party correspondence, on political police and other government files, and on the local press—both Nazi and non-Nazi. A few of the Nazi files for Lower Saxony are in the West German Federal Archive (Bundesarchiv) in Koblenz, but the vast majority of these files are in the Gauarchiv of Hanover-South–Brunswick; of these, a large part survived the war and are now in the Hanover branch of the Lower Saxony State Archive (Niedersächsisches Staatsarchiv). The *Gau* archives of *Gau* Hanover-East and *Gau* Weser-Ems were destroyed during the war and only one or two files have survived. The party files contain correspondence between the *Gau* head-quarters and the Reich head-quarters in Munich, and between the *Gau* head-quarters and the district (*Kreis*) and local branch (*Ortsgruppe*) leaders. They contain both personal letters and organizational and propaganda directives in the form of circulars. Unfortunately, much of the material for the period 1927–33 is routine and it is particularly difficult to assess the relations between the *Gaue* and the Munich head-quarters. Lastly, the personal files of those Nazis who played a significant role in Lower Saxony were examined in the Berlin Document Centre.

Additional relevant material can be found in the files of the various government offices. The files of the *Oberpraesidium* in Hanover contain reports from the *Regierungspräsidenten* in the Province of Hanover and correspondence between the *Oberpräsident* and the Prussian Ministry of the Interior in Berlin. The files of the six *Regierungspräsidenten* (Aurich, Hanover, Hildesheim, Lüneburg, Osnabrück and Stade) contain correspondence between the *Regierungspräsidenten* and the *Landräte* and reports to the *Oberpräsident*. Above all, they contain the fortnightly political police reports for their particular areas. These reports record the activities of movements of the extreme Left and Right. Finally, the files of the state governments of Brunswick, Oldenburg and Schaumburg-Lippe contain correspondence with the Reich Ministry of the Interior in Berlin, fortnightly political police reports and other police reports. They also contain minutes of the *Landtag* debates.

The local press in Lower Saxony was very extensive. Even small towns had at least one and very often two papers and the cities even more. Faced with this predicament, the author concentrated firstly on reading those Nazi papers which have survived, and secondly on reading the papers of those areas which were of most significance for the growth of Nazism in Lower Saxony before 1933.

A valuable source for the period before 1925 is the autobiographical accounts by the two co-founders of the Hanover branch of the NSDAP, Wenzel and Seifert, and especially the account written by the first *Gauleiter* of Göttingen, Ludolf Haase, with the title 'Der Aufstand in Niedersachsen'. This account was mimeographed in 1942 and circulated to former comrades.

My attempts to interview the few leading National Socialists of the *Kampf-*

zeit in Lower Saxony, who are still alive, were unsuccessful. I am, however, grateful to the Herren Oberkreisdirektoren of Ammerland, Diepholz, Stade and Wittmund, and to Herr Landrat a.D. Reinhard Oncken, Wittmund, and Herr Bürgermeister a.D. Brüning, Diepholz for granting me interviews.

UNPUBLISHED SOURCES

(1) *Niedersächsisches Staatsarchiv*

  (a) Hannover

    Hann. Des. 310 I. NSDAP Gauarchiv Hannover-Süd–Braunschweig.

    Hann. Des. 122a. Oberpraesidium Hannover.

    Hann. Des. 80 Hann II. Regierungspraesidium Hannover.

    Hann. Des. 80 Hildesheim II. Regierungspraesidium Hildesheim.

    Hann. Des. 80 Lüneburg II and III. Regierungspraesidium Lüneberg.

  (b) Aurich

    Rep. 21a Regierungspraesidium Aurich.

    Rep. 31a Landratsamt Leer.

    Rep. 109 Staatsanwaltschaft Aurich.

    Depositum L I Kreisverein Aurich der Deutschnationalen Volkspartei.

  (c) Bückeburg

    Schaumburg Des. L 4 Landtagsverhandlungen.
                  Staatsministerium.

  (d) Oldenburg

    39 Landtagsverhandlungen.

    131 Ministerium für Kirchen und Schulen.

    136 Staatsministerium.

    205 Stadtarchiv Oldenburg.

  (e) Osnabrück

    Rep. 116 Regierungspraesidium Osnabrück.

    Erwerbungen Nr. 11 Landesverband Osnabrück der Deutschnationalen Volkspartei.

  (f) Stade

    Rep. 80p. Regierungspraesidium.

  (g) Wolfenbüttel

    12 A Neu Staatsministerium.

    133 A Neu Polizeipraesidium Braunschweig.

    126 Neu Kreisdirektion Braunschweig

    127 Neu Kreisdirektion Wolfenbüttel

BIBLIOGRAPHY

(2) *Stadtarchiv Braunschweig*

G X 9 Der Bürgerbund Braunschweig.
Akten 1919–33.
G X 6 Deutsche Volkspartei, Landesverband Braunschweig.
VIII Politische Plakatsammlung.

(2a) *Stadtarchiv Göttingen*

XXV 153 ⎫
XXVII 156 ⎭ Repatorium der Polizeidirektion.

(3) *Bundesarchiv, Koblenz*

Sammlung Schumacher. NSDAP Parteikorrespondenz 1925–33.
NS 1 Akten des Reichsschatzmeisters der NSDAP.
NS 22 Akten des Reichsorganisationsleiters der NSDAP.
R 72 Der Stahlhelm. Bund der Frontsoldaten. Der Salzgau.

(4) *Staatsarchiv Düsseldorf*

Reg.Düsseldorf. Regierungspraesidium Düsseldorf.

(5) *Berlin Document Center*

NSDAP personal files.

(6) *Forschungsstelle für die Geschichte des Nationalsozialismus in Hamburg*

Miscellaneous material, including a memorandum by Hinrich Lohse—'Der Fall Strasser' and the minutes of a conversation with Karl Kaufmann, *Gauleiter* of Hamburg.

MICROFILMED DOCUMENTS

Hoover Institution NSDAP Hauptarchiv Microfilm Collection

Reel 3	Folder 79 Partei und Verein von 1920–3.
	Folders 81–2 Aufrufe zu Versammlungen 1919–34. Berichte. Wahlkampf. Propaganda.
Reel 4	Folder 109 Parteitagungen 1920, 1921 der DSP.
Reel 6	Folder 141 Hannover-Süd–Braunschweig.
Reel 7	Folder 163 Weser-Ems.
Reel 15	Folders 278–83 NSBO.
	Folders 284–9 Reichspropagandaleitung.
Reel 16	Folder 297 SA Norddeutschland 1923.
	Folder 298 SA Oberkommando. Allgemeines 1923.
	Folders 302–7 SA Befehle 1926–32
Reel 17	Folder 316 SA Braunschweig.
	Folder 329 SS Allgemeines.

BIBLIOGRAPHY

Reel 18	Folder 333 Reichsführung der HJ 1924–27.
Reel 26	Folder 514 Persönliche Berichte und Erinnerungen.
	Folder 522 Einsendungen von Behoerden A-L.
Reel 27	Folder 525 Korrespondenz mit Behoerden betr. Sicherstellung von Akten HJ.
	Folders 528–31 Kampferlebnisse der alten Garde der NSDAP.
Reels 41/2	Folder 839 DSP.
Reel 43	Folder 877 Welfenpartei.
Reel 44	Folders 893–5 Volck–Fobke–Haase–Heinze–Hitler Correspondence.
	Folder 896 Strasser–Haase–Fobke–v. Pfeffer Denkschriften.
	Folders 897–905 Fobke.
Reel 46	Folders 951–3 Darré Rundschreiben.
Reel 47	Folder 984 Braunschweiger Tageszeitung.
	Folder 1017 Göttinger Nachrichten.
	Folder 1018 Göttinger Tageblatt.
Reel 48	Folder 1033 Hildesheimer Beobachter.
	Folder 1074 Niedersachsen-Stürmer.
	Folder 1075 Niedersächsischer Beobachter.
	Folder 1261 Bernhard Rust 1926–32.
Reel B	Folder 5 Personalakte Adolf Hitler Reg. Rat. Braunschweig Staatsministerium.
	90A Verbotszeit der Partei 1923–33 Files of Braunschweiger Staatsministerium.
	91 Neugruendung des NSDAV.
	Folders 1408–9 Regierung Erfurt betr. Dietrich Klagges.

National Archives Microfilm Collection
T-81
Reel 1 NSDAP 1932.
Reels 90–1 SA 1923 and 1932.
Reel 116 Völkisch movement 1924.
Reel 159 Völkisch movement 1924.
Reels 164, 175–6 NSDAP Kreisleitung Eutin (Oldenburg).
T-84
Reel 4 NSDAP 1923.

2. PUBLISHED SOURCES

(a) *The Press*
NSDAP: *Völkischer Beobachter* 1921–33.
Nationalsozialistische Briefe 1925–6.
Niedersächsischer Beobachter 1929–31 (only available from 1929–31).
Niedersachsen-Stürmer 1930–2 (incomplete).
Niedersächsische Tageszeitung 1931–3 (founded 1931).

BIBLIOGRAPHY

OTHERS: Brunswick
Braunschweigische Landeszeitung 1930–3.
Volksfreund 1930–3.
Oldenburg
Der Ammerländer 1927–30.
Nachrichten für Stadt und Land 1930–3.
Kr. Wittmund
Anzeiger für Harlingerland 1923–4.
Osnabrück
Der Stadtwächter 1929–31.
Göttingen
Göttinger Tageblatt 1919–21.
1929–30.

(b) *Documentary Material*

Das Programm der NSDAP und seine Weltanschauliche Grundgedanken, von Dipl. Ing. Gottfried Feder. (München 1932).
Der Nationalsozialismus: Dokumente 1933–1945, hrsg. von Walther Hofer (Frankfurt 1957).
ERNST DEUERLEIN, *Der Aufstieg der NSDAP 1919–1933 in Augenzeugenberichten* (Düsseldorf 1968).
Dokumente der Zeitgeschichte (Dokumente der Sammlung Rehse aus der Kampfzeit) hrsg. von Adolf Dresler und Fritz Maier (München 1941).
Die Zerstörung der deutschen Politik. Dokumente, 1871–1933, hrsg. von Harry Pross (Frankfurt 1959).
Ausgewählte Dokumente zur Geschichte des Nationalsozialismus. Herausgegeben von Dr. Hans-Adolf Jacobsen und Dr. Werner Jochmann (Bielefeld 1966).
JOHANN DORNER, *Bauernstand und Nationalsozialismus* (München 1930) (NS Bibliothek, Heft 15).
KARL FIEHLER, *Nationalsozialistische Gemeindepolitik* (München 1933).
W. JOCHMANN, *Nationalsozialismus und Revolution. Ursprung und Geschichte der NSDAP in Hamburg. Dokumente* (Frankfurt 1963).
Landesversammlung (Brunswick Landtag), *Verhandlungen, Niederschriften und Sitzungsberichte 1927/1930 and 1930–1933.*
Nationalsozialistisches Jahrbuch. Hrsg. unter Mitwirkung der Hauptparteileitung der NSDAP (München 1927, 1928, 1931, 1933).
Partei-Statistik. Stand 1 Januar 1935. Herausgeber Der Reichsorganisationsleiter der NSDAP.
Rednerinformation 1932, hrsg. von der Reichspropagandaleitung der NSDAP (München 1932).
A. ROSENBERG, *Wesen, Grundsätze und Ziele der Nationalsozialistischen Deutschen Arbeiterpartei* (München, 1923).
G. RÜHLE, Das Dritte Reich. *Dokumentarische Darstellung des Aufbaues der Nation. Bd. I Die Kampfahre 1918–1933* (Berlin, 1936).
A. TYRELL, *Führer befiehl … Selbstzeugnisse aus der 'Kampfzeit' der NSDAP. Dokumentation und Analyse* (Düsseldorf, 1969).

BIBLIOGRAPHY

(c) *Memoirs and Speeches, etc.*

H. BOLM, *Hitler-Jugend in einem Jahrzehnt. Ein Glaubensweg der nieder-sächsischen Jugend* (Braunschweig, 1938).

PHILIPP BOUHLER, *Kampf um Deutschland. Ein Lesebuch für die deutsche Jugend* (Berlin, 1938).

R. W. DARRÉ, *Erkenntnisse und Werden. Aufsätze aus der Zeit vor der Macht-ergreifung*, 2 Auflage (Goslar, 1940).

R. W. DARRÉ, *Neuadel aus Blut und Boden* (München, 1934).

R. W. DARRÉ, *Um Blut und Boden. Reden und Aufsätze*, 3 Aufl. (München, 1941).

R. W. DARRÉ, *Im Kampf um die Seele des deutschen Bauern* (Berlin, 1934).

OTTO DIETRICH, *Mit Hitler in die Macht. Persönliche Erlebnisse mit meinem Führer*, 20 Aufl. (München, 1935).

ANTON DREXLER, *Mein Politisches Erwachen. Aus dem Tagebuch eines deutsch-en sozialistischen Arbeiter*, 4 Aufl. (München, 1923).

HANS FALLADA, *Bauern, Bonzen und Bomben*, Neuausgabe (Hamburg, 1964).

A. GIMBEL and K. HEPP eds., *So kämpften wir! Schilderungen aus der Kampf-zeit der NSDAP in Gau Hessen-Nassau* (Frankfurt, 1941).

JOSEPH GOEBBELS, *Kampf um Berlin. Der Anfang*, 9 Auflage (München, 1936).

JOSEPH GOEBBELS, *Die Zweite Revolution. Briefe an Zeitgenossen* (Zwickau, 1926).

JOSEPH GOEBBELS, *Lenin oder Hitler? Eine Rede, gehalten am 19. Februar 1926 im Opernhaus in Königsberg* (Zwickau, 1926).

JOSEPH GOEBBELS, *Vom Kaiserhof zur Reichskanzlei* (München, 1934).

Das Tagebuch von Joseph Goebbels 1925/6, hrsg. von H. Heiber (Stuttgart, 1961).

LUDOLF HAASE,'Aufstand in Niedersachsen. Der Kampf der NSDAP 1921/ 1924' (Mimeographed 1942).

ERNST HANFSTAENGEL, *Hitler. The Missing Years* (London, 1957).

HANS HENNIGSEN, *Niedersachsenland. Du wurdest unser! Zehn Jahre National-sozialismus im Gau Ost-Hannover* (Harburg–Wilhelmsburg, 1935).

Adolf Hitler, *Mein Kampf*, Translation (New York, 1939).

Hitler's Secret Conversations (New York, 1961).

The Speeches of Adolf Hitler, ed. Norman H. Baynes, vol. 1 (London, 1942).

Adolf Hitlers Reden, hrsg. Ernst Boepple (München, 1933).

WERNER JOCHMANN, *Im Kampf um die Macht. Hitlers Rede vor dem Hamburger Nationalklub von 1919* (Frankfurt, 1960).

WALTER KIEHL, ed., *Mann an der Fahne. Kameraden erzählen von Dr. Ley* (München, 1938).

A. KREBS, *Tendenzen und Gestalten der NSDAP. Erinnerungen an die Früh-zeit der Partei* (Stuttgart, 1959).

KURT LUDECKE, *I knew Hitler. The Story of a Nazi who Escaped the Blood Purge* (New York, 1937).

JULIUS LIPPERT, *Im Strom der Zeit. Erlebnisse und Eindrücke* (Berlin, 1942).

WALTHER LUETGEBRUNE, *Neu-Preussens Bauernkrieg* (Hamburg, 1931).

GUSTAV NOSKE, *Erlebtes aus Aufstieg und Niedergang einer Demokratie* (Zü-rich, 1947).

BIBLIOGRAPHY

FRIEDRICH PLÜMER, *Die Wahrheit über Hitler und seinen Kreis* (Munich, 1925).

HEINZ PREISS, *Die Anfänge der völkischen Bewegung in Franken*, Inaugural Dissertation (Erlangen, 1937).

HERMANN RAUSCHNING, *Hitler Speaks. A Series of Political Conversations with Adolf Hitler on his Real Aims* (London, 1939).

HERMANN RAUSCHNING, *The Revolution of Nihilism. Warning to the West* (New York, 1939).

ERNST RÖHM, *Die Geschichte eines Hochverräters*, 7, Auflage (München, 1934).

ALFRED ROSENBERG, *Blut und Ehre. Ein Kampf für die deutsche Wiedergeburt. Reden und Aufsätze von 1919–1933* (München, 1939).

ALFRED ROSENBERG, *Kampf um die Macht. Aufsätze von 1921–1932* (München, 1937).

ALFRED ROSENBERG, *Schriften und Reden* (München, 1943).

SERGE LANG and ERNST VON SCHENK, *Portrait eines Menschheitsverbrechers, nach den hinterlassenen Memoiren des ehemaligen Reichsministers Alfred Rosenberg* (St. Gallen, 1947).

Rückblick auf die Geschichte der Ortsgruppe Göttingen der NSDAP anlässlich des 15-jährigen Bestehens im Göttinger Tageblatt 6/7 February 1937.

ERNST VON SALOMON, *Die Geächteten*, Neuausgabe (Hamburg, 1962).

ERNST VON SALOMON, *Der Fragebogen* (Hamburg, 1951).

RICHARD SCHERINGER, *Das Grosse Los, unter Soldaten, Bauern und Rebellen* (Hamburg, 1959).

EUGEN SCHMAHL and WILHELM SEIPEL, *Entwicklung der völkischen Bewegung* (Giessen, 1933).

KURT SCHMALZ, *Nationalsozialisten ringen um Braunschweig* (Braunschweig, 1933).

PETER SCHMIDT, *Zwanzig Jahre Soldat Adolf Hitlers. Zehn Jahre Gauleiter* (Köln, 1941).

OTTO SCHMIDT-HANNOVER, *Umdenken oder Anarchie* (Göttingen, 1959).

ARNO SCHROEDER, *Mit der Partei vorwärts. Zehn Jahre Gau Westfalen-Nord* (Detmold, 1940).

RUDOLF VON SEBOTTENDORF, *Bevor Hitler kam. Urkündliches aus der nationalsozialistischen Bewegung* (München, 1933).

OSWALD SPENGLER, *Preussentum und Sozialismus* (München, 1919).

OSWALD SPENGLER, *Briefe 1913–1936*, ed. M. Koktanek (Munich, 1963).

GREGOR STRASSER, *Kampf um Deutschland. Reden und Aufsätze eines Nationalsozialisten*, 2 Aufl (München, 1932).

OTTO STRASSER, *Hitler and I* (London, 1940).

FRITZ THYSSEN, *I Paid Hitler* (London, 1941).

FRITZ WENZEL, *Unser Reichsbauernführer R. Walther Darré und seine Mitkämpfer. Der Sieg von Blut und Boden. Dargestellt für Volk und Jugend* (Berlin, 1934).

SECONDARY SOURCES

THEODORE ABEL, *The Nazi Movement. Why Hitler Came to Power* (New York, 1965).

BIBLIOGRAPHY

A. ACKERMANN, *Die wirtschaftlichen und sozialen Verhältnisse des Bremischen Bauerntums 1870–1930*, Dissertation (Leipzig, 1935).

WILLIAM S. ALLEN, *The Nazi Seizure of Power. The Experience of a Single German Town 1930–1935* (London, 1965).

WERNER T. ANGRESS, 'The Political Role of the Peasantry in the Weimar Republic', in *Review of Politics*, 1959.

KARL ANLAUF, *Die Revolution in Niedersachsen* (Hanover, 1920).

HANNAH ARENDT, *The Origins of Totalitarianism* (New York, 1951).

HEINRICH BENNECKE, *Hitler und die SA* (München, 1962).

VOLKER R. BERGHAHN, *Der Stahlhelm, Bund der Frontsoldaten, 1919–1935* (Düsseldorf, 1967).

L. BERGSTRAESSER, *Die Geschichte der politischen Parteien in Deutschland* (München, 1952).

H. P. BLEUEL and ERNST KLINNERT, *Deutsche Studenten auf dem Weg ins Dritte Reich* (Gütersloh, 1968).

K. D. BRACHER, *Die Auflösung der Weimarer Republik* (Villingen, 1960).

K. D. BRACHER, *Die deutsche Diktatur. Enstehung, Struktur, Folgen des National-Sozialismus* (Köln, 1969).

ERNEST BRAMSTED, *Goebbels and National Socialist Propaganda 1925–1945* (London, 1965).

HANS-CHRISTIAN BRANDENBURG, *Die Geschichte der H. J. Wege und Irrwege einer Generation* (Köln, 1968).

MARTIN BROSZAT, *Der Nationalsozialismus. Weltanschauung, Program, und Wirklichkeit* (Stuttgart, 1960).

MARTIN BROSZAT, 'Die Anfänge der Berliner NSDAP 1926/7', in *Vierteljahreshefte für Zeitgeschichte*, 1960.

MARTIN BROSZAT, *Der Staat Hitlers* (München, 1969).

HANS BUCHHEIM, 'The SS—Instrument of Domination' in H. Krausnick, H. Buchheim, M. Broszat, H-A. Jacobsen, *Anatomy of the SS State* (London, 1968).

ALAN BULLOCK, *Hitler. A Study in Tyranny* (London, 1962).

F. L. CARSTEN, *The Reichswehr and Politics 1918–1933* (Oxford, 1966).

NORMAN COHN, *The Pursuit of the Millennium* (London, 1962).

W. CONZE, 'Die Krise des Parteienstaates in Deutschland' in *Historische Zeitschrift*, 1954.

R. DAHRENDORF, *Society and Democracy in Germany* (London, 1968).

Die Landwirtschaft Niedersachsens 1914–1964, hrsg. Albrect Thaer Gesellschaft (Celle, 1964).

Die Wirtschaftsstruktur im Bezirk des Landesarbeitsamtes Niedersachsen. Wirtschaftswissenschaftliche Gesellschaft zum Studium Niedersachsens. Reihe A. Heft 14 (Hannover, 1930).

A. DIX, *Die deutschen Reichstagswahlen 1871–1930 und die Wandlungen der Volksgliederung* (Tübingen, 1930).

MANFRED DÖRR, *Die Deutschnationale Volkspartei 1925–1928*, Dissertation (Marburg, 1964).

BERNHARD EHRENFEUCHTER, *Politische Willensbildung in Niedersachsen zur Zeit des Kaiserreiches*, Dissertation (Göttingen, 1951).

BIBLIOGRAPHY

K. D. ERDMANN, 'Die Geschichte der Weimarer Republik als Problem der Wissenschaft' in *Vierteljahreshefte für Zeitgeschichte*, 1955.

THEODOR ESCHENBURG, *Die Improvisierte Demokratie. Gesammelte Aufsätze zur Weimarer Republik* (München, 1963).

ERICH EYCK, *A History of the Weimar Republic* (London, 1962–4).

F. FABIAN, *Die Verschuldung der deutschen Landwirtschaft vor und nach dem Kriege* (Barby, 1930).

F. FELDMANN, *Geschichte des Ortsvereins Hannover der Sozialdemokratische Partei Deutschlands vom Gründungsjahre 1864 bis 1933* (Hannover, 1952).

P. FLEISCH, *Erlebte Kirchengeschichte. Erfahrungen in und mit der hannoversche Landeskirche* (Hannover, 1952).

GÜNTER FRANZ, *Die politischen Wahlen in Niedersachsen 1867–1949* (Bremen, 1957).

G. FRANZ-WILLING, *Die Hitler-Bewegung. I. Der Ursprung 1919–1922* (Hamburg, 1962).

HELMUT GÄTSCH, *Die Freien Gewerkschaften in Bremen 1919–1933* (Bremen, 1969).

THEODOR GEIGER, *Die Soziale Schichtung des deutschen Volkes* (Stuttgart, 1932).

ALEXANDER GERSCHENKRON, *Bread and Democracy in Germany* (Berkeley/L.A., 1943).

HANS GERTH, 'The Nazi Party: Its Leadership and Composition', in *American Journal of Sociology*, 1940.

HELGE GREBING, *Der Nationalsozialismus, Ursprung und Wesen* (München, 1959).

RUDOLF HEBERLE, *Social Movements* (New York, 1951).

RUDOLF HEBERLE, *Landbevölkerung und Nationalsozialismus. Eine soziologische Untersuchung der politischen Willensbildung in Schleswig-Holstein 1918 bis 1932* (Stuttgart, 1963).

H. HEIBER, *Joseph Goebbels* (München, 1965).

KONRAD HEIDEN, *Geschichte des Nationalsozialismus. Die Karriere einer Idee* (Berlin, 1932).

KONRAD HEIDEN, *Der Führer. Hitler's Rise to Power* (London, 1944).

LEWIS HERTZMANN, *DNVP. Right-Wing Opposition in the Weimar Republic 1918–1924* (Lincoln, 1963).

THEODOR HEUSS, *Hitlers Weg. Eine historisch-politische Studie über den Nationalsozialismus* (Stuttgart, 1932).

HEINZ HÖHNE, *Der Orden unter dem Totenkopf. Die Geschichte der SS*, (Gütersloh, 1967).

H. H. HOFMANN, *Der Hitlerputsch. Krisenjahre deutscher Geschichte* (Munich, 1961).

J. B. HOLT, *German Agricultural Policy 1918–1934* (Chapel Hill, 1936).

KLAUS HORNUNG, *Der Jungdeutscher Orden* (Düsseldorf, 1958).

HARALD HÜNER, *Die Wirtschaftlichen und gesellschaftlichen Grundlagen des Bauerntums in der Landschaft der mittleren Aller von etwa 1880 bis 1932* (Hildesheim und Leipzig, 1937).

BIBLIOGRAPHY

PETER HÜTTENBERGER, *Die Gauleiter, Studie zum Wandel des Machtgefüges in der NSDAP* (Stuttgart, 1969):

MICHAEL JOVY, *Deutsche Jugendbewegung und Nationalsozialismus, Versuch einer Klärung ihrer Zusammenhänge und Gegensätze*, Dissertation (Köln, 1952).

WALTER H. KAUFMANN, *Monarchism in the Weimar Republic* (New York, 1953).

ARNE KLÖNNE, *Hitlerjugend. Die Jugend und ihre Organisationen im Dritten Reich* (Hannover/Frankfurt, 1960).

EBERHARD KLÜGEL, *Die Lutherische Landeskirche Hannover und ihr Bischof 1933–1945* (Berlin and Hamburg, 1964).

E. KRAFT, *80 Jahre Arbeiterbewegung zwischen Meer und Moor. Ein Beitrag zur Geschichte der politischen Bewegungen in Weser-Ems* (Bremen, 1952).

ALFRED KRUCK, *Geschichte des Alldeutschen Verbandes 1890–1939* (Wiesbaden, 1954).

KARL KÜHLING, *Osnabrück 1925–1933. Von der Republik bis zum dritten Reich* (Osnabrück, 1963).

REINHARD KÜHNL, 'Zur Programmatik der nationalsozialistischen Linken. Das Strasserprogramm von 1925/1926' in *Vierteljahreshefte für Zeitgeschichte*, 1966.

REINHARD KÜHNL, *Die nationalsozialistische linke 1925–1930* (Meisenberg, 1967).

WALTER Z. LAQUEUR, *Young Germany. A History of the German Youth Movement* (London, 1962).

DANIEL LERNER, *The Nazi Elite* (Stanford, 1951).

WERNER LIEBE, *Die deutschnationale Volkspartei 1918–1924* (Düsseldorf, 1956).

S. M. LIPSET, *Political Man* (London, 1960).

CHARLES P. LOOMIS and J. ALLEN BEAGLE, 'The Spread of German Nazism in Rural Areas', in *American Sociological Review*, 1946.

WERNER MASER, *Die Frühgeschichte der NSDAP* (Bon, 1965).

ERICH MATHIAS and RUDOLF MORSEY, eds., *Das Ende der Parteien 1933* (Düsseldorf, 1963).

PETER MELCHER, 'In Couleur und Braunhemd. Die Studentenschaft in der Weimarer Republik', in *Politikon*. Göttinger Studentenzeitschrift für Niedersachsen No. 9, pp. 7–10.

ROBERT MICHELS, *Umschichtungen in den herrschenden Klassen nach dem Kriege* (Stuttgart–Berlin, 1934).

FRIEDRICHE MEINECKE, *The German Catastrophe* (Boston, 1963).

A. MILATZ, *Wähler und Wahlen in der Weimarer Republik* (Bonn, 1965).

RUDOLF MORSEY, 'Hitler als Braunschweiger Regierungsrat', in *Vierteljahreshefte für Zeitgeschichte*, 1960.

WERNER E. MOSSE, ed., *Entscheidungsjahr 1932. Zur Judenfrage in der Weimarer Republik* (Tübingen, 1965).

FRANZ NEUMANN, *Behemoth: The Structure and Practice of National Socialism* (London, 1942).

SIGMUND NEUMANN, *Die deutschen Parteien. Wesen und Wandel nach dem Kriege* (Berlin, 1932).

BIBLIOGRAPHY

E. Neusüss-Hunkel, *Die SS* (Hannover/Frankfurt, 1956).

ERNST NOLTE, *Three Faces of Fascism* (London, 1965).

JEREMY NOAKES, 'Conflict and Development in the NSDAP 1924–1927' in *Journal of Contemporary History* (October, 1966).

DIETRICH ORLOW, 'The Organizational History and Structure of the NSDAP 1919–1923', in *Journal of Modern History*, 1965.

TALCOTT PARSONS, *Essays in Sociological History*. Revised Edition (New York, 1964).

AUGUST PETERS, *Die Wirtschaftssysteme der Lüneburger Heide* (Dessau, 1928).

JAMES K. POLLOCK, 'An Areal Study of the German Electorate 1930–1933', in *American Political Science Review*, vol. 38 (1944).

JAMES K. POLLOCK, 'The German Reichstag Election of 1930', *American Political Science Review*, vol. 24 (1930).

HANS PRILOP, *Die Vorabstimmung in Hannover 1924. Untersuchungen zur Vorgeschichte und Geschichte der deutsch-hannoverischen Partei*, Dissertation (Hamburg, 1954).

P. G. J. PULZER, *The Rise of Political Anti-Semitism in Germany and Austria* (London, 1964).

EVA G. REICHMANN, *Hostages of Civilization. The Social Sources of National Socialist Anti-Semitism* (London, 1950).

K. ROHE, *Das Reichsbanner Schwarz-Rot-Gold* (Düsseldorf, 1966).

ERNST-AUGUST ROLOFF, *Braunschweig und der Staat von Weimar* (Braunschweig, 1964).

ERNST-AUGUST ROLOFF, *Bürgertum und Nationalsozialismus 1930–1933. Braunschweigs Weg ins Dritte Reich* (Hannover, 1961).

ARTHUR ROSENBERG, *Geschichte der Weimarer Republik* (Frankfurt, 1961).

WOLFGANG SCHÄFER, *NSDAP. Entwicklung und Struktur der Staatspartei des Dritten Reiches* (Hannover, 1956).

URSULA SCHELM-SPANGENBERG, *Die Deutsche Volkspartei im Lande Braunschweig* (Braunschweig, 1964).

GERHARD SCHILDT, *Die Arbeitsgemeinschaft Nordwest. Untersuchungen zur Geschichte der NSDAP 1925/26*, Diss. (Freiburg, 1964).

D. SCHOENBAUM, *Hitler's Social Revolution, Class and Status in Nazi Germany 1933–1939* (London, 1969).

OTTO-ERNST SCHÜDDEKOPF, *Linke Leute von Rechts. Die National revolutionären Minderheiten und der Kommunismus in der Weimarer Republik* (Stuttgart, 1960).

H. J. SCHULZE, *Oldenburgs Wirtschaft einst und jetzt* (Oldenburg, 1965).

H. SCHWARZWÄLDER, *Die Machtergreifung der NSDAP in Bremen 1933*, (Bremen, 1966).

E. A. SHILS, 'Authoritarianism "Right" and "Left"' in R. Christie and M. Jahoda, eds., *Studies in the Scope and Method of 'The Authoritarian Personality'* (Glencoe, Ill., 1954).

WILLIAM L. SHIRER, *The Rise and Fall of the Third Reich* (London, 1960).

KURT SONTHEIMER. *Antidemokratisches Denken in der Weimarer Republik. Die politishen Ideen des deutschen Nationalismus zwischen 1918 und 1933* (München, 1962).

BIBLIOGRAPHY

FRITZ STERN, *The Politics of Cultural Despair. A Study in the Rise of the Germanic Ideology* (Berkeley, 1961).

G. STOLTENBERG, *Politische Strömungen im schleswig-holsteinischen Landvolk 1918–1933* (Düsseldorf, 1962).

HEINRICH STRIEFLER, *Deutsche Wahlen in Bildern und Zahlen. Eine soziographische Studie über die Reichstagswahlen der Weimarer Republik* (Düsseldorf, 1946).

The Third Reich, U.N.E.S.C.O., 1955.

KARL THIEME, hrsg. *Judenfeindschaft. Darstellung und Analysen* (Frankfurt, 1963).

ERWIN TOPF, *Die Grüne Front* (Berlin, 1933).

ERNST TROELTSCH, *Spektator-Briefe. Aufsätze über die deutsche Revolution und die Weltpolitik 1918/1922* (Tübingen, 1924).

THILO VOGELSANG, *Reichswehr, Staat und NSDAP. Beiträge zur deutschen Geschichte 1930–1932* (Stuttgart, 1962).

R. G. L. WAITE, *Vanguard of Nazism. The Free Corps Movement in Postwar Germany 1918–1923* (Cambridge/Mass., 1952).

A. G. WHITESIDE, 'The Nature and Origins of National Socialism', in *Journal of Central European Affairs*, 1957.

S. J. WOOLF, ed., *European Fascism* (London, 1968).

ULRICH WÖRTZ, *Programmatik und Führerprinzip. Das Problem des Strasser-Kreises in der NSDAP*, Dissertation (Erlangen, 1966).

G. WURZBACHER and R. PFLAUM, *Das Dorf im Spannungsfeld industrieller Entwicklung* (Stuttgart, 1954).

Z. A. B. ZEMAN, *Nazi Propaganda* (Oxford, 1964).

INDEX

INDEX

INDEX

Munich, Nazi headquarters in, 13, 17, 20–2, 27, 37–8, 56, 64–5, 68–9, 71–7, 81–2

National Bolshevism, 85
National Liberal Party, 5, 117, 247
Nationalsozialistische Arbeitsgemeinschaft, 53, 57–9, 63
Nationalsozialistische Betriebszellenorganisation, 174–82
Nationalsozialistische Briefe, 71–2, 74, 77
Nationalsozialistische Deutscher Studentenbund (NSDSt.B), 196–200
Nationalsozialistischer Deutscher Wirtschaftsbund, 128, 163, 170
Nationalsozialistische Freiheitsbewegung, 53, 58–9, 61–2, 65, 68, 93
Nationalsozialistische Freiheitspartei, 47, 51
Nationaler Sozialist, 76
Nationalverband deutscher Offiziere, 39
Nazi Party (NSDAP), two stages in rise of, 1–2; problem of sources for, 3; founding of Hanover City branch, 14–17; Hitler seizes power in (1921), 15; early propaganda, 18–19; outside Hanover 1921–3, 20–2; in Göttingen 1921–2, 22–3; unique characteristics of, 24–5; the ban in Prussia, 28; developments in Hanover 1923, 30–4; developments in Göttingen 1923–4, 34–7; Hitler *putsch*, 38–40; conflict with the DVFP, 30–1, 34–7, 41–55; the re-founding of the, 60–5; the Arbeitsgemeinschaft North West, 68–83; rivalry with the DVFB, 89–92; the issue of participation in elections, 67–8, 71–2, 83–4, 93; local organization, 95–101; reorientation of, 104–8; the Mittelstand campaign 1928–30, 121–9; in local government, 129–38; 1928 reorganization, 139–40; activism, 141–3; administration, 145–6; in Young Plan campaign, 147–8; in 1930 election, 148–55; developments in organization, 156–60; the Gauleiter and Kreisleiter, 160–2; specialized Nazi organizations, 162–5; the agrarpolitischer Apparat, 165–70; the Mittelstand department, 170–3; other Nazi

professional departments, 173–4; the SA, 182–7; the SS, 187–90; the NSBO, 174–82; the Hitler Youth, 190–5; the Nazi Student league, 196–200; propaganda, 201–221; in government, 222–32; crisis of 233–8; November 1932 election, 238–41; the Strasser affair, 241–5
Finances, 93–5, 105, 143–6, 234–5, 243
Membership, 16–17, 23, 28, 60–1, 104, 140–1, 159
Gau Hanover-North (1925–8), 63, 65, 74, 89, 91, 93–5, 98–102, 104–106, 121, 126, 128, 139
Gau Hanover-South (Göttingen) (1925–8), 63, 65, 74, 89–90, 140
Gau Lüneburg-Stade (1925–8), 63, 74, 91–2, 126
Gau Hanover-East (1928–45), 140–2, 145, 159, 161–2, 166–7, 178, 184, 187, 189, 238
Gau Hanover-South–Brunswick (1928–45), 140–6, 151–2, 157–60, 164–8, 170–4, 178–9, 186–7, 191–193, 201–4, 206, 208, 211, 215–17, 233–5, 237–8, 240, 243–4
Gau Weser-Ems (1928–45), 140–2, 145, 159, 166, 178, 194, 202, 238
Gau Berlin, 74, 96 fn. 2, 175, 190, 193
Gau Westphalia, 63, 72, 74, 81, 140 fn. 1, 238
Neustadt-Gödens, 21
Niedersachsen-Stürmer, 151, 184
Niedersächsischer Beobachter, 1923–4, 33; 1925–31, 76, 102–3, 135, 142, 151, 203
Niedersächsischer Handwerkerbund, 110, 138 fn. 2
Niedersächsische Tageszeitung, 204
Nienburg, 20, 100, 235
Norden, 4, 92, 117
Nordwestdeutscher Handwerkerbund, 171–2
Northeim, 3, 23, 35, 63
Noske, G., 18
Nuremberg, 13, 39, 57

Oberkirchenrat, 228
Oberlindober, H., 174
Oldenburg (city of), 3, 10, 90–1, 106, 134, 228

270

INDEX

Oldenburg (Free State of), 63, 122; economic structure of, 3–4; political background of, 6, 112; early Nazi activity in, 21, 25, 29; Nazi membership in, 91; Mittelstand protest movement in, 108–9; Landvolk in, 120; Nazi activity in 1928, 120–2; Young Plan vote, 147; 1930 election in, 153–4; Chamber of Agriculture election, 168–9; 1932 presidential election, 214; July 1932 election in, 218; Nazi success in, 220.

Oldenburg Landtag, 133 fn. 7, 202, 225–7, 230, 232

Organization Consul, 28

Orgesch (Organization Escherich), 34, 38

Osnabrück (city of), 4, 90, 97, 136–8, 154, 175, 207

Osnabrück (Regierungsbezirk), 3, 63, 212

Oven, General von, 39

Pan-German League, 9

Papen, F. von, 233, 239–40, 242

Pauly, J., 227, 229, 231

Peasantry, 105–27, 219–20

Peine, 3–4, 100–1, 190

Pfeffer, F. von, 72–3, 76–8, 82, 84, 188–189

Plümer, F., 69

Poland, 109, 247

Pollock, J., 152

Pomerania, 45

Preiss, H., 159–60

Press, the, 100–1, 203–5, 214

Progressive Party, 5, 117, 246

Protestants, 207–8, 223–4, 228

Prussian Landtag, 215

Quindel, G., 43

Ramin, J. von, 21

Rathenau, W., 28

Rauschning, H., 169

Reichsbanner, 194, 216

Reichsführerschaft, 48, 52–3, 57, 59–60, 62

Reichshammerbund, 9–10

Reichskommissar für Überwachung der Öffentlichen Ordnung, 29 fn. 5, 61 fn. 2, 104

Reichskriegsflagge, 93

Reichstag, 1920 election, 112; May 1924 election, 43, 109, 114–15, 117; December 1924 election, 57, 93, 118; 1928 election, 119–23 1930 election, 148–55; July 1932 election, 217–20; November 1932 election, 233, 241

Reichswehr, 39, 66

Reinhardt, E., 142

Reventlow, Graf E. von, 60–1, 105

Rheden-Rheden, von H., 94, 166–8

Riepenhausen, Major von, 39

Riese, A., 102

Röhm, E., 48, 93

Rönck, H., 198

Röver, C., 90, 121, 134, 225 fn. 4, 227

Rohe, K., 250 fn. 3

Rosenberg, A., 41–2, 44, 47–50, 73

Rosikat, Dr., 106

Rossbach, G., 31–2

Roth, A., 9

Rüthnick, Dr., 21

Ruhr, the, 101

Rupprecht, Prince, 39

Russia, 72, 80, 84

Rust, B., 46–7, 60, 62–3, 67, 72, 75–6, 78–80, 84, 91, 98, 101–3, 106, 165, 168, 172, 188, 205–6, 242

SA, 24–5, 92–3, 182–8

SS, 187–90

Salder (Amtsbezirk), 105

Salzburg, 16, 41–2

Sassenberg, Polizei-Major, 224

Sauckel, F., 128

Sauckel, Frau, 66 fn. 3

Schandelah, 144–5

Schaumberg-Lippe, 3, 63, 140

Schemm, H., 163

Schierbaum, Dr., 136–7

Schlageter, 34

Schlageter-Gedächtnis-Bund, 34, 40

Schleicher, K. von, 242

Schlesische Langesellschaft, 106

Schleswig-Holstein, 45, 48, 60, 69, 108, 118–20, 124

Schleswig Holsteinische Landespartei, 113–14

Schmalz, K., 133

Schmidt, H., 133

Schmidt-Nordstemmen, 171

Schneider, A., 133

Schneider, Dipl. Ing., 160

Schrader, K., 171

INDEX

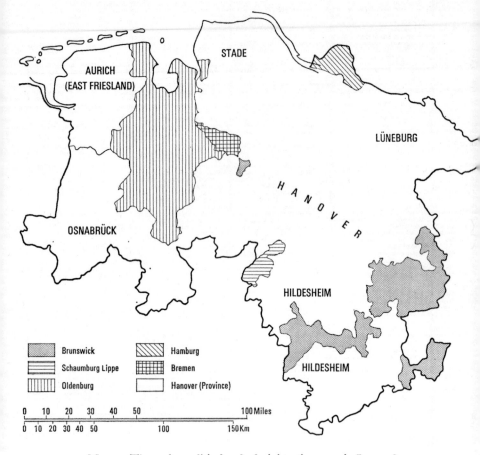

MAP I The major political and administrative areas in Lower Saxony

Cuxhaven
Land Hadeln
Norden Wittmund
Aurich
Friesland
Wilhelms haven
Wesermünde
Stade
Hamburg
Harburg
Emden
Leer
Ammerland
Wesermarsch
Bremervörde
Osterholz
Harburg Land
Lüneburg
enburg City
Bremen
Rotenburg
Verden
Soltau
Uelzen
Dannenberg
Oldenburg
Oldenburg County
Delmen horst
Gf. Hoya
Aschendorf-Hümmling
Cloppenburg
Fallingbostel
Celle
Meppen
Vechta
Gf. Diepholz
Nienburg
Hanover City
Neustadt
Celle Town
Gifhorn
Gt. Bentheim
Bersenbrück
Wittlage
Burgdorf
Lingen
Osnabrück City
Schaumburg-Lippe
HANOVER
Peine
Braunschweig
Helm stedt
Melle
Gf. Schaumburg
Springe
Hildesheim
Wolfenbüttel
Osnabrück
Hameln
Alfeld
Goslar County
Goslar Town
Holzminden
Gandersheim
Zellerfeld
Einbeck
Osterode
Blankenburg
Hann-Münden
Northeim
Göttingen
Duderstadt

0 10 20 30 40 50   100 Miles
0 10 20 30 40 50   100   150 Km

MAP 2 The *Kreise* in Lower Saxony in 1932

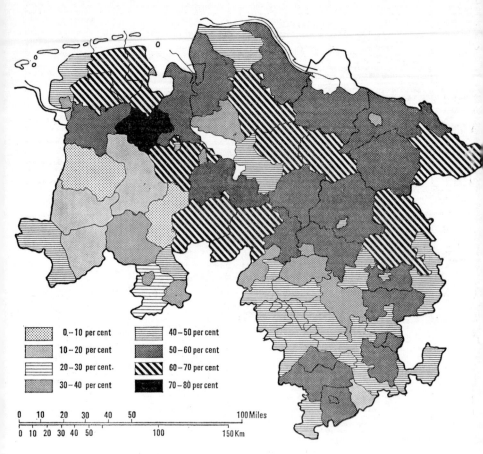

MAP 3   The Nazi vote in Lower Saxony in the July 1932 Reichstag election

Legend:

0 – 10 per cent	40 – 50 per cent
10 – 20 per cent	50 – 60 per cent
20 – 30 per cent.	60 – 70 per cent
30 – 40 per cent	70 – 80 per cent

Scale:

0   10   20   30   40   50   100 Miles

0   10   20   30   40   50   100   150 Km